ERIN DUNIGAN, MCSE, MCT
ALAIN GUILBAULT, MCSE, MCT
BRIAN KOMAR, MCSE, MCT
LARRY PASSO, MCSE, MCT
BARRIE SOSINSKY

MCSE
TRAINING GUIDE

WINDOWS NT WORKSTATION 4.0

New Riders Publishing, Indianapolis, Indiana

MCSE Training Guide: Windows NT Workstation 4.0

By Erin Dunigan, Alain Guilbault, Brian Komar, Larry Passo, and Barrie Sosinsky

Published by:
New Riders Publishing
201 West 103rd Street
Indianapolis, IN 46290 USA

Printed in the United States of America 1 2 3 4 5 6 7 8 9 0

Library of Congress Cataloging-in-Publication Data

CIP data available upon request

Warning and Disclaimer

This book is designed to provide information about Windows NT Workstation 4.0. Every effort has been made to make this book as complete and as accurate as possible, but no warranty or fitness is implied.

The information is provided on an "as is" basis. The authors and New Riders Publishing shall have neither liability nor responsibility to any person or entity with respect to any loss or damages arising from the information contained in this book or from the use of the disks or programs that may accompany it.

New Riders is an independent entity from Microsoft Corporation, and not affiliated with Microsoft Corporation in any manner. This book and CD-ROM may be used in assisting students to prepare for a Microsoft Certified Professional Exam. Neither Microsoft Corporation, its designated review company, nor New Riders warrants that use of this book and CD-ROM will ensure passing of the relevant Exam.

Publisher *David Dwyer*

Executive Editor *Mary Foote*

Managing Editor *Sarah Kearns*

Acquisitions Editor
Stephanie Layton

Development Editor
Nancy Warner

Project Editor
Brad Herriman

Copy Editor
Keith Cline

Technical Editor
Christoph Wille, MCSE, MCSD

Software Product Developer
Steve Flatt

Software Acquisitions and Development
Dustin Sullivan

Team Coordinator
Amy Lewis

Manufacturing Coordinator
Brook Farling

Book Designer
Glenn Larsen

Cover Designer
Dan Armstrong

Cover Production
Casey Price

Director of Production
Larry Klein

Production Team Supervisor
Laurie Casey

Graphics Image Specialists
Steve Adams, Debi Bolhuis, Kevin Cliburn, Sadie Crawford, Wil Cruz, Tammy Graham, Oliver Jackson

Production Analysts
Dan Harris
Erich J. Richter

Production Team
Lori Cliburn, Aleata Howard, Kristy Nash, Laure Robinson, Elizabeth SanMiguel, Scott Tullis, Maureen West

Indexer
Kevin Fulcher

About the Authors

Erin Dunigan is a Senior Systems Engineer with QuickStart Technologies, a Microsoft Solution Provider Partner and Authorized Technical Education Center. She is a Microsoft Certified Systems Engineer (MCSE) and a Microsoft Certified Trainer (MCT) who specializes in Microsoft Exchange Server and Windows NT. In addition to training and consulting, Erin also writes for *Microsoft Certified Professional Magazine,* covering such topics as exam preparation products, as well as reviewing new exams as they release. Erin lives in Los Angeles, California where she can be close to the mountains in the winter and the beach in the summer.

Alain Guilbault is a Microsoft Certified Systems Engineer (MCSE) and a Microsoft Certified Trainer (MCT). Alain obtained his certifications for NT 3.51 and NT 4.0 while working as a full time technical instructor and IT coordinator for an international training company. He has been in the computer training arena for the last five years. He currently lives with his wife Sara in Calgary, Alberta Canada.

Brian Komar is a trainer and consultant with Online Business Systems. He holds a Bachelor of Commerce degree and several professional designations, including: Microsoft Certified Trainer (MCT), Fellow Life Management Institute (FLMI) and Microsoft Certified Systems Engineer (MCSE). Brian's six years of experience in the Information Technology industry are supported by strong business skills and a background in accounting and actuarial services. Online Business Systems is a consulting firm with offices in Winnipeg, Minneapolis, and Calgary. Online develops complete, practical computer solutions

You can reach Brian by email at bkomar@online-can.com.

Online Business Systems is an international company dedicated to providing complete Information Technology (IT) consulting services. Online's vision of success revolves around leadership, exceptional work quality and employee education. As one of the 50 Best Managed Private Companies in Canada, Online has a high level of integrity and works hard at being a complete solution provider for their clients.

Larry Passo is a Senior Systems Engineer for QuickStart Technologies, a Microsoft Solution Provider Partner and Authorized Technical Education Center, at their headquarters in Newport Beach, California. With over 20 years of experience in the computer industry as a developer, design engineer, and network specialist, Larry holds certifications as both a Microsoft Certified Systems Engineer and as a Microsoft Certified Trainer. He provides advanced training and consulting for a variety of Microsoft operating systems and the Microsoft BackOffice family of server products and is a frequent contributor to Microsoft Certified Professional magazine. Larry and his wife, Debra, live in Irvine, California.

Barrie Sosinsky is the author of more than 40 computer books, and has written over 80 articles for major computer magazines. He is a contributor to BackOffice Magazine, writing feature articles and book reviews. Barrie's company, Killer Apps (Medfield, MA), develops database solutions, Web sites, and technical documentation for clients. He has done projects for several universities, large hospitals, and corporations. He is the father of two children, Alexandra, 5, and Joseph, 4 months. Barrie and his wife, Carol Westheimer, live in Medfield,

Cliff Strauss is a consultant with Online Business Systems. He holds a Bachelor of Computer Science degree and has over four years of development experience. With particular expertise in Microsoft Visual Studio, Cliff has worked on a variety of projects in the health care and financial industries.

Trademark Acknowledgments

All terms mentioned in this book that are known to be trademarks or service marks have been appropriately capitalized. New Riders Publishing cannot attest to the accuracy of this information. Use of a term in this book should not be regarded as affecting the validity of any trademark or service mark.

Contents at a Glance

Table of Contents

Introduction

MCSE Training Guide: Windows NT Workstation 4.0 is designed for advanced end users, service technicians, and network administrators who are considering certification as a Microsoft Certified Systems Engineer (MCSE) or as a Microsoft Certified Product (MCP) Specialist. The Windows NT Workstation 4.0 exam ("Exam 70-73: Implementing and Supporting Microsoft Windows NT Workstation 4.0") tests your ability to implement, administer, and troubleshoot systems that incorporate Windows NT Workstation, as well as your ability to provide technical support to users of Microsoft Windows NT Workstation.

Who Should Read This Book

This book is designed to help advanced users, service technicians, and network administrators who are working for MCSE certification prepare for the MCSE "Implementing and Supporting Microsoft Windows NT Workstation 4.0" exam (#70-73).

This book is your one-stop-shop. Everything you need to know to pass the exam is in here, and it has been certified by Microsoft. You do not *need* to take a class in addition to buying this book to pass the exam. Your personal study habits, however, may benefit from taking a class in addition to buying this book.

This book can also help advanced users and administrators who are not studying for the MCSE exam but are looking for a single-volume reference on Windows NT Workstation 4.0.

How This Book Helps You

This book takes you on a self-guided tour of all the areas covered by the MCSE Windows NT Workstation 4.0 exam and teaches you the specific skills you need to achieve your MCSE certification. You will also find helpful hints, tips, real-world examples, exercises, and references to additional study materials. Specifically, this book is set up to help you in the following ways:

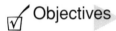 Objectives

▶ **Organization.** This book is organized by major exam topics (seven in all) and exam objectives. Every objective you need to know for the "Implementing and Supporting Microsoft Windows NT Workstation 4.0" exam is covered in this book; a margin icon, like the one in the margin here, helps you quickly locate these objectives. Pointers at different elements direct you to the appropriate place in the book if you find you need to review certain sections.

▶ **Deciding how to spend your time wisely.** Pre-chapter quizzes are at the beginning of each chapter to test your knowledge of the objectives contained within that chapter. If you already know the answers to those questions, you can make a time-management decision accordingly.

▶ **Extensive practice test options.** Plenty of questions are at the end of each chapter to test your comprehension of material covered within that chapter. An answer list follows the questions so that you can check yourself. These practice test options help you decide what you already understand and what requires extra review on your part. The accompanying CD-ROM also contains a sample test engine that gives you an accurate idea of what the test is really like.

The test engine on the accompanying CD-ROM gives you a chance to practice for the certification exams. The questions on the CD-ROM provide a more thorough and comprehensive look at what your certification exams are really like.

Note   For a complete description of the test engine, please see Appendix D, "All About TestPrep."

For a complete description of what you can find on the accompanying CD-ROM, see Appendix C, "What's on the CD-ROM."

Understanding What the Implementing and Supporting Microsoft Windows NT Workstation 4.0 Exam (#70-73) Covers

The "Implementing and Supporting Microsoft Windows NT Workstation 4.0" exam (#70-73) covers seven main topic areas, arranged in accordance with test objectives. The exam objectives, listed by topic area, are covered in the following sections.

Planning

- ▶ Create unattended installation files

- ▶ Plan strategies for sharing and securing resources

- ▶ Choose the appropriate file systems to use in a given situation:

    - ▶ NTFS

    - ▶ FAT

    - ▶ HPFS

- ▶ Security

- ▶ Dual-boot systems

Installation and Configuration

- ▶ Install Windows NT Workstation on an Intel platform in a given situation

▶ Set up a dual-boot system in a given situation

▶ Remove Windows NT Workstation in a given situation

▶ Install, configure, and remove hardware components for a given situation. Hardware components include the following:

> ▶ Network adapter drivers
>
> ▶ SCSI device drivers
>
> ▶ Tape device drivers
>
> ▶ UPS
>
> ▶ Multimedia devices
>
> ▶ Display drivers
>
> ▶ Keyboard drivers
>
> ▶ Mouse drivers

▶ Use Control Panel applications to configure a Windows NT Workstation computer in a given situation

▶ Upgrade to Windows NT Workstation 4.0 in a given situation

▶ Configure server-based installation for wide-scale deployment in a given situation

Managing Resources

▶ Create and manage local user accounts and local group accounts to meet given requirements

▶ Set up and modify user profiles

▶ Set up shared folders and permissions

▶ Set up permissions on NTFS partitions, folders, and files

▶ Install and configure printers in a given environment

Connectivity

▶ Add and configure the network components of Windows NT Workstation

▶ Use various methods of access network resources

▶ Implement Windows NT Workstation as a client in a NetWare environment

▶ Use various configuration to install Windows NT Workstation as a TCP/IP client

▶ Configure and install dial-up networking in a given situation

▶ Configure Microsoft Peer Web Services in a given situation

Running Applications

▶ Start applications on Intel and RISC platforms in various operating system environments

▶ Start applications at various priorities

Monitoring and Optimization

▶ Monitor system performance by using various tools

▶ Identify and resolve a given performance problem

▶ Optimize system performance in various areas

Troubleshooting

▶ Choose the appropriate course of action to take when the boot process fails

▶ Choose the appropriate course of action to take when a print job fails

▶ Choose the appropriate course of action to take when the installation process fails

▶ Choose the appropriate course of action to take when an application fails

▶ Choose the appropriate course of action to take when a user cannot access a resource

▶ Modify the Registry using the appropriate tool in a given situation

▶ Implement advanced techniques to resolve various problems

Hardware and Software Needed

As a self-paced study guide, much of this book expects you to use Windows NT Workstation 4.0 and follow along through the exercises while you learn. Microsoft designed Windows NT Workstation 4.0 to operate in a wide range of actual situations, and the exercises in this book encompass that range. Some of the exercises require only a single stand-alone computer running Windows NT Workstation. Others (those that explore some of the Windows NT Workstation networking options) require a small Microsoft network. Some exercises refer to a pair of computers (one running Windows NT Workstation, and one running Windows NT Workstation and Windows NT Server) configured as described in the following sections.

Computer 1

▶ Computer on the Microsoft Hardware Compatibility List (such as Intel 80486/33 or higher)

▶ 486DX 33 MHz (or better) processor for Windows NT Workstation

▶ 12 MB RAM minimum for x86-based systems (16 MB recommended)

▶ 16 MB RAM minimum for RISC-based systems

▶ 200 MB (or larger) hard disk for Windows NT Workstation

▶ 3.5-inch 1.44-MB floppy drive

- VGA (or Super VGA) video adapter

- VGA (or Super VGA) monitor

- Mouse or equivalent pointing device

- Two-speed (or faster) CD-ROM drive

- Network Interface Card (NIC)

- Presence on an existing network, or use of a two-port (or more) mini-port hub to create a test network

- MS-DOS 5.0 or 6.x and Microsoft Windows for Workgroups 3.x pre-installed

- Microsoft Windows 95 (CD-ROM version)

Computer 2

- Computer on the Microsoft Hardware Compatibility List

- 486DX2 66-MHz (or better) processor for Windows NT Server

- 16 MB of RAM (minimum) for Windows NT Server

- 340-MB (or larger) hard disk for Windows NT Server

- 3.5-inch 1.44-MB floppy drive

- VGA (or Super VGA) video adapter

- VGA (or Super VGA) monitor

- Mouse or equivalent pointing device

- Two-speed (or faster) CD-ROM drive (optional)

- Network Interface Card (NIC)

- Presence on an existing network, or use of a two-port (or more) mini-port hub to create a test network

- MS-DOS 5.0 or 6.x and Microsoft Windows for Workgroups 3.x pre-installed

► Microsoft Windows 95 (floppy version)

► Microsoft Windows NT Server (CD-ROM version)

Computers 1 and 2 should be running at least MS-DOS 5.0 and Windows for Workgroups 3.11 at the start. In fact, it is best if the computers have only MS-DOS 5.0 and Windows for Workgroups 3.11 at the beginning. Otherwise, you may be tempted to use a computer that contains real work and files that cannot be replaced easily. These computers should be test computers. You should not be afraid to format the hard drive and start over should it be necessary.

It is somewhat easier to get access to the necessary computer hardware and software in a corporate business environment. It is harder to allocate enough time within the busy workday to complete a self-study program. Most of your study time may occur after normal working hours, away from the everyday interruptions and pressures of your regular job. If you have access to only a single, non-networked computer, you cannot complete all the networking exercises.

Tips for the Exam

Remember the following tips as you prepare for the MCSE certification exams:

► **Read all the material.** Microsoft has been known to include material not specified in the objectives. This course has included additional information not required by the objectives in an effort to give you the best possible preparation for the examination, and for the real-world network experiences to come.

► **Complete the exercises in each chapter.** They will help you gain experience using the Microsoft product. All Microsoft exams are based on experience, and require you to have used the Microsoft product in a real networking environment. Exercises for each objective are placed at the end of each chapter.

▶ **Complete all the questions in the "Review Questions" sections.** Complete the questions at the end of each chapter—they will help you remember key points. Although questions are fairly simple, be warned: Some questions may have more than one answer.

Note

Although this book is designed to prepare you to take and pass the "Implementing and Supporting Microsoft Windows NT Workstation 4.0" certification exam, there are no guarantees. Read this book, work through the exercises, and take the practice assessment exams.

When taking the real certification exam, make sure you answer all the questions before your time limit expires. Do not spend too much time on any one question. If you are unsure about an answer, answer the question as best you can and mark it for later review when you have finished all the questions. It has been said, whether correctly or not, that any questions left unanswered will automatically cause you to fail. Good luck.

Remember, the object is not to pass the exam, it is to understand the material. After you understand the material, passing is simple. Knowledge is a pyramid; to build upward, you need a solid foundation. The Microsoft Certified System Engineer program is designed to ensure that you have that solid foundation.

Good luck!

New Riders Publishing

The staff of New Riders Publishing is committed to bringing you the very best in computer reference material. Each New Riders book is the result of months of work by authors and staff who research and refine the information contained within its covers.

As part of this commitment to you, the NRP reader, New Riders invites your input. Please let us know if you enjoy this book, if you have trouble with the information and examples presented, or if you have a suggestion for the next edition.

Please note, though: New Riders staff cannot serve as a technical resource during your preparation for the Microsoft MCSE certification exams or for questions about software- or hardware-related problems. Please refer to the documentation that accompanies Windows NT Workstation or to the applications' Help systems.

If you have a question or comment about any New Riders book, there are several ways to contact New Riders Publishing. We respond to as many readers as we can. Your name, address, or phone number never becomes part of a mailing list and is not used for any purpose other than to help us continue to bring you the best books possible. You can write us at the following address:

New Riders Publishing
Attn: Publisher
201 W. 103rd Street
Indianapolis, IN 46290

If you prefer, you can fax New Riders Publishing at 317-817-7448.

You also can send e-mail to New Riders at the following Internet address:

    networking@mcp.com

If you have technical problems with the CD-ROM, contact Macmillan Computer Publishing at the following Internet address:

    support@mcp.com

NRP is an imprint of Macmillan Computer Publishing. To obtain a catalog or information, or to purchase any Macmillan Computer Publishing book, call 800-428-5331.

Thank you for selecting *MCSE Training Guide: Windows NT Workstation 4.0*!

C h a p t e r

Planning an Effective Implementation

This chapter helps you prepare for the exam by covering the following objectives:

 Objectives

▶ Creating unattended installation files.

▶ Planning strategies for sharing and securing resources.

▶ Choosing the appropriate file system to use in a given situation. File systems and situations include NTFS, FAT, HPFS, security, and dual-boot systems.

Test Yourself! Before reading this chapter, test yourself to determine how much study time you will need to devote to this section.

1. As a network administrator of a 500-user network, you need to roll out Windows NT Workstation 4.0 to all the machines in your network. You have standardized hardware across departments. You want to make the installation of Windows NT Workstation unattended. You also need to roll out Office 97 as part of this rollout. What should you do?

2. You need to create home directories for the 250 users in your network as a location for the users to store personal files. Where should you install these directories? How should you make them available to users?

3. Lesley needs to work on some confidential files on her Windows NT Workstation. She shares a machine with Scott, who cannot have access to these files. How can Lesley make these files secure so that Scott cannot access them while he is sitting at the machine?

4. Roger wants to dual-boot his Windows 95 system with Windows NT Workstation 4.0. His drive is divided into three partitions: C, D, and E. How should Roger format these partitions for use within both Windows NT and Windows 95?

5. Kelley moves a file from one NTFS partition on her local hard drive to another partition on her local hard drive. What happens to the file's permissions?

6. Jack wants to fully automate the installation of 50 Windows NT Workstation 4.0 computers. What files does he need to use for these installations to make them automated and capable of setting specific parameters on a per-computer basis?

Effective planning prior to implementation of Windows NT Workstation 4.0 is critical. This chapter focuses on planning the unattended installation of Windows NT Workstation 4.0, planning how to most effectively share and secure resources, and how to plan the appropriate file system to use on your Windows NT Workstation.

This chapter discusses the following planning topics:

- ▶ Creating and using unattended answer files and uniqueness database files.

- ▶ Using sysdiff to create snapshot files, difference files, and INF files.

- ▶ Planning the use of built-in Windows NT Groups.

- ▶ Sharing folders for use as users' home directories, shared application folders, and common access folders.

- ▶ Choosing the right file system (FAT, NTFS, HPFS) for use in various situations, including dual-boot systems and file security.

In terms of the number of questions that appear on the exam, planning tends to be one of the major topic areas on the Windows NT Workstation exam. Understanding how planning applies to an effective implementation of Windows NT Workstation should help you significantly in passing the exam.

Answers are located at the end of the chapter...

Creating Unattended Installation Files

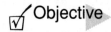 **Objective** One way that planning assists in rolling out Windows NT Workstation is in the creation and implementation of an unattended installation of the Windows NT Workstation operating system. This keeps the team doing the rollout from having to visit every computer to install the operating system manually either from a CD or from a shared network installation point.

Files Used for Unattended Installation

In a relatively small environment, one with less than 50 machines, manually installing Windows NT Workstation might be an option. In any larger environment, however, time is better spent on developing an unattended installation plan for rolling out Windows NT. Based on the size of an environment (number of workstations to install), using an unattended installation could save significant time in the total installation process.

Although doing an unattended installation can take more time "up front," it is time well spent if it decreases the total time of the migration process. Some of the files and tools related to this unattended installation process are the following:

▶ Unattended answer file (Unattend.txt)

▶ Uniqueness database file (UDF)

▶ Sysdiff

An unattended installation gives a network administrator the ability to both *customize* and *automate* the installation of Windows NT as follows:

Customize—User- or organization-specific information can be tailored to a particular installation by using a combination of unattended answer files and uniqueness database files.

Automate—Using an unattended answer file and a uniqueness database file enables the administrator to perform a "hands free" installation of Windows NT.

Windows NT 4.0 uses a combination of an unattended answer file, along with uniqueness database files to do both the customization and automation of the installation of Windows NT Workstation. A third utility used in the installation process, sysdiff, enables the administrator to automate the installation of other applications in addition to the operating system itself. Using these three tools, an administrator can perform an entire installation of the operating system and all needed applications.

Answer Files

Using an answer file frees the administrator from having to sit at a particular computer, manually replying to the prompts of the setup program. That manual approach is fine if you are only installing a few machines, but it can become quite time consuming if you are rolling out Windows NT Workstation in a large-scale environment.

An unattended answer file is a text file implemented as part of the Windows NT setup process by using the /u switch after the Winnt (or Winnt32) command. The syntax of this command is as follows:

```
Winnt /u:answer file /s:source path where NT is being installed
on an non-NT machine
```

or

```
Winnt32 /u:answer file /s:source path where NT is being installed
on an existing NT machine
```

Where:

/u is the switch specifying that this is an unattended installation

answer file is the name of the answer file that you have created. (The default name of the sample answer file is Unattend.txt)

/s is the switch to point to the location of the Windows NT installation files

source path is the location of the Windows NT installation files (the I386 directory for an Intel installation)

Tip

In Windows NT 4.0, you can list two /s:*source path* locations for a particular installation. If, for example, you have two network locations that include the Windows NT installation files, you can point to both of them and thus draw from both locations to speed up the installation.

The main purpose of the unattended answer file is to use it to reply to the prompts that the end user or person doing the installation usually must manually respond to as part of the setup process. You can use the same unattended answer file across a number of installations. If you are using an unattended answer file only, however, it is difficult to completely automate the setup process because of the unique information required to install Windows NT Workstation. An example of that data that needs to be unique in an installation is the NetBIOS computername of that NT Workstation.

One possible solution to this problem of supplying unique information is to indicate the computername as part of the unattended answer file. After the installation finishes, you must then go to all the installed machines and change the computername to one that is unique on the network or in the domain. This solution is not the best solution because it requires "touching" every machine that has been installed, after the installation process (see fig. 1.1). To perform the installation in this manner, after each machine is installed the administrator must do the following:

1. Log on to the computer using the default administrator account created during installation.

2. Go to the Start menu, Settings, Control Panel, to the Network applet.

3. Click on the Change button next to the computer name to provide a unique name.

4. If this machine is to belong to a domain, you must change the domain name from the workgroup into which the machine was originally installed.

Figure 1.1

The Control Panel, Network applet is used to change the computer name and domain name on a Windows NT workstation.

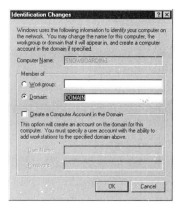

In addition to changing the computer name after the installation, you must also change the domain membership after the installation as well. Because all the installed computer names must be identical, none of the machines could have joined the domain during the installation process. Thus you must add them to the domain after changing the computer names. This requires a significant amount of post-installation work for the administrator in a medium-to-large sized environment. Although this option works in a smaller LAN environment, this is not the most efficient solution for most larger network environments.

A second option is to have the installation process stop and prompt the user during the network portion of the setup so that this unique information can be added at that time. If your goal is to fully automate the installation process, however, you do not want the installation to stop in the middle and wait for user input.

Uniqueness Database Files (UDF)

One solution to the problem of providing unique information in the unattended answer file for the installation process is to create what is called a uniqueness database file or UDF. A UDF is a text file that enables you to supply the information that must be unique to each computer or each user. Uniqueness database files are used in conjunction with an unattended answer file to provide a complete installation of Windows NT Workstation without any user intervention during the setup process. The uniqueness database file provides the capability to specify per-computer parameters for the installation, such as computername or user name.

The UDF is used to merge or to replace sections of the unattended answer file during the GUI portion of the Windows NT setup process. For the installation of Windows NT Workstation 4.0, you can use one unattended answer file for the information that applies to all installations, and one or more UDF files to specify the settings intended for a single computer or for a group of computers. It is possible to have one UDF that contains settings for multiple computers or users within it.

Sysdiff

In addition to installing Windows NT Workstation, you may need to install various applications as well. If those applications do not support a scripted installation, you can use the sysdiff utility to install those applications on the destination computers. By using sysdiff, you can automate the installation of all desired applications. This enables you to not only automate and customize the installation of the operating system, but also the installation of all applications required for your environment. Sysdiff is used to perform the following:

▶ Create a snapshot file

▶ Create a difference file

▶ Apply the difference file

Sysdiff is also alternatively used to

▶ Create an INF file

▶ Dump the contents of a difference file

Creating an Unattended Answer File

An unattended answer file is just a text file that answers the prompts of the setup program during installation so that no one has to manually answer the setup prompts on every machine. A sample unattended answer file, called Unattend.txt, is included with the Windows NT Workstation CD. You can use it as a template for creating or customizing an unattended installation file.

You can also use the Windows NT Setup Manager, a graphical application included with the Windows NT Workstation Resource Kit CD, to create an unattended answer file.

Modifying the Unattend.txt Sample File

On the Windows NT Workstation 4.0 CD, open the Unattend.txt file with any text editor such as Notepad. In general, the information found in the Unattend.txt can be categorized as section heading, parameters, and values associated with those parameters. Most of the actual section headings are predefined and do not need to be changed. If necessary, however, you can add additional sections. An example of the format used follows here:

```
[section]
;comments
;comments
parameter=value
```

Information in the Unattend.txt file is divided into main sections. You may or may not choose to modify all these sections, depending on your particular environment. Those sections are as follows:

[Unattended]—This section is used during text mode setup and can only be modified in the answer file. This is the section that tells the setup that this is an unattened setup. This section is used to specify settings such as whether this is an upgrade install, what file system to use, and the path for the installation.

[OEMBootFiles]—This section is used to specify OEM boot files and can only be specified in the answer file, not in the UDF.

[MassStorageDrivers]—This section is used to specify SCSI drivers to install, and is used during the text mode portion of setup. If this section is missing, setup tries to detect SCSI devices on the computer. This section can only be specified in the answer file, not in the UDF.

[DisplayDrivers]—This section contains a list of display drivers to be loaded by the text mode setup process. If this section is missing, setup tries to detect the display devices on the computer.

[KeyboardDrivers]—This section includes a list of keyboard drivers to be loaded by setup. This setting can only be specified in the answer file, not in the UDF.

[PointingDeviceDrivers]—This section contains a list of pointing device drivers to be used during setup, and is run during the text mode portion of setup. This section must be specified in the answer file, not in the UDF.

[OEM_Ads]—This section can be used to modify the default user interface of the setup program. It is used to modify the banner, background bitmap, and logo used during the GUI portion of setup.

[GuiUnattended]—This section is used to specify settings for the GUI portion of setup. It can be used to indicate the time zone, and to hide the administrator password page.

[UserData]—This section is used to provide user-specific data such as user name, organization name, and computer name, as well as product ID.

[LicenseFilePrintData]—This section is only valid when installing Windows NT Server. It enables you to specify the licensing option you want to use for your Windows NT server.

[Network]—This section is used to specify network settings such as network adapters, services, and protocols. If this section is missing, networking won't be installed. This is the section used to specify the domain or workgroup to join, as well as to create a computer account in the domain.

 Caution

If a [Network] section is not specified in your unattended answer file, no networking for Windows NT Workstation will be installed. If the computer you are installing does not have a CD-ROM, and you are installing across the network, you will have a Windows NT system that has no way to connect to the installation files to add the networking components.

If the [Network] section is specified, but is empty, the user is presented with a number of different error messages during the installation.

[Modem]—This section is used to identify whether a modem should be installed. This section must be specified if you want to install modems by using RAS in unattended mode.

[Display]—This section is used to indicate specific display settings for the display adapter being installed. These settings must be correct and supported by the adapter.

[DetectedMassStorage]—This section is used to specify which mass storage devices setup should recognize, even if they are not currently connected to the system during installation. This setting must be specified in the answer file, not in the UDF.

 Note

The sections of the unattended answer file that pertain to individual user settings are the most likely candidates for including in a UDF. Those are: [GuiUnattended], [UserData], and [Network].

Those items that can only be specified in the answer file and not the UDF must be the same for all installations from that answer file. If, for example, you have a need to install different keyboard drivers or SCSI drivers on various machines, this requires you to create a different answer file for each of those instances. For the exam, you must have a good understanding of what scenario would require you to modify a UDF file, and what would require you to use multiple unattended answer files.

Using Setup Manager to Create an Unattended Answer File

Setup Manager is a graphical application that comes on the Windows NT Workstation Resource Kit CD. You can use it to graphically create an unattended answer file instead of editing the template file Unattend.txt directly. You can specify the following three areas in the Setup Manager:

▶ General Setup

▶ Network Setup

▶ Advanced Setup

General Setup

The *General Setup Options* dialog box is used to specify the installation directory, display settings, time zone, license mode, user information, computer role, and general information for hardware detection and upgrade information (see fig. 1.2).

Figure 1.2

The General Setup Options dialog box contains parameters for user settings and general information.

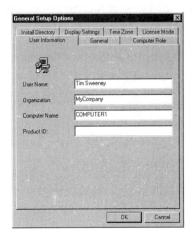

The following items are found within the General Setup Option dialog box:

- ▶ **User Information.** This tab contains fields for the user's name, organization name, computer name, and product ID.

- ▶ **General.** The General tab contains settings for whether or not to confirm hardware as part of the installation as well as the capability to run a program with setup. It also includes specifications if this is an upgrade installation. The upgrade options available are as follows:

  - ▶ **Prompt User for Windows NT Installation to upgrade.** This is used if there is more than one installation of Windows NT on the machine.

  - ▶ **Upgrade the current single Windows NT installation.** This is used when upgrading a single Windows NT installation.

  - ▶ **Upgrade the first Windows NT installation found.** This is used if there is more than one installation of

Windows NT on the machine and you do not want the user prompted as to which to use.

▶ **Upgrade Windows 3.1 or Windows for Workgroups.** This is used when upgrading Windows 3.x.

▶ **Computer Role.** The options for computer role are as follows:

▶ **Workstation in Workgroup.** This option is used if installing Windows NT Workstation into a workgroup. You use this option in either a smaller environment with no domains or in an environment in which you will later add the computer to the domain.

▶ **Workstation in Domain.** If this option is selected, an additional prompt to create a computer account in the domain appears.

▶ **Server in Workgroup.** This option is used when installing a member server.

▶ **Server in Domain.** If this option is selected, an additional prompt to create a computer account in the domain appears.

▶ **Primary Domain Controller.** This option is used when installing the first domain controller in a domain.

▶ **Backup Domain Controller.** This option is used when installing an additional domain controller into the domain.

▶ **Install Directory.** The options for the install directory are either to use the default directory, to prompt the user for the directory, or to use a particular directory that you specify.

▶ **Display Settings.** You can have the display settings automatically configured, or set them to be configured at logon.

▶ **Time Zone.** You can select the time zone for the user location from a list.

▶ **License Mode.** This is used if installing Windows NT Server. It is used to specify the license settings for the Windows NT server.

Networking Options

The *Networking Options* dialog box is used to specify the adapters, protocols, services, modem settings, and whether this portion of the GUI setup should be manual or automatic (see fig. 1.3).

Figure 1.3

The Networking Options dialog box contains settings for specifying network adapters, protocols, and services.

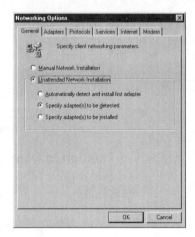

The settings that you can configure through the Network Options dialog box are as follows:

- ▶ **General.** This tab enables you to specify whether the networking components will be configured manually or unattended. It can be configured to either automatically configure the first detected adapter, or to search for particular adapters.

- ▶ **Adapters.** The Adapters tab enables you to specify which adapters will be detected.

- ▶ **Protocols.** The Protocols tab enables you to specify which protocols are installed and what configuration parameters are used.

- ▶ **Services.** The Services tab enables you to specify which services are installed and what their configuration parameters are. Services include RAS, CSNW, and SNMP.

- ▶ **Internet.** The Internet tab is used only when installing Windows NT Server.

- ▶ **Modem.** The modem tab is used only if the RAS service is installed on the Services tab.

Advanced Options

The *Advanced Options* dialog box is used to specify device drivers to install, the file system to use, and the banner and background information to use during the GUI portion of setup. As figure 1.4 shows, this section is also used to control the reboots during the setup process as well as to skip the display of the administrator password page.

Figure 1.4

The Advanced Options dialog box is used to specify additional device drivers and advertisement information during the GUI portion of setup.

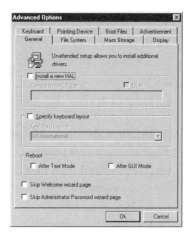

You can configure the following settings through the Advanced Options dialog box:

▶ **General.** This tab enables you to specify skipping the welcome page, setting the administrator password, and enables you to specify the automatic reboot after text and GUI modes of setup, as well as keyboard layout and HAL type.

▶ **File System.** This tab enables you to keep the current file system or convert to NTFS as part of the installation.

▶ **Mass Storage.** This tab enables you to specify a list of driver descriptions.

▶ **Display.** This tab enables you to specify a list of display driver descriptions.

▶ **Keyboard.** This tab enables you to specify a list of keyboard driver descriptions.

▶ **Pointing Device.** This tab enables you to specify a list of pointing device driver descriptions.

▶ **Boot Files.** This tab enables you to specify a list of boot files.

▶ **Advertisement.** This tab enables you to specify banner text during the GUI portion of installation, a logo graphics file, and a background graphics file.

You can use a combination of Setup Manager to configure most of the settings for the unattended answer file, and then a text editor to make changes to that file directly.

Creating Uniqueness Database Files

The uniqueness database file extends the functionality of the un-attended answer file, enabling the specification of per-computer settings. Its function is to merge with sections of the answer file to provide these computer-specific settings. The UDF is a text file that should be located with the other Windows NT installation files on the distribution server.

The UDF contains two sections—one for Unique IDs and one for the Unique ID parameters. The first section identifies which areas of the answer file will be replaced or modified. It is used to specify the particular users or computers which will have unique informa-tion specified. The Unique ID parameters section contains the actual data that will be merged into the answer file, such as the computer name or time zone information.

The syntax used when specifying a UDF is as follows:

```
Winnt /u:answerfile /s:x:\ /udf:userid,x:\udf.txt
```

or

```
Winnt32 /u:answerfile /s:x:\ /udf:userid,x:\udf.txt
```

Where:

answerfile represents the name of the unattended answer file.

/s points to the source path of the Windows NT installation files.

/udf indicates the unique ID and the path to the UDF file.

The first section of the UDF lists the Uniqueness IDs. Following the Uniqueness IDs are the sections that they refer to. For example:

```
[UniqueIDs]
User1 = UserData, GuiUnattended, Network
User2 = UserData, GuiUnattended, Network
[User1:UserData]
FullName = "User 1"
OrgName = "MyCompany"
ComputerName = "Computer1"
[User1:GuiUnattended]
TimeZone = "(GMT-08:00) Pacific Time (US & Canada); Tijuana"
[User1:Network]
JoinDomain = "DomainName"
[User2:UserData]
FullName = "User 2"
OrgName = "MyCompany"
ComputerName = "Computer2"
[User2:GuiUnattended]
TimeZone = "(GMT-08:00) Pacific Time (US & Canada); Tijuana"
[User2:Network]
JoinDomain = "OtherDomain"
```

So, how do you combine the use of the unattended answer file and the UDF? For each environment (similar hardware, certain department, certain geography), create a single unattended answer file. Additionally, create at least one UDF file that specifies the unique IDs of all machines that will be installed. For each Unique ID, indicate those parameters that should be defined on a per-computer basis or per-user basis.

Note   Understanding how the unattended answer file and UDFs function is important for the exam. Not only is it one of the exam objectives, but there tends to be quite a few questions on this area on the exam.

Using Sysdiff

Sysdiff, unlike the unattended answer file and the uniqueness database file, is not used to actually install the Windows NT operating system itself. Instead, it is used to install applications after the operating system is in place. You can use it in conjunction with these files to create a fully automated install of both the operating system and your applications.

This tool gives you the ability to track the changes between a standard installation of Windows NT Workstation and an installation that has been modified to your particular environment. It does this by creating a *snapshot* of your system before the changes. The snapshot is of the freshly installed Windows NT Workstation, as has been configured from the automated installation. After you have made the desired changes to your system (adding applications), sysdiff then records a *difference file*, which tracks the changes that were made.

 Note

The sysdiff utility is for Windows NT 4 only. Therefore do not try to use it to install Windows 95 or Windows NT 3.51.

Creating a Snapshot File

The first step in running sysdiff is to install Windows NT Workstation on to a sample system. After the operating system is installed, you use sysdiff to take a snapshot of that reference machine. The command to take a snapshot of the system is as follows:

```
Sysdiff /snap [/log:log file] snapshot file
```

Where:

> *log file* is the name of an optional log file that can be created by sysdiff.

> *snapshot file* is the name of the file that will contain the snapshot of the system.

This process creates the snapshot file. This snapshot file is then used as the original configuration. This original configuration is the baseline for comparing with the changed system.

The reference machine (the one that you are taking a snapshot of) must be the same platform (x86, Alpha, and so on) as the destination computers (the ones that will be installed unattended). Additionally, the Windows NT root directory (d:\winnt, for example) must be the same on the reference machine and the target machines that will have the difference file applied

This process creates the snapshot file, which is then used as the original configuration for comparison.

 Caution

> When propagating the directory structure, sysdiff does not copy empty directories. As a workaround, you can either copy a temporary file into those directories or copy them as part of the Windows NT installation.

Creating a Difference File

After the snapshot has been taken, install all applications needed on the machine. After the applications have been installed, you then apply the second step of sysdiff, which is to create the difference file. The difference file is created by using the following command:

```
Sysdiff /diff [/c:title] [/log:log file] snapshot file difference
file
```

Where:

/c:*title* is the title for the difference file.

log file is the name of an optional log file that can be created by sysdiff.

snapshot file is the name of the file that contains the snapshot of the system. This file must be created from the same snapshot file created with the /snap command. If you use a file created on another system, sysdiff will not run.

difference file is the name of the file that contains the changes from when the snapshot was created to the current configuration of the system.

This mode uses the snapshot file (the original configuration) created in the first step to determine the changes in the directory structure and the Registry entries created by the application installations. These are what will be added to the difference file.

 Caution

Make certain that you do not change the computer name of the reference machine after you have started the sysdiff process. If you do, you must re-create the snapshot and the difference file.

Applying the Difference File

The final step in the sysdiff process is to apply the difference file to a new installation as part of the unattended setup. This is done with the following command:

```
Sysdiff /apply /m [/log:log file] difference file
```

Where:

/m makes the changes made to the menu structure map to the Default User profile structure, rather than to the currently logged on user. Otherwise, these menu changes would only be made to one user account, not globally on the system. And that one user account may not even exist on the destination workstation.

log file is the name of an optional log file sysdiff uses to write information regarding the process. This is good to use for troubleshooting if sysdiff fails during the apply process.

difference file is the file created by the /diff command. The Windows NT root must be the same (d:\winnt, for example) as the system that created the difference file. This means that all the unattended installs that you will perform using this difference file must be identical in the location of this system root.

You do not have to run this command as part of the unattended installation. You can run it at any time after Windows NT Workstation is installed. To make the installation of Windows NT and your applications fully automated, you might want to have it run as part of the install.

Because this difference file contains all the files and Registry settings for the applications you installed, it can be quite large (depending on how many applications you install). Applying such a potentially large package as part of the installation can add a significant amount of time to your setup process. One way of alleviating that is to create an INF file from this difference file.

Creating an INF File

An INF file created from the difference file contains only the Registry and the initialization file directives. It is, therefore, significantly smaller than the difference file itself. The command to initiate the INF portion of the installation is as follows:

```
Sysdiff /inf /m [/u] sysdiff_file oem_root
```

Where:

> */m* makes the changes made to the menu structure map to the Default User profile structure rather than to the currently logged on user. Otherwise, these menu changes would only be made to one user account, not globally on the system. And that one user account may not even exist on the destination workstation.

> */u* indicates that the INF be generated as a Unicode text file. The default is to generate the file using the system ANSI codepage.

> *Sysdiff_file* is the path to the file created by the /diff process.

> *Oem_root* is the path of a directory. This is where the OEM structure required for the INF will be created, and where the INF will be placed.

This command creates the INF file as well as a OEM directory structure, which contains all the files from the difference file package. You should create this directory under the I386 directory (if installing x86 machines) on the distribution server. If the directory is not under the I386 directory, you can move it.

 Caution

> The initial phase of Windows NT installation is DOS based and cannot copy directories whose path names are longer than 64 characters. Make certain that the directory length under the OEM directory does not exceed that.

Using the INF File

To use this INF file after it has been created, you must add a line to the file Cmdlines.txt under the OEM directory. This line is used to invoke the INF that you created. The format of the command is as follows:

```
"RUNDLL32 syssetup,SetupInfObjectInstallAction section 128 inf"
```

Where:

> *section* specifies the name of the section in the INF file.

> *inf* specifies the name of the INF file. This needs to be specified as a relative path.

Using an INF file rather than the entire difference file package can save you time in your unattended installation.

Dumping the Difference File

You can use the /dump option to dump the difference file into a file that you can review. This command enables you to read the contents of the difference file. The syntax of this command is as follows:

```
Sysdiff /dump difference file dump file
```

Where:

> *difference file* specifies the name of the difference file that you want to review.

> *dump file* specifies the name you want to give to the dump file.

After creating the dump file, you can view it with any text editor such as Notepad.

Planning Strategies for Sharing and Securing Resources

 When installing Windows NT Workstation 4.0, another consideration is how resources will be made available to users while also remaining secure. Giving users access to resources does not require "giving away the shop." To effectively share and secure resources for Windows NT Workstation, you must understand the built-in groups and what rights those give the users within them, as well as how sharing one folder affects the other folders in the hierarchy below it.

Built-In NTW Groups

Windows NT Workstation has five built-in groups added as part of the installation process. You can utilize these built-in groups to give users certain rights and abilities on the Windows NT system. These groups are as follows:

▶ Users

▶ Power Users

▶ Administrators

▶ Guests

▶ Backup Operators

When administering user accounts and assigning user rights, it is typically easier to assign rights to a group rather than to an individual. Table 1.1. identifies and explains the default rights initially assigned to users or groups on a Windows NT workstation.

Table 1.1

Definition of Default User Rights		
User Right	Enables	Granted to
Access this computer from the network	A user to connect to the computer over the network.	Administrators, Everyone, Power Users
Back up files and directories	A user to back up files and directories. (This right supersedes file and directory permissions.)	Administrators, Backup Operators
Change the system time	A user to set the clock of the internal computer.	Administrators, Power Users
Force shutdown from a remote system	A user to shut down a remote computer	Administrators, Power Users
Load and unload device drivers	A user to install and remove device drivers.	Administrators
Log on locally	A user to log on at the computer from the computer keyboard.	Administrators, Backup Operators, Guests, Everyone, Power Users, Users
Manage auditing and security log	A user to specify what types of resource access (such as file access) are to be audited, and to view and clear the security log. This right does not enable a user to set system auditing policy using **Audit** on the User Manager	Administrators

User Right	Enables	Granted to
	Policy menu. Members of the Administrators group can always view and clear the security log.	
Restore files and directories	A user to restore backed-up files and directories. This right supersedes file and directory permissions.	Administrators, Backup Operators
Shut down the system	A user to shut down Windows NT.	Administrators, Backup Operators, Power Users, Users, Everyone
Take ownership of files or other objects	A user to take ownership of files, directories, printers, and other objects on the computer. This right supersedes permissions protecting objects.	Administrators

Table 1.1 lists the definition of what each default user right enables a user to do. You can use the existing groups on Windows NT Workstation to give a user the ability to perform any of these tasks, or you can add that user's account to the list of accounts with permissions (see fig. 1.5).

Figure 1.5

In User Manager, the Policies menu, User Rights, you can modify the default user rights assigned in Windows NT.

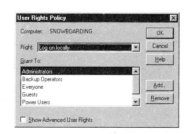

When trying to determine whether to add a particular user account to the list of default user rights or to just add the user to an existing Windows NT Workstation group that has that right, it is helpful to know which groups are assigned certain rights by default. Table 1.2 shows this.

Table 1.2

Assignment of Default User Rights

Rights	Admin	Power Users	Users	Guests	Every-one	Backup Opera-tors
Access this computer from the network	X	X			X	
Back up files and directories	X					X
Change the system time	X	X				
Force shut-down from a remote system	X	X				
Load and unload device drivers	X					
Log on locally	X	X	X	X	X	X
Manage auditing and security log	X					
Restore files and directories	X					X
Shut down the system	X	X	X		X	X

Rights	Admin	Power Users	Users	Guests	Every-one	Backup Opera-tors
Take owner-ship of files or other objects	X					

In addition to these default user rights, Windows NT also has built-in user capabilities. You cannot modify these built-in capabilities. The only way to give a user one of these abilities is to put that user in a group that has the capability. If you want to give a user the right to create and manage user accounts on a Windows NT workstation, for example, you must put that user into either the Power Users or the Administrators group to give him that ability. Table 1.3 lists the built-in capabilities on Windows NT Workstation.

Table 1.3

Built-In User Capabilities

Built-in Capabilities	Admin	Power Users	Users	Guests	Every-one	Backup Opera-tors
Create and manage user accounts	X	X				
Create and manage local groups	X	X				
Lock the Workstation	X	X	X	X	X	X
Override the lock of the workstation	X					
Format the hard disk	X					

continues

Table 1.3 Continued

Built-In User Capabilities

Built-in Capabilities	Admin	Power Users	Users	Guests	Every-one	Backup Opera-tors
Create Common Groups	X	X				
Share and stop Sharing Directories	X	X				
Share and stop Sharing Printers	X	X				

These built-in user rights on Windows NT Workstation are important in understanding how to give users access to perform certain tasks on the system.

Users

The Users group provides the user with the necessary rights to use the computer as an end user. By default, all accounts created on Windows NT Workstation get put into the Users group, except for the built-in Administrator and Guest accounts.

Power Users

The Power Users group gives members the ability to perform certain system tasks without giving the user complete administrative control over the machine. One of the tasks a Power User can perform is the sharing of directories. An ordinary user on Windows NT Workstation cannot share directories (see table 1.2).

Administrators

The Administrators group has full control over the Windows NT workstation. This account has the most control on the computer. As a member of the Administrators group, however, the user does not automatically have control over all files on the system. If using an NTFS partition, a file's permissions could be to restrict access from the Administrator. If the Administrator needs to access the file, she can take ownership of the file and then access it.

Guests

The Guests group is used to give someone limited access to the resources on the Windows NT workstation. The Guest account is automatically added to this group.

Note

The Guest account is disabled by default on Windows NT Workstation 4.0. This is a change from Windows NT 3.51, which enabled the Guest account by default for the workstation.

Backup Operators

The Backup Operators group gives a user the ability to back up and restore files on the Windows NT system. A user has the right to back up any files or directories that she has access to without being part of this group. By being a part of the Backup Operators group, a user has the ability to back up and restore files that normally the user would not have access to.

Special Groups

In addition to the default groups created on Windows NT Workstation, Windows NT Workstation uses four other special groups. You cannot assign users to these groups. That assignment happens as part of the Windows NT functionality. These special groups are as follows:

▶ Network

▶ Interactive

▶ Everyone

▶ Creator Owner

The *Network* group contains any user who is accessing this computer from across the network rather than sitting down at the computer locally. If Kelley is connecting to a shared printer on your Windows NT Workstation, for example, Kelley is part of the network group accessing your machine.

The *Interactive* group refers to the user who is logged on locally to the Windows NT workstation. Thus in the preceding example where Kelley is accessing your shared printer, on her own machine Kelley is logged on interactively, but to your machine she is part of the Network group.

Everyone refers to any user who accesses the Windows NT workstation. This includes all users defined on the computer or domain, as well as guests, interactive, network users, and users from other domains.

Creator Owner refers to the user account that created a resource, such as a file or printer. The Creator Owner automatically has full control over the resource that he created.

Sharing Home Directories for Users' Private Use

One of the issues that you have to decide in the planning process is whether to give your users their own home directories or personal directories for storing information either on the server or on their local workstation. A home directory is used as a location for a user to be able to store his or her own data or files, and only that particular user has access to the directory.

 Note An Administrator always has the ability to "take ownership" of a user's home directory in the case that she or he might need to if, for instance, the user has left the company and the files need to be retrieved (see Chapter 3, "Managing Resources").

One decision you must make when planning the structure of users' home directories is whether those directories should be on the user's local machine or on the server. Both of these can be good options, for varying reasons, as listed in table 1.4.

Table 1.4

Benefits of Storing Users' Home Directories on the Server versus the Local Computer

Server-Based Home Directories	Local Home Directories
Are centrally located so that users can access them from any location on the network.	Available only on the local machine. If user is a *roaming user*, information is not accessible from other systems.
If a regular backup of the server is being done, information in up users' home directories is also backed up.	Often users' local workstations are not backed regularly as part of a scheduled backup process. If the user's machine fails, the user cannot recover the lost data.
Windows NT does not provide a way to limit the size of a user's directory. Thus if a lot of information is being stored in home directories, it uses up server disk space.	If a user stores a lot of information in his home directory, the space is taken up on his local hard drive rather than the server.
If the server is down, the user won't have access to her files.	The user has access to his files regardless of whether the server is up, because the files are stored locally.
Some network bandwidth is consumed due to the over-the-network access of data or files.	No network traffic is generated by a user accessing his or her files.

Structure

Typically when you are creating home directories on the server for users, it is best to centralize those directories under one directory (for example, called "Users"). If you have five users in your company—named Tina, Mark, Carla, Corey, and Fritz—your directory structure would look like that shown in figure 1.6.

Figure 1.6

The directory structure of five users' home directories.

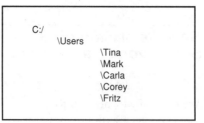

If you were to share these directories at the "users" level, you would have the problem that all directories would be accessible to all users. Thus if Tina wanted to access Mark's directory, using this setup, you could not prevent her from doing so. If you use share permissions only, you must share each user's directory individually at the folder level. In this case, therefore, you would share Tina's directory to just Tina, Mark's to just Mark, and so on. (For a more thorough discussion of NTFS versus Share permissions, see Chapter 3, "Managing Resources.")

Permissions

To share each individual user's home directory separately at the folder level is probably tedious, especially if you have a large environment with many users. One way around this problem is to create the "Users" directory on an NTFS partition rather than a FAT partition. By doing that, you can use NTFS permissions for each specific directory (for example, the directory called "Tina"), and then share with share permissions the top level "Users" directory to the Users group. By combining NTFS and share permissions in this manner, you can solve the problem of giving individual access, without a lot of extra work on the part of the administrator. Table 1.5 lists the directory permissions.

Table 1.5

Directory Structure Permissions for Users' Home Directories Using NTFS and Share Permissions		
Directory	User/Group	Permission
\Users	Users	Full Control
\Tina	Tina	Full Control
\Mark	Mark	Full Control

Directory	User/Group	Permission
\Carla	Carla	Full Control
\Corey	Corey	Full Control
\Fritz	Fritz	Full Control

This example provides a situation where all users can access the top level Users folder, but only a particular user can access his or her own home directory. Only Fritz has full control to his own home directory, for example. Because Fritz is not listed in the directory permissions for Carla's home directory, he does not have access to it or anything inside of it.

Sharing Application Folders

Another resource you may have to plan for is to give your users access to shared network applications. Shared application folders are typically used to give users access to applications that they will run from a network share point. Another option is to have users run applications locally from their own computers. Table 1.6 shows a comparison.

Table 1.6

Shared Network Applications versus Locally Installed Applications

Shared Network Applications	Locally Installed Applications
Take up less disk space on the local workstation.	Use more local disk space.
Easier to upgrade/control.	Upgrades must "touch" every machine locally.
Use network bandwidth.	Use no network bandwidth for running applications.
Slower response time because applications are accessed from the server.	Faster, more responsive.
If the server is down, users can't run applications.	Users can run applications regardless of server status.

As you can see, there are advantages and disadvantages to both shared network and locally installed implementations.

Structure

If you choose to use shared network applications, you must plan your server directory structure so that these folders can be shared in the most efficient and secure method. If, for example, you use a shared copy of Word, Excel, and PowerPoint, your directory structure might look something like that shown in figure 1.7.

Figure 1.7

The directory structure of shared applications folders.

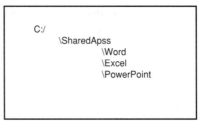

```
C:/
      \SharedApss
            \Word
            \Excel
            \PowerPoint
```

In this example, you want all your users to be able to access these folders for running applications, but you do not want them to be able to change the permissions or delete any files from within these directories. A group (the "Applications group") is in charge of updates to these applications. That group, therefore, needs the ability to modify the application directories, but not to modify the permissions on the directory structure.

Permissions

The permissions on this shared network applications directory structure need to allow the Applications group to make updates to files within any of the three directories as needed, and to allow the users to access the directories to execute the applications. To do this, set up the directory structure like that shown in table 1.7.

Table 1.7

Directory Structure Permissions for Shared Network Applications

Directory	Group	Permission
\SharedApps	Administrators	Full Control
	Applications group	Change
	Users	Read

Directory	Group	Permission
\Word	Inherited from Shared Apps	Inherited from SharedApps
\Excel	Inherited from Shared Apps	Inherited from SharedApps
\PowerPoint	Inherited from Shared Apps	Inherited from SharedApps

Because you are sharing the top-level folder *SharedApps*, you do not need to share the lower-level folders *Word*, *Excel*, and *Power-Point* unless you want them to be individually available to users. By giving administrators full control, you give them the ability not only to add files but also to change the permissions on the directory structure. By giving the Applications group the change permission, you are allowing them to upgrade the applications in these directories as needed.

Sharing Common Access Folders

Another situation that you may face when planning how to appropriately share and secure resources is the need to have a directory structure, which allows for certain groups to work together on files and have access to directories based on this group membership. You might have a top-level directory called *Departments*, for example, with subdirectories of Sales, Accounting, Human-Resources, and Finance.

Structure

To create a directory structure to support the need for certain groups to share access over certain directories, you may want to create your directory structure like that shown in figure 1.8.

Figure 1.8

The directory structure of company departments' common access folders.

```
C:\Departments
            \Sales
            \Accounting
            \HumanResources
            \Finance
```

By creating the departmental folders under one main folder, you centralize the administration of the folder hierarchy. This structure enables you to have a common location for the sales personnel to store their files and access information. Because you may not want the sales personnel to access the accounting data, however, you need to plan your shared directories accordingly.

Permissions

To set share permissions on this folder hierarchy, you need to assign permissions separately to each directory, as shown in table 1.8.

Table 1.8

Directory Structure Permissions for Common Access Folders		
Directory	Group	Permission
\Departments	Administrators	Full Control
\Sales	Sales	Change
\Accounting	Accountants	Change
\HumanResources	HR	Change
\Finance	Finance	Change

Giving the Administrators group Full Control over the Departments share makes the administration of the shared hierarchy possible and enables the administrators to have access to all the shared folders below the top-level folder Departments. No specific department can be given access at the Departments level, because you do not want any department having access to any other department's data. Because this is the case, you need to share each departmental folder at the folder level, and only to that particular department. The Sales folder, for example, is shared to the Sales group with Change permission. The Sales group will probably need to add or modify data in this directory, but not modify the directory itself, or the directory's permissions. Because of this, the Sales group is given the Change permission rather than Full Control. (For a more thorough definition of share permissions, see Chapter 3, "Managing Resources.")

Choosing the Appropriate File System to Use in a Given Situation

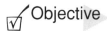 Objective   Windows NT Workstation 4.0 has support for two file systems: FAT and NTFS. Windows NT 3.51 contained support for HPFS (the High Performance File System used with OS/2), but that support has been eliminated in the latest release.

Windows NT 4.0 supports the use of either or both the NTFS and FAT file systems. An important decision in planning your Windows NT Workstation environment is which file system to use. Which file system you use on each workstation or each partition within a workstation depends on the needs of your particular environment. Some of the issues to consider when choosing a file system are the following:

▶ Performance

▶ Size of partition

▶ Recoverability

▶ Dual-boot capabilities

▶ Security

▶ Compressing files

Using Disk Administrator

Disk Administrator is the primary tool used when creating, removing, formatting, and viewing disk partitions on Windows NT Workstation. It is a graphical tool for managing disk configuration. Disk Administrator enables you to do the following:

▶ View physical disks on your system.

▶ View partition sizes.

▶ Create and delete partitions.

▶ View free space available.

▶ View file systems used for each partition.

▶ Create and delete logical drives within an extended partition.

▶ Format partitions.

▶ View logical drives within an extended partition.

▶ Change drive letter assignments.

▶ Save and restore disk configuration information.

Understanding how to use Disk Administrator is important in both planning and implementing Windows NT Workstation.

Primary Partitions

A *partition* is an area of a physical disk that functions as though it were a separate unit. There is a limit of four partitions per physical disk.

A *primary partition* is a partition on which you can load the files needed to boot a particular operating system. A primary partition cannot be sub-partitioned. Thus if you want multiple partitions on your system, make certain not to use all available free space for the primary partition. There can be up to four primary partitions per physical disk. A primary partition is needed for the Windows NT system partition.

▶ **System Partition.** The volume that contains the files needed to load Windows NT Workstation (Ntldr, Ntdetect.com, and so on). Only a primary partition can be used as the system partition. This primary partition must be marked active.

▶ **Boot Partition.** The volume that contains the Windows NT operating system files (\winnt directory and subdirectories). This can be the same volume as the system partition, but does not have to be.

Creating a Primary Partition with Disk Administrator

Using Disk Administrator, follow these steps to create a new primary partition.

1. To launch Disk Administrator, go to the Start button, Programs, Administrative Tools, Disk Administrator.

2. Select the area of free space that you would like to create as a primary partition.

3. Go to the Partition menu and choose Create.

4. Enter in the size of the primary partition that you would like to create.

5. Before you can format this new partition, you must save the change you have made by going to the Partition menu and choosing Commit Changes Now.

6. After you have committed the changes, you can go to the Tools menu and choose Format to format the new partition.

7. Select a file system that you would like to use for the new partition and click on OK to format the partition.

8. This new drive is now available in My Computer or the Windows NT Explorer.

Extended Partitions

An *extended partition* is created from free space on the physical disk and can be sub-partitioned into multiple logical drives. An extended partition is not assigned a drive letter or formatted with a file system. Only the logical drives within the extended partition can be assigned a drive letter or formatted with a particular file system. Creating an extended partition enables you to avoid the four-partition limitation.

Note

There can only be one extended partition per physical disk, so plan your partitions accordingly. If you have three primary partitions, and create an extended partition that does not include all the free space available on the drive, you could end up wasting the remaining free space.

Creating multiple logical drives within the extended partition enables you to format each drive with a particular file system as needed. If you create a single logical drive within the extended partition, within Windows NT you cannot change the partition information without deleting the logical drive and then re-creating logical drives.

 Tip

> Some third-party partition managers, such as Partition Magic, enable you to change the size of an existing partition without deleting the partition or losing data. Keep in mind, however, that it is always a good idea to back up important data before resizing partitions.

If you have multiple physical disks, it is possible to have a disk that only has an extended partition on it and no primary partitions. To do this, you must have at least one physical disk that has a primary partition for the Windows NT system partition.

Creating an Extended Partition with Disk Administrator

You can use Disk Administrator to create an extended partition by following these steps:

1. To launch Disk Administrator, go to the Start button, Programs, Administrative Tools, Disk Administrator.

2. Select the area of free space that you would like to create as an extended partition.

3. Go to the Partition menu and choose Create Extended.

4. Enter in the size of the extended partition that you would like to create.

5. Before you can use this new partition, you must save the change you have made by going to the Partition menu and choosing Commit Changes Now.

6. After you have committed the changes, you can create logical drives within this extended partition and format them as needed.

7. These new logical drives are now available in My Computer or the Windows NT Explorer.

Tip

Windows NT knows of the existence of an extended partition because the System ID byte in the Partition Table entry is set to 5.

Within an extended partition, you can create any number of logical drives. This limit is typically reached due to the number of available drive letters.

Default Drive Letter Assignment

Although you can change the drive letter assignments in Disk Administrator, by default Windows NT letters drives in a particular order. That order is as follows:

1. Windows NT first checks the first physical disk for a primary partition. The first primary partition on the first physical disk gets the drive letter C.

2. Windows NT then checks all remaining disks for the first primary partition, and that is assigned a drive letter.

3. After this process of lettering the first primary partition is completed for all physical disks, Windows NT then assigns drive letters to the logical drives in the extended partitions on each physical disk, starting with the first physical drive in the system.

4. Finally, after all logical drives are assigned drive letters, all remaining primary partitions on all drives are assigned drive letters.

Understanding how Windows NT assigns drive letters can help you in troubleshooting as well as managing your system.

The High Performance File System (HPFS)

High Performance File System (HPFS) is the file system used with OS/2. Windows NT 3.51 supported partitions formatted with the HPFS file system, although it did not support formatting new drives as HPFS. In Windows NT 4.0, the support for HPFS has been eliminated entirely. Thus if you have a system that currently has an HPFS partition, you need to format that drive as either FAT or NTFS before installing Windows NT Workstation 4.0 or upgrading to Windows NT 4.0. You must remove the HPFS partition before setting up Windows NT 4.0. Otherwise, you cannot proceed with the installation. You can do this in one of two ways:

▶ Format the HPFS partition to either FAT or NTFS

▶ Convert the HPFS partition to NTFS prior to the installation

The option you choose depends on what is stored on the existing HPFS drive.

 Caution

Reformatting the drive erases all existing data on the drive. Therefore, do not choose this option unless you have made a backup of the data or choose not to keep the existing data.

Formatting an HPFS Partition

If you choose to format the existing HPFS drive as either FAT or NTFS, you must make certain to back up the existing data on the drive that you want to keep.

If the HPFS drive is your system partition (the one that you boot from) or your boot partition (the one that contains the Windows NT operating system files), you cannot reformat that partition from within Windows NT.

To format the system partition, you need to follow these steps:

1. Create a DOS bootable floppy.

2. Boot the computer from the floppy.

3. Use the DOS format command with the /s option to format the drive FAT and make it bootable to DOS.

4. From DOS, launch the Windows NT installation.

If the \winnt directory is not on the system partition (the one that you just formatted), you didn't blow away Windows NT by formatting the system partition. If you can boot off a Windows NT bootable floppy, you can run the upgrade from within Windows NT rather than DOS.

To format the boot partition, you need to follow these steps:

1. If the system partition is FAT, boot to DOS.

2. After booting under DOS, format the boot partition with the DOS format command.

3. From DOS, launch the Windows NT installation

 Caution If you are reformatting your system partition, make certain that you have either a DOS bootable or Windows NT bootable floppy available so that you can restart your computer after you have reformatted.

If the HPFS partition that you are trying to delete is not your system or boot partition, you can reformat the partition within the Windows NT Disk Administrator program (see fig. 1.9).

Figure 1.9

You can use the Windows NT Disk Administrator program (in Windows NT 3.51) to format an HPFS drive as either FAT or NTFS.

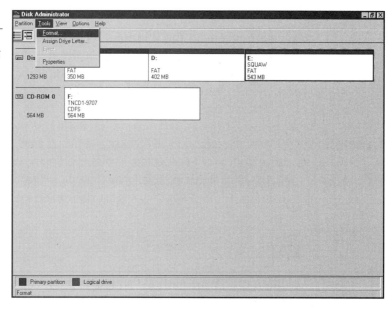

If there are any files in use on the HPFS partition being formatted, the format command prompts you to close those files in use on the drive.

After you have reformatted the drive, you are ready to upgrade the system to Windows NT Workstation 4.

Converting an HPFS Partition

If you do not want to lose the data on your HPFS partition, you can use the convert command (from within Windows NT 3.51) to convert the HPFS partition to NTFS before you upgrade to Windows NT 4.0. The convert command is run from the command line with the following syntax:

```
Convert drive: /FS:NTFS /v
```

Where:

> *drive* is the drive letter of the HPFS partition you want to convert
>
> */FS:NTFS* specifies the file system that you want to convert to (NTFS is the only option)
>
> */v* runs in verbose mode

You cannot convert the Windows NT boot partition while you are running Windows NT. If the boot partition is the partition you are attempting to convert, you receive a prompt to convert it the next time the machine is rebooted.

 Caution

> Converting a drive to NTFS can take a long time, especially if the drive is large or fragmented. The convert command does not display any status information. It may, therefore, appear to be hung up, when in actuality it is still converting the file system.

FAT

Windows NT Workstation 4 supports the FAT file system. This file system is named after its method of organization, the File

Allocation Table. The File Allocation Table resides at the top, or beginning of the volume. Two copies of the FAT are kept in case one is damaged. FAT supports the following four attributes:

- ▶ Read only

- ▶ Archive

- ▶ System

- ▶ Hidden

Understanding the Benefits

The FAT file system is typically a good option for a small-sized partition. Because FAT is required for DOS, it is also a good option for a dual-boot system with Windows 95 or Windows 3.x. The FAT file system on Windows NT has a number of benefits over using FAT on a DOS-based system. Used under Windows NT, the FAT file system supports the following:

- ▶ Long file names up to 255 characters.

- ▶ Multiple spaces.

- ▶ Multiple periods.

- ▶ File names are not case-sensitive, but they do preserve case.

The FAT file system has a fairly low fill-system overhead, which makes it good for smaller partitions.

Knowing the Limitations

Although the FAT file system is necessary for dual-boot configurations, there are some significant limitations to using it with Windows NT. Those include the following:

- ▶ **Inefficient for larger partitions.** There are two reasons that FAT is inefficient on larger partitions (over about 200 MB). One reason is that FAT uses a linked list for its directory structure. If a file grows in size, the file may become fragmented on the disk and will have slower access time for retrieving the file because of fragmentation. The other reason is the default cluster size used on a FAT partition. For partitions up to 255 MB, FAT uses a 4 K cluster size. For partitions greater than 512 MB, however, FAT uses 16 K cluster sizes and up to 256 K cluster sizes for drives above 8192 MB on Windows NT 4. Thus if you are using FAT under Windows NT and have a partition that is 800 MB and you have a lot of smaller (under 32 K) files on the drive, you could end up wasting a lot of space on the drive due to the cluster size.

▶ **Has no Local Security.** The FAT file system does not support local security, so there is no way to prevent a user from accessing a file if that user can log on locally to the workstation.

▶ **Does not support compression under Windows NT.** Although the FAT file system supports compression by using DriveSpace or DoubleSpace, neither of those are supported under Windows NT. For this reason, there is no way to use compression on FAT under Windows NT.

Whether you choose to use the FAT file system depends on what needs you have on your particular workstation.

Using NTFS

NTFS tends to be the preferred file system for use under Windows NT if your environment can support it (you don't need to dual-boot, for instance). Only Windows NT supports NTFS.

Understanding the Benefits

Using NTFS has many benefits, including the following:

▶ **Support for long file names.** NTFS supports long file names up to 255 characters long.

▶ **Preservation of case.** NTFS is not case-sensitive, but it does have the capability to preserve case for POSIX compliance.

▶ **Recoverability.** NTFS is a recoverable file system. It uses transaction logging to automatically log all file and directory updates so that in the case of a power outage or system failure this information can be used to redo failed operations.

▶ **Security.** NTFS provides the user with local security for protecting files and directories.

▶ **Compression.** NTFS supports compression of files and directories to optimize storage space on your hard disk.

▶ **Size.** NTFS partitions can support much larger partition sizes than FAT. NTFS can support partitions up to 16 exabytes in size. (An exabyte is a little larger than one billion gigabytes.)

Using NTFS gives you security and enhanced functionality compared with the FAT file system.

Knowing the Limitations

The main limitation with NTFS is compatibility with other operating systems and overhead. If needing to dual-boot, or if you have a partition size smaller than about 200 MB, you should use FAT rather than NTFS.

Comparison of FAT and NTFS

There are benefits to using both FAT and NTFS partitions on Windows NT Workstation. Many of these are dependent on your particular configuration and what you need to support. Table 1.9 provides a comparison of the two file systems.

Table 1.9

Comparison of NTFS and FAT File Systems		
Feature	FAT	NTFS
File name length	255	255
Compression	No	Yes
Security	No	Yes
Dual-boot capabilities with non-Windows NT systems	Yes	No
File/partition size	4 GB	16 EB
Recommended partition size	0–200 MB	100 MB–16 EB

continues

Table 1.9 Continued

Comparison of NTFS and FAT File Systems

Feature	FAT	NTFS
Can use it to format a floppy	Yes	No
Recoverability (transaction logging)	No	Yes

NTFS and FAT are both supported file systems under Windows NT 4.0. Your decision on which to use depends on what scenario you must support.

Using Compression

NTFS compression is used to make more efficient use of limited hard disk space. If you need more space on your hard disk and do not wish to purchase an additional drive, you can use NTFS compression to fit more information on your existing disk. The compression state of a folder does not necessarily reflect the compression state of the files in that folder. It is possible to have a folder that is compressed, and yet none of the files within that folder are compressed. To use NTFS compression under Windows NT Workstation 4.0, you can either initiate it through the file or folder properties or through the command line using the compact utility.

 Caution

There is a utility called compress that enables you to compress folders and files. It is not recommended that you use this file for compression because you cannot open a file that has been compressed with this utility.

Implementing Compression Through File or Folder Properties

To compress a file or folder within Windows NT 4.0, you can go to the properties for that file or folder on an NTFS drive. To implement compression through the properties, follow these steps:

1. Use the secondary (right-click) mouse button to click on the file or directory.

2. Choose the Properties option from the Context menu.

3. On the General Properties tab, click on the check box next to Compress to mark the compression attribute.

This compresses that file or folder and potentially any subfolders underneath it.

Implementing Compression Through the Command Line

To compress a file or folder through the command line, use the compact command. The syntax of the command is as follows:

```
compact [/c] [/u] [/s[:folder]] [/a] [/i] [/f] [/q] [filename
[...]]
```

Where:

none displays the compression state of the current folder.

/c compresses the specified folder or file.

/u uncompresses the specified folder or file.

/s[:folder] specifies that the requested action (compress or uncompress) be applied to all subfolders of the specified folder or to the current folder if none is specified.

/i ignores errors.

/f forces compression or uncompression of the specified folder or file.

/a displays files with the hidden or system attribute.

/q reports only the most essential information.

filename specifies a pattern, file, or folder. You can use multiple file names and wild cards.

You may choose to use the command line utility rather than the Properties tab for the file or folder if you want to implement compression as part of a batch file.

Caution The command line utility, compact, automatically compresses all files and subfolders when you change the compression attribute of a folder without prompting you beforehand. If you do not wish to do that, you can use the Graphical Properties tab for that file or folder.

Implementing Security

When talking about security as it relates to file systems, it is necessary to define what is meant by security. The NTFS file system gives you the ability to implement "local security." *Local security* is defined as being able to restrict access to a file or directory to someone who is sitting at the keyboard of that particular machine. Even if someone can log on to your Windows NT workstation locally or interactively, for example, you can still prevent them from accessing your files and directories if you use NTFS security.

NTFS is the only file system used with Windows NT 4 that has the ability to provide local security. The FAT file system can only secure a directory with share level permissions, not local permissions. Share level permissions apply only to users accessing the directory across the network. Because of this, share level permissions cannot prevent David, logged on locally, from accessing your files or directories.

Choosing Dual-Boot Scenarios

If you want to dual-boot between Windows NT 4.0 and any other non-Windows NT operating system, you must use the FAT file system for universal access across operating systems. The NTFS file system is only accessible by Windows NT. Thus if you are dual-booting with Windows 95, the NTFS partition will not be visible under Windows 95.

If you have a machine that you dual-boot between Windows NT Workstation 4.0 and Windows 95, you can use an NTFS partition if you choose to, even though it is inaccessible from within Windows 95. You must make sure in doing this, however, that you do not format your active partition (your C drive) or the partition that has the windows directory on it. Otherwise, you can't boot into Windows 95.

If you choose to dual-boot between Windows 95 and Windows NT Workstation 4.0, any applications that you have installed under one operating system must be reinstalled under the other operating system as well.

 Caution

> If you are using the FAT32 file system with Windows 95, you must remove it before installing Windows NT for dual-boot. The FAT32 file system for Windows 95 is inaccessible from within Windows NT.

Moving or Copying Files

When moving or copying files across partitions, and using NTFS permissions, you must be careful or you may lose the NTFS permissions on the file. Table 1.10 lists what happens to NTFS file permissions when a file is moved or copied across or within a partition.

Table 1.10

Results on File Permissions from Moving or Copying Files Within and Across Partitions

Action	File Permissions
Move file across NTFS partition	Inherited from new directory
Move file within NTFS partition	Retain permissions
Copy file across NTFS partition	Inherited from new directory
Copy file within NTFS partition	Inherited from new directory
Move file to FAT partition	NTFS permissions lost
Copy file to FAT partition	NTFS permissions lost

Files moved within an NTFS partition do not actually move; the pointer to the file is just moved. Because of this, the original file remains and its file permissions are still intact.

When moving a file across NTFS partitions, however, the permissions are not retained, but are instead inherited from the destination directory. The reason is that this action is actually a copy, and then delete. The copy/delete process creates a new file in the destination directory, and that new file thus inherits the permissions of the directory to which it is moved.

Copying a file either within or across NTFS partitions always creates a new file as part of the copy process. Because of this, the new file inherits the permissions of the directory to which it is copied.

Moving or copying a file from an NTFS partition to a FAT partition causes it to lose its file permissions altogether. This is because the FAT file system does not support NTFS file permissions. Whenever a file is moved or copied to a FAT partition, the file no longer contains any of the NTFS permissions or attributes, such as the compression attribute.

Note

The same rules apply when you are talking about moving or copying compressed files or folders from one partition to another as apply to NTFS permissions. In Table 1.10, replace the words "NTFS Permissions" with "Compression."

Key Terms and Concepts

Table 1.11 identifies key terms from this chapter. Review the key terms and make certain that you understand each term for the exam.

Table 1.10

Key Terms: Planning an Effective Implementation	
Term	Covered in Section…
Unattended Answer File	Creating Unattended Installation Files
UDF	Creating Unattended Installation Files
Sysdiff	Creating Unattended Installation Files

Term	Covered in Section...
Difference File	Creating Unattended Installation Files
Built-in Windows NT Groups	Built-in NTW Groups
Primary Partition	Choosing the Appropriate File System to Use in a Given Situation
Extended Partition	Choosing the Appropriate File System to Use in a Given Situation
HPFS	Choosing the Appropriate File System to Use in a Given Situation
FAT	Choosing the Appropriate File System to Use in a Given Situation
NTFS	Choosing the Appropriate File System to Use in a Given Situation
Compact	Using Compression
Compress	Using Compression

Exercises

These exercises provide practice for you to work with recordsets first-hand. The operations are fairly simple ones, with results being printed in the Debug window for the sake of simplicity. All four lab exercises are run from databases included on the Windows NT Workstation CD-ROM.

Exercise 1.1: Using the Setup Manager to Create an Unattended Answer File

The following exercise helps you work with the Setup Manager to create an unattended answer file. This sample file could be used to automate an installation of Windows NT Workstation.

Objective

To create an unattended answer file using the Setup Manager utility on the Windows NT Workstation CD-ROM.

Time Estimate: 30 Minutes

Steps

1. Log on to Windows NT Workstation as an administrator.

2. Insert the Windows NT Workstation CD into the CD-ROM drive. From the CD, click on the Support/deptools/i386 directory. Launch Setup Manager by double-clicking on it.

3. Click on the General button. Fill in the following fields on the User Information tab:

User Name	**Your name**
Organization Name	MyCompany
Computername	MyComputer
Product ID	Leave blank

Fill in the following information on the Computer Role tab:

Role Workstation in Workgroup

Workgroup Name Sierras

On the Time Zone tab, select your time zone from the list. Click on the OK button.

4. Click on the Networking Setup button. On the General tab, select Automatically detect and install first adapter. Click on the OK button.

5. Click on the Advanced Setup button. On the Advertisement tab, Banner text, type in **This is a customized NT Setup**. On the General tab, put a check mark in the following check boxes:

▶ Reboot After Text Mode

▶ Reboot After GUI Mode

▶ Skip Welcome Wizard Page

▶ Skip Administrator Password Page

Then click on OK.

6. Click on the Save button and save this file as c:\custom.txt. Exit out of Setup Manager.

7. Launch Notepad from the Start button, Programs, Accessories menu. From the File menu, choose Open. In the File Name field, type in **c:\custom.txt**. Review the contents of the file.

8. Exit Notepad and log off Windows NT Workstation.

Exercise 1.2: Assigning User Rights to a User Account

This exercise helps you understand the rights of built-in Windows NT Workstation groups by examining the user rights within User Manager and testing to see what happens when they are changed.

Objective

The objective of this exercise is to familiarize you with the different user rights given to groups under Windows NT and to give you practice modifying those rights.

continues

Time Estimate: 40 Minutes

Steps

1. Log on to Windows NT Workstation with the built-in Administrator account.

2. Launch User Manager by going to the Start menu, Programs, Administrative Tools, User Manager.

3. Within User Manager, click on the Policies menu and choose User Rights.

4. What groups can log on locally to the Windows NT workstation by default?

5. What groups can change the system time?

6. Close out of the User Rights dialog box. Within User Manager, create a new user account by clicking on the User menu and choosing New User. Fill in the following fields:

Username	MarinaS
Full Name	Marina Sugar
Password	Blank
Description	User
User Must Change Password at next logon	Uncheck

7. Click on the Add button to create the user account for MarinaS.

8. From the Policies Menu, choose User Rights. From the list of user rights, select Change the System Time. Click on the Add button to add the new account MarinaS to the list of accounts with the right to change the system time.

9. Log off of Windows NT Workstation.

10. Log on as MarinaS with a blank password.

11. On the taskbar, double-click on the clock.

12. Change the time to 12:00 AM. Were you successful?

13. Log off of Windows NT.

14. Log on as the default administrator.

15. Launch User Manager by going to the Start menu, Programs, Administrative Tools, User Manager.

16. Within User Manager, click on the Policies menu and choose User Rights.

17. From the list, select Change the System Time. Remove the account for MarinaS from the list of accounts with the right to change the system time.

18. Close out of the User Rights dialog box. Exit out of User Manager.

19. Log off Windows NT Workstation.

20. Log on as MarinaS with a blank password.

21. Double-click on the clock on the taskbar. Change the system time to 2:30 PM. Were you successful?

22. Log off Windows NT Workstation.

Exercise 1.3: Creating a Partition Using Disk Administrator and Converting an Existing FAT Partition to NTFS

This exercise teaches you how to work with partitions and Disk Administrator. (This lab exercise requires that you either have unpartitioned space on your hard disk or that you have a FAT partition that you can convert to NTFS.)

Objective

This exercise teaches you how to work with Disk Administrator to create an NTFS partition and to convert a FAT partition to NTFS.

Time Estimate: 30 Minutes

continues

Exercise 1.3: Continued

Steps

Creating an NTFS Partition from Free Space

1. Log on to Windows NT Workstation as an administrator.

2. Launch Disk Administrator from the Start button, Programs, Administrative Tools group.

3. If this is the first time that you have run Disk Administrator, it prompts you to write a signature on the disk. Accept the defaults when prompted.

4. Within Disk Administrator, how many partitions do you have? How many primary? How many secondary? How can you tell the difference within Disk Administrator?

5. Select an area of free space, signified by diagonal lines, by clicking on it. From the Partition menu, choose Create. From the Create dialog box, select the size you wish to use for your new partition. Make certain that it is at least 10 MB.

6. Click on the new partition, and then on the Partition menu choose Commit Changes Now. When prompted to save the changes, click on Yes. A dialog box appears indicating that disks were updated successfully. Click on OK.

7. With the new partition selected, go to the Tools menu and choose Format. Under File System, select NTFS. Within the Format dialog box, click on Start. Click on OK to the Warning message. Click on OK in the format complete message. Click on Close to exit the Format dialog box.

Converting a FAT Partition

1. Log on to Windows NT Workstation as an administrator.

2. Launch Disk Administrator by going to the Start button, Programs, Administrative Tools, Disk Administrator.

3. View the partitions on your system to determine which is a FAT partition. You will convert this partition to NTFS. If you do not wish to convert an existing partition, create a new FAT partition with Disk Administrator.

4. Close Disk Administrator. Go to a command prompt and type **convert** *drive letter:* **/fs:ntfs**, and then press Enter. Windows NT begins the conversion process. If files are in use on this partition, you receive a message that `Convert cannot gain exclusive access to your drive, would you like to schedule it to be converted the next time the system restarts`. Type **Y** to answer Yes and press Enter. Exit the command prompt by typing **Exit**. Restart Windows NT Workstation by clicking on the Start button, Restart the Computer. When the computer reboots, it will convert the drive to NTFS. After the conversion has happened, the system restarts again and boots into Windows NT Workstation.

Exercise 1.4:   Copying a File from an NTFS Partition to a FAT Partition

This exercise shows you the effects of copying and moving files to and from an NTFS partition. (This lab exercise requires that you have both a FAT and NTFS partition on your Windows NT Workstation. For instructions on how to create an NTFS partition, see exercise 1.3)

Objective

This exercise helps you to see the effects of moving a file from an NTFS partition to a FAT partition.

Time Estimate: 20 Minutes

Steps

1. Log on to Windows NT Workstation as an administrator.

2. Launch Windows NT Explorer from the Start menu, Programs group.

3. On an NTFS partition, create a new folder called Test.

4. Right-click on the Test folder and select the Properties.

5. Click on the Security tab and then the Permissions button.

continues

6. From the Directory Permissions dialog box, click on the Add button. From the list of names, select the Guests group and then click on the Add button. From the list of names, select the Administrators group and then click on the Add button. After both groups show up under Add names, click on OK to close the Add Users and Groups dialog box.

7. Within the Directory Permissions dialog box, select the Everyone group and click on Remove. Select the Administrators group. In the Type of Access drop-down box, select Full Control. Select the Guests group. In the Type of Access drop-down box, select No Access. Click on OK to close the Directory Permissions dialog box. Click on OK to close the Test Properties dialog box.

8. Within the Test folder, create a new text document by clicking on the File menu, New and selecting text document from the list. Name this document Mammoth.txt. Get the properties for Mammoth.txt by clicking on the file and then going to File, Properties. From the Mammoth Properties dialog box, select the Security tab and then the Permissions button. What are the permissions for this file? Are they the same as the directory? Why or why not?

9. Close the file Permissions dialog box and close the Mammoth Properties dialog box. Open My Computer and position the window on the screen so that you can see it as well as the window for the Test folder containing Mammoth.txt. Drag Mammoth.txt and drop it on to the root of a FAT partition.

10. Open the FAT partition that you copied the file to by double-clicking on it from within the My Computer window. Find Mammoth.txt and select it. Get the properties for it by clicking on File Properties. What happened to the permissions?

Review Questions

The following questions test your knowledge of the material in this chapter.

1. Problem: You are in charge of your company's rollout of Windows NT Workstation 4.0. You need to install 500 machines that will all be part of the same domain and will use TCP/IP. You have identical hardware, and want Windows NT installed identically on all machines.

   Required Result: To install Windows NT Workstation on all machines so that it is configured correctly so that once installed it works on the network.

   Optional Result: Install in the shortest time possible.

   Optional Result: Install with no user intervention.

   Solution: You decide to create one unattended answer file to use for the installation. You will not use UDFs. You will manually install the network settings during the installation.

   A. This solution fulfills the required result as well as both optional results.

   B. This solution fulfills the required result and one of the optional results.

   C. This solution fulfills the required result but neither of the optional results.

   D. This solution does not meet the required result.

2. Problem: You are in charge of your company's rollout of Windows NT Workstation 4.0. You need to install 500 machines that will all be part of the same domain and will use TCP/IP. You have identical hardware, and want Windows NT installed identically on all machines.

   Required Result: To install Windows NT Workstation on all machines so that it is configured correctly so that once installed it works on the network.

Optional Result: Install in the shortest time possible.

Optional Result: Install with no user intervention.

Solution: Create one unattended answer file and one UDF file specifying the computer names and use those for the installation. Use DHCP for configuring TCP/IP.

    A. This solution fulfills the required result as well as both optional results.

    B. This solution fulfills the required result and one of the optional results.

    C. This solution fulfills the required result but neither of the optional results.

    D. This solution does not meet the required result.

3. Problem: You are in charge of your company's rollout of Windows NT Workstation 4.0. You need to install 500 machines that will all be part of the same domain and will use TCP/IP. You have identical hardware, and want Windows NT installed identically on all machines.

Required Result: To install Windows NT Workstation on all machines so that it is configured correctly so that once installed it works on the network.

Optional Result: Install in the shortest time possible.

Optional Result: Install with no user intervention.

Solution: Install Windows NT Workstation from the CD directly.

    A. This solution fulfills the required result as well as both optional results.

    B. This solution fulfills the required result and one of the optional results.

    C. This solution fulfills the required result but neither of the optional results.

    D. This solution does not meet the required result.

4. Margie wants to upgrade her OS/2 system to Windows NT Workstation 4.0. It is a 486, with 32 MB RAM, a 6x CD-ROM, and 1.2 GB hard disk, with 500 MB free. Her system is formatted as one drive, with the HPFS file system. What steps should she take to upgrade this machine?

   A. Run winnt /b from the Windows NT Workstation CD.

   B. Run setup from the Windows NT Workstation CD.

   C. Run winnt32 /b from the Windows NT Workstation CD.

   D. Format the drive as FAT, and then install Windows NT Workstation.

5. Pat wants to prevent others who use his workstation from accessing files he has been working on. How can Pat restrict access to those who will be sitting at his system?

   A. Store the files in the briefcase. The briefcase has a "security" option that enables him to password protect them.

   B. Format his workstation with FAT. FAT has built-in support for restricting access based on user accounts.

   C. Format his workstation with NTFS. NTFS has built-in support for restricting access based on user accounts.

   D. Store the files on the desktop. The desktop has a security option that enables him to password protect them.

6. Joyce has a dual-boot system with Windows 95 and Windows NT Workstation 4. She needs to run both operating systems to test out an application she is writing. She is running out of space on her C drive and would like to take advantage of the extra space gained by compression. What should Joyce do?

   A. Get the Windows 95 Plus Pack, which comes with a compression agent.

   B. Use DOS DoubleSpace to compress the drive.

C. Format the drive NTFS and use the compress command to compress the drive.

D. You cannot support this configuration.

7. How can you create an unattended answer file? (Choose all that apply.)

A. Use the Setup Manager on the Windows NT Resource Kit

B. Use the System Policy Editor installed with Windows NT Workstation

C. Create the file with a text editor such as Notepad

D. Use the sample Unattend.txt as a template file and customize it to your environment.

8. How can you create a uniqueness database file? (Choose all that apply.)

A. Use the Setup Manager on the Windows NT Resource Kit.

B. Use the System Policy Editor installed with Windows NT Workstation.

C. Create the file with a text editor such as Notepad.

D. Use the sample Unattend.txt as a template file and customize it to your environment.

9. Winnie needs to be able to share files on her Windows NT workstation with other users on the network. To do this, what built-in group on Windows NT Workstation should she be made a member of?

A. Users

B. Power Users

C. Guests

D. Domain Administrators

10. Harry is an administrator of a 200-person network. He needs to set up home directories for all the users on the network. The data that users will be storing in their home directories is sensitive and should not be viewed by other users. This data is vital to the company's business. Users will need to access this data from anywhere on the network. How should Harry set up the home directories?

    A. Create a directory called *Users* on a FAT partition on the server and put each user's home directory underneath it. Share the "Users" directory to all Users.

    B. Create a "common" directory on the server for all users to store their files.

    C. Create a directory called "Users" on an NTFS partition on the server and put each user's home directory underneath it. Share the "Users" directory to all Users. The NTFS permissions will allow only each specific user to access his or her home directory.

    D. Create a home directory on each user's workstation.

11. Fred has a Windows NT 3.51 workstation he needs to upgrade to Windows NT 4.0. It is a Pentium 100 with 32 MB RAM, 1.2 GB hard disk, an 8x CD. It is currently partitioned with the following:

    ▶ C drive that is FAT and the system partition

    ▶ D drive that is HPFS and contains the boot partition

    ▶ E drive that is NTFS and contains data files

    What should he do to upgrade this system?

    A. Connect to the network share with the Windows NT Workstation 4.0 files and run winnt32 /b to install Windows NT.

    B. Use Disk Administrator to format drive D: as FAT, and then connect to the network share with the Windows NT Workstation 4.0 files and run winnt32 /b to install Windows NT.

    C. Use Disk Administrator to convert drive D: to FAT, and then connect to the network share with the Windows NT Workstation 4.0 files and run winnt32 /b to install Windows NT.

    D. From a command prompt, use the convert command to convert drive D to NTFS. After the system has rebooted, connect to the network share with the Windows NT Workstation 4.0 files and run winnt32 /b to install Windows NT.

12. What is the name of the partition where the Windows NT operating system files are located?

13. What is the name of the partition where the files needed to boot Windows NT are located?

14. What are two benefits of using FAT over NTFS?

15. What are three benefits of using NTFS over FAT?

16. What are three benefits of using HPFS over NTFS?

17. Under Windows NT 4.0, FAT supports long file names up to:

    A. 175 characters

    B. 8.3 characters

    C. 255 characters

    D. It depends on the size of the partition

18. Kirk has a dual-boot Windows 95 and Windows NT Workstation 4.0 system. It is configured with the following drive partitions:

    ▶ C drive is FAT and is the system partition.

    ▶ D drive is FAT and contains the Windows 95 operating system files.

    ▶ E drive is FAT and contains the Windows NT Workstation operating system files.

    ▶ F drive is used for storing data.

He decides to take advantage of all the functionality of NTFS and converts drive E to NTFS. What will happen the next time he tries to boot into Windows 95?

   A. Nothing, the system will boot into Windows 95 as before.

   B. The system will boot into Windows 95 safe mode.

   C. The system cannot boot into Windows 95 because of the conversion.

   D. The system will no longer give the option to boot into Windows 95. Modify the Boot.ini file to re-enable this option.

19. Tempest has a dual-boot Windows 95 and Windows NT Workstation 4.0 system. It is configured with the following drive partitions:

   ▶ C drive is FAT and is the system partition. It is also where the Windows 95 files are installed.

   ▶ D drive is FAT.

   ▶ E drive is FAT and contains the Windows NT Workstation operating system files.

   ▶ F drive is used for storing data.

She decides to take advantage of all the functionality of NTFS and converts drive C to NTFS. What will happen the next time she tries to boot into Windows 95?

   A. Nothing, the system will boot into Windows 95 as before.

   B. The system will boot into Windows 95 safe mode.

   C. The system cannot boot into Windows 95 because of the conversion.

   D. The system will no longer give the option to boot into Windows 95. Modify the Boot.ini file to re-enable this option.

20. Eric moves a file from his D drive to his C drive. His D drive is formatted NTFS and is compressed. His C drive is using the FAT file system. What will happen to the file when it is copied to the C drive?

    A. It will remain compressed.

    B. It will no longer be compressed.

    C. It will be converted to FAT compression.

    D. It will be compressed using the DOS DriveSpace utility.

21. Mitch has a system configured with Windows 95 and Office 97. He would like to dual-boot with Windows NT Workstation 4.0 and still be able to use his office applications. His machine has 32 MB RAM, 1 GB hard disk formatted with FAT32, and is a Pentium 100. What should he do to upgrade his machine?

    A. Install Windows NT 4.0 using the winnt32 command, and then reinstall Office 97 under Windows NT.

    B. Upgrade Windows 95 to Windows NT Workstation by deleting his Windows directory after he installs Windows NT Workstation.

    C. Install Windows NT 4.0 using the winnt32 command, and then reinstall Office 97 under Windows NT.

    D. Mitch cannot install Windows NT Workstation on this machine in its current configuration.

Review Answers

1. C is correct. To create one unattended answer file and stop during the network prompts will fulfill the required result of having Windows NT installed properly, but it does not fulfill either of the optional results because it is not the quickest option and it does prompt for user intervention. For more information, refer to " Creating an Unattended Answer File."

2. A is correct. By using one unattended answer file and a UDF file, you can automate the install with no user intervention and have it ready to function on the network after the install is complete. For more information, refer to "Creating an Unattended Answer File."

3. C is correct. Although this method will get Windows NT Workstation installed, and does meet the required result, it does not meet either of the optional results for shortest time taken or for no user intervention. For more information, refer to "Creating Unattended Installation Files."

4. D is correct. This is the only option, because the drive is formatted HPFS. For more information, refer to "The High Performance File System."

5. C is correct. The only way to implement local security is through using NTFS permissions to restrict access to the files. For more information, refer to "Choosing the Appropriate File System to Use in a Given Situation."

6. D is correct. While dual-booting Windows 95 and Windows NT Workstation, you cannot implement compression through either operating system without sacrificing access by the other operating system. For more information, refer to "Choosing the Appropriate File System to Use in a Given Situation."

7. A, C, and D are correct. You can create an unattended answer file through the Setup Manager, by using the template Unattend.txt, or by creating it with Notepad. For more information, refer to "Creating Unattended Installation Files."

8. C is correct. To create a UDF, use any text editor such as Notepad. For more information, refer to "Creating Unattended Installation Files."

9. B is correct. To be able to share resources, Winnie needs to be a member of the Power Users group. Users on Windows NT Workstation do not have the right to share directories. Domain administrators do have that ability, but that group is not a Windows NT Workstation group. For more information, refer to "Planning Strategies for Sharing and Securing Resources."

10. C is correct. To most easily set up the users' home directories so that only each particular user can access his or her home directory, Harry should put the Users directory on an NTFS partition. This will put the appropriate rights in place after the Users directory is shared and the users' home directories are created. For more information, refer to "Sharing Home Directories for Users' Private Use."

11. D is correct. The D drive must be converted before the upgrade. This must be done as a convert, because the D drive contains the boot partition. For more information, refer to "Choosing the Appropriate File System to Use in a Given Situation."

12. Boot partition. For more information, refer to "Choosing the Appropriate File System to Use in a Given Situation."

13. System partition. For more information, refer to "Choosing the Appropriate File System to Use in a Given Situation."

14. Dual-boot, smaller partition size. For more information, refer to "Choosing the Appropriate File System to Use in a Given Situation."

15. Compression, Security, Partition size. For more information, refer to "Choosing the Appropriate File System to Use in a Given Situation."

16. There are none. HPFS is not supported under Windows NT Workstation 4.0. For more information, refer to "Choosing the Appropriate File System to Use in a Given Situation."

17. C is correct. There is support for file names up to 255 characters under Windows NT. For more information, refer to "Choosing the Appropriate File System to Use in a Given Situation."

18. A is correct. Because Kirk formatted drive E, which has Windows NT installed on it, that conversion will not affect Windows 95. The only result Kirk will see from this is that he will not be able to access drive E from within Windows 95. For more information, refer to "Choosing the Appropriate File System to Use in a Given Situation."

19. C is correct. Because Tempest converted the C drive, which had Windows 95 installed on it, she will no longer be able to boot into Windows 95. For more information, refer to "Choosing the Appropriate File System to Use in a Given Situation."

20. B is correct. Because Eric moved the file from NTFS to FAT, the file lost the compression attribute. For more information, refer to "Choosing the Appropriate File System to Use in a Given Situation."

21. D is correct. Because Mitch's system is formatted with FAT32, he cannot install Windows NT Workstation on it. For more information, refer to "Choosing the Appropriate File System to Use in a Given Situation."

Answers to Test Yourself Questions at the Beginning of the Chapter

1. Use an unattended answer file with a single UDF file that specifies the per-computer settings. To install Office 97, use sysdiff to take a snapshot of the original (post-installation) configuration and then create a difference file after Office 97 has been installed. For more information, refer to "Creating Unattended Installation Files."

2. Most likely you will want to create the users' home directories on the server so that they will be backed up and can be accessed from any location in the network. You should make them available to users through a combination of NTFS and Share permissions so that you do not have to share each individual folder to each user. For more information, refer to "Sharing Home Directories for Users' Private Use."

3. Lesley should store the files on an NTFS partition. NTFS has local security, which enables Lesley to restrict access to the files, even from someone who is sitting locally at the machine. For more information, refer to "Choosing the Appropriate File System to Use in a Given Situation."

4. Roger will need to format all partitions with the FAT file system because that is the only file system that can be read by both Windows NT Workstation and Windows 95. He should not format partitions with NTFS or FAT32; otherwise, they will be inaccessible to one of the operating systems. For more information, refer to "Choosing the Appropriate File System to Use in a Given Situation."

5. It depends on what file system the destination partition is using. If the destination partition is FAT, the file permissions will be lost because FAT does not support those permissions. If the destination partition is NTFS, the file will inherit the permissions of the destination partition rather than retain its own permissions. The only time a file retains its own permissions is in the event that it is moved within a partition. For more information, refer to "Choosing the Appropriate File System to Use in a Given Situation."

6. Minimally Jack will need to use an Unattend.txt and a UDF, which specifies the per-computer settings for each of the 50 machines. If Jack's environment is not standardized in terms of hardware or installation directory, he may need to use multiple unattended answer files as well. For more information, refer to "Creating Unattended Installation Files."

C h a p t e r

Installing and Configuring Windows NT Workstation 4.0

This chapter prepares you for the exam by covering the following objectives:

 Objectives

▶ Installing Microsoft Windows NT Workstation 4.0 on an Intel platform in a given situation.

▶ Removing Microsoft Windows NT Workstation 4.0 in a given situation.

▶ Upgrading to Windows NT Workstation 4.0 in a given situation.

▶ Configuring server-based installation for wide-scale deployment in a given situation.

▶ Installing, configuring, and removing hardware components for a given situation. Hardware components include the following:

Network adapter drivers

SCSI device drivers

Tape device drivers

UPS

Multimedia devices

Display drivers

continues

Keyboard drivers

Mouse drivers

▶ Using Control Panel applications to configure a Microsoft Windows NT Workstation 4.0 computer in a given situation.

Installation of operating systems and applications software on client desktops is one of the most time consuming activities performed by many network administrators. Being able to efficiently carry out these functions can lead to large time savings (try calculating the time you could gain by saving an hour at each of 200 client desktops).

Test Yourself! Before reading this chapter, test yourself to determine how much study time you will need to devote to this section.

1. You have an MS-DOS system with a CD-ROM drive configured as drive D. What command should you use to install Windows NT Workstation 4.0?

2. You have a Windows 95-based computer that uses compressed drives. What do you have to do before you upgrade it to Windows NT Workstation 4.0?

3. You want to set up a computer to dual-boot Microsoft Windows NT Workstation 4.0 and Microsoft Windows NT Server 4.0. What do you need to do to use the same 32-bit application program with both versions of the operating system?

4. You want to remove Windows NT Workstation 4.0 from your computer that was set up to dual-boot with Windows 95. You delete all the Windows NT operating systems files and the hidden files in the system partition. You receive the following error message, however, when you boot your computer:

   BOOT: Couldn't find NTLDR.

   Please insert another disk.

   How do you fix this problem?

5. What program should you use to install a new network adapter card: Windows Setup or Control Panel?

6. What program should you use to install a new SCSI host adapter card: Windows Setup or Control Panel?

7. Your UPS unit is being deactivated when Windows NT Workstation 4.0 boots. Which file needs to be modified to prevent your UPS unit from being turned off?

Answers are located at the end of the chapter...

Installing Windows NT Workstation on an Intel Platform

 **Objective** ▶

Before you try to install Microsoft Windows NT Workstation 4.0, you must be able to answer the following questions:

1. Is your hardware on the Microsoft Windows NT 4.0 Hardware Compatibility List (HCL)?

2. Does your hardware meet the minimum requirements for processor, RAM, and hard disk space?

3. Are you attempting to install Microsoft Windows NT Workstation 4.0 on a "clean" system, or are you planning to upgrade a computer with an existing operating system?

4. If you are upgrading a computer with an existing operating system, will the Microsoft Windows NT 4.0 operating system be replacing the other operating system? Or, do you want to be able to use both operating systems and be able to switch between them by "dual-booting"?

5. What file system(s) do you want to use: FAT or NTFS?

6. Will your Windows NT Workstation 4.0 be a member of a workgroup or be a member of a domain?

7. Which type of installation do you want to perform: typical, portable, compact, or custom?

8. Where are the installation files that you will use to install Microsoft Windows NT Workstation 4.0 located: on a local floppy/CD-ROM, or on a network-distribution server?

After you have determined what your answers are to the preceding questions, write them down. Your answers help you to choose the proper options during the setup process.

Key Concepts ▶

The Hardware Compatibility List (HCL) specifies all the computer systems and peripheral devices that have been tested for operation with Microsoft Windows NT 4.0. Devices not listed on the HCL can cause intermittent failures or, in extreme cases, system crashes.

Using the Windows NT Hardware Qualifier Tool (NTHQ.EXE)

One way to make sure that all your hardware is on the official Hardware Compatibility List (HCL) is to execute the Windows NT Hardware Qualifier Tool (NTHQ.EXE), which is only available for Intel x86-based computers, or compatibles. A batch file (Makedisk.bat) that actually creates a special MS-DOS bootable disk that contains NTHQ.EXE can be found in the \Support\HQTool folder on the Windows NT Workstation 4.0 installation CD. You can find full instructions on how to create the special bootable disk and then use NTHQ in Exercise 2.1.

NTHQ presents detected hardware devices in four categories: System, Motherboard, Video, and Others. The Others category is used for device types that the tool cannot positively identify. If the system has an old PCI adapter that does not support PCI version 2.0 or later, for example, the tool might not be able to identify its device type. Click on the appropriate tabs to view detection results for each category or save the results to a text file named Nthq.txt. You should then check the list of detected devices with the Windows NT 4.0 HCL to avoid unpleasant surprises during installation. The information in Nthq.txt is also very useful in avoiding IRQ conflicts when adding new hardware because, unlike Windows 95, Windows NT does not support Plug and Play. A portion of an actual Nthq.txt file is reproduced in the sidebar. Note that IRQ, DMA, and I/O addresses for detected devices are detailed in the Nthq.txt file.

Key Concepts

Plug and Play (PnP) devices can, with the proper operating system, be automatically configured to work with any combination of other peripheral devices. Windows NT 4.0 does not support PnP automatic configuration of devices; Windows 95 does.

The following is part of the data generated by the Windows NT Hardware
Qualifier tool (NTHQ.EXE):

```
Hardware Detection Tool For Windows NT 4.0 Beta 2

Master Boot Sector Virus Protection Check
Hard Disk Boot Sector Protection: Off.
No problem to write to MBR

ISA Plug and Play Add-in cards detection Summary Report

No ISA Plug and Play cards found in the system
ISA PnP Detection:  Complete

Legacy Detection Summary Report

System Information
Device: System board
Computer Name: Toshiba
Machine Type: IBM PC/AT
Machine Model: fc
Microprocessor: Pentium
Conventional memory: 655360
Available memory: >=48
Can't locate BIOSName
BIOS Version: 430CDS  V6.30   TOSHIBA
BIOS Date: 01/09/97
Bus Type: ISA

Device: Standard 101/102-Key or Microsoft Natural Keyboard
Hardware ID (for Legacy Devices): *PNP0303
I/O: 60 - 60
I/O: 64 - 64
IRQ: 1

Device: Standard PS/2 Port Mouse
Hardware ID (for Legacy Devices): *PNP0F0E
IRQ: 12

Device: Chips & Tech. Super VGA
Hardware ID (for Legacy Devices): *PNP0930
I/O: 3b0 - 3bb
I/O: 3c0 - 3df
Memory: a0000 - affff
```

```
Memory: b8000 - bffff
Memory: e4000 - effff


Device: Standard Floppy Disk Controller
Hardware ID (for Legacy Devices): *PNP0700
I/O: 3f2 - 3f5
IRQ: 6
DMA: 2


Enumerate all IDE devices


IDE Devices Detection Summary Report
Primary Channel: master drive detected
Model Number: TOSHIBA MK1301MAV
Type of Drive: Fixed Drive
Disk Transfer Rate: >10Mbs
Number of Cylinders: 2633
Number of Heads: 16
Number of Sectors Per Track: 63
Number of unformatted bytes per sector Per Track: 639
LBA Support: Yes
DMA Support: Yes
Drive Supports PIO Transfer Cycle Time Mode:   1
Drive Supports Fast PIO Mode: 3
Drive Supports Fast PIO Mode: 4


Secondary Channel: ATAPI device as a master drive detected
Model Number: TOSHIBA CD-ROM XM-1502B
Firmware Revision: 2996
Protocol Type: ATAPI
Device Type: CD-ROM drive
LBA Support: Yes
DMA Support: Yes
Drive Supports PIO Transfer Cycle Time Mode:   1
Drive Supports Fast PIO Mode: 3


IDE/ATAPI: Complete
PCI Detection: Complete


================End of Detection Report====================
Adapter Description: Chips & Technologies Super VGA
Listed in Hardware Compatibility List: Yes


Adapter Description: Joystick/game port
Listed in Hardware Compatibility List: Yes
```

Tip

If you have several different computers that you would like to examine with the NTHQ utility, follow these steps:

1. Boot the first computer with the NTHQ floppy.

2. Execute the NTHQ program, as described in Exercise 2.1.

3. Rename the Nthq.txt to computername.TXT.

4. Use the same NTHQ floppy on the next computer.

5. Repeat, as necessary, on all your computers.

Minimum Requirements for Installation

You must make sure that your computer hardware meets the minimum requirements for the installation of Windows NT Workstation 4.0 (see table 2.1). If your hardware does not meet the minimum requirements, you also need to make the necessary upgrades before you attempt to install Windows NT Workstation 4.0. If your computer has devices not listed in the HCL, you should check with the devices' manufacturers to see whether device drivers that support Windows NT 4.0 are available. Unlike with Windows 95, you cannot use older 16-bit device drivers with Windows NT. If you cannot obtain the proper device drivers, you cannot use unsupported devices after you install Windows NT.

 Tip

If you have unsupported devices, see whether they emulate another device that has drivers for Windows NT 4.0. Then try to use the drivers for the emulated device (for example, standard VGA for video, Sound Blaster for audio, Novell NE2000-compatible for generic network adapter cards).

Table 2.1

Windows NT Workstation 4.0 Minimum Installation Requirements	
Component	Minimum Requirement
CPU	32-bit Intel x86-based (80486/33 or higher) microprocessor or compatible (the 80386 microprocessor is no longer supported)
	Intel Pentium, Pentium Pro, or Pentium II microprocessor
	Digital Alpha AXP-based microprocessor
Memory	Intel x86-based computers: 12 MB RAM
	RISC-based computers: 16 MB RAM
Hard disk	Intel x86-based computers: 110 MB
	RISC-based computers: 148 MB
Display	VGA or better resolution
Other drives	Intel x-86 based computers require a high-density 3½ floppy and a CD-ROM drive (unless you are planning to install Windows NT over a network).
Optional	Network adapter card
	Mouse or other pointing device, such as a trackball

Microsoft Windows NT 4.0 actually requires slightly more hard disk space during the installation process to hold some temporary files than it requires after installation. If you don't have at least 119 MB of free space in your partition, the Setup routine displays an error message and halts. The Setup routine also displays an error message and halts if you attempt to install Windows NT Workstation 4.0 to a Windows NT software-based volume set or stripe set (RAID 0). If you have a hardware-based volume set or stripe set, you might be able to install Windows NT Workstation 4.0 on it; ask your manufacturer.

Keep in mind that Table 2.1 lists the *minimum* requirements for installation of Windows NT Workstation 4.0. After you install your actual application software and data, you will probably find out that your actual hardware requirements are higher than these minimum values.

 Caution

> If you are upgrading a Windows 95-based computer to Windows NT Workstation 4.0, make sure that you do not have any compressed drives and that you are not using FAT32. FAT32 is the new, optional, partitioning format that is only supported by Windows 95 OEM Service Release 2 (which is also called Windows 95b). Windows 95 compressed drives and FAT32 partitions cannot be accessed by Windows NT.

Installation Options

During installation, you can make use of your knowledge from Chapter 1, "Planning an Effective Installation," to decide whether you want to change the partitioning of your hard disk and/or convert hard disk partitions from FAT to NTFS.

Regardless of whether you install Microsoft Windows NT Workstation 4.0 locally via the three floppies and the CD, or you install by means of a network connection to a network distribution server, you have four setup options: Typical, Portable, Compact, and Custom. These four setup options install varying components from several categories (see table 2.2).

Table 2.2

Varying Components in Four Setup Options				
	Typical	Portable	Compact	Custom
Accessibility options	X	X	None	All options
Accessories	X	X	None	All options
Communications programs	X	X	None	All options

	Typical	Portable	Compact	Custom
Games			None	All options
Windows Messaging			None	All options
Multimedia	X	X	None	All options

 Note

Compact Setup is designed to conserve hard disk space and installs no optional components. The only way to install Windows Messaging or games during installation is to choose Custom Setup. You can change installation options after installation via the Add/Remove Programs application in Control Panel.

Beginning the Installation

You actually have several choices on how to install Microsoft Windows NT Workstation 4.0. These are as follows:

▶ Locally, via three Setup floppies and a CD

▶ Locally, using the CD and creating and using the three Setup floppies

▶ Over the network, creating and using the three Setup floppies

▶ Over the network, not requiring any Setup floppies

Step-by-step instructions on the actual installation procedures are detailed in Exercises 2.2, 2.3, and 2.4. After you install Microsoft Windows NT Workstation 4.0, you then need to install all your applications.

Installing Windows NT Workstation 4.0 on an Intel Computer with an Existing Operating System

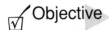 **Objective**

If your computer already has an existing operating system with support for CD-ROM, you can install Windows NT Workstation 4.0 directly from the installation CD. All you have to do is to execute WINNT.EXE, which is a 16-bit program compatible with MS-DOS, Windows 3.x, and Windows 95. WINNT.EXE is located in the \I386 folder on the Microsoft Windows NT Workstation 4.0 CD. It performs the following steps:

▶ Creates the three Setup boot disks (requires three blank, high density, formatted disks)

▶ Creates the WIN_NT.~LS temporary folder and copies the contents of the \I386 folder to it

▶ Prompts the user to restart the computer from the first Setup boot disk

You can also modify the installation process (see table 2.3).

Table 2.3

Switch	Effect
	Modifying the WINNT.EXE Installation Process
/b	Do not make the three Setup boot disks. Create a temporary folder named WIN_NT.~BT and copy the boot files that would normally be copied to the three floppies to it. The contents of the temporary folder are used rather than the Setup boot disks to boot the machine when the user is prompted to restart the computer.
/c	Skip the check for available free space.
/I:*inf_file*	Specify the name of the Setup information file. The default file name is Dosnet.inf.
/f	Do not verify files as they are copied.

Switch	Effect
/l	Create a log file called $WINNT.LOG that will list all errors that occur as files are being copied to the temporary directory.
/ox	Create the three Setup boot disks and then stop.
/s:*server_path*	Specify the location of the installation source files.
/u	Allow all or part of an installation to proceed unattended as detailed in Chapter 1. The */b* option for floppyless install is automatically invoked and the */s* option for location of the source files must be used. The */u* option can be followed with the name of an answer file to fully automate installation.
/udf	Use during an unattended installation to specify settings unique to a specific computer that are contained in a uniqueness data file, as detailed in Chapter 1.
/w	This *undocumented* flag enables the WINNT.EXE program to execute in Windows instead of requiring execution from a MS-DOS command prompt.
/x	Do not create the three Setup boot disks. You must already have the three boot disks.

Note

There is also a 32-bit version of the installation program called WINNT32.EXE that is used to upgrade earlier versions of Windows NT and cannot be used to upgrade Windows 95. WINNT32.EXE does not support the /f, /c, or /l options. See the section entitled "Upgrading to Windows NT Workstation 4.0" for more information.

Key Concepts

WINNT.EXE and WINNT32.EXE are the installation programs for Windows NT.

Setting Up a Dual-Boot System

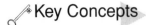**Key Concepts**

Dual-boot systems are computers that have more than one operating system installed. When a dual-boot system is restarted, the user can choose which system he would like to start.

If you are in the process of transitioning your users to Windows NT Workstation, they might feel better if they could continue to use their previous operating system for a limited period of time. Additionally, they might need to be able to execute applications that are not compatible with Windows NT. Another possibility is that you might need to support users running different operating systems and you need to be able to use only one computer. If you need to solve any of these problems, you may want to set up a dual-boot system.

Dual-booting is a term for having more than one operating system on a single computer. A dual-boot system also has, typically, a boot menu that appears whenever the computer is restarted. The boot menu then enables users to choose which of the available operating systems they would like to start.

It is possible to install Windows NT Workstation 4.0 to operate as a dual-boot system. The other operating system can be any version of MS-DOS, Microsoft Windows, or even OS/2.

Caution

Although it is possible to set up a dual-boot system with Windows 95 and Windows NT, this configuration is not recommended. In this configuration, you must install all your Windows applications twice—once for each operating system. No system or application settings are migrated or shared between the two operating systems.

Removing Windows NT Workstation

 **Objective**

To remove Windows NT Workstation from a computer, you must first determine whether there are any NTFS partitions on the computer. If there are any NTFS partitions on the computer, you must remove them because Windows 95 or MS-DOS cannot use them. If the NTFS partitions contain only data and no Windows NT system files, you can use the Windows NT Disk Administrator program to remove them. If the NTFS partitions contain Windows NT system files, or if they are logical drive(s) in an extended partition, the MS-DOS FDISK utility cannot be used to remove them and you should use the procedure detailed in Exercise 2.5.

After you have removed all the NTFS partitions, you need to start the computer with a Windows 95 or MS-DOS system disk that contains the Sys.com file. Then type the command **sys c:** to transfer the Windows 95 or MS-DOS systems files to the boot track on drive C. You then need to remove all the remaining Windows NT Workstation files, as follows:

▶ All paging files (C:\Pagefile.sys)

▶ C:\BOOT.INI, C:\BOOTSECT.DOS, C:\NTDETECT.COM, C:\NTLDR (these are hidden, system, read-only files)

▶ The *winnt_root* folder

▶ The c:\Program files\Windows Windows NT folder

 Caution

If you fail to remove the Windows NT boot track from your computer, the following error message appears when you restart your computer:

BOOT: Couldn't find NTLDR.

Please insert another disk.

You can now install your choice of operating systems on your computer.

Upgrading to Windows NT Workstation 4.0

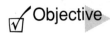 **Objective**   If you are upgrading an earlier version of Microsoft Windows NT Workstation to Microsoft Windows NT Workstation 4.0, you need to use the 32-bit version of the installation program WINNT32.EXE. WINNT32.EXE was previously explained in the section entitled "Installing Windows NT Workstation 4.0 on an Intel Computer with an Existing Operating System." Installations of any version of Windows NT Server cannot be upgraded to Windows NT Workstation 4.0 and you must install into a new folder and re-install all of your Windows applications.

If Windows NT Workstation 3.x is upgraded to Windows NT Workstation 4.0, all the existing Registry entries are preserved, including the following:

▶ User and Group settings

▶ Preferences for applications

▶ Network settings

▶ Desktop environment

To upgrade Windows NT Workstation 3.x to Windows NT Workstation 4.0, install to the same folder as the existing installation and answer yes to the upgrade question that you are asked during the installation process, and then follow the instructions.

 Caution   Because of differences in hardware device support and differences in the internal structure of the Registry, there is no upgrade path from Microsoft Windows 95 to Microsoft Windows NT 4.0. You need to perform a new install of Windows NT to a new folder and then re-install all your Windows applications. No system or application settings are shared or migrated. After your installation of Microsoft Windows NT Workstation 4.0 and applications is complete, you should delete the Windows 95 directory.

For a significant performance increase for the file transfer portion of a network-based upgrade of a previous version of Windows NT Workstation to Windows NT Workstation 4.0, use multiple /s switches with WINNT32.EXE to specify multiple servers that contain the source files (see the next section).

Configuring Server-Based Installation for Wide-Scale Deployment

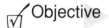 Objective

The quickest way to install Windows NT Workstation 4.0 on a large number of computers is to use a network distribution server as the source of the installation files (especially when you need to install Windows NT Workstation 4.0 on computers that have network connectivity but don't have CD-ROM drives).

Procedures to set up a network distribution server include the following:

1. Use the Windows NT Explorer, Windows 95 Explorer, or the MS-DOS XCOPY command to copy the I386 folder from the Windows NT Workstation 4.0 CD to a folder on the network server. Make sure that you also copy all the subfolders.

   Share the folder on the network server with the appropriate permissions that will allow authorized users to access the files.

2. You could also share the I386 folder on the Windows NT Workstation 4.0 CD, but that method causes your installations to be performed significantly slower and should only be used if you must conserve hard disk space on your network server.

Keep in mind that if you use Windows NT Explorer or Windows 95 Explorer to copy the files, the default options must be changed to allow for hidden files and system files with extensions such as .dll, .sys, and .vxd to be displayed and copied. In the View, Options dialog box, select Show all files in the settings for the Hidden Files list (see fig. 2.1).

Figure 2.1

Displaying hidden and system files in Windows NT Explorer.

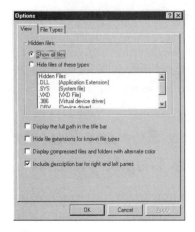

If you are using WINNT32.EXE to upgrade an existing copy of Windows NT, you can use more than one network server to significantly speed up the rate at which the installation files are downloaded to your client computers. If you set up two network servers called SERVER1 and SERVER2 with installation shares called NTW, for example, the proper command line option to use both servers during the installation process is:

WINNT32 /B /S:\\SERVER1\NTW /S:\\SERVER2\NTW

Installing, Configuring, and Removing Hardware Components

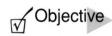 Some configurable hardware components in Windows NT Workstation include the following:

- ▶ Network adapter drivers

- ▶ SCSI device drivers

- ▶ Tape device drivers

- ▶ UPS

- ▶ Multimedia devices

- ▶ Display drivers

- ▶ Keyboard drivers

- ▶ Mouse drivers

This section covers each of the preceding items, which are accessible via programs in Control Panel (see fig. 2.2). The discussion looks at how you can configure these types of devices in Windows NT.

Figure 2.2

The default options in Control Panel.

Working with Network Adapter Drivers

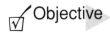

You can configure network adapters by double-clicking on the Network icon in the Control Panel and then selecting the Adapters tab (see fig. 2.3).

Figure 2.3

Viewing the current network adapters.

Windows NT 4.0 allows for an unlimited number of network adapters as discussed in Chapter 4, "Connectivity." You can also configure each network adapter separately. To configure a specific network adapter, select the Adapters tab of the dialog box and then click on the Properties button. Figure 2.4 shows a sample network adapter properties dialog box. The actual dialog boxes for network adapter properties are manufacturer-specific, so your system may look different than this example.

Figure 2.4

Specifying the hardware settings for a network adapter.

You also need to make sure that you have the proper device drivers for your network adapter. Windows NT 4.0 is compatible with any device drivers compliant with Network Driver Interface Specification (NDIS) version 4.0 or version 3.0. Windows NT cannot use any 16-bit legacy device drivers or device drivers from Windows 95, which uses NDIS 3.1 drivers.

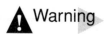 Warning

When you modify the settings in the Network Adapter Properties dialog box, be careful to select the proper settings. Microsoft Windows NT does not support Plug and Play and has no way to determine whether the values that you select are correct. Incorrect values in this dialog box can lead to loss of network connectivity and, in extreme cases, can cause system crashes.

Working with SCSI Device Drivers

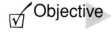 Objective

The user interface for viewing configuration information on SCSI host adapters in Windows NT 4.0 has now been moved to the Control Panel.

To view device properties, open the SCSI Adapters dialog box (see fig. 2.5). Select the Devices tab, select the device, and then click on the Properties button. You can then view information on the device properties and the revision data on its device drivers (see fig. 2.6).

Figure 2.5

Viewing SCSI and IDE adapters and devices.

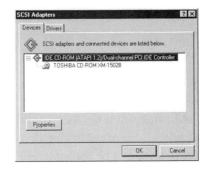

Figure 2.6

Viewing the settings for a SCSI or IDE device.

 Tip

In spite of the fact that the dialog box is titled SCSI Adapters, this is also where you can view and modify information on your IDE adapters and devices as well. You must restart Windows NT 4.0 if you add or delete any SCSI or IDE adapters.

Working with Tape Device Drivers

 **Objective**

The user interface for viewing configuration information on tape devices in Windows NT 4.0 has been moved to the Control Panel (see fig. 2.7).

Figure 2.7

*Viewing config-
ured tape
devices.*

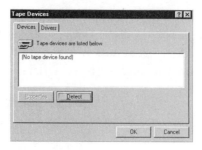

If you want to have Windows NT 4.0 automatically detect tape
devices, click on the Devices tab, and then click on Detect. If you
would rather view device properties, click on Properties. You can
also add and remove device drivers by using the Add and Remove
buttons that can be found by selecting the Drivers tab. You do not
have to restart Windows NT if you add or delete any tape devices.

Working with UPS

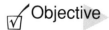 Objective

An Uninterruptible Power Supply (UPS) provides backup power
in case your local power source fails. Power for UPS units is typically provided by batteries that are continuously recharged and
are rated to provide power for a specific (usually highly limited)
period of time. Figure 2.8 shows the UPS option in Control Panel.

Figure 2.8

*Configuring your
Uninterruptible
Power Supply
(UPS).*

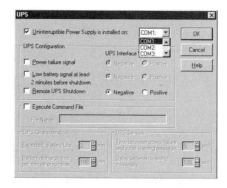

During a power failure, the UPS service of Windows NT communicates with the UPS unit until one of the following events occur:

▶ Local power is restored.

▶ The system is shut down by the UPS service or by an administrator.

▶ The UPS signals to Windows NT that its batteries are low.

During a power failure, the Windows NT Server service is paused (which prevents any new users from establishing sessions with the server). Any current users are warned to save their data and to close their open sessions. All users are notified if normal power is restored.

 Caution

Communication between the UPS and the Windows NT system is via a standard RS-232 port. The cable is not, however, a standard cable. A special UPS cable *must* be used for proper communications between the UPS system and your computer.

You must be sure to test the UPS unit after it has been configured. On startup of Intel-based computers, NTDETECT.COM sends test messages to all serial ports to determine whether a serial mouse is attached. Some UPS units misinterpret these test messages and shut down. To prevent your UPS unit from having this problem, add the /NoSerialMice switch to the Boot.ini file.

Working with Multimedia Devices

 **Objective**

Use the Multimedia icon in Control Panel to install, configure, and remove multimedia devices. Categories of multimedia devices that can be modified include audio, video, MIDI, and CD music (see fig. 2.9). There is also a Devices tab that enables you to view information on all the multimedia devices and drivers installed on your system (see fig. 2.10).

Figure 2.9

Viewing properties of multimedia devices.

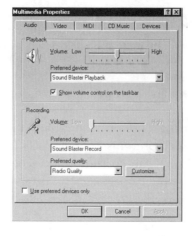

Figure 2.10

Viewing the current multimedia devices.

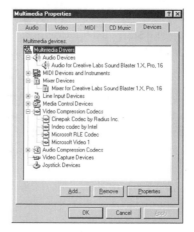

Drivers for sound cards must be installed after you have successfully installed Windows NT and cannot be configured during an unattended install. For step-by-step instructions on how to install a sound driver, see Exercise 2.9.

Working with Display Drivers

Use the Settings tab of the Display program in Control Panel to choose display options, including refresh frequency, font sizes, video resolution, and the number of colors (see fig. 2.11).

Figure 2.11

Viewing the display properties.

The Settings tab also enables you to choose options for your display (see table 2.4).

Table 2.4

Options for Configuring Display Settings	
Option	Description
Color Palette	Lists color options for the display adapter.
Desktop Area	Configures screen area used by the display.
Display Type	Displays options about the display device driver and allows installation of new drivers.
Font Size	Allows selection of large or small display font sizes.
List All Modes	Gives the option to configure color, desktop area, and refresh frequency simultaneously.
Refresh Frequency	Configures the frequency of the screen refresh rate for high-resolution drivers only.
Test	Tests screen choices. If you make changes and do not test them, you are prompted to test your choices when you try to apply them.

Whenever you make changes to your display driver settings, you are prompted to test them before they are saved. If you ignore the test option and save incompatible values, your screen may become unreadable. You can restore normal operations by restarting your computer and then selecting the VGA option from the Boot menu. The VGA option forces your video card into 16-color standard VGA. You can then try different values in the Display Properties dialog box.

 Caution

> Be careful when changing your settings for your display driver. In extreme cases, it is possible to damage your display card or monitor with incorrect settings.

Working with Keyboard Drivers

 **Objective**

Figure 2.12 shows the Keyboard program in Control Panel. The options that you can configure in the three tabs of the Keyboard program are the following:

▶ **Speed.** Controls repeat character delay, character repeat rate, and cursor blink speed.

▶ **Input Locales.** Specifies the proper international keyboard layout.

▶ **General.** Enables you to view and/or change the keyboard driver. You might want to change your keyboard driver if you need to support an international keyboard, or if your prefer a Dvorak style keyboard rather than the standard QWERTY keyboard.

Figure 2.12

Viewing the properties of your keyboard.

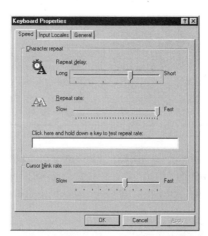

Tip   You can specify keyboard options to configure a system to match the capabilities of a physically impaired user in the Accessibility Options program in Control Panel.

Working with Mouse Drivers

 **Objective**   Use the Mouse program in Control Panel to change mouse options, including Buttons, Pointers, Motion, and General (see fig. 2.13).

Figure 2.13

Viewing your mouse settings.

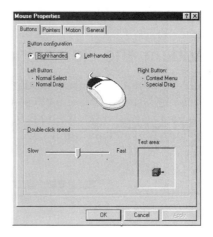

Table 2.5 details the various options that you can configure with the Mouse program.

Table 2.5

Configuring Mouse Options

Tab	Available Options
Buttons	Configure mouse for right-hand or left-hand operation and double-click speed
Pointers	Choose the pointer shapes to associate with various system events
Motion	Control pointer speed and select whether you want the mouse pointer to snap to the default button in dialog boxes
General	View current mouse driver and change to new mouse driver, if desired

All the mouse options detailed in table 2.5, with the exception of the mouse driver, are configurable individually for each user account and are saved in the user's profile.

Using Control Panel Applications to Configure Windows NT Workstation

 **Objective**

In addition to the Control Panel applications used to configure hardware that were described in the section entitled "Installing, Configuring, and Removing Hardware Components," you can use several other options to configure Windows NT Workstation.

Adding and Removing Programs

You can modify the installation option (Typical, Portable, Compact, or Custom) that you chose when you installed Windows NT Workstation 4.0 by choosing the Add/Remove Programs program in Control panel and then selecting the Windows NT Setup tab (see fig. 2.14).

Figure 2.14

Adding and removing optional components.

The Windows NT Setup tab enables you to add and delete optional components and applications in the following categories:

- ▶ Accessibility options

- ▶ Accessories

- ▶ Communications

- ▶ Games

▶ Multimedia

▶ Windows messaging

Note that the check boxes as depicted actually can have the following three states:

▶ **Clear boxes.** Indicate that *none* of the selected components or applications in that category is installed.

▶ **Clear and checked boxes.** Indicate that *all the* selected components or applications in that category are installed.

▶ **Gray and checked boxes.** Indicate that *some* of the selected components or applications in that category are installed. For details on which of the components or applications are actually installed, click on the Details button.

You can also add and remove applications from your system by choosing the Add/Remove Programs program in Control panel and then selecting the Install/Uninstall tab. You could attempt to delete a program by deleting the appropriate program folder, but you will fail to remove any files that program needs that are in different folders, as well as any Registry entries that had been made by that program.

Modifying Date/Time or Time Zone

You can also use the Control Panel to modify your computer's date and time or to change which time zone it is located in (see fig. 2.15). You must be an administrator or power user or have been granted the Change the System Time user right to be able to access this dialog box.

Figure 2.15

Setting your time, date, and time zone.

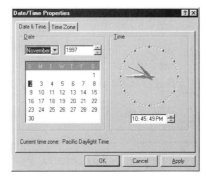

Exercises

The following exercises detail step-by-step procedures on various ways to install and configure Windows NT Workstation 4.0 on your computer. Other lab exercises show you how to use many of the options in Control Panel to configure a current installation of Windows NT Workstation 4.0.

Exercise 2.1: Creating and Using an NTHQ Boot Floppy

This exercise shows you how to create a Windows NT Hardware Qualifier NTHQ boot floppy. You then use the NTHQ boot floppy to examine the hardware configuration of your computer.

Objective

Determine whether the hardware in your computer is supported by Windows NT

Time Estimate: 20 minutes

Steps

1. Insert the Windows NT Workstation 4.0 CD into your CD-ROM drive.

2. Type **D:** at the command prompt to switch the default drive to the CD-ROM drive (or whatever the correct drive letter is for your computer).

3. Type **CD \Support\HQTool** to switch to the HQTool directory.

4. Insert a formatted 3 ½ inch floppy into floppy drive A.

5. Type **Makedisk** at the command prompt.

6. After the Makedisk utility finishes transferring all the necessary files to the floppy, reboot your computer, leaving the floppy that you just made in drive A.

7. When the NTHQ dialog box appears, click on Yes to approve device detection.

8. Click on Yes to approve comprehensive detection.

9. Wait for system detection to complete and then click on the various buttons at the bottom of the screen and observe the details that were detected for the various devices in your computer.

10. Click on the Save button at the bottom of the screen.

11. Click on OK to save the detection results to A:\NTHQ.TXT.

12. Click on the Exit button at the bottom of the screen.

13. Remove the floppy from drive A.

14. Reboot your computer.

15. Reinsert the NTHQ floppy into your floppy drive.

16. View the contents of A:\NTHQ.TXT.

Exercise 2.2:   Installing Windows NT Workstation 4.0 from CD on a Computer Without an Existing Operating System

This exercise shows you how to perform a CD-based installation of Windows NT on a computer that doesn't have an existing operating system.

Objective

Install Windows NT Workstation on an Intel platform

Time Estimate: 70 minutes

Steps

1. Before starting installation, verify that your hardware (especially your CD-ROM drive) is listed on the Windows NT HCL.

2. Locate your Windows NT Workstation 4.0 CD and the three floppies that came with it.

3. Insert the Windows NT Workstation CD into the CD-ROM drive.

4. Insert the Windows NT Workstation Setup Boot Disk into your floppy drive and restart your computer.

continues

5. When prompted, insert Windows NT Workstation Setup Disk #2.

6. At the Windows NT Workstation Setup – Welcome to Setup screen, press Enter to start the installation process.

7. Press Enter to detect mass storage devices.

8. When prompted, insert Windows NT Workstation Setup Disk #3.

9. Press Enter to approve the list of detected mass storage devices. (Don't worry if your IDE hard disk controller isn't detected, the installation process should proceed just fine anyway).

10. Press Page Down, repeatedly, until you reach the last page of the Windows NT Licensing Agreement.

11. Press F8 to approve the Windows NT Licensing Agreement.

12. Press Enter to approve the list of detected hardware components.

13. Select the desired installation partition and then press Enter.

14. Press Enter to not convert the installation partition to NTFS.

15. Press Enter to install to the default directory named \WINNT.

16. Press Enter to examine the hard disk for errors.

17. Wait for hard disk examination.

18. Wait while files are copied.

19. When prompted, remove the floppy disk from the drive and press Enter to restart the computer and begin the graphical portion of the setup process.

20. When the computer restarts, click on Next.

21. Select the typical option for installation and then click on Next.

22. Enter your name and organization, and then click on Next.

23. Enter your CD-ROM key, and then click on Next.

24. Enter your computer name (specify a computer named **Test**), and then click on Next. The maximum length for a computer name is 15 characters.

25. Enter and confirm the password for the administrator account, and then click on Next. Make sure that you write down your selected password and keep it in a secure location. If you forget your administrator password, you will find yourself locked out of your own system and you will have to reinstall Windows NT to restore access.

26. Click on Yes to create an Emergency Repair Disk (ERD).

27. Click on Next to install the most common components.

28. Click on Next to install Windows NT Networking.

29. Specify whether your computer will be participating in a network, and then click on Next. If your computer will not be participating in a network, skip ahead to step 36.

30. Click on Start Search For Your Adapter, or Select From List.

31. Select your adapter from the list, and then click on Next.

32. Make sure that NetBEUI is the only specified protocol, and then click on Next.

33. Click on Continue to approve the network card settings. (Remember that Windows NT 4.0 doesn't support Plug and Play and your network card settings *must* be correct.)

34. Click on Next to start the network.

35. Click on Next to install the computer named Test into a workgroup named Workgroup.

36. Click on Next to finish setup.

37. Select the proper time zone, and then click on Close.

38. Click on OK to approve the detected video adapter.

continues

---

39. Click on Test to test the video adapter.

40. Click on OK to start the video test and wait five seconds.

41. Click on Yes (if you saw the bitmap properly).

42. Click on OK to save the video settings.

43. Click on OK in the Display Properties dialog box.

44. Wait while files are copied.

45. Wait while the configuration is saved.

46. Insert a floppy that will become your ERD, and then click on OK.

47. Wait while the ERD is formatted and files are copied.

48. Wait while the temporary configuration files are removed.

49. Press the button to restart your computer. The installation process is now complete.

Exercise 2.3: Upgrading an Existing System to Windows NT Workstation 4.0 from CD-ROM Without the Setup Disks

This exercise shows you how to re-create the Setup disks and then upgrade an existing system to Windows NT Workstation 4.0 from CD-ROM.

Objective

Install Windows NT Workstation on an Intel platform

Time Estimate: 80 minutes

Steps:

1. Format three high-density floppies and label them as follows:

   Windows NT Workstation Setup Boot Disk

   Windows NT Workstation Setup Disk #2

   Windows NT Workstation Setup Disk #3

2. Place the Windows NT Workstation 4.0 CD in the CD-ROM drive. (This exercise assumes that your CD-ROM drive is drive D.)

3. From a command prompt, type **D:\I386\WINNT** to upgrade a 16-bit system, or type **D:\I386\WINNT32** to upgrade a previous version of Windows NT.

4. Insert Windows NT Workstation Setup Disk #3, into the floppy drive.

5. When prompted by the Windows NT 4.0 Upgrade/ Installation screen, click on Continue.

6. Wait while files are copied.

7. When prompted, insert Windows NT Workstation Setup Disk #2.

8. When prompted, insert Windows NT Workstation Setup Boot Disk.

9. When prompted, leave the Windows NT Workstation Setup Boot Disk in the drive and restart your computer.

10. Wait while the computer restarts and files are copied.

11. When prompted, insert Windows NT Workstation Setup Disk #2.

12. At the Windows NT Workstation Setup – Welcome to Setup screen, press Enter to start the installation process.

13. Press Enter to detect mass storage devices.

14. When prompted, insert Windows NT Workstation Setup Disk #3.

15. Press Enter to approve the list of detected mass storage devices. (Don't worry if your IDE hard disk controller isn't detected. The installation process should proceed just fine anyway.)

16. Press Page Down, repeatedly, until you reach the last page of the Windows NT Licensing Agreement.

continues

17. Press F8 to approve the Windows NT Licensing Agreement.

18. Press Enter to approve the list of detected hardware components.

19. Select the desired installation partition, and then press Enter.

20. Press Enter to not convert the installation partition to NTFS.

21. Press Enter to install to the default directory named \WINNT.

22. Press Enter to examine the hard disk for errors.

23. Wait for hard disk examination.

24. Wait while files are copied.

25. When prompted, remove the floppy disk from the drive and press Enter to restart the computer and begin the graphical portion of the setup process.

26. When the computer restarts, click on Next.

27. Select the typical option for installation, and then click on Next.

28. Enter your name and organization, and then click on Next.

29. Enter your CD-ROM key, and click on Next.

30. Enter your computer name (specify a computer named **Test**), and click on Next.

31. Enter and confirm the password for the administrator account, and then click on Next.

32. Click on Yes to create an Emergency Repair Disk (ERD).

33. Click on Next to install the most common components.

34. Click on Next to install Windows NT Networking.

35. Specify whether your computer will be participating in a network, and then click on Next. If your computer will not be participating in a network, skip ahead to step 42.

36. Click on Start Search For Your Adapter, or Select From List.

37. Select your adapter from the list, and then click on Next.

38. Make sure that NetBEUI is the only specified protocol, and then click on Next.

39. Click on Continue to approve the network card settings. (Remember that Windows NT 4.0 doesn't support Plug and Play, and your network card settings *must* be correct.)

40. Click on Next to start the network.

41. Click on Next to install the computer named Test into a workgroup named Workgroup.

42. Click on Next to finish setup.

43. Select the proper time zone, and then click on Close.

44. Click on OK to approve the detected video adapter.

45. Click on Test to test the video adapter.

46. Click on OK to start the video test and wait five seconds.

47. Click on Yes (if you saw the bitmap properly).

48. Click on OK to save the video settings.

49. Click on OK in the Display Properties dialog box.

50. Wait while files are copied.

51. Wait while the configuration is saved.

52. Insert a floppy that will become your ERD, and then click on OK.

53. Wait while the ERD is formatted and files are copied.

54. Wait while the temporary configuration files are removed.

55. Press the button to restart your computer.

56. The installation process is now complete.

Exercise 2.4:   Installing Windows NT Workstation 4.0 from a Network Server

This exercise details how to upgrade an existing MS-DOS system to Microsoft Windows NT Workstation 4.0 when the installation files are located on a network server.

Objective

Install Windows NT Workstation on an Intel platform

Time Estimate: 60 minutes

Steps:

1. Format three high-density floppies and label them as follows:

   Windows NT Workstation Setup Boot Disk

   Windows NT Workstation Setup Disk #2

   Windows NT Workstation Setup Disk #3

2. From a command prompt, enter the appropriate command to connect a network drive to drive letter X. The appropriate command for a Microsoft based network would be:

   NET USE X: **server**\ *sharename*

3. Change to drive X.

4. Start the Windows NT installation process by typing **WINNT** and pressing Enter.

5. Insert Windows NT Workstation Setup Disk #3 into the floppy drive.

6. When prompted by the Windows NT 4.0 Upgrade/ Installation screen, click on Continue.

7. Wait while files are copied.

8. When prompted, insert Windows NT Workstation Setup Disk #2.

9. When prompted, insert Windows NT Workstation Setup Boot Disk.

10. When prompted, leave the Windows NT Workstation Setup Boot Disk in the drive and restart your computer.

11. Wait while the computer restarts and files are copied.

12. When prompted, insert Windows NT Workstation Setup Disk #2.

13. At the Windows NT Workstation Setup – Welcome to Setup screen, press Enter to start the installation process.

14. Press Enter to detect mass storage devices.

15. When prompted, insert Windows NT Workstation Setup Disk #3.

16. Press Enter to approve the list of detected mass storage devices. (Don't worry if your IDE hard disk controller isn't detected. The installation process should proceed just fine anyway.)

17. Press Page Down, repeatedly, until you reach the last page of the Windows NT Licensing Agreement.

18. Press F8 to approve the Windows NT Licensing Agreement.

19. Press Enter to approve the list of detected hardware components.

20. Select the desired installation partition, and then press Enter.

21. Press Enter to not convert the installation partition to NTFS.

22. Press Enter to install to the default directory named \WINNT.

23. Press Enter to examine the hard disk for errors.

24. Wait for hard disk examination.

25. Wait while files are copied.

continues

Exercise 2.4: Continued

26. When prompted, remove the floppy disk from the drive and press Enter to restart the computer and begin the graphical portion of the setup process.

27. When the computer restarts, click on Next.

28. Select the typical option for installation, and then click on Next.

29. Enter your name and organization, and click on Next.

30. Enter your CD-ROM key, and then click on Next.

31. Enter your computer name (specify a computer named **Test**), and then click on Next.

32. Enter and confirm the password for the administrator account, and then click on Next.

33. Click on Yes to create an Emergency Repair Disk (ERD).

34. Click on Next to install the most common components.

35. Click on Next to install Windows NT Networking.

36. Specify whether your computer will be participating in a network, and then click on Next. If your computer will not be participating in a network, skip ahead to step 43.

37. Click on Start Search For Your Adapter, or Select From List.

38. Select your adapter from the list, and then click on Next.

39. Make sure that NetBEUI is the only specified protocol, and then click on Next.

40. Click on Continue to approve the network card settings. (Remember that Windows NT 4.0 doesn't support Plug and Play, and your network card settings *must* be correct.)

41. Click on Next to start the network.

42. Click on Next to install the computer named **Test** into a workgroup named Workgroup.

43. Click on Next to finish setup.

44. Select the proper time zone, and then click on Close.

45. Click on OK to approve the detected video adapter.

46. Click on Test to test the video adapter.

47. Click on OK to start the video test and wait five seconds.

48. Click on Yes (if you saw the bitmap properly).

49. Click on OK to save the video settings.

50. Click on OK in the Display Properties dialog box.

51. Wait while files are copied.

52. Wait while the configuration is saved.

53. Insert a floppy that will become your ERD, and then click on OK.

54. Wait while the ERD is formatted and files are copied.

55. Wait while the temporary configuration files are removed.

56. Press the button to restart your computer.

57. The installation process is now complete.

Exercise 2.5: Removing NTFS Partitions

This exercise gives instructions on how to remove Windows NT from a computer where there are NTFS partitions that are logical drives in extended partitions. Logical NTFS partitions cannot be removed using FDISK.

Objective

Remove Windows NT Workstation

Time Estimate: 30 minutes

Steps

1. Insert the Windows NT Workstation Setup Boot Disk into your floppy drive and restart your computer. (If you don't have the three Setup Boot Disks, you can create them with the command WINNT /OX.)

continues

Exercise 2.5: Continued

2. When prompted, insert Windows NT Workstation Setup Disk #2.

3. At the Windows NT Workstation Setup - Welcome to Setup screen, press Enter to start the installation process.

4. Press Enter to detect mass storage devices.

5. When prompted, insert Windows NT Workstation Setup Disk #3.

6. Press Enter to approve the list of detected mass storage devices. (Don't worry if your IDE hard disk controller isn't detected, the installation process should proceed just fine anyway.)

7. Press Page Down, repeatedly, until you reach the last page of the Windows NT Licensing Agreement.

8. Press F8 to approve the Windows NT Licensing Agreement.

9. Press Enter to approve the list of detected hardware components.

10. Select the desired installation partition and then press Enter.

11. Specify that you want to convert the desired partition from NTFS to FAT.

12. After the conversion to FAT completes, press F3 to exit from the setup program.

13. Restart your computer with a MS-DOS system disk that contains the Sys.com program.

14. From a command prompt, type **SYS C:**, which transfers a MS-DOS boot sector to the hard disk.

Exercise 2.6: Changing Hardware Settings for a Network Adapter

This exercise shows the necessary steps to change the hardware settings for a network adapter.

Objective

Install, configure, and remove network adapter drivers

Time Estimate: 10 minutes

Steps

1. Double-click on the Network program in Control Panel.

2. Click on the Adapters tab.

3. Select the desired network adapter in the Network Adapters section.

4. Click on Properties.

5. Modify the network card properties to the desired settings, and then click on OK.

6. Click on Close in the Network dialog box.

7. Wait while your bindings are recalculated.

8. Click on Yes to restart your computer.

Exercise 2.7: Adding Additional SCSI Adapters

This exercise shows how to add additional SCSI adapters to a computer already running Windows NT 4.0.

Objective

Install, configure, and remove SCSI device drivers

Time Estimate: 10 minutes

Steps

1. Double-click on the SCSI Adapters program in Control Panel.

2. Click on the Drivers tab.

3. Click on Add.

4. Wait while the driver list is being created.

5. Select the appropriate SCSI adapter from the list, or click on Have Disk.

continues

Exercise 2.7: Continued

6. Insert the installation CD or the device manufacturer's installation disk when prompted, and then click on OK.

7. Click on Close to close the SCSI Adapters box.

Exercise 2.8: Adding Tape Devices

This exercise shows how to add tape devices to a computer already running Windows NT Workstation 4.0.

Objective

Install, configure, and remove tape device drivers

Time Estimate: 10 minutes

Steps

1. Double-click on the Tape Devices program in Control Panel.

2. Click on Detect to see whether your tape drive can be automatically detected.

3. If your tape drive is not automatically detected, click on the Drivers tab.

4. Click on Add.

5. Select the appropriate SCSI adapter from the list, or click on Have Disk.

6. Click on OK.

7. Insert the installation CD or the device manufacturer's installation disk when prompted, and then click on OK.

8. Click on Close to close the Tape Devices dialog box.

Exercise 2.9: Installing a Sound Card

This exercise leads you through the steps to install a driver for a sound card.

Objective

Install, configure, and remove multimedia devices

Time Estimate: 10 minutes

Steps

1. Double-click on the Multimedia program in Control Panel.

2. Click on the Devices tab.

3. Click on Add.

4. Select the appropriate device from the list (or Unlisted or Updated Driver if you have a manufacturer's installation disk).

5. Click on OK.

6. Place the installation CD (or manufacturer's installation disk) in your drive and click on OK.

7. Configure the appropriate hardware settings for your sound card in all the dialog boxes that occur.

8. Restart your computer when prompted.

Exercise 2.10:   Configuring Display Settings

This exercise leads you through the steps to change your display settings.

Objective

Install, configure, and remove display devices

Time Estimate: 10 minutes

Steps

1. Double-click on the Display program in Control Panel.

2. Click on the Settings tab in the Display Properties dialog box.

3. Click on Display Type.

4. In the Display Type dialog box, click on Change.

5. Select the appropriate device from the list (or Have Disk if you have an manufacturer's installation disk).

6. Click on OK.

continues

Exercise 2.10: Continued

7. Place the installation CD (or manufacturer's installation disk) in your drive and click on OK.

8. In the Display Type dialog box, click on Close.

9. Click on Test to test the new video settings.

10. Click on OK and wait five seconds to perform the video test.

11. Click on Yes (if you saw the test bitmap correctly).

12. In the Display Properties dialog box, click on OK.

13. If prompted, restart the computer.

Exercise 2.11: Adjusting Keyboard Drivers

This exercise shows you how to adjust the repeat delay and the repeat speed for your keyboard.

Objective

Install, configure, and remove keyboard drivers

Time Estimate: 5 minutes

Steps

1. Double-click on the Keyboard program in Control Panel.

2. Adjust the Repeat delay to the desired setting.

3. Adjust the Repeat rate to the desired setting.

4. Click on OK to save your settings.

Exercise 2.12: Configuring Your Mouse

This exercise leads you though the steps of configuring your mouse.

Objective

Install, configure, and remove mouse drivers

Time Estimate: 5 minutes

Steps

1. Double-click on the Mouse program in Control Panel.

2. Click on the Buttons tab to specify right-handed or left-handed operation, and then double-click on Speed.

3. Click on the Pointers tab to specify the desired style for the mouse pointer.

4. Click on the Motion tab to specify pointer speed and snap to default.

5. Click on the General tab to view the current mouse driver.

6. Click on OK to save your mouse settings.

Exercise 2.13: Adding Additional Optional Components

This exercise shows you how to add any additional optional components that you didn't select when you installed Windows NT Workstation 4.0.

Objective

Use Control Panel applications to configure a Windows NT Workstation computer

Time Estimate: 10 minutes

Steps

1. Double-click on the Add/Remove program in Control Panel.

2. Click on the Windows NT Setup tab.

3. Click on the appropriate category from the displayed list.

4. Click on Details.

5. Click on the optional component(s) that you want to add.

6. Click on OK.

continues

Exercise 2.13: Continued

7. Click on OK in the Add/Remove Properties dialog box.

8. If prompted, insert the installation CD in your CD-ROM drive, and then click on OK.

Exercise 2.14: Modifying Your System Time

This exercise shows you how to change your system time, date, and/or time zone.

Objective

Use Control Panel applications to configure a Windows NT Workstation computer

Time Estimate: 5 minutes

Steps

1. Double-click on the Date/Time program in Control Panel.

2. Change the month, date, and time, as desired.

3. Click on the Time Zone tab to select the proper time zone and the settings for daylight savings time.

4. Click on OK to save the new date/time settings.

Review Questions

The following questions test your knowledge of the material in this chapter:

1. Mitch has a system configured with Windows 95 and Office 97. He would like to dual-boot with Windows NT Workstation 4.0, and still be able to use his office applications. His machine has 32 MB RAM, a 1 GB hard disk formatted with FAT32, and is a Pentium 100. What should he do to upgrade his machine?

   A. Install Windows NT 4.0 using the WINNT32 command, and then reinstall Office 97 under NT.

   B. Upgrade Windows 95 to Windows NT Workstation by deleting his Windows directory after he installs Windows NT Workstation.

   C. Install Windows NT 4.0 using the WINNT32 command, and then reinstall Office 97 under NT.

   D. Mitch cannot install Windows NT Workstation on this machine in its current configuration.

2. You want to install Microsoft Windows NT Workstation 4.0 on 10 Microsoft Windows for Workgroups computers that are connected to your Microsoft Windows NT Server 4.0. What is the fastest way to perform the installation?

   A. Using floppies

   B. Using the Setup Boot floppies and CD

   C. Over the network

   D. Over the network specifying the /b option for WINNT

3. You want to upgrade a Windows 95 computer to Windows NT Workstation 4.0. You have the installation CD and a CD-ROM drive. What program should you use to perform the upgrade?

   A. SETUP

   B. WINNT

   C. WINNT32

   D. UPGRADE

4. You want to upgrade a Windows NT Workstation 3.51 computer to Windows NT Workstation 4.0. You have the installation CD and a CD-ROM drive. What program should you use to perform the upgrade?

   A. SETUP

   B. WINNT

   C. WINNT32

   D. UPGRADE

5. You are setting up a network-based distribution server so that you can perform over-the-network based installations of Microsoft Windows NT Workstation 4.0. What program should you use to place the necessary files on your server? Choose two.

   A. SETUP /A

   B. XCOPY

   C. SERVER MANAGER

   D. Explorer

6. What version of network adapter drivers does Microsoft Windows NT Workstation 4.0 support? Choose two.

   A. ODI

   B. NDIS 3.0

   C. NDIS 3.1

   D. NDIS 4

7. You need to re-create the three Setup Boot Disks that originally came with your installation CD. What command enables you to re-create the disks without installing Windows
   NT Workstation 4.0?

   A. /b

   B. /a

   C. /ox

   D. /x

8. How do you configure network hardware and software?

   A. Use Windows Setup.

   B. In Control Panel, click on the Network program.

   C. In Control Panel, click on the Devices program.

   D. In Control Panel, click on the Services program.

9. What command will use a script file to install Windows NT?

   A. Netsetup

   B. Setup setup.txt

   C. WINNT /U:setup.txt /s:\\server1\ntwWINNT32 /b

10. You need to upgrade a computer from Windows 95 to Windows
    NT Workstation 4.0. It is Pentium based, has 32 MB of RAM
    and 750 MB of free hard disk. What method should you use?

    A. Run WINNT and install Windows NT Workstation 4.0
       in the same directory as Windows 95.

    B. Run WINNT and install Windows NT Workstation 4.0
       in a different directory from Windows 95.

    C. Run WINNT32 and install Windows NT Workstation
       4.0 in the same directory as Windows 95.

    D. Run WINNT32 and install Windows NT Workstation
       4.0 in a different directory from Windows 95.

    E. You cannot perform this upgrade.

11. When you upgrade a computer from a previous version of Windows NT Workstation, which Registry settings are preserved? Choose all that apply.

    A. User and group accounts.

    B. All desktop settings.

    C. Network adapter settings and protocols.

    D. You cannot perform this upgrade.

12. You need to upgrade a computer from Windows 95 to Windows NT Workstation 4.0. It is Intel 386 based, has 32 MB of RAM and 750 MB of free hard disk. What method should you use?

    A. Run WINNT and install Windows NT Workstation 4.0 in the same directory as Windows 95.

    B. Run WINNT and install Windows NT Workstation 4.0 in a different directory from Windows 95

    C. Run SETUP and install Windows NT Workstation 4.0 in the same directory as Windows 95.

    D. Run SETUP and install Windows NT Workstation 4.0 in a different directory from Windows 95.

    E. You cannot perform this upgrade.

13. What is the maximum length of a computer name?

    A. 15

    B. 12

    C. 32

    D. 256

14. What is the minimum RAM required to install Windows NT Workstation 4.0 on an Intel processor?

    A. 4 MB

    B. 12 MB

    C. 16 MB

    D. 32 MB

15. You need to install the Windows Messaging system when you install Windows NT Workstation 4.0. Which Setup option should you choose?

    A. Compact

    B. Portable

    C. Typical

    D. Custom

16. Your computer has Windows 95 installed. You wish to install Windows NT Workstation 4.0 and configure it to dual-boot both operating systems. Which of the following statements are true? Choose two.

    A. You must re-install all your 32-bit Windows applications before they will run under Windows NT Workstation 4.0.

    B. Do nothing after you install Windows NT Workstation 4.0. All your 32-bit Windows applications will continue to execute.

    C. All your user profile settings will be migrated from Windows 95 to Windows NT 4.0 Workstation.

    D. None of your user profile settings will be migrated from Windows 95 to Windows NT Workstation 4.0.

17. You have 50 Pentium-based computers with network cards that you wish to upgrade to Windows NT Workstation 4.0. To prepare for over-the-network installations, which folder on the installation CD needs to be shared?

    A. \I386

    B. \NETSETUP

    C. OEMSETUP

    D. \WINNT

18. When performing an over-the-network based installation of Windows NT Workstation 4.0, what is the name of the temporary folder that contains the installation files?

    A. WIN_NT.TMP

    B. $WINNT.LS

    C. WIN_NT.~LS

    D. WIN_NT.TMP

19. You need to upgrade a computer from Windows NT 3.51 Workstation to Windows NT Workstation 4.0. It is Pentium based, has 32 MB of RAM and 750 MB of free hard disk. What method should you use?

    A. Run WINNT and install Windows NT Workstation 4.0 in the same directory as Windows NT 3.51

    B. Run WINNT and install Windows NT Workstation 4.0 in a different directory from Windows NT 3.51

    C. Run WINNT32 and install Windows NT Workstation 4.0 in the same directory as Windows NT 3.51

    D. Run WINNT32 and install Windows NT Workstation 4.0 in a different directory from Windows NT 3.51

    E. You cannot perform this upgrade.

20. What switch needs to specified along with the /s switch to enable an unattended installation of Windows NT Workstation 4.0?

    A. /b

    B. /u

    C. /oem

    D. /ox

Review Answers

1. D is correct. Because Mitch's system is formatted with FAT32 he cannot install Windows NT Workstation on it. For more information, refer to the section entitled "Minimum Requirements for Installation."

2. D is correct. Performing an over the network installation with the /b option does not waste time creating the three Setup Boot Disks and reading them back. For more information, refer to the section entitled "Installing Windows NT Workstation 4.0 on an Intel Computer with an Existing Operating System."

3. B is correct. You cannot use WINNT32 with Windows 95. For more information, refer to the section entitled "Installing Windows NT Workstation 4.0 on an Intel Computer with an Existing Operating System."

4. C is correct. You cannot use WINNT to upgrade Windows NT. For more information, refer to the section entitled "Installing Windows NT Workstation 4.0 on an Intel Computer with an Existing Operating System."

5. B and D are both correct. There is no SETUP /A option for Windows NT and Server Manager is used for other functions. For more information, refer to the section entitled "Installing Windows NT Workstation 4.0 on an Intel Computer with an Existing Operating System."

6. B and D are both correct. ODI and NDIS 3.1 are types of network device drivers that are supported by Windows 95. For more information, refer to the section entitled "Working with Network Adapter Drivers."

7. C is correct. For more information, refer to the section entitled "Installing Windows NT Workstation 4.0 on an Intel Computer with an Existing Operating System."

8. B is correct. For more information, refer to the section entitled "Working with Network Adapter Drivers."

9. C is correct. For more information, refer to the section entitled "Installing Windows NT Workstation 4.0 on an Intel Computer with an Existing Operating System."

10. B is correct. There is no upgrade path from Windows 95 and you can only use WINNT32 when you are upgrading previous versions of Windows NT. For more information, refer to the section entitled "Upgrading to Windows NT Workstation 4.0."

11. A, B, and C are all correct. When you upgrade a previous version of Windows NT, all Registry settings are preserved. For more information, refer to the section entitled "Upgrading to Windows NT Workstation 4.0."

12. E is correct. Windows NT WWorkstation 4.0 is not supported on Intel 386 microprocessors. For more information, refer to the section entitled "Upgrading to Windows NT Workstation 4.0."

13. A is correct. For more information, refer to Exercise 2.2.

14. B is correct. For more information, refer to the section entitled "Minimum Requirements for Installation."

15. D is correct. You can only install the messaging components if you choose a custom installation. For more information, refer to the section entitled "Installation Options."

16. A and D are both correct. For more information, refer to the section entitled "Setting Up a Dual-Boot System."

17. A is correct. There is no upgrade path from Windows 95 to Windows NT. For more information, refer to the section entitled "Configuring Server-Based Installation for Wide-Scale Deployment."

18. C is correct. For more information, refer to the section entitled "Installing Windows NT Workstation 4.0 on an Intel Computer with an Existing Operating System."

19. C is correct. The 16-bit version of the installation program does not work under Windows NT. For more information, refer to the section entitled "Upgrading to Windows NT Workstation 4.0."

20. B is correct. For more information, refer to the section entitled "Installing Windows NT Workstation 4.0 on an Intel Computer with an Existing Operating System."

Answers to Test Yourself Questions at the Beginning of the Chapter

1. d:\I386\WINNT /b is the command you should use to install Windows NT Workstation 4.0. For more information, refer to the section entitled "Installing Windows NT Workstation 4.0 on an Intel Computer with an Existing Operating System."

2. Windows NT Workstation 4.0 cannot access Windows 95 compressed partitions. You have to uncompress the compressed drives. For more information, refer to the section entitled "Minimum Requirements for Installation."

3. To execute 32-bit applications in a dual-boot configuration, you must install them twice. Boot the computer with Windows NT Workstation 4.0, and then install the application. Then boot the computer with Windows NT Server 4.0 and reinstall the application. For more information, refer to the section entitled "Setting Up a Dual-Boot System."

4. You can restore the Windows 95 boot track by booting the computer with a Windows 95 boot disk and executing the SYS command. For more information, refer to the section entitled "Removing Windows NT Workstation."

5. Control Panel is where you can find the options to install new network adapters. (In Windows NT 3.51, you would have used Windows Setup.) For more information, refer to the section entitled "Working with Network Adapter Drivers."

6. Control Panel is where you find the options to install new SCSI host adapters. (In Windows NT 3.51, you would have used Windows Setup.) For more information, refer to the section entitled "Working with SCSI Device Drivers."

7. Boot.ini is the file that needs to be modified to prevent your UPS from being deactivated (add the NoSerialMice option). For more information, refer to the section entitled "Working with UPS."

Chapter 3

Managing Resources

This chapter helps you prepare for the exam by covering the following objectives:

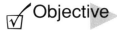 Objective

- ▶ Create and manage local user accounts and local group accounts to meet given requirements

- ▶ Set up and modify user profiles

- ▶ Set up shared folders and permissions

- ▶ Set permissions on NTFS partitions, folders, and files

- ▶ Install and configure printers

Managing resources is important in the administration of Windows NT Workstation. Managing resources refers to the computer accounts on the workstation, both for users and groups, as well as the resources on the workstation. Being able to set appropriate permissions either to allow or restrict access to resources based on a user or group account is key to an effective implementation of Windows NT Workstation. Resources refer not only to files and directories on the Windows NT Workstation, but to printers as well.

Test Yourself! Before reading this chapter, test yourself to determine how much study time you will need to devote to this section.

1. You set up a shared directory called Information. You assign the following permissions to the shared directory:

Account	Permission
CherriL	Change
Users	Read
Operations	Full Control

   If CherriL is a member of the Users group and a member of the Operations group, what are CherriL's effective permissions for the shared directory if she is sitting locally at the workstation?

2. You set up a shared directory called Information. You assign the following permissions to the shared directory:

Account	Permission
CherriL	Change
Users	Read
Operations	Full Control

   If CherriL is a member of the Users group and a member of the Operations group, what are CherriL's effective permissions for the shared directory if she is accessing it from across the network?

3. You set up NTFS permissions on a directory called Sales Data. You assign the following NTFS permissions to the directory:

Account	Permission
JasonM	Read
Users	Read
Sales	Full Control

If JasonM is a member of the Users group and a member of the Sales group, what are JasonM's effective permissions for this directory if he is sitting locally at the workstation?

4. You set up a directory called Market Research. You assign the following NTFS and Share permissions to the directory:

Account	NTFS Permissions	Share Permissions
CarlaH	Change	Change
Users	Read	Read
Marketing	Full Control	Full Control

If CarlaH is a member of the Users group and a member of the Marketing group, what are CarlaH's effective permissions for this directory if she is sitting locally at the workstation?

5. You set up a directory called Market Research. You assign the following NTFS and Share permissions to the directory:

Account	NTFS Permissions	Share Permissions
CarlaH	Change	Change
Users	Read	Read
Marketing	Full Control	No Access

If CarlaH is a member of the Users group and a member of the Marketing group, what are CarlaH's effective permissions for this directory if she is accessing the Market Research directory from across the network?

6. Your boss tells you to delete the account for SpenceB because SpenceB is leaving the company. You delete the account. Two hours later your boss calls you to tell you he was wrong—SpenceB was just going on vacation, not leaving the company and he needs his account back. You re-create his account, giving it the same name as before. In the afternoon, SpenceB calls you to tell you he cannot access his files in his home directory or other files in shared directories that he used to be able to access. What is the problem?

7. You receive a call from your boss who is quite angry because the report that he needs will not print. He tells you that all that is coming out of the printer is "garbage text" on multiple pages. What do you think the problem is?

8. You receive a call from your boss who is quite angry because the report that she needs will not print. She tells you that nothing is coming out of the printer. You look at the print queue for the printer and see five other documents behind it waiting to print. What should you do to troubleshoot this problem?

9. You want to add a shortcut to the Start menu so that it will be available to all users who log on to that workstation. How should you do that?

10. You want to have the same desktop settings no matter where you log on within your Windows NT domain. All the client machines are Windows NT Workstation 4.0. How can you set this up?

Answers are located at the end of the chapter...

Implementing Local User and Group Accounts

Objective   Windows NT has a mandatory logon. That means that every user who wants to use a Windows NT Workstation must have a logon name and password before he or she can use Windows NT Workstation. Whether you are in a small workgroup or a large domain, it is a good idea to plan the implementation of user accounts as well as local group accounts. Local group accounts are used to give multiple users access to resources. If you have a particular resource such as a printer, it is easier to give access to a group rather than each user individually. When planning your user and group accounts, you need to accomplish a few tasks, such as the following:

- ▶ Planning user and group accounts

- ▶ Creating user and group accounts

- ▶ Managing user and group accounts

Each one of these tasks is important for an effective implementation of Windows NT Workstation.

Planning User Accounts

Before creating user accounts, it is a good idea to plan how you will implement user accounts under Windows NT Workstation. Planning user accounts includes what password requirements you wish to implement, your naming convention, the location of a user's home directory, and whether to grant dial-in access to users.

Modifying Account Policy

How often do you want users to have to change their passwords? What do you want to have happen if there are multiple bad logon attempts? How many passwords do you want "remembered?" All these items are manipulated with the Account Policy. The Account Policy is configured within User Manager by choosing Account from the Policies menu (see fig. 3.1).

Figure 3.1

*You can modify
password options
within the Ac-
count Policy
screen of User
Manager.*

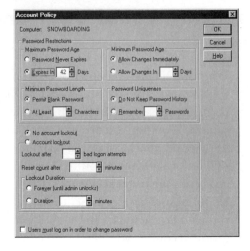

The following is a list of the password restrictions available:

Maximum Password Age. This option enables you to specify how long a user's password is valid. The default is that
passwords expire in 42 days.

 Tip

> If the Account Policy is set so that the password expires and
> the user's account is specified so that the password never
> expires, the user setting overrides the Account Policy setting.

Minimum Password Age. This specifies how long a user
must keep a particular password before she can change it
again. If you force a user to change her password, and you
leave this set to Allow Changes Immediately, after the user
has changed her password she can change it right back to
the old one. If you are trying to implement password changes for security reasons, this breaks down your security. For
that reason, you may want to set a minimum password age.

Minimum Password Length. The default on Windows NT
is to allow blank passwords. Once again, for security reasons
you may not want to allow this. You can set a minimum password length of up to 14 characters, which is the maximum
password length allowed under Windows NT.

Password Uniqueness. If you want to force users to use different passwords each time they change their passwords, you can set a value for password uniqueness. If you set the password uniqueness value to remember two passwords, when a user is prompted to change her password she cannot use the same password again until changing her password for the third time.

The following is a list of the Account Lockout options:

Lockout after bad logon attempts. Setting a value for this option prevents the account from being used after this number is reached, even if the right password is finally used. If you set this value to five, which is the default when enabling Account Lockout, on the sixth attempt—even if the user (or hacker) types in the correct user name and password—he cannot log on to Windows NT.

Reset counter after. This value specifies when to refresh the counter for bad logon attempts. The default value is 30 minutes. That means if Account Lockout is set to five and a user tries to logon unsuccessfully four times and then tries again in 45 minutes, the counter will have been reset and the account will not be locked out.

Lockout Duration. This value specifies how long the account should remain locked out if the lockout counter is exceeded. It is generally more secure to set Lockout Duration to forever so that the administrator must unlock the account. That way the administrator is warned of the activity on that account.

Users must log on to change password. This setting requires a user to log on successfully before changing his password. If a user's password expires, the user cannot log on until the administrator changes the password for the user.

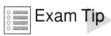 Exam Tip

For the exam, you should be familiar with the Account Policy screen and how to configure each option on it.

When planning an account policy, it is important to give your environment the required security, but also make the password requirements manageable. If you forced users to change their passwords every day, and set the password history to remember 24 passwords (the maximum), you might have a situation where users start writing them down and sticking them on the monitor or under the keyboard or in the desk drawer. That would compromise your security rather than enhance it.

Utilizing a Naming Convention

Planning your naming convention is also another important part of creating user accounts. If you are going to be implementing Windows NT Workstation in a domain environment, the user names need to be unique in the domain. If you are implementing Windows NT Workstation as a stand-alone machine, user names must be unique on that machine.

You must implement a naming convention to allow for this uniqueness in names. You might choose to use employee identification numbers as logon names. In a very large company where each employee is given a unique employee number, this may be a good way of ensuring uniqueness. In a smaller company, you may choose to use a naming convention of first name last initial. If you had an employee named Kendra McCormick, her logon name would be KendraM. If, later on, your company hired a Kendra McClarty, you would have to determine how to handle this user. You cannot use the name KendraM because that is already used. One option is to add a number to the user name, making it KendraM1. Another option is to add the second letter of the last name, to make it KendraMc. In a larger environment, this type of naming convention can become unwieldy due to the possibility of having so many duplicate names.

It is probably pretty likely that you would have more than one StephenR, for instance, in a 10,000 user company. In the case of a larger environment, it may make more sense to use a first initial, last name naming convention. In this environment if you had a user named David Kayano, his user name would be DKayano. An even better way to implement a naming convention for a large

company is to take a few letters of the first name, the middle initial, and the last name. Even with this naming convention, you
may have duplicates, so you would need to account for that possibility. In a large environment, it may be likely that you may have
more than one user named Mike Smith, for instance.

Designing a Home Directory Location

Whether you will grant users home directories for storing personal information is another issue you must consider when planning
user accounts. A home directory is designed to be a storage location available only to that particular user for storing his or her
own files.

You can create a home directory either on the local Windows NT
Workstation or on a remote location such as a Windows NT Server. When deciding whether to create a user's home directory locally or remotely, you must take into account the needs of your
environment. Do users "roam" from machine to machine in your
network? If so, you need to store a user's home directory centrally
so that the user can access it potentially from anywhere in the
network. If you are in a workgroup of just Windows NT Workstations, however, you would most likely just create user home directories on each Windows NT Workstation locally because there is
no central server to create them on.

If you choose to create the home directories on a Windows NT
Server, you must give the users access to the Shared Users directo-
ry on the server. For more information on this, see Chapter 1,
"Planning an Effective Implementation."

Granting Dial-In Permission

If you have users who will be working from home or who travel
and are on the road and need to access your network remotely,
you need to grant those users dial-in access. Windows NT does not
by default grant the right to dial in to the network remotely. You
must, if called for, specifically grant it to them.

Note

If you are creating user accounts for a Windows NT Workstation rather than a domain, granting the dial-in permission only applies to that one Windows NT Workstation.

The call back options for dial-in access are as follows:

No call back. This setting disables call back for a particular user account. If this is set, the user initiates the phone call with the RAS server and the user is responsible for the phone charges.

Set By Caller. This enables the remote user to specify the number for the server to call back the user. This is typically used to have the server responsible for the phone charges, rather than the user.

Preset To. When set, this specifies a number for the server to call the user back when the user initiates a dial-in session. This tends to be used for security so that a user is called back at a pre-defined number only.

 Tip

Don't set Preset To in the Dial-in permissions if a user will be traveling and calling from a hotel or other location with a switchboard rather than a direct line.

Built-In User Accounts

 **Objective**

Windows NT Workstation creates the following two built-in user accounts when installed:

▶ Administrator

▶ Guest

You can use these two built-in accounts for administration of Windows NT Workstation and to allow guest access to the Windows NT Workstation.

Tip   Windows NT Workstation 3.51 created an additional user account when installed that was called the Initial User account. Windows NT Workstation 4.0 no longer creates that account during installation. Be careful of questions referring to this Initial User account on the exam that may try to trick you.

▶ **Administrator.** The default Administrator account has full power over the Windows NT Workstation. It has the right to create user accounts, delete them, share resources, stop sharing them, format partitions, create partitions, set password policies, and use the administrative tools of Windows NT. This default Administrator account is always created on Windows NT, so it is a good idea to rename this account after installation if you have concerns about security.

▶ **Guest.** This built-in account on Windows NT is used for people who do not have accounts on the Windows NT Workstation or the domain that the workstation is a part of if in a domain environment. This account has the least privilege on the Windows NT Workstation and is not allowed to share resources, create users, or manage user policies. This account is only used for allowing the user to log on to the Windows NT Workstation, and may be used to allow the user to access resources on that system or on the network. You may choose to rename this built-in account after installation for security purposes.

 Tip   You can rename both the built-in accounts on Windows NT Workstation, but you cannot delete them. If you try to delete either of them, an error message appears stating that you cannot delete the account.

Accounts You Create

Along with the accounts created on Windows NT Workstation during installation, you must create additional user accounts on that workstation for those who need to log on to that Windows NT Workstation—or accounts in the domain if the workstation is participating in a domain environment. You must create an account for every user who will log on to the Windows NT Workstation, unless the user will be using the Guest account or the default Administrator account. Under Windows NT, logging on the workstation is mandatory to gaining access to any resources on it, unlike Windows 95 which has the capability to cancel out of the logon screen. Within Windows NT Workstation, a user must have a valid user name and password; otherwise, he cannot log on to the machine.

Creating User Accounts

After you have planned your account policy, naming convention, and user account settings, you are ready to actually start creating user accounts. To create user accounts, you must be logged on with an account that has that right. On a Windows NT Workstation, the only two groups that can create user accounts are the Administrators group and the Power Users group. To create a user account in User Manager, see figure 3.2.

Figure 3.2

User Manager is used to create user accounts.

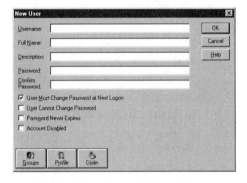

You must configure many items when creating a new user account. The following sections discuss these items.

Setting User Information

Within the User Information section, one field is required. That field is the Username. The Username can be a maximum of 20 characters and cannot contain special characters. Special characters are defined as the following:

" / \ [ ] : ; l = , + * ? < >

The Full Name and Description fields are used just for informational purposes. If you choose to pre-assign a password to users when creating their accounts, you specify that password in the Password field as well as the Confirm Password field. The password in Windows NT can be up to 14 characters long. If you have specified an account policy that requires a minimum password length, you must enter in a password at least that long when creating the user account.

Establishing Password Options

The password options are not required fields when creating a new user account. You may choose to implement some of these options, however, when creating user accounts. These options are as follows:

▶ **User Must Change Password at Next Logon.** When this is selected (which is the default when creating new users), the user is prompted to change his password when he logs on to Windows NT. This setting is not compatible with the account policy that forces a user to log on to change his password. If both are selected, the user must contact the administrator to change the password.

▶ **User Cannot Change Password.** Setting this option prevents a user from changing her password. If this setting as well as User Must Change Password are selected, you get an error message stating that you cannot check both options for the same user when you attempt to add the account.

▶ **Password Never Expires.** You can use this option to override the setting for password expiration in the Account Policy. This option tends to be used for accounts that will be assigned to services, but can also be granted to user accounts as well. If you have this option selected as well as User Must Change Password at Next Logon, a warning tells you that the user will not be required to change her password.

▶ **Account Disabled.** Rather than deleting a user's account when he or she leaves the company, it is a good idea to disable the account instead. If the user will be replaced, it is likely that the new individual hired will need the same rights and permissions that the previous user did. By disabling the account, you prevent the previous employee from being able to access your Windows NT Workstation or domain. When the new individual is hired, you can then rename the old account to the new name and have the user change the password.

▶ **Account Locked Out.** This option is visible only if you have Account Lockout enabled in the Account Policy. You, as an administrator, can never check this box—it will be grayed out. The only time this box is available is if a user's account has been locked out due to hitting the set number of bad logon attempts. If the Lockout Duration is set to forever, the administrator must go into that user's account and uncheck the Account Locked Out check box.

Configuring a User Environment Profile

You can use the User Environment Profile Settings, under the Profile button within the properties for the user's account to manage the user's working environment. Figure 3.3 shows the settings that you can modify through this button.

Figure 3.3

You use the Profile button to configure the user's working environment.

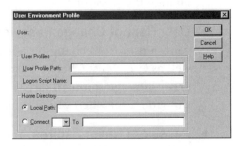

When determining how to create and configure your user accounts for Windows NT Workstation, it is important to understand the settings that you can define for the user's environment. These are as follows:

▶ **User Profile Path.** This setting is used to specify a path for a user profile to be available centrally on a server or to assign a mandatory user profile for this user. To use a roaming or mandatory user profile, you must create a share on a server and then specify the path to that share in the user's profile, where the path follows the syntax of:

```
\\servername\sharename\profilename
```

For more information on mandatory user profiles, see the section entitled "Mandatory User Profiles" later in this chapter.

▶ **Logon Script Name.** This setting is used to specify a logon script to be used if desired. If a logon script is specified, it will be launched when the user logs on to the Windows NT Workstation. If the logon script is in a subdirectory of the machine's logon script path (typically c:\winnt\system32\repl\import\scripts), you must specify that subdirectory within the logon script name (for example, users\LailaL.bat). Logon scripts can have the extension cmd, bat, or exe.

▶ **Home Directory.** To specify a home directory for a user's personal use, specify it here. This home directory can be either local or remote, by using the connect option. If you choose to use a remote home directory (for a discussion of local verses remote home directories, see Chapter 1, "Planning an Effective Implementation"), you must select a drive letter and specify the path to that remote share, such as:

\\servername\users\JillB

If you choose to use local home directories, specify the full path in this setting such as:

C:\users\JillB

 Tip   If you are trying to specify home directories for multiple users simultaneously, you can use the variable %username% in place of the user's name.

The settings within the User Environment Profile can enable you to manage both the location of the user's profile, as well as the location of the user's home directory. A decision needs to be made regarding both of these settings—if you are in a Windows

NT domain environment—as to whether you will choose to centrally store these items, or allow them to be stored on each individual user's workstation.

Using a Template Account

You can use a template account if you have certain information that must be specified for multiple user accounts that you will create. If you have a group of sales people that you will be creating Windows NT accounts for, for instance, you may want the description field for all of them to be Sales Representative. You could manually add that to each user account that you create, but that would be unnecessary effort if you had a lot of accounts to create. Instead, you could create a user account called Template that had the description field filled in. In addition to the description field, you could put this Template account in the Sales group and specify the home directory and logon script settings (see fig. 3.4).

Figure 3.4

You can create a template user account to make creating user accounts more efficient.

 Tip

You can use the variable %username% for the user's home directory. By using this variable, you can specify it in the template account. When each user is created, it pulls that information from his or her user name.

After the Template account has been created, you can now use that account to create the user accounts for the Sales Representatives. To create these accounts, complete the following steps:

1. Highlight the Template account in User Manager.

2. On the User menu, choose Copy.

3. Enter in the Username and Full Name for this new account.

A template account can then also be created for other groups of user accounts that will need to have the same information referenced regarding description, groups, home directories, logon scripts, user profile paths, or dial-in access.

Managing User Accounts

 After user accounts have been created, it may be necessary to manage them. This management can include renaming user accounts or deleting user accounts. It is important to understand when renaming a user account is recommended versus when deleting a user account is the appropriate course of action.

Renaming User Accounts

When a user account is created in Windows NT, it is given a unique identification called a security identifier (SID). This SID is designed to be unique in all of space and time. It is not based on the user's name, so renaming the user account does not make a difference to NT. If you have a CIO who has left the company and you hire a new CIO, by renaming the old account to the name of the new CIO you can retain all the existing rights and permissions that the original account had. It is likely that the new CIO would need the same rights and permissions as the former one, so this would save you the work of reassigning those.

Deleting User Accounts

In Windows NT it is not usually a good idea to delete a user account. If CindyF has permissions to a particular directory, and you accidentally delete her user account, you cannot just re-create another account called CindyF. When the original CindyF account was created, it was given a SID, which was unique in all of space and time. When you deleted her account, you deleted the SID. When you re-created her account, even though it appeared to be the same user name, the SID that was created was different.

 The SID (security identifier) is created when the user account is created and is uniquely tied to that particular user account. If you choose to delete and re-create the user account, it will have a different SID.

It is the SID that is used for resource access, so CindyF no longer will have access to that directory until you add the new account for her to the list of directory permissions. Because of this issue with the SID, it is generally better to disable an account using the User Manager than to delete the account. In the case of the CIO who left the company, you would probably want to disable that account so that the CIO would not be able to have access to your network. When the new CIO is hired, enable the account and rename it to the name of the new CIO. If you had deleted the account, you would have to re-create all of the rights and permissions that the former CIO had.

Planning Local Group Accounts

Local group accounts are used to organize users to give them rights on the workstation, as well as to give them access to resources. Built-in local groups are used to give users the rights to perform certain actions on the workstation. Local groups that you create are used to logically organize users to give them the ability to access a particular resource such as a folder or a printer.

 Note

Local groups are the only type of group created on Windows NT Workstation. Windows NT Server installed as a domain controller contains local groups as well as global groups.

Built-in Local Groups

If you want to give a user the ability to create additional user accounts, to create disk partitions, format those partitions, and share directories, you can put that user in the Administrators built-in group to give the user those rights. The following list describes the four built-in groups on Windows NT Workstation. Assigning users to these built-in groups can help you manage Windows NT Workstation.

> ▶ **Administrators.** The Administrators group has full control over the Windows NT Workstation. This account has the most control on the computer. As a member of the Administrators group, however, the user does not automatically have

control over all files on the system. If using an NTFS partition, a file's permissions could be to restrict access from the administrator. If the administrator needs to access the file, she can take ownership of the file and then access it. Administrative privilege is one of three different levels of privilege that you can assign to a user in Windows NT. It is the highest level of privilege that can be assigned within Windows NT.

▶ **Guests.** The Guests group is used to give someone limited access to the resources on the Windows NT Workstation. The Guest account is automatically added to this group. The Guest group is one of the three levels of privilege that you can assign to a Windows NT user account.

▶ **Users.** The Users group provides the user with the necessary rights to use the computer as an end user. By default, all accounts created on Windows NT Workstation are put into the Users group, except for the built-in Administrator and Guest accounts. User privilege is one of the three levels of privilege that you can assign in Windows NT.

▶ **Power Users.** The Power Users group gives members the ability to perform certain system tasks without giving the user complete administrative control over the machine. One of the tasks a power user can perform is the sharing of directories. An ordinary user on Windows NT Workstation cannot share directories.

For more information on the default rights and abilities of these built-in groups, see the section entitled "Built-In Groups" in Chapter 1, "Planning an Effective Implementation."

Local Groups You Create

If you have to assign permissions to a shared resource or implement NTFS permissions on directories or printers, you may want to consider creating additional group accounts. The built-in groups can be used to give users certain rights on the workstation or in the domain, but you may have a need to allocate access to resources based on department or geographical location. In that situation, you may choose to create a group for each department, each city, or each logical grouping of users to which you may need to assign rights. If you have a printer that you need to share to the Education Department, for example, it might make more sense to put all those users in the Education Department into a group and assign that group access to the printer.

Creating Local Group Accounts

 **Objective**

To create a local group account, you must be logged on to Windows NT with an account that has administrative permissions. The tool used for creating user accounts is User Manager on Windows NT Workstation and User Manager for Domains on a Windows NT domain. To create a local group account on Windows NT Workstation, you must fill in the fields as shown in figure 3.5.

Figure 3.5

To create a local group account on Windows NT Workstation, use User Manager.

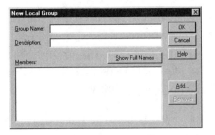

 Tip

If you have a user account highlighted when you go to create a new local group, that user account will automatically be put in that group. This can be used as a shortcut when creating local groups. If you would like to have more than one user account automatically added to the group, you can highlight multiple user accounts by holding down the Ctrl key.

To create a new local group, complete the following steps:

1. Highlight those accounts that you would like to be a part of this group by selecting them and holding down Ctrl.

2. Within User Manager, go to the User menu and choose New Local Group.

3. Type in a Group name for this group and optionally a description.

4. Add any additional user accounts to this group by clicking on the Add button.

5. Click on the OK button to create the local group.

You can now use this local group to assign permissions to resources such as a directory or a printer.

Managing Local Group Accounts

It may be necessary to manage your local group accounts after they have been created. This management could be in the form of adding additional user accounts to the group, renaming the group, or deleting the group. If you need to add additional users to a local group, you can do that when you create the user account by selecting the Groups button within the user properties or after you have created the user account by double-clicking on the local group account within User Manager. To add a user account to the local group, click on the Add button and select the desired user account.

Renaming Local Group Accounts

You cannot rename a local group account. If you decide that you want to change the name of a group, you must create a new group with the new name. You must then give this group the appropriate rights to resources.

Deleting Local Group Accounts

If you choose to delete a group account, that group will be gone forever. In the same way that an individual user account is given a SID when it is created, so is a group account. If you delete the group accidentally, you must re-create the group and reassign all the permissions for the group. Deleting a group does not delete the individual user accounts within the group, just the group itself.

Tip

You cannot delete any of the built-in system groups on NT. This includes Administrators, Power Users, Users, Guests, Backup Operators, and the Replicator.

Setting Up and Modifying User Profiles

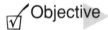 **Objective**

User profiles are automatically created when a user logs on to Windows NT. A user profile establishes the settings that contribute to a user's working environment. This includes such things as wallpaper, desktop shortcuts, and network connections. The user's profile contains all user-definable settings for the user's environment.

 Tip

On Windows NT Workstation, a user profile is automatically created for every user who logs on to the workstation. This is unlike Windows 95, which enables you to select whether to use user profiles. This is the type of issue you may see brought up in a test question.

Understanding User Profiles

User profiles are used to enable each user on Windows NT to store his own individual settings for his own work environment. User profiles are primarily used for convenience, but can be used by an administrator to establish control over the user's environment. (For more information, see the section entitled "Mandatory User Profiles.") A user profile can be stored either locally on the user's Windows NT Workstation or centrally on a server so as to be accessible from any location in the network. User profiles, if stored on the server and set as roaming user profiles, can be accessed from any machine on the network running Windows NT 4.0.

 Caution

User profiles for Windows NT Workstation 4.0 are not interchangeable with user profiles for Windows NT Workstation 3.51 or Windows 95. If you have a user who uses all three operating systems, that user must have three different user profiles, one for each operating system.

User Profile Settings

So, what can be stored in a user profile? Items that relate to a user's own working environment are stored in a user profile. Table 3.1 identifies these items.

Table 3.1

Items Included in a User's Profile	
Item	Description
Accessories	Any user-specific settings that affect the user's environment such as Calculator, Clock, Notepad, and Paint.
Control Panel	Any user-defined settings defined within the Control Panel such as Mouse Pointers, Modem Dialing Properties, and Mail and Fax properties.
Printers	Any printer connections made within Windows NT Workstation to network printers.
Start menu	Any personal program groups and their properties such as the working directory.
Taskbar	Any taskbar settings such as Always on Top or Auto Hide.
Windows NT Explorer	Any user-specific settings for Windows NT Explorer such as whether to view the toolbar, to show large icons, and how to arrange icons.

Items managed on a per-user basis that define the user's working environment are a part of the user's profile settings.

User Profile Directory Structure

By default in Windows NT Workstation, when a user logs on to the workstation a user profile is stored locally on that machine for the user. This profile is created under the user's name in the Profiles folder under the Windows NT root directory. The first time a user logs on to the computer, this directory is created for that user.

The user's profile inherits the settings of the Default User directory structure, discussed later in the section entitled "Default User." Also combined into the user's profile are the groups common to all users, found in the All Users directory structure. After the user logs off the Windows NT Workstation, any changes that the user made to her environment while logged on are saved to the user's profile. Below the user's directory within the Profiles directory is a structure of settings relating to the user's profile. Table 3.2 describes that structure.

Table 3.2

Folders Within a User's Profile Directory

Folder	Description
Application Data	Any application specific data. The contents of this folder are determined by application vendors.
Desktop	Any desktop items such as shortcuts, folders, documents, or files.
Favorites	A listing of favorite locations such as Internet URLs for different web sites.
NetHood	Any shortcuts to Network Neighborhood items.
Personal	Any shortcuts to program items.
PrintHood	Shortcuts to printers.
Recent	Shortcuts to recently used items.
SendTo	Shortcuts to items in the SendTo Context menu. You can add items to this folder such as Notepad or printers.
Start menu	Shortcuts to the program items found in the Start menu.
Templates	Shortcuts to any template items.

The NetHood, PrintHood, Recent, and Templates folders are not visible by default. If you would like to display these folders, you must go into the View menu within Windows NT Explorer and choose Options, the View tab, and then the Show All Files radio button. This displays these hidden folders.

All Users

The All Users public folder is used for Start menu shortcuts that apply to all users of the Windows NT Workstation. These settings are not added to the user's profile, but they are used in conjunction with it to define the user's working environment. The common program groups, common to all users who log on to the Windows NT Workstation, are stored under the All Users directory. If you would like to add a menu shortcut to a Windows NT Workstation, you can do that by adding it to the All Users folder.

 Note

Only members of the Administrators group can add items to the All Users folder for common access.

Default User

The Default User folder contains the settings that each new user who logs on to the workstation inherits the first time he or she logs on. If no preconfigured profile exists for a user when he logs on, he inherits the settings from the Default User folder; those settings are copied into that user's new profile directory. Any changes that the user makes while logged on are saved into his user profile, leaving the Default Users folder unchanged.

Setting Various User Profiles

Setting User Profiles can help you to configure the environment for your users. User profiles can be used to restrict users, or as a convenience for users to retain their own settings when they move from one machine to another throughout your network. Setting user profiles falls under three main categories: mandatory user profiles, local user profiles, and roaming user profiles.

Mandatory User Profiles

You may have a situation in which you do not want users to have the convenience of storing their own desktop settings in personal or individual profiles, but instead need to have a more consistent working environment. You can use mandatory user profiles when a higher level of control is required than just the standard user profile environment. The user cannot change mandatory user profiles. A mandatory user profile is created by the administrator and can be assigned to one or more users. User profiles are configured through the Control Panel, System icon (see fig. 3.6).

Figure 3.6

User profiles are managed through the System properties.

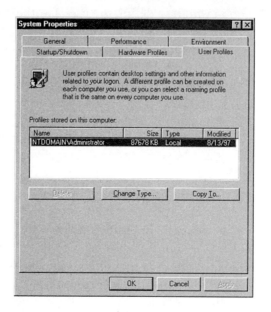

 Tip

In Windows NT 4.0, user profiles are configured through the Control Panel, System icon, User Profiles tab. In Windows NT 3.51, user profiles were manipulated through the Setup Editor. Because this is a change from Windows NT 3.51 to Windows NT 4.0, it is good test material.

Because it cannot be changed, it remains consistent from one log on to the next. In addition, because a mandatory user profile cannot be changed, it can be used for multiple users in your network. You can use mandatory user profiles to present a consistent working environment for certain departments or for all users in your company.

Local User Profiles

The term local user profiles refers to a user's profile that is created on the Windows NT Workstation that she is logging on to. Local user profiles are the default in Windows NT Workstation, and are created the first time that a user logs on to a Windows NT Workstation. Local user profiles are stored locally on the Windows NT Workstation, under the Profiles directory. If a user only uses one machine and will never need to have his settings while sitting at another Windows NT Workstation, a local user profile might be what you would choose for that user.

Roaming User Profiles

Local user profiles are allowed in Windows NT. If you will have users who must "roam" from one Windows NT Workstation computer to another in your environment, however, you may not choose to use local user profiles. A roaming user profile is configured by the administrator to allow the user to retain her own settings wherever she might land on the network, as long as it is another Windows NT 4.0 machine. When the user makes a change to a roaming personal profile, that change gets saved on the server where the profile is stored. If the user is logged on to two machines simultaneously, the last session to be logged off will be the settings retained for the user's profile. If the administrator decides to create a roaming mandatory profile, the user cannot change it. A roaming mandatory profile can be used for multiple users. If the administrator needs to make a change to the profile, she needs to make the change only once and it will affect all users who have that mandatory profile.

Creating a User Profile

Now that you are aware of the different reasons to use mandatory or roaming user profiles with NT Workstation, you must actually implement user profiles. To create a user profile, complete the following steps:

1. Log on to Windows NT Workstation with an account that has administrative permissions.

2. Create a test user account.

3. Log off and log on as the test user account. This creates a folder under the Profiles directory for that test user.

4. Configure the desktop environment as you would like it to be for the new mandatory profile.

5. Log off and log back on with the administrative account.

6. Create a centralized location for storing user profiles on a server and share that directory (for example, servername\Profiles\username).

7. Go into the Control Panel, System icon, and select the User Profiles tab.

8. Select the profile for the test user and click on Copy To. Under Copy Profile To, enter in the path to the shared profiles directory: (**\\servername\Profiles\username**)

9. Under Permitted to Use, make sure the right user name is selected.

10. Within the folder that you created for the test user's roaming profile, rename the file Ntuser.dat to **Ntuser.man** to make the profile mandatory.

11. Launch User Manager and double-click on the test user's account.

12. Click on the Profile button and enter in the path to the mandatory profile: (**\\servername\Profiles\username**)

User profiles—regardless of whether they are used for convenience for the user or to restrict user actions—can be helpful in managing the NT Workstation environment.

Testing a User Profile

To test the creation of a user profile, log on to the Windows NT Workstation as a user who has been assigned a mandatory user profile. If you receive the proper settings while logged on as that user, your test has been successful. If you do not receive those settings, go back to the Control Panel, System, User Profiles tab to determine whether you have set up the user's profile properly.

Also, check the properties of that user account within User Manager to make sure you have indicated the path to the user account properly. Third, check the actual directory structure on the machine storing the profile to verify that the share point has been set up correctly as well as that the profile has been copied to the correct folder.

Setting Up Shared Folders and Permissions

 Objective

To allow remote access of your resources, you must make them available on the network to other users on other computers. Making some resources available on the network does not mean that you have to make all resources available on the network. Windows NT enables you to selectively choose which folders you want to allow access to and which you want to remain private to that workstation.

To share a folder in Windows NT means to make that folder available to other users on the network. If you have a resource that you want others to access, you must choose to share that resource. Sharing can only be done at the folder or directory level—it cannot be done at the individual file level. Thus if you want to share only one file, you must create a folder and put just that one file into the folder. After you put the file in the folder, you then need to share that folder. After a folder is shared, users with rights to that shared folder have access to all the files and subfolders beneath it as well.

Planning Shared Folders

When planning shared folders it is important to structure your directories appropriately as well as plan the naming convention that you will use for the share names.

Location of Resources

When you share a directory, all files and folders below that directory are shared with the same access permissions as the parent directory. Because of this, you need to plan where to locate resources to be able to grant access only to the resources you choose to. Figure 3.7 shows an example of planning the location of resources.

Figure 3.7

The location of shared re-sources.

In the example in figure 3.7, you as the administrator must decide how you want to implement sharing of these application folders. If you want users to have the same access to each of the application folders, you could create the share at the SharedApps level. If, however, you want users to only have access to certain applications but not others, you would have to create the shared folder at each application folder such as Word or Excel.

Naming Convention for Shared Folders

When deciding a naming convention for sharing resources, the type of clients in the environment must be considered. If all clients are Windows 95 or Windows NT, using long share names is possible. If your environment contains Windows 3.x clients or DOS clients, you must take that into account when determining your naming convention for shared resources. Windows 3.x clients and DOS clients cannot view long share names, so in that situation you must keep the share names to 8.3 characters or less. Also, when creating shared folders, it is a good idea to use share names that are intuitive as to what is found within that shared resource. Using the share name Share01 does not really describe what the resource is.

Establishing Shared Folder Permissions

Windows NT provides four different levels of permission that you can give to users who will access your shared folder. You can use these permissions at either a user or a group level, depending on the needs of your environment. These permissions are as follows:

▶ **No Access.** If a user or group is given the No Access permission to a shared folder, that user or group cannot even open the shared folder, although he will see the shared folder on the network. The No Access permission overrides all other permissions that a user or group might have to the folder.

▶ **Read.** The Read permission allows the user or group to display files and subfolders within the shared folder. It also allows the user or group to execute programs that might be located within the shared folder.

▶ **Change.** The Change permission allows the user or group to be able to add files or subfolders to the shared folder as well as append or delete information from existing files and subfolders. The Change permission also encompasses everything included within the Read permission.

▶ **Full Control.** If a user or group is given the Full Control permission, that user or group has the ability to change the file permissions, to take ownership of files, and to perform all tasks allowed by the Change permission.

Enabling Folder Sharing

To share a folder for others to access on the network, you must have the right to share folders. This right is not given to ordinary users (members of the Users group) in Windows NT Workstation. To share a network resource under Windows NT, you must be a member of one of the following groups:

▶ Power Users (on Windows NT Workstation)

▶ Administrators (on Windows NT Workstation or Server)

▶ Server Operators (on Windows NT Domain Controller)

If you are not a member of one of those groups, you must be added to one of those groups before you can share resources.

Sharing a Folder Locally

To share a folder locally, meaning that you are sitting at the workstation that holds the folder you would like to share, right-click on the folder and choose the Sharing option. This brings up the properties of the folder, with the focus on the Sharing tab (see fig. 3.8).

Figure 3.8

The Sharing tab of a folder within My Computer.

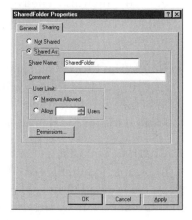

To locally create a shared folder, complete the following steps:

1. Click on the Shared As radio button.

2. Enter the Share Name you would like to use. (Remember that DOS and Windows 3.x clients cannot access share names longer than 8 characters.)

3. Optionally, enter in a comment to describe this shared resource.

4. Optionally, set a user limit for the number of simultaneous connections.

Tip

Windows NT Workstation has a built-in limit of 10 inbound network connections. Selecting a higher number in the User Limit section does not increase this number.

5. Assign permissions to the shared folder.

Sharing a Folder Remotely

To share a folder remotely, meaning that you would like to attach to a remote server or workstation and share its resources out to the network, you must use Server Manager, which comes with the Client-Based Network Tools for Windows NT Workstation. Server Manager is a tool that you can use to create remote shared directories (see fig. 3.9).

Figure 3.9

You can create shared directories on a remote machine by using Server Manager.

To remotely create a shared folder using Server Manager, follow these steps:

1. Highlight the computer on which you would like to create the shared folder.

2. On the Computer menu, choose Shared Directories.

3. From the Shared Directories dialog box, click on the New Share button.

4. Enter the share name that you want to use for this new share.

5. Enter the path to the share. This is the path as it would be specified according to the remote machine. If you wanted to share the directory C:\Info, for example, that is what you would type. Because there is no Browse button available, you must know the path that you would like to share.

6. Optionally, enter a comment to describe the shared resource.

7. Optionally, set a user limit for the shared resource. If the resource is on a Windows NT Workstation, remember that the maximum number of inbound connections is 10. If the resource is on a Windows NT Server, the number of inbound connections is unlimited.

8. Click on the Permissions button to set the permissions for the shared resource.

9. Click on OK to create the shared resource.

Setting Permissions on a Shared Folder

To set permissions on a shared folder, highlight the folder and right-click on it. From the Context menu, choose Sharing. From the folder properties, Sharing tab, click on the Permissions button. This button is only available if the folder is being shared. By default in Windows NT, the share permissions are set to the group Everyone Full Control (see fig. 3.10).

Figure 3.10

The default permissions on a shared folder are Everyone Full Control.

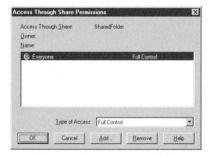

These default share permissions should be changed if there is a need for security because the group Everyone includes just that— everyone from your workstation or domain or from other domains. To change the default permissions, click on the Add button. By default just groups are shown. To grant access to a specific user account, click on the Show Users button. After you have selected the appropriate user or group, from the Type of Access field, select the access you want to assign to that user or group. After you have granted permissions to the user or group to make the share more secure, you should remove the permission for Everyone Full Control.

Caution

Make sure before removing the permissions for Everyone Full Control that you have added another user or group to have access to the shared directory or else you may have a situation in which the directory is shared but no one has been granted access.

Managing Shared Folders

It is likely that after you have created your shared folders you may need to manage them at a later point. Managing folders includes creating a new share from an existing share, stop sharing a folder, modifying permissions on a shared folder, and modifying the share name after a folder has been shared.

Creating a New Share

One of the needs that falls under managing shared folders is the need to create a new share after a directory has already been shared. The steps to creating a new share are slightly different than creating the shared directory from the beginning; the differences are important to understand both for the real-life need for implementation and for the exam. When you configure a new share for an existing shared directory, a new button called New Share appears (see fig. 3.11).

Figure 3.11

Creating a new share from an existing shared directory.

To create a new share from an existing shared directory, complete the following steps:

1. Right-click on the existing shared folder and choose the Sharing option.

2. Click on the New Share button. (Notice that you cannot change the existing share name through this dialog box.)

3. This enables you to enter in the new share name, any comments, and set the permissions for this new shared directory.

4. Click on OK to close the New Share dialog box. Click on OK to close the folder's properties dialog box and create the new share.

Many reasons may prompt you to re-share an existing shared directory. Perhaps you want to assign the permissions differently to the two directories, or you may need to add another reference to the share for additional departments' use.

Stop Sharing

After a directory has been shared, it may be necessary to stop sharing that directory. It might be that the information found in the directory is no longer up to date and no longer needs to be accessed by users in your company. It may be that you decide that there is no longer a need for sharing that information. Whatever the reason, it is possible to stop sharing a directory after it has already been shared. To stop sharing a directory on Windows NT Workstation, complete the following steps:

1. Right-click on the directory that you would like to stop sharing and choose Sharing from the Context menu.

2. Click on the Not Shared radio button.

3. Click on OK. This stops sharing the directory.

Note

One way to prevent any access to your Windows NT Workstation is to stop the Server service, through Control Panel, Services. This also stops the Computer Browser service, but is the most effective way of preventing access to your workstation.

Modifying Permissions on a Shared Directory

After you have set up your shared directories, you may need to change the directory permissions at a later time. This could be because you have added another local group that now needs permissions to the resource, because the resource needs have changed in your environment, or because you may now want to be more restrictive as to who has access to this resource. To modify the permissions of a shared directory after it has been shared, complete the following steps:

1. Right-click on the shared directory and choose Sharing from the Context menu.

2. On the Sharing tab, click on the Permissions button.

3. Add or remove groups as needed from the list of users and groups with permissions.

To change permissions on a shared directory, you must be logged on with an account that has the right to change those permissions. The groups that have that right are the Administrators group and the Power Users group.

Modifying Share Names

Another aspect of managing shared resources is the potential need to change the name of a shared resource after it has been shared. To change the name of a share, you must actually get rid of the first share (stop sharing it) and create a new share with the new name. The order in which you do this is not critical—you can create a new share (as described in "Creating a New Share" earlier in this chapter) or you can stop sharing the resource (as described in "Stop Sharing" earlier in this chapter), and then re-create the share (as described in "Sharing a Folder" earlier in this chapter). You cannot modify a share name without re-creating the share.

How Shared Folder Permissions Apply

When setting up permissions on shared folders, it is important to understand how those permissions will apply, or how those permissions will be implemented in your environment. Before you set up shared folder permissions, you need to know how user and group permissions will interact, as well as how the No Access permission can override any other permission set for that user or group.

User and Group Permission Interaction

You can grant shared folder permissions to both users and groups. Because of this, you might have a situation in which a user is given access to a shared resource, and a group that the user is a member of is also given access. There also might be a scenario where a user is a member of more than one group that has been given access to the resource. In those cases, you need to understand how user and group permissions interact in shared folder permissions. Table 3.3 shows an example of this.

Table 3.3

Example of User and Group Shared Folder Permissions

Account	Permission
BillC	Read
Democrats	Change
Politicians	Full Control

In table 3.3, a user named BillC is a member of both the Democrats and the Politicians groups. BillC is given Read, Democrats are given Change, and Politicians are given Full Control. Because BillC is a member of both groups, his effective permission is Full Control, the cumulative permission of all the groups to which he belongs. Whenever combining user and group permissions for a shared folder, the effective permission is always the cumulative permission, or least restrictive, except in the case of No Access.

Using the No Access Permission on a Shared Folder

The No Access permission is unique in that it can override all other permissions granted for a user or group if it exists in the list of permissions for that user. If No Access is listed in the permissions, that overrides all other permissions (see table 3.4).

Table 3.4

Account	Permission
Example of User and Group Shared Folder Permissions	
BillC	Full Control
Democrats	Change
Politicians	No Access

In table 3.4, BillC is a member of the Democrats and the Politicians groups. Even though BillC's account has been given Full Control, the Politicians group has been assigned the No Access permission. Because BillC is a Politician, his effective permission is No Access. If BillC needs to have access to the folder, he will either need to be taken out of the Politicians group, or the permission for the Politicians group needs to be changed. One way to give BillC access, but to still restrict access for the Politicians group, is to set the permissions as seen in table 3.5.

Table 3.5

Account	Permission
Example of User and Group Shared Folder Permissions	
BillC	Full Control
Democrats	Change
Politicians	

In table 3.5, the effective permissions for BillC are Full Control. Politicians have not been granted the No Access permission; they have just not been specified in the list of permissions. This means that users who are members of the Politicians group still do not have access to the shared folder, but BillC's effective permissions are Full Control.

Setting Permissions on NTFS Partitions, Folders, and Files

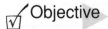 Objective ▶

One of the benefits of using NTFS on a Windows NT Workstation is the added security that NTFS enables you to take advantage of under Windows NT. NTFS permissions enable you to get beyond the security limitations of shared folder permissions (that they are effective only when accessing the directory from across the network) and implement local security on both the folder and the file level. Shared folder permissions can only be assigned at the folder level. NTFS permissions can also apply to a user who is accessing a shared network resource as well as a local resource. NTFS permissions are applicable only on an NTFS partition—they are not available on FAT partitions.

Planning NTFS Folder and File Permissions

Before implementing NTFS permissions, it is necessary to have a good understanding of what they are and of how they will effect the resource permissions that you choose to assign. When a partition is formatted with NTFS, automatically all files and folders on that partition have their permissions set to Everyone Full Control. It is important to understand these default NTFS permissions, especially if you are concerned about implementing security in your Windows NT environment. You may want to remove this Everyone Full Control permission. Be careful, however, how you do that. If you just remove Everyone Full Control, but don't add any groups to have NTFS permissions, you can end up with a system that cannot be logged on to. In assigning NTFS permissions, it is usually a good idea to assign Full Control to the Administrators group. If you choose to remove Everyone Full Control, but you still want validated users to be able to access the files and folders on an NTFS partition, replace Everyone Full Control with Users Full Control. The permissions you choose to assign depend on what the resource is that you are trying to protect. With application folders, for example, you may not want users to have Full Control to add or delete anything to or from that folder.

NTFS Permissions

You can assign NTFS permissions to files or folders. Table 3.6 describes each NTFS permission and what it allows a user to do.

Table 3.6

Standard NTFS Permissions

Permission	Folder	File
Read (R)	Display the folder and subfolders, attributes, and permissions	Display the file, its attributes, and permissions
Write (W)	Add files or folders, change attributes for the folder, and display permissions	Change file attributes and add or append data to the file
Execute (X)	Make changes to subfolders, display permissions, and display attributes	Run a file if it is an executable and display attributes and permissions
Delete (D)	Remove the folder	Remove the file
Change Permission (P)	Modify folder permissions	Modify file permissions
Take Ownership (O)	Take ownership of the folder	Take ownership of a file

These NTFS permissions are combined into standard groupings of NTFS permissions at both the file and the folder level.

NTFS File Permissions

NTFS file permissions are a combination of the various NTFS permissions. You can set NTFS file permissions on a per-file basis; they override NTFS folder permissions if there is a conflict. Table 3.7 shows the standard NTFS file permissions.

Table 3.7

Standard NTFS File Permissions	
Standard File Permission	Individual NTFS Permissions
No Access	(None)
Read	(RX)
Change	(RWXD)
Full Control	(All Permissions)

These standard NTFS file permissions are combinations of the individual NTFS permissions.

NTFS Folder Permissions

NTFS folder permissions are also combined into a standard set of permissions. Table 3.8 shows the NTFS folder permissions. When listing NTFS folder permissions, they are typically followed by two sets of parenthesis. The first set represents the standard permissions on the folder itself. The second set represents the permissions inherited by any file created within that folder.

Table 3.8

Standard NTFS Folder Permissions	
Standard Folder Permissions	Individual NTFS Permissions
No Access	(None) (None)
Read	(RX) (RX)
Change	(RWXD) (RWXD)
Add	(WX) (Not Specified)
Add & Read	(RWX) (RX)
List	(RX) (Not Specified)
Full Control	(All) (All)

Those permissions that have "Not Specified" listed under the file permissions indicate that that particular permission does not apply at a file level, only at a folder level. The List permission, for example, allows you to display that which is contained within a folder—it allows you to list all the files within the folder. That permission would not make sense at a file level, only at a folder level.

Setting NTFS Permissions

The default NTFS permission when a partition is created is Everyone Full Control. Thus to be able to use NTFS permissions, you must choose to set them on either a file or a folder level. NTFS permissions can enhance shared folder permissions that you may have already implemented on your Windows NT Workstation. You set NTFS permissions through the properties of a file or folder from the Security tab. Figure 3.12 shows an example of setting NTFS permissions.

Figure 3.12

Setting NTFS permissions.

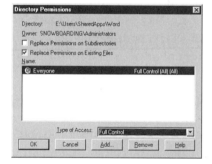

Keep in mind that to set NTFS permissions you must have the right to do so.

Requirements to Assign NTFS Permissions

Not just any user on Windows NT can assign NTFS permissions. To assign NTFS permissions, you must be a part of a group that has been given that right, or your user account must be given that right. By default, the group Everyone is assigned Full Control when an NTFS partition is created. If that default permission is left, part of the Full Control permission includes the right to Change Permissions (P). Suppose that the default Everyone Full Control is changed. To assign NTFS permissions, you must either be:

▶ **The owner of the file or folder.** You must be the one who created it.

▶ **Given Full Control.** This includes the ability to Change Permissions (P).

▶ **Given Special Access to Change Permissions (P).** A user can be assigned just this one permission to a file or folder.

▶ **Given Special Access to Take Ownership (O).** With the ability to Take Ownership, a user can then give himself the right to Change Permissions (P). (For a description of Taking Ownership, see the section entitled "Taking Ownership of Files or Folders" later in this chapter.)

To be used effectively, users must be educated regarding what the various NTFS permissions are. Not only that, they must also know how NTFS permissions apply—at a file and folder level—and how they enhance shared folder permissions.

How NTFS Permissions Apply

Because NTFS permissions can be implemented at both a file and a folder level, you must have an understanding of how these two levels interact. In addition to the standard NTFS permissions, you can also use other combinations of NTFS permissions in certain scenarios.

File and Folder Permission Interaction

If a file is created within a folder that has NTFS permissions set, the default is for the file to inherit the permissions of the folder in which it is created. It is possible, though, to assign different permissions to a file that contradict the permissions of the folder in which it is created. Assume, for example, that you create an environment as shown in table 3.9.

Table 3.9

Example of NTFS File and Folder Permission Interaction

Resource	User or Group Account	Permission
Folder: Test	Everyone	Full Control
File: Top Secret	MyAccount	Full Control

You create a folder called Test on an NTFS partition. The default permissions for the Test folder are Everyone Full Control. You decide to leave those default permissions. After creating the folder, you decide to create a Word document within it called Top Secret. You have information in that file that you do not want anyone else to see, so you decide to remove Everyone Full Control from the file permissions and add just your own user account with Full Control. Because no other user account but yours is specified, no on else has access to that file—or do they? The folder permission is Everyone Full Control—what do you think the effective file permissions are? If another user wants to read what is in Top Secret, will she be able to? File permissions always override folder permissions, so in the case of the Top Secret file, only the account MyAccount has Full Control to that file and can access it. All other users are denied access. Even though Everyone has Full Control at the folder level, because there is only one account specified at the file level, that effectively excludes all other accounts.

User and Group Permission Interaction

With NTFS permissions, as with shared folder permissions, user and group permissions interact so that the cumulative permission is the effective permission. NTFS permissions can be granted to both users and groups. Because of this, you might have a situation in which a user is given access to a resource through NTFS permissions, and a group which the user is a member of is also given access through NTFS permissions. There also might be a scenario with NTFS permissions where a user is a member of more than one group that has been given different NTFS permissions to the resource. In those cases, you need to understand how user and group permissions interact in NTFS permissions. Table 3.10 shows an example of this interaction, using the same user account and groups from the discussion on shared folder permissions.

Table 3.10

Example of User and Group NTFS Permissions

Account	File Permission
BillC	Read
Democrats	Change
Politicians	Full Control

In table 3.10, BillC is a member of both the Democrats and the Politicians groups. For a particular file, the NTFS permissions are set so that BillC is given Read, Democrats are given Change, and Politicians are given Full Control to the file. Because BillC is a member of both groups, his effective NTFS permission is Full Control, the cumulative permission of all the groups to which he belongs. Whenever combining user and group NTFS permissions, the effective permission is always the cumulative permission, or least restrictive, except in the case of the No Access permission.

Using Special Access Permissions

The Special Access permission is a combination of the individual NTFS permissions that is not one of the standard NTFS permissions. Typically, the standard permissions are what you will assign to files or folders, but it is possible that you may want to implement a customized version of the individual NTFS permissions. If you need to assign individual permissions, you can assign Special Access permissions. The Special Access permissions are the same for both files and folders—they are just a listing of the individual NTFS permissions (see fig. 3.13).

Figure 3.13

Assigning Special Access permissions.

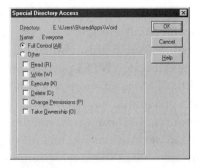

To assign Special Access permissions to a file or a folder, complete the following steps:

1. Right-click on the file or folder and select the properties from the Context menu.

2. Click on the Security tab and then on the Permissions button.

3. Under the type of access, select Special File or Folder Access.

4. Select the Other radio button and then check each individual NTFS permission that you would like to use.

Special directory access can be used when you have a situation that requires customizing the NTFS permissions assigned to a resource.

Taking Ownership of Files or Folders

Taking ownership of files or folders is one of the NTFS permissions that can be assigned through special directory or file permissions. Whoever creates a file or a folder is the owner of that file or folder. As the owner, that individual has Full Control to that file or folder. This includes the ability to assign permissions to it as well as access it and allow others to access it through sharing.

There may be a scenario where a user is the owner of a file or a number of files and then leaves the company. You or the user's replacement may need to access those files. If the user restricted access to those files so that only he had permissions to them, you must Take Ownership of the user's files. To Take Ownership, you have to have been given that right through the NTFS permissions. If the user removed everyone but himself from the list of permissions on the resource, only an administrator can Take Ownership of the files.

Administrators can always Take Ownership, even if they have been given No Access to the file or folder. There is no way to give ownership to another user or group, only the capability to give the permission to take ownership. Because of this, if an administrator takes ownership of a user's files, that administrator will remain the owner. The administrator cannot give back ownership to the user to try to "cover up" the fact that he took ownership of the files.

This prevents any user or administrator from altering or creating files or folders and then making it look like those files or folders belong to another user.

To give someone the right to take ownership, that person must be granted either Full Control, Take Ownership special permission, or Change Permission special permission. Then you must change the resource permissions so that they can take ownership.

Using the No Access Permission for NTFS Permissions

If the No Access permission is set, that overrides all others. Even if the user himself is given Full Control, but a group he belongs to is given No Access, his permission is No Access.

As in shared folder permissions, in NTFS permissions the No Access permission is unique in that it can override all other permissions granted for a user or group if it exists in the list of permissions for that user or group. If No Access is listed in the NTFS permissions, that overrides all other permissions (see table 3.11).

Table 3.11

Using No Access in NTFS Permissions

Account	File Permission
BillC	Full Control
Democrats	Change
Politicians	No Access

In table 3.11, BillC is a member of the Democrats and the Politicians groups. Even though BillC's account has been given Full Control to the file, the Politicians group has been assigned the No Access NTFS permission. Because BillC is a Politician, his effective NTFS permission is No Access. If BillC needs to have access to the file, he will either need to be taken out of the Politicians group, or the NTFS permission for the Politicians group needs to be changed. One way to give BillC access, but to still restrict access for the Politicians group is to set the NTFS file permissions (see table 3.12).

Table 3.12

Example of NTFS File Permissions

Account	File Permission
BillC	Full Control
Democrats	Change
Politicians	

In table 3.12, the effective NTFS permissions for BillC are Full Control. Politicians have not been granted the No Access permission, they have just not been specified in the list of NTFS permissions. This means that users who are members of the Politicians group still do not have access to the file, but BillC's effective NTFS permissions are Full Control.

File Delete Child

File Delete Child refers to a specific scenario relating to NTFS permissions under Windows NT. If a user has been given the NTFS No Access permission to a particular file, but Full Control to the directory that contains the file, the user can actually delete the file even though he doesn't even have the ability to read the file. This is true only when the user actually tries to delete the file, not when he attempts to move it to the Recycle Bin. This situation is called File Delete Child. It is a part of Windows NT due to requirements of POSIX compliance. To get around this problem of a user being able to delete a file that he should not have access to, follow these steps:

1. Get the properties for the directory that contains the file.

2. Instead of selecting Full Control as the directory permission, select Custom.

3. When the list of Custom Options displays, put a check in each check box. This is the same as Full Control, except that it bypasses the File Delete Child problem.

4. Make sure the file permissions are still set to No Access for that user.

Combining Shared Folder and NTFS Permissions

When combining shared folder permissions with NTFS permissions, it is important to understand when each of these permissions is effective. Shared folder permissions apply only to those users accessing the directory from across the network. Shared folder permissions do not apply to the user sitting interactively on the machine. NTFS permissions, on the other hand, do apply to the user sitting locally at the machine and also apply to the user accessing the computer from across the network. When combining shared folder permissions and NTFS permissions, it is always the most restrictive permission that is the effective permission (see table 3.13).

Table 3.13

Example of Shared Folder Permissions and NTFS Permissions

Account	Shared Folder Permission	NTFS Permission
BillC	Full Control	Read
Democrats	Read	Change
Politicians	Change	Read

In table 3.13, BillC is a member of two groups—Democrats and Politicians. Two sets of permissions have also been applied in table 3.13—shared folder permissions and NTFS permissions. When determining a user's effective permissions, you must first determine the effective shared folder permissions, and then determine the effective NTFS permissions, and then compare the two.

In this example, BillC's effective shared folder permissions would be Full Control because it is the cumulative permission that is the effective permission. In the case of the NTFS permissions, BillC's effective permission would be Change because it is the cumulative of the NTFS permissions. What would be BillC's permissions if he is sitting locally at the Windows NT Workstation? (Hint: Do shared folder permissions apply if the user is sitting locally at the workstation?) BillC's effective permissions if he were sitting locally at the workstation would be Change because only NTFS permissions apply locally. What would BillC's effective permissions be if he were accessing this resource from across the network? If BillC were accessing this resource from across the network, you must combine the shared folder permissions and the NTFS permissions and take the *most restrictive*. Therefore, BillC's effective permissions if he were accessing this resource from across the network would be Change.

Table 3.14 shows another example of combining shared folder permissions and NTFS permissions.

Table 3.14

Example of Shared Folder Permissions and NTFS Permissions

Account	Shared Folder Permission	NTFS Permission
BillC	Full Control	Full Control
Democrats	No Access	Change
Politicians	Change	Read

In table 3.14, BillC is again a member of both the Democrats and the Politicians groups and is given Full Control at the share level. This time, however, the Democrats group has been given No Access at the share level.

What are BillC's effective permissions if he is accessing this resource from across the network? For shared folder permissions, the effective permission is the cumulative permission, except in the case of No Access. Thus even though BillC has Full Control, he has No Access because No Access is in the list of permissions for the resource.

What are BillC's local permissions if he were sitting at the workstation rather than accessing it from across the network? For the NTFS permissions, BillC's cumulative permission is Full Control.

Share permissions do not apply when a user is sitting locally at the workstation. Thus if BillC were sitting locally at the machine, he would have Full Control to the resource. If he were accessing it from across the network, however, he would have No Access.

Understanding the interaction between shared folder permissions and NTFS permissions is critical to understanding how to manage the security of resources in your Windows NT environment. The first level is understanding how user and group permissions apply in terms of shared folder permissions.

Note

Shared folder permissions are the only security that you can implement on a FAT partition.

The second level in understanding permissions is to understand how user and group permissions apply for NTFS permissions, as well as understanding how NTFS file and folder permissions relate. Finally, the last issue in understanding permissions is to understand how shared folder and NTFS permissions interact depending on how the user is accessing the resource. Keep the following rules in mind to help you with permissions:

▶ When combining user and group permissions for shared folders, the effective permission is the cumulative permission.

▶ When combining user and group permissions for NTFS security, the effective permission is the cumulative permission.

▶ When combining shared folder permissions and NTFS permissions, the most restrictive permission is always the effective permission.

▶ With NTFS permissions, file permissions override folder permissions.

▶ Using NTFS permissions is the only way to provide local security.

▶ Shared folder permissions are the only way to provide security on a FAT partition and are effective only when being accessed from across the network.

Installing and Configuring Printers in a Given Environment

☑ Objective ▶   Printing questions tend to be one of the most frequent trouble-shooting questions that come up in a network environment. Why can't you print to that printer? Why is the print job garbled? What do you need to do to print? How do you set print permissions? How do you configure printing in your environment? To effectively manage and install printers in your Windows NT environment, these questions need to be answered and understood.

Printing Vocabulary

Before you can discuss printing under Windows NT, you must know the language used when talking about printing. You must understand at least a few terms before a discussion of printing will be meaningful. Those terms are as follows:

▶ **Printer.** A printer is the software component for printing. It is also referred to as a logical printer. It is the software interface between the application and the print device.

▶ **Print Device.** This term refers to the actual hardware that the paper comes out of. This is what you would traditionally think of as a printer. In Windows NT terminology, however, it is called a print device.

▶ **Print job.** The print job refers to that which is sent to the print device. It contains both the data and the commands for print processing.

▶ **Print spooler.** The print spooler is a collection of DLLs (Dynamic Link Libraries) that accept, process, schedule, and distribute the print jobs.

▶ **Creating a printer.** Creating a printer refers to defining a printer from your Windows NT Workstation. When you are creating a printer, you are specifying that the machine on which you are creating it will be the print server for that print device. Creating a printer is necessary when no other

Windows NT system has created the printer yet, or when the print device is on a non-Windows NT operating system such as Windows 95.

▶ **Connecting to a printer.** Connecting a printer is necessary when the print device has already been defined by another Windows NT system and a printer has been created on that Windows NT system. If that is the case, to use the created printer, from your Windows NT Workstation you just need to connect to the printer.

▶ **Print server.** The print server is the computer that has created the printer on which the printer is defined. Typically this is a Windows NT server; a Windows NT Workstation or even a Windows 95 system, however, can act as a print server.

▶ **Print queue.** The print queue refers to the list of print jobs waiting to print on the print server.

▶ **Printer driver.** The printer driver is the software that enables applications to communicate properly with the print device.

▶ **Spooling.** The process of storing documents on the hard disk and then sending them to the printer. After the document has been stored on the hard disk, the user regains control of the application.

These terms are all central to the understanding of how to install and configure printing in a Windows NT environment so that it works effectively.

Installing a Printer

The first step to implementing effective printing in your Windows NT environment is to install a printer. Before you install a printer, you should check the Windows NT Hardware Compatibility List (HCL) to make sure that the print device is on it. If Windows NT does not have a printer driver for the print device, you must get a Windows NT 4.0-compatible printer driver for that device. To install a printer, you must also be logged on with an account that has the right to install or create a printer. The groups in Windows NT Workstation that have that right are as follows:

▶ Administrators

▶ Power Users

To install a printer in Windows NT 4.0, the Add Printer Wizard is used.

 Tip

Print Manager is no longer used in Windows NT 4.0—the Add Printer Wizard is used in its place. Be careful of exam questions that refer to configuring or adding printers by using Print Manager.

When you install a printer, you have the option to either install the printer to My Computer or to a Network Print Server. You receive both options when you use the Add Printer Wizard to install a printer.

My Computer (Creating a Printer)

When installing a printer locally (when the print device is connected to LPT1, for instance), you use the My Computer option. Also, when installing a network printer (one that your computer accesses indirectly across the network) that will be managed by your computer, you select the My Computer option. Using My Computer designates the machine that the printer is being installed on as the print server.

 Note

Remember that if you are using Windows NT Workstation as a print server, Windows NT Workstation accepts only 10 inbound network connections simultaneously. If you must support more than that, you may want to consider installing a Windows NT Server to act as the print server.

A printer can be installed using the My Computer option as seen in figure 3.14.

Figure 3.14

Installing a printer using the My Computer option.

To install a printer using My Computer, complete the following steps:

1. Log on to Windows NT with an account that the right to install a printer.

2. Go to the Printers folder off of the Start menu, Settings.

3. Double-click on the Add Printer icon.

4. Select the My Computer radio button to install the printer.

5. Select which port should be used to access the print device. If the print device is local to the machine, select the local LPT port. If the print device is a network print device, select the appropriate port to connect to the print device. (For more information on printer ports, see the section entitled "Configuring Printer Ports" in this chapter.)

6. Select the appropriate printer driver. If the right driver for your print device is not on the list, select the Have Disk button and install the correct driver from a floppy or other location.

7. In the next dialog box, you can enter a name for the printer. This is called a friendly name and is for your own use. This name cannot be more than 31 characters when combined with the print server name.

8. Select whether you want this to be the default printer for Windows-based applications.

9. If you would like to share this printer on the network, select the Shared radio button and select additional operating systems to make the printer available to. (For more discussion on sharing a printer, see the section entitled "Sharing a Printer" in this chapter.)

10. The final question of the Add Printer Wizard is whether you would like to print a test page. Printing a test page enables you to determine whether the printer has been installed properly and the print device is functioning.

If you have a print device locally attached to your Windows NT Workstation or you are doing the initial definition of a network print device, you will use the My Computer, or Creating a Computer option in the Add Printer Wizard.

Network Print Server (Connecting to a Printer)

If a printer has already been defined and you just need to send a print job to it from your Windows NT Workstation, you can use the Network Print Server option to install that network printer. This is done when the print device is being managed by another Windows NT 4.0 system. Connecting to a printer using the Network Print Server option can be seen in figure 3.15.

Figure 3.15

Using the Network Print Server option to install a printer.

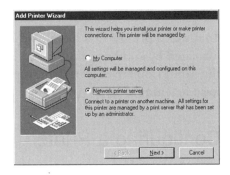

If the print device is being managed by a non-Windows NT 4.0 computer (server or workstation), you must create the printer on your own system using the My Computer option. To connect to an installed printer, complete the following steps:

1. Log on to Windows NT with an account that has the right to install a printer.

2. Go to the Printers folder off of the Start menu, Settings.

3. Double-click on the Add Printer icon.

4. Select the Network Print Server radio button to install the printer.

5. From the list of available print servers, select the one that has the printer you would like to install by double-clicking on that print server or by typing in the full path in the printer field. For example:

   \\printserver\printer

6. Select whether you want this to be the default printer for all Windows-based applications.

7. Click on Finish to set up the printer.

Note

Notice that when installing a printer using the Network Print Server option you never have to specify the printer driver as you do when installing a printer using the My Computer option. That is because the driver is automatically downloaded to your workstation from the print server when you select the Network Print Server option.

To install a printer that has already been defined and is being managed by another print server, use the Network Print Server in the Add Printer Wizard to have the driver downloaded to your local machine.

Configuring a Printer

Configuring a printer refers to the management of the printer after it has been installed. Configuring a printer includes the following:

▶ Configuring printer ports

▶ Sharing a printer

▶ Setting printer permissions

- ▶ Scheduling when a printer is available

- ▶ Modifying the spool settings

- ▶ Setting the print priority

Configuring a printer is essential in being able to administer printing effectively.

Configuring Printer Ports

When you install a printer by using the My Computer option on your Windows NT Workstation, you have the option to set a printer port. This would be a local LPT port if the print device is local to your machine, or an additional port if it is a network print device that you will manage from your machine. If you are creating a printer for a network print device, you must use a port compatible with that device. If you will be creating a printer for an HP Jet Direct print device using DLC, for example, you will first need to install the DLC protocol on the machine acting as the print server. After the DLC protocol is installed, you will then have the option within the printer's ports tab to configure a port for the HP Jet Direct print device. Additionally, if you have multiple print devices that are the same or compatible, you may choose to use the Ports tab to set up a printer pool (see fig. 3.16).

Figure 3.16

Setting up a printer pool.

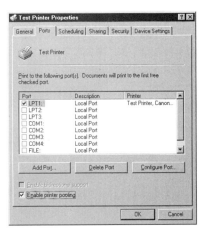

Setting up a printer pool is a way of taking advantage of similar hardware and speeding up printing for your users.

Caution

Make sure if you implement a printer pool that all the print devices are physically near each other. There is no way to specify which device a print job will be printed on with a printer pool. Thus if the devices are on different floors, you may have just implemented a good employee fitness plan as they go from floor to floor looking for their documents.

A *printer pool* is one printer servicing multiple print devices. Because you are using the same printer (printer driver), the devices must be the same or compatible.

Sharing a Printer

It is likely that in your Windows NT environment you will need to share printers for users' use. Sharing a printer can be done during the installation or creation of the printer, or it can be done after the printer has already been installed (see fig. 3.17).

Figure 3.17

Sharing a printer.

Note

You can only share a printer that has been defined by your computer. You cannot share a printer that you connect to using the Network Print Server option.

To share a printer defined by your workstation, complete the following steps:

1. Log on to Windows NT with an account that has administrative permissions.

2. Open the Printers folder by going to the Start button, Settings, Printers folder.

3. Right-click on the printer you want to share and choose the Sharing option from the Context menu.

4. Click on the Shared radio button and type in a share name for the printer.

5. If you have only Intel platforms using Windows NT 4.0 in your environment, click on OK to share the printer. When another Windows NT 4.0 Workstation tries to print to your shared printer, the printer driver is downloaded to the other machine automatically.

6. If you have other clients such as Windows 95 or Windows NT 3.51 or other platforms of Windows NT 4.0, you can select those operating systems from the list of alternate drivers.

7. After you have selected those alternate operating systems from the list, you receive a prompt for the location of the drivers for each operating system. This is so the drivers for each operating system that you have selected can be downloaded when the client tries to print to your printer.

Note Each time a Windows NT Workstation prints to your printer, there will be a verification that the client's printer driver is the current printer driver. Thus if you need to update the printer driver, update it on the print server and it will be downloaded automatically to the client workstations. When a Windows 95 client prints to your shared printer, however, it only downloads the driver the first time that it prints to it.

Sharing a printer is necessary for your users to be able to print to it. Setting up a shared printer for other operating systems can assist your users in printing to your shared printer.

Note   Windows 3.x clients must install their own drivers locally. Printer drivers for Windows 3.x are not installed when a printer is shared.

Setting Printer Permissions

Printer permissions are divided into the following four levels of permissions:

▶ Full Control

▶ Manage Documents

▶ Print

▶ No Access

By default, all users are given the Print permission; the creator owner is given Manage Documents permission; administrators are given Full Control. As you will see in this chapter, you may want to change these default printer permissions after the printer has been installed. Table 3.15 shows the capabilities granted with each of the four levels of print permission.

Table 3.15

Capabilities Granted with Printer Permissions				
Capability	Full Control	Manage Documents	Print	No Access
Print Documents	X	X	X	
Pause, resume, restart, and cancel the user's own documents	X	X	X	
Connect to a printer	X	X	X	
Control job settings for all documents	X	X		

Capability	Full Control	Manage Documents	Print	No Access
Pause, restart, and delete all documents	X	X		
Share a printer	X			
Change printer properties	X			
Delete printers	X			
Change printer permissions		X		

Figure 3.18

Setting printer permissions.

You can assign your own permissions to a printer (see fig. 3.18).

To assign or change printer permissions, complete the following steps:

1. Log on with an account that has Full Control to the printer.

2. Go to the Printers folder and get the properties for the printer.

3. Select the Security tab, and then the Permissions button.

4. Add or remove users or groups from the list of permissions to the printer.

Understanding how to set printer permissions is crucial to implementing printing security in your Windows NT environment.

Scheduling Printing

Scheduling printing enables you to set the available printing times on a per-printer basis. If, for instance, your Accounting Department needs to print large printer-intensive documents but you do not want the printer to be bogged down during the day, you can create a printer for the Accounting group that is scheduled to be available only from 7 p.m. until 7 a.m. so that those documents do not dominate the printer during the day (see fig. 3.19).

Figure 3.19

Setting the scheduling options for a printer.

Setting the scheduling options helps you to control the traffic on your shared printer and gives you the ability to distribute that traffic most efficiently.

Modifying Spool Settings

You can also set spool settings on a per-printer basis. You can configure spool settings to make the printing process more efficient. The spool settings that can be set are as follows:

Spool print documents so program finishes printing faster. If you choose this option, the documents will spool. This option has two choices within it:

▶ **Start printing after last page is spooled.** Documents will not print until they are completely spooled. The application that is printing is not available during the spooling. This requires that you have adequate space on the partition of the spool directory to hold the entire print job.

> ▶ **Start printing immediately.** Documents will print before they have spooled completely which speeds up printing.

Print directly to the printer. This prevents the document from spooling. This speeds up printing, but is not an option for a shared printer, which would have to support multiple incoming documents simultaneously.

Hold mismatched documents. This prevents incorrect documents from printing. Incorrect documents are those that do not match the configuration of the printer.

Print spooled documents first. Spooled documents will print ahead of partially spooled documents, even if they have a lower priority. This speeds up printing.

Keep documents after they have printed. Documents remain in the spooler after they have been printed.

Setting the spool settings to fit your environment can greatly increase the efficiency of your printing.

Setting Print Priority

Setting priorities on printers enables you to assign different preferences on different groups. If you want to make sure that all documents printed by management print ahead of documents from regular employees, for example, you could set that up. To implement printer priorities, complete the following steps:

1. Define two or more printers pointing to the same print device from the same print server.

2. Connect both printers to the same port to the print device.

3. Set a different priority for each of the printers.

4. Assign permissions to the printers based on the priorities set.

If you wanted to set up the previously described scenario for the management to have a higher priority than the rest of the users, for example, you could set up one printer called Management Printer (see fig. 3.20).

Figure 3.20

Setting priorities on a shared printer.

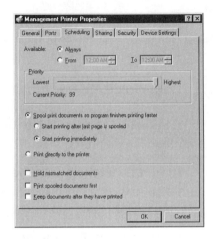

To make sure that management's print jobs have the highest priority, give it a priority of 99 (the highest priority). Then set up another printer called Users Printer and give it the default priority of 1 (the lowest). What is to keep ordinary users from printing to the management printer after they find out that it has a higher priority? The permissions that you set on the Security tab. On the management printer, remove the permission Everyone Print and replace it with Management Print. That way if you are not in the group called Management, you cannot print to the high priority printer. Assigning priorities to different printers enables you to manage the printing environment within Windows NT.

Managing Printing

Managing printing refers to those tasks that need to be performed after the printer is installed and configured for your environment. These are the day-to-day tasks that may need to be performed in a Windows NT printing environment.

Pausing and Resuming a Printer

Pausing and resuming a printer might be necessary for troubleshooting printing problems. You may want to pause a printer if you want to prevent garbled output from spanning multiple pages if a user has the wrong printer driver configured. To pause a printer, complete the following steps:

1. Open the Printers folder by going to the Start button, Settings, Printers.

2. Double-click on the printer to open it.

3. From the Printer menu, choose Pause Printing.

After the printer has been paused and the problem has been solved, you must resume the printer. To resume a printer that has been paused, complete the following steps:

1. Open the Printers folder by going to the Start button, Settings, Printers.

2. Double-click on the printer to open it.

3. From the Printer menu, choose Pause Printing. This removes the check mark next to it and resumes the printer.

Pausing and resuming a printer is not a typical event, but might be needed in troubleshooting situations.

Redirecting Printing

Redirecting printing refers to the capability to change which print device a printer prints to. You can redirect a printer to either a local or a remote print device. You may need to redirect a printer if there is a problem with the print device and it needs to be taken offline for maintenance. Redirecting a printer redirects all documents sent to that printer. There is no way to redirect on a document-by-document basis. To redirect documents to a remote print device, complete the following steps:

1. Open the Printers folder by going to the Start button, Settings, Printers.

2. Right-click on the printer that needs to be redirected and select the properties.

3. Click on the Ports tab.

4. Click on the Add Port button.

5. Click on Local Port, and then click on New Port.

6. For the Port Name, enter in the UNC path to the other printer (**printserver\printer2**, for example).

Note

> Both the original and the new printer must use the same printer driver for redirecting to work properly. Also, remove the original port so that the printer does not attempt to print to the old port.

7. Documents will be redirected to the new printer.

Redirecting documents is one issue in managing printing within Windows NT. It is typically used for troubleshooting situations. Why wouldn't you just tell all your users to print to the new printer while the original is being serviced? You could, but that would mean redefining the printer settings on all client machines in your environment. By redirecting printing, you make the change one time on the print server and it is invisible to the clients.

Troubleshooting Printing

In addition to the previously covered items of troubleshooting printing, there are a few more issues that you must understand in troubleshooting printing, both in a support environment and for the exam.

Spooler Service

The Spooler service is what controls the print spooling process under Windows NT. If your users cannot print to a printer and there are documents in the print queue that will not print and cannot be deleted (even by the administrator), you may need to stop and restart the Spooler service (see fig. 3.21).

Figure 3.21

Stopping and restarting the Spooler service can clear a jammed print queue.

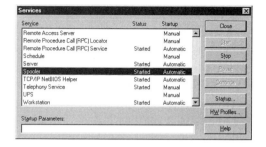

To stop and restart the spooler service, complete the following steps:

1. Open the Control Panel by Start menu, Settings, Control Panel.

2. Click on the Spooler service in the list of services.

3. Click on Stop. When prompted to verify that you want to stop the service, click on Yes.

4. After the service has been stopped, click on the Start button within the Services dialog box to restart the Spooler service.

Note

While the Spooler service is stopped, no one can print to the shared printer.

Stopping and restarting the Spooler service clears just the jammed print job from the queue and then allows the other print jobs to continue printing.

Spool Directory

In addition to the Spooler service in Windows NT, there is also a *spool directory*, which is the location on the hard disk where print jobs are stored while spooling. By default this directory is found under the Windows NT Root\system32\spool\printers directory.

Note

This one directory is used for spooling all printers defined on the print server.

If you notice the hard disk thrashing or documents not printing or not reaching the print server, check to make sure that available space exists on the partition where the spool directory is located. If there is not sufficient disk space (minimally about 5 MB free, more if there are complex print jobs) available, you must free up some disk space. If that is not possible, you must move the spool directory to another location. You can do this by going into the Server Properties within the Printers folder (see fig. 3.22).

Figure 3.22

You can change the location of the spool directory.

To change the spool directory, complete the following steps:

1. Open the Printers folder by going to the Start button, Settings, Printers.

2. From the File menu, choose Server Properties.

3. On the Advanced tab, type in the new location for the spool directory.

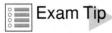 **Exam Tip**

In Windows NT 3.51, there was no graphical interface for changing the spool directory. It could only be changed in the Registry. Because this is something different in Windows NT 4.0, watch for it on the exam.

Key Terms and Concepts

Table 3.16 identifies key terms from this chapter. Review the key terms and make sure that you understand each term for the exam.

Table 3.16

Key Terms: Managing Resources	
Term	Covered in Section...
Account Policy	Implementing Local User and Group Accounts
Built-in user accounts	Implementing Local User and Group Accounts
SID	Implementing Local User and Group Accounts
Local group accounts	Implementing Local User and Group Accounts
User profiles	Setting Up and Modifying User Profiles
Shared folder permissions	Setting Up Shared Folders and Permissions
NTFS permissions	Setting Permissions on NTFS Partitions, Folders and Files
No Access permission	Setting Permissions on NTFS Partitions, Folders, and Files
File Delete Child	Setting Permissions on NTFS Partitions, Folders, and Files
Printer	Installing and Configuring Printers in a Given Environment
Print device	Installing and Configuring Printers in a Given Environment
Spooling	Installing and Configuring Printers in a Given Environment

continues

Table 3.16 continued

Key Terms: Managing Resources

Term	Covered in Section...
Print server	Installing and Configuring Printers in a Given Environment
Printer pool	Installing and Configuring Printers in a Given Environment
Scheduling printing	Installing and Configuring printers in a Given Environment
Printer priorities	Installing and Configuring Printers in a Given Environment
Spooler service	Installing and Configuring Printers in a Given Environment

Exercises

Exercise 1.1:   Creating User Accounts Using a Template Account

This exercise teaches you how to create a template account to use for creating user accounts with similar configuration settings. It also teaches you how to create a location for users' home directories, as well as a new local group.

Objective

Create and manage local user accounts and local group accounts to meet given requirements

Time Estimate: 40 minutes

Steps

To create a local group, follow these steps:

1. Log on to Windows NT with an account that has administrative permissions.

2. Launch User Manager by Start button, Programs, Administrative Tools, User Manager.

3. Create a new local group by User menu, New Local Group.

4. In the Group Name field, type **Sales**.

5. In the Group Description field, type **Sales Representatives**.

6. Make sure there are no user accounts included in the group. (You add the user accounts later in the lab.)

7. Click on OK to create the local group.

To create a Users directory to store users' home directories, follow these steps:

1. Log on to Windows NT with an account that has administrative permissions.

2. Launch Windows NT Explorer by Start button, Programs, Windows NT Explorer.

continues

3. Create a new folder off the C drive called **Users**.

4. Right-click on the Users folder and choose the Sharing option. Leave the defaults and click on OK to share the Users folder.

To create the template account, follow these steps:

1. Log on to Windows NT with an account that has administrative permissions.

2. Launch User Manager by Start button, Programs, Administrative Tools, User Manager.

3. Create a new user account by User menu and choosing New User.

4. In the Username field, type **Sales_Template**.

5. In the Description field, type **Sales Representative**.

6. Click on the Profile button. For the Home Directory, select Connect to and enter the path of the home directory, **\\server\users\%username%**, where server is the name of your Windows NT Workstation. Then click on OK.

7. Click on the Dialin button. Click on the check box to grant dial-in permission to the user. Click on OK and then OK to create the user account.

To create additional accounts using the template, follow these steps:

1. Log on to Windows NT with an account that has administrative permissions.

2. Launch User Manager by Start button, Programs, Administrative Tools, User Manager.

3. Click on the Sales_Template account to highlight it.

4. With the Sales_Template account highlighted, click on the User menu and choose Copy.

5. Enter **Sales1** for the Username. Notice that the description is already filled in for this user.

6. Go to the Profile button. Notice that the Home Directory is already filled in for this user.

7. Go to the Dialin button. Notice that the dial-in permissions are already granted for this user.

8. Click on OK to create this user account.

9. Exit User Manager.

Exercise 1.2: Implementing User Profiles

This exercise shows you how to create a profile for a user.

Objective

Set up and modify user profiles

Time Estimate: 35 minutes

Steps

To create a test user profile, follow these steps:

1. Log on to Windows NT with an account that has administrative permissions.

2. Launch User Manager by going to the Start button, Programs, Administrative Tools, User Manager.

3. Create a new user called User Profile. Accept the defaults except for the User Must Change Password check box. Uncheck that so that User Profile will not have to change the password.

4. Log off and log on as User Profile.

5. Make a change to the wallpaper on the system by going to the Control Panel, Display, Background tab.

continues

6. Log off and log back on as the account with administrative permissions.

7. Go to the User Profiles tab by going to Start, Settings, Control Panel, System and selecting it.

8. What profiles are stored on your machine?

9. Exit from the System icon.

To create a shared profiles directory, follow these steps:

1. Log on to Windows NT with an account that has administrative permissions.

2. Create a directory on the C drive called **Profiles**.

3. Share the Profiles directory, leaving the default settings.

4. Within that directory create a folder called **TestProfile**.

To test using the User Profile, follow these steps:

1. Log on to Windows NT with an account that has administrative permissions.

2. Launch User Manager by going to the Start button, Programs, Administrative Tools, User Manager.

3. Create a new user called **TestProfile**. Accept the defaults except for the User Must Change Password check box. Uncheck that so that User Profile will not have to change the password.

4. Click on the Profile button. For the User Profile Path, type in the path that you created to the Profiles directory: **\\server\profiles\testprofile**, where server is your computer name.

5. Click on OK to create the user account and exit User Manager.

6. Go to the User Profiles tab by going to Start, Settings, Control Panel, System and selecting it.

7. Under Profiles Stored on This Computer, click on the profile for Profile User and click on Copy To.

8. In the Copy To field, type the network path to the folder you created: **server\profiles\profile**, where server is your computer name.

9. For Permitted to Use, click on the Change button and select the account for Test Profile.

10. Log off Windows NT and log on as Test Profile.

11. What settings do you get?

Exercise 1.3:   Creating and Managing Shared Directories

This exercise shows you how to create a shared directory, set the permissions for it, and manage the shared directory after it is created.

Objective

Set up shared folders and permissions

Time Estimate: 25 minutes

Steps

1. Log on to Windows NT Workstation as an account with administrative permissions on that workstation.

2. On an NTFS partition (or FAT if you do not have NTFS), create a directory called **Antigua**.

3. Right-click on the directory and choose Sharing from the Context menu.

4. Click on the Shared As button and leave the share name as Antigua.

5. In the Comment field, type **This is a Shared Directory**.

6. Click on the Permissions button.

continues

Exercise 1.3: Continued

7. Remove the group Everyone from the list of shared permissions. Add Administrators with Full Control and Users with Read access.

8. Click on OK to create the shared directory.

9. Double-click on the Network Neighborhood icon on your desktop. Double-click on your computer. Does Antigua show up?

10. Close Network Neighborhood.

11. Launch Windows NT Explorer. Right-click on the Antigua directory and choose Sharing from the Context menu.

12. Click on the New Share button to create a new share.

13. Type **Guatemala** for the new share name. For the Comment, type **Second Share**.

14. Click on the Permissions button and remove the Everyone Full Control permission. Do not add any other permissions.

15. Click on OK. You receive a prompt with a warning that your shared directory will be inaccessible because you have removed all the permissions. Click on the Yes button to continue.

16. Double-click on the Network Neighborhood icon on your desktop. Double-click on your computer. Does Antigua show up? Does Guatemala show up?

17. Double-click on Guatemala. What happens?

18. Close Network Neighborhood.

Exercise 1.4: Implementing NTFS Permissions and Using No Access

This lab helps you set up NTFS permissions on folders and files and see how the No Access permission works. (This lab requires that you have an NTFS partition on your Windows NT Workstation.)

Objective

Set up permissions on NTFS partitions, folders, and files

Time Estimate: 35 minutes

Steps

1. Log on to Windows NT Workstation as an account with administrative permissions on that workstation.

2. Launch Windows NT Explorer. Right-click on the Antigua directory created in the preceding lab and choose Properties from the Context menu.

3. Click on the Security tab. Click on the Permissions button.

4. What are the default NTFS permissions for the Antigua directory?

5. Remove the group Everyone Full Control.

6. Click on the Add button and add Administrators Full Control.

7. Click on the Add button and add Users Read access.

8. Log off Windows NT.

9. Log on with an account that has user permissions.

10. Launch Windows NT Explorer. Double-click on the Antigua directory. Can you open it?

11. On the File menu, choose New, Folder to create a new folder within the Antigua directory. Were you successful? Why or why not?

12. Log off Windows NT.

13. Log on to Windows NT Workstation as an account with administrative permissions on that workstation.

14. Launch Windows NT Explorer. Right-click on the Antigua directory created in the preceding lab and choose Properties from the Context menu.

continues

Exercise 1.4: Continued

15. Click on the Security tab. Click on the Permissions button.

16. Highlight the Users group and change the permission from Read to No Access.

17. Log off Windows NT.

18. Log on with an account that has user permissions.

19. Launch Windows NT Explorer. Double-click on the Antigua directory. Can you open it? Why or why not?

20. Log off Windows NT.

Exercise 1.5: Printer Installation and Configuration

This lab walks you through installation and configuration of a printer in Windows NT Workstation.

Objective:

Install and configure printers

Time Estimate: 35 minutes

Steps:

To install and share a printer, follow these steps:

1. Log on to Windows NT Workstation as an account with administrative permissions on that workstation.

2. Open the Printers folder by going to the Start button, Settings, Printers.

3. Double-click on the Add Printer Wizard.

4. Leave the default of My Computer and click on Next.

5. Click on Enable Printer Pooling, and then click on LPT2 and LPT3.

6. From the list of printers, select HP on the left and then HP LaserJet 4 on the right. Click on Next.

7. For the printer name, type **My Printer**.

8. When prompted to share the printer, click on the Shared radio button. Do not share the printer to other operating systems.

9. When prompted to print a test page, select No.

10. Click on Finish. When prompted, enter the path to the Windows NT Workstation installation files.

To set printer permissions, follow these steps:

1. Log on to Windows NT Workstation as an account with administrative permissions on that workstation.

2. Open the Printers folder by going to the Start button, Settings, Printers.

3. Right-click on My Printer and choose the Properties from the Context menu.

4. Click on the Security tab and the Permissions button.

5. What are the default permissions for your newly created printer?

6. Click on the Add button and select an existing Windows NT Workstation group to add to the list of permissions. Under Type of Access, select Manage Documents.

7. Click on OK to exit the printer properties for My Printer.

To set the schedule for a printer, follow these steps:

1. Log on to Windows NT Workstation as an account with administrative permissions on that workstation.

2. Open the Printers folder by going to the Start button, Settings, Printers.

continues

3. Right-click on My Printer and choose the Properties from the Context menu.

4. Click on the Scheduling tab and set the printer to be available from 6 p.m. to 5 a.m.

5. Set the priority to 50.

6. For the spool settings, select to print spooled documents first.

7. Close the properties for My Printer.

To view the spool directory location, follow these steps:

1. Log on to Windows NT Workstation as an account with administrative permissions on that workstation.

2. Open the Printers folder by going to the Start button, Settings, Printers.

3. From the File menu, choose Server Properties.

4. Click on the Advanced tab.

5. What is the location of the spool directory?

6. Close the Printers folder.

To stop and restart the Spooler service, follow these steps:

1. Log on to Windows NT Workstation as an account with administrative permissions on that workstation.

2. Launch the Control Panel by going to the Start button, Settings Control Panel.

3. Double-click on the Services icon.

4. Find the Spooler service in the list and highlight it.

5. Click on the Stop button and continue when prompted.

6. After the Spooler service has been stopped, go to the properties of My Printer, to the General tab.

7. Click on the Print Test Page button. What message did you get?

8. Restart the Spooler service.

9. Log off of Windows NT.

Review Questions

The following questions test your knowledge of the material in this chapter.

1. If you are concerned about security in your network, what can you do to make the default Administrator and the default Guest accounts more secure? (Choose all that apply.)

   A. Delete them and create new ones

   B. Delete the built-in Guest account and change the password for the built-in Administrator account

   C. Create difficult passwords for both accounts

   D. Rename both accounts

2. What directories are created when a user logs on to a Windows NT Workstation for the first time?

   A. Default User

   B. All Users

   C. A directory called Users

   D. A directory named after that user

3. What is the difference between a roaming user profile and a local user profile?

4. What is the difference between a personal user profile and a mandatory user profile?

5. What does it mean if the Account Locked Out check box is checked for a user's account?

   A. That user chose to have his account locked out by indicating it in his user profile.

   B. Someone has exceeded the number of bad logon attempts allowed by the Account Policy.

   C. Another administrator checked that for the user's account because he will be on leave for three months.

   D. It is the default setting when you create a user account.

6. What are the built-in group accounts on Windows NT Workstation?

    A. Administrators

    B. Users

    C. Power Users

    D. Account Operators

    E. Print Operators

7. You have a user who will be on a leave of absence for six months. What should you do with his user account?

    A. Delete it and re-create it when he returns.

    B. Rename the account so that no one else can use it.

    C. Disable the account while the user is gone.

    D. Leave the account alone.

8. What group do you have to be a member of to be able to share resources on a Windows NT Workstation? (Choose all that apply.)

    A. Administrators

    B. Power Users

    C. Users

    D. Server Operators

9. You want to set up both shared folder permissions and NTFS permissions on your Windows NT Workstation computer. You have two FAT partitions and would like to create the shares on the C drive. What should you do?

    A. First set the share permissions, and then the NTFS permissions.

    B. First set the NTFS permissions, and then set the Shared Folder permissions.

    C. You cannot share folders on a FAT partition.

    D. You cannot implement NTFS permissions on a FAT partition.

10. You have a shared folder with the following permissions:

Account	Permissions
KelleyD	Full Control
Sales	Change
Users	Read

If KelleyD is a member of the Sales and the Users group, what are KelleyD's effective permissions?

A. Full Control.

B. Change.

C. Read.

D. You cannot determine.

11. You have assigned the following NTFS permissions on a folder:

Account	Permissions
KelleyD	Full Control
Sales	Change
Users	Read

If KelleyD is a member of the Sales and the Users group, what are KelleyD's effective permissions?

A. Full Control.

B. Change.

C. Read.

D. You cannot determine.

12. You have a shared folder with the following permissions:

Account	Shared Folder Permissions	NTFS Permissions
KelleyD	Full Control	
Sales	Read	Change
Users	No Access	Read

If KelleyD is a member of the Sales and the Users group, what are KelleyD's effective permissions when accessing this resource locally?

   A. Full Control.

   B. Change.

   C. No Access.

   D. You cannot determine.

13. You have a shared folder with the following permissions:

Account	Shared Folder Permissions	NTFS Permissions
KelleyD		
Sales	Read	Change
Users		Read

If KelleyD is a member of the Sales and the Users group, what are KelleyD's effective permissions when accessing this resource from across the network?

   A. No Access.

   B. Change.

   C. Read.

   D. You cannot determine.

14. What is a print device?

15. What is a printer?

16. What is a printer pool?

17. You want to print to a printer managed by a Windows NT Server 4.0. What should you do?

    A. Use Print Manager to connect to the printer.

    B. Use Print Manager to create a printer.

    C. Use the Add Printer Wizard to connect to the printer.

    D. Use the Add Printer Wizard to create a printer.

18. What is File Delete Child?

19. What groups on a Windows NT Workstation have the right to take ownership?

    A. Users.

    B. Administrators.

    C. Account Operators.

    D. Print Operators.

20. What is the appropriate method of clearing a jammed print job from the queue?

    A. Delete the printer and re-create it.

    B. Stop the printer service.

    C. Delete the spool directory.

    D. Stop and restart the Spooler service.

Review Answers

1. C and D are correct. The default Administrator and Guest accounts cannot be deleted, so they should be renamed and given difficult passwords to prevent them from being hacked. For more information, see the section entitled "Implementing Local User and Group Accounts."

2. D is correct. When a user logs on to a Windows NT Workstation for the first time, a profile directory is created for that user and is named after that user's logon name. For more information, see the section entitled "Setting Up and Modifying User Profiles."

3. A roaming user profile is available to the user from any Windows NT 4.0 Workstation on the network. A local user profile is only available on the user's local workstation. For more information, see the section entitled "Setting Up and Modifying User Profiles."

4. A personal user profile is used to store the user's personal settings. It is mainly used for convenience for the user to be able to store her own settings. A mandatory user profile does not allow the user to save any changes made to the profile. For more information, see the section entitled "Setting Up and Modifying User Profiles."

5. B. The only way the Account Locked Out box can be checked is by exceeding the number set for bad logon attempts. For more information, see the section entitled "Implementing Local User and Group Accounts."

6. A, B, and C are correct. Account Operators and Print Operators are default groups on Windows NT Server installed as a domain controller, not on Windows NT Workstation. For more information, see the section entitled "Implementing Local User and Group Accounts."

7. C is correct. Because the user will be coming back to the company, you should disable the account so that it will not be used while he is gone. Do not delete the user account because that will delete the SID as well. For more information, see the section entitled "Implementing Local User and Group Accounts."

8. A and B are correct. Only Administrators and Power Users can share directories on Windows NT Workstation. For more information, see the section entitled "Setting up Shared Folders and Permissions."

9. D is correct. You cannot use NTFS permissions on a FAT partition. For more information, see the section entitled "Setting Permissions on NTFS Partitions, Folders, and Files."

10. A is correct. When combining user and group permissions, the effective permissions are the cumulative permissions. For more information, see the section entitled "Setting Up Shared Folders and Permissions."

11. A is correct. When combining user and group permissions, the effective permissions are the cumulative permissions. For more information, see the section entitled "Setting Permissions on NTFS Partitions, Folders, and Files."

12. A is correct. When combining user and group permissions the effective permissions are the cumulative permissions. The shared folder permissions do not apply because KelleyD is sitting locally at the computer. For more information, see the section entitled "Setting Permissions on NTFS Partitions, Folders, and Files."

13. C is correct. When combining user and group permissions the effective permissions are the cumulative permissions. For more information, see the section entitled "Setting Permissions on NTFS Partitions, Folders, and Files."

14. A print device is the actual hardware that the paper comes out of. For more information, see the section entitled "Installing and Configuring Printers in a Given Environment."

15. A printer is the software component that interfaces between the application and the print device. For more information, see the section entitled "Installing and Configuring Printers in a Given Environment."

16. A printer pool is defined as one printer pointing to multiple print devices. Those devices must be of the same type. For more information, see the section entitled "Installing and Configuring Printers in a Given Environment."

17. C is correct. Because the printer is already managed by the Windows NT Server, all the user needs to do is to use the Add Printer Wizard to connect to the printer. For more information, see the section entitled "Installing and Configuring Printers in a Given Environment."

18. File Delete Child refers to a specific scenario relating to NTFS permissions under Windows NT. If a user has been given the NTFS No Access permission to a particular file, but full control to the directory that contains the file, the user is actually able to delete the file even though he does not even have the ability to read the file. For more information, see the section entitled "Setting Permissions on NTFS Partitions, Folders, and Files."

19. B is correct. By default only the Administrators group has the right to take ownership of files or folders. For more information, see the section entitled "Setting Permissions on NTFS Partitions, Folders, and Files."

20. D is correct. The appropriate course of action when troubleshooting jammed print jobs is to stop and restart the Spooler service. For more information, see the section entitled "Installing and Configuring Printers in a Given Environment."

Answers to Test Yourself Questions at the Beginning of the Chapter

1. CherriL's permissions are Full Control. The share permissions that you assign do not apply to her because she is sitting locally at the machine. Share permissions only apply when a user is accessing the resource from across the network. For more information, see the section entitled "Setting Up Shared Folders and Permissions."

2. CherriL will have Full Control to the resource because her effective permissions are the cumulative permissions. Because the Operations group has Full Control, and she is a member of that group, and she is accessing the resource from across the network, CherriL will have Full Control. For more information, see the section entitled "Setting Up Shared Folders and Permissions."

3. JasonM's effective permissions to the directory are Full Control. With NTFS permissions, the effective permissions are cumulative for user and group permissions. Because he is sitting locally at the machine, the NTFS permissions apply to him. For more information, see the section entitled "Setting Up Shared Folders and Permissions."

4. CarlaH's effective permissions are Full Control. That is because those are her cumulative NTFS permissions. Shared folder permissions do not apply because CarlaH is sitting locally at the machine. For more information, see the section entitled "Setting Up Shared Folders and Permissions."

5. CarlaH's effective permissions are No Access. That is because she is accessing the resource from across the network. Thus both shared folder permissions and NTFS permissions apply because there is a No Access permission granted to the Marketing group which CarlaH is a part of. Any time there is a No Access in a user's permissions, that overrides all other permissions. For more information, see the section entitled "Setting Up Shared Folders and Permissions."

6. When you deleted the account for SpenceB, the SID was also deleted. A SID is uniquely tied to a particular user account and is unique in history. Because of that, when you re-create the account for SpenceB, even though the account has the same name, there is a new SID. Because there is a new SID and the old SID is no longer valid, the user's resource rights must be redefined. For more information, see the section entitled "Setting Up Shared Folders and Permissions."

7. Typically when there is "garbage text" coming out of the print device it is due to the wrong printer driver being used or a corrupt printer driver. Reinstall the printer driver to fix the problem. For more information, see the section entitled "Installing and Configuring Printers in a Given Environment."

8. The problem is probably that a print job is stuck in the queue. To remove a jammed print job from the queue, go to Control Panel, Services and stop and restart the Spooler service. That is the appropriate method for troubleshooting a jammed print job. For more information, see the section entitled "Installing and Configuring Printers in a Given Environment."

9. Add the shortcut to the All Users folder under the Profiles directory. This adds the shortcut to the Start menu for all current and new users to log on to the Windows NT Workstation. For more information, see the section entitled "Setting Up and Modifying User Profiles."

10. Set up your User account to have a roaming user profile. Place that profile in a central location such as a server. (Note: This assumes that you are using Windows NT Workstation in a domain environment.) For more information, see the section entitled "Setting Up and Modifying User Profiles."

Chapter 4

Connectivity

This chapter helps you prepare for the exam by covering the following objectives:

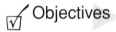 Objectives

> ▶ Add and configure the network components of Windows NT Workstation
>
> ▶ Use various methods to access network resources
>
> ▶ Implement Windows NT Workstation as a client in a NetWare environment
>
> ▶ Use various configurations to install Windows NT Workstation as a TCP/IP client
>
> ▶ Configure and install Dial-Up Networking in a given situation
>
> ▶ Configure Peer Web Services in a given situation

A *local area network* (LAN) is a collection of computers in a specific area that are connected by a communications network. LANs can range in size from just two computers to hundreds, or thousands of computers in a single location. Networks can also consist of LANs in multiple locations connected into a *wide area network* (WAN). It is also common for computer networks to include non-Microsoft based computers, such as Novell NetWare, Apple Macintosh, or Unix-based computers. Connectivity with the Internet is also increasingly important. For a Windows NT Workstation 4.0 to participate in various LAN and WAN configurations, you must be able to properly configure its network components.

Before reading this chapter, test yourself to determine how much study time you need to devote to this section.

Test Yourself! Before reading this chapter, test yourself to determine how much study time you will need to devote to this section.

1. You have an older network adapter card that only has drivers for Windows for Workgroups, can you use it with Windows NT Workstation 4.0?

2. You have two networks that use the NetBEUI protocol. You connect the two networks with a router, but computers on the different networks can't connect to each other. What is wrong?

3. You have installed the NWLink IPX/SPX Compatible Transport protocol on your computer, but you cannot establish a session with a NetWare file server. What other component do you need to install?

4. What are network bindings?

5. How many network adapter cards can you put into a single Windows NT Workstation 4.0 computer?

6. What is a Browse Master?

7. What command should you type at a command prompt to redirect port LPT1: to a network printer named HP5 located on a print server named PRINTSERVE?

8. When do you need to specify a default gateway on a computer configured for TCP/IP?

9. You have a computer configured for IPX, and you cannot make a connection to a Unix SLIP server. What is your problem?

10. You need to set up a web server for your department. Which component of Windows NT Workstation 4.0 is well suited for your purposes?

Answers are located at the end of the chapter...

The Windows NT Networking Model

Before reviewing how to configure the network components of Windows NT, it is important to examine the underlying components that make up the networking architecture. The networking architecture is made of several different interlocking layers in which lower levels affect those levels higher than they are. Knowledge of how all the different levels work together is important in understanding how the Windows NT networking architecture enables the various computers in a network to communicate.

All the networking components of Windows NT Workstation 4.0 are built into the operating system (although some of them are not installed automatically and must be manually configured). Any Windows NT Workstation 4.0–based computer can participate as:

▶ A client or a server in a *distributed application* environment

▶ A client or a server in a *peer-to-peer networking* environment

The built-in networking components enable Windows NT Workstation 4.0 to share files, printers, and applications with other networked computers (including other computers that aren't based on Windows NT).

Key Concepts

A *distributed application*, also referred to as a client/server application, has its component pieces executing on more than one computer. A *front-end* process running on a client computer, communicates with a *back-end* process that runs on a server.

Key Concepts

A *peer-to-peer network* enables any computer to connect to files and printers on any other computer in the network, not just to specialized servers.

Windows NT Networking versus the OSI Reference Model

The *Open Systems Interconnection* (OSI) model is one technique that you can use to understand the networking architecture of Windows NT. The OSI model was developed by the *International Standards Organization* (ISO) and is a layered architecture that standardizes how various computers in a network should exchange information with each other.

The components of the Windows NT networking architecture can be organized into three categories: network adapter card drivers, transport drivers, and file system drivers. The advantages of this modular design are increased flexibility and reliability because it is much easier to test and to change a small module than the entire block of network software. Also, each layer only needs to be written to be compatible with the layers immediately above it and below it in the overall architecture, which makes adding new capabilities much easier. Figure 4.1 compares the Windows NT network architecture model with the OSI model.

Figure 4.1

Windows NT network architecture versus the OSI model.

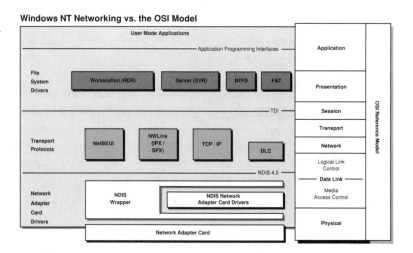

The OSI model is only a theoretical model. There is not a one-to-one match between the layers of the OSI model and the layers of the Windows NT network architecture.

Note

NDIS-Compatible Network Adapter Card Drivers

The bottom layer of the Windows NT network architecture, as shown in figure 4.1, is the network adapter card driver. These drivers must be 32-bit and compliant with the Network Device Interface Specification (NDIS) 3.0 or 4.0.

Key Concepts

> The *Network Device Interface Specification* (NDIS) is the specification that controls how network adapter card drivers need to be written. Windows NT 4.0 supports NDIS 3.0 and 4.0.

Caution

> Windows NT cannot use older 16-bit device drivers or the 32-bit NDIS 3.1–compliant drivers that were developed for Windows 95.

Because the adapter card drivers and any protocols being used are completely independent of each other, protocols can be substituted without changing adapter card drivers.

NDIS 4.0

NDIS 4.0 is an updated version, for Microsoft Windows NT 4.0, of the boundary layer that defines the interaction of network protocols and network adapter card drivers. Any network protocol compliant with NDIS 4.0 can communicate with any network card driver compliant with NDIS 4.0.

The initial connection made between each protocol being used and the network card driver is referred to as network *binding*. The actual set of networking components used is called the *protocol stack*. If you have more than one network adapter in your computer, each adapter card's protocol stack can be configured individually.

In Windows NT 4.0, NDIS 4.0 enables the following:

▶ An unlimited number of network adapter cards.

▶ An unlimited number of network protocols can be bound to a single network adapter card.

▶ Independence between protocols and adapter card drivers.

▶ Communication linkages between adapter cards and their drivers.

 Tip

Windows NT 4.0 can also use drivers written to be compliant with the NDIS 3.0 specification that was used by Windows NT 3.x.

Network Protocols

The network protocols, as shown in figure 4.1, control the communications between computers on a network. Different network protocols provide varying communications services and capabilities.

 Caution

Windows NT Workstation 4.0 doesn't support AppleTalk connectivity. Only Windows NT Server 4.0 can be configured with Services for Macintosh.

TCP/IP

Transmission Control Protocol/Internet Protocol (TCP/IP) is the default protocol for Windows NT 4.0 and is an industry standard suite of protocols used for wide area networks (WANs) and the Internet. TCP/IP is commonly used in wide area networks that consist of a variety of computer types.

Microsoft's implementation of TCP/IP provides a number of advantages, including the following:

▶ Routing support

▶ Connectivity with the Internet

▶ Interoperability with most operating systems and computer types

▶ Support for Dynamic Host Configuration Protocol (DHCP)

▶ Support for Windows Internet Name Service (WINS)

▶ Support for Simple Network Management Protocol (SNMP)

NWLink IPX/SPX Compatible Transport

NWLink IPX/SPX Compatible Transport is Microsoft's NDIS-compliant version of Novell's Internetwork Packet Exchange (IPX/SPX). NWLink can be used for communications between Windows NT-based computers and MS-DOS, Windows 3.x, and OS/2-based computers.

The advantages of NWLink include the following:

▶ Routing support

▶ Supported by a wide variety of other operating systems

▶ Large installed base

 Caution

NWLink is only a transport protocol and by itself it doesn't enable a Windows NT Workstation 4.0–based computer to access files and/or printers on a Novell NetWare server, or to act as a file and/or print server to NetWare clients. To access files and/or printers on a NetWare server, you must also use a NetWare-compatible redirector, such as Microsoft Client Services for NetWare (see the section entitled "File System Drivers").

NetBEUI

NetBIOS Extended User Interface (NetBEUI) was originally developed to support small departmental LANs of up to 150 users. Because it was assumed that these small departmental LANs would be connected by gateway devices, no support for routing was included. If you want to connect two or more NetBEUI-based LANs, you must use a bridge rather than a router. Although it is possible to configure some routers to function with NetBEUI, that configuration is usually not a good choice. NetBEUI is typically used only by Microsoft-based computers.

The main characteristics of NetBEUI are as follows:

- ► No routing support

- ► Fast performance on small LANs

- ► Small memory overhead

- ► No tuning options

Although the names seem similar, don't make the common mistake of confusing the NetBEUI transport protocol with the NetBIOS API. NetBIOS and NetBEUI serve quite different functions in the networking components of Windows NT (see the section entitled "Network Application Program Interfaces").

DLC

Data Link Control (DLC) is not used for general networking by Windows NT Workstation 4.0. The main use for DLC by Windows NT is for connectivity to printers directly attached to the network, such as Hewlett Packard JetDirect devices. Additional software is required for connectivity to Systems Network Architecture (SNA) mainframes.

Even if you are planning on using another protocol such as TCP/IP or NWLink to communicate with your printers directly attached to your network, you must install the DLC protocol. Some of the networking components needed to establish network sessions with network attached printers are only installed when and if the DLC protocol is installed.

Transport Driver Interface

The *Transport Driver Interface* (TDI) boundary layer, as previously seen in figure 4.1, provides the connection between the file system drivers and the individual transport protocols. The TDI standard enables transport protocols to be added or removed from a system independently of any file systems that might be in use. TDI is a Microsoft standard.

File System Drivers

File system drivers are used to access files. Whenever an application attempts to access a file, the I/O Manager determines if the I/O request is for a local disk or for a network resource. If the request is for a network resource, a redirector then passes it to the appropriate network components. The default redirector included with Windows NT Workstation 4.0 is called the Workstation service. It is possible for a Windows NT Workstation 4.0 to have more than one redirector to enable network communications with non-Microsoft-based servers, such as Unix or Novell NetWare.

In addition to the Workstation service, Windows NT Workstation 4.0 also includes a component called the Server service. The Server service is responsible for responding to I/O requests from other computers on the network that have been passed up to it by the lower network components.

 Note   Don't confuse the Workstation service and the Server service with the products Windows NT Workstation 4.0 and Windows NT Server 4.0. Both products have both services and can function as either a client or a server during network sessions.

Network Application Program Interfaces

An *application program interface* (API) is the set of routines that an application program uses to request and carry out lower level services performed by the operating system. The two network

APIs used by Windows NT to establish communications sessions and to transfer data to other computers in a network are as follows:

- ▶ **NetBIOS—Network Basic Input/Output System.** The original network API supported by Microsoft. NetBIOS was originally developed by IBM.

- ▶ **Windows Socket—also called WinSock.** A newer network API originally developed by the Unix community. It is now also supported by Microsoft.

File and Print Sharing Process

Figure 4.2 details the interaction between the Workstation service, at a client, and the Server service, at a server, as a client attempts to open a file at the server. Note that to simplify this example, it is assumed that the user at the client computer has the necessary security authorization to access the file on the server.

Figure 4.2

Windows NT network I/O.

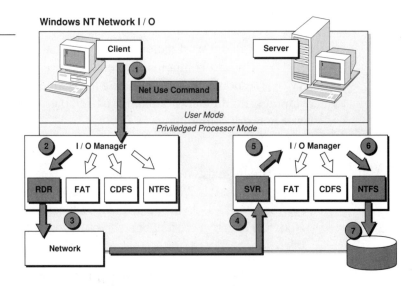

The sequence of operation in figure 4.2 is as follows:

1. A client initiates a file open command (via a program option or at a command prompt).

2. The I/O Manager, at the client, determines that the file is located remotely.

3. The Workstation service, at the client, passes the I/O request to the lower level networking layers, which send the request to the remote server.

4. The Server service, at the server, receives the I/O request asking to open a file that resides at the server.

5. The Server service, at the server, passes the I/O request to the I/O Manager.

6. The I/O Manager, at the server, passes the I/O request to the local file system driver.

7. The local file system driver, at the server, performs the desired action.

An acknowledgment is then sent back to the requesting client. In this process, either computer could be Windows NT Workstation 4.0 or Windows NT Server 4.0.

 Caution

Although Windows NT Workstation 4.0 can function as a network server, the Microsoft End User License Agreement (EULA) limits usage to 10 concurrent inbound sessions. There are no limitations on outbound sessions from Windows NT Workstation 4.0.

You should deploy Windows NT Server 4.0 if you need more than 10 concurrent inbound sessions.

Distributed Processing

In distributed processing applications, sometimes called *client/server* applications, computing requirements are divided into pieces that run on more than one computer. The minimal *front-end* processes run on a client and the resource intensive (CPU and/or hard disk) *back-end* processes are executed on a server. The server shares its processing power by executing applications on the request of clients. Microsoft SQL Server and Microsoft Exchange Server are examples of distributed applications.

Note
Computers based on Windows NT Workstation 4.0 or Windows NT Server 4.0 can perform the role of either the client or the server in a client/server application.

Interprocess Communications Mechanisms

In a distributed processing application, a network connection that enables data to flow back and forth between the client and the server needs to be established. Table 4.1 lists the various types of network connections that can be established.

Table 4.1

Types of Interprocess Communications

IPC Mechanism	Typical Uses
Named Pipes	Named pipes establish a guaranteed, bidirectional communications channel between two computers. After the pipe is established, either computer can read data from or write data to the pipe.
Mailslots	Mailslots establish a uni-directional communications channel between two computers. Receipt of the message is not guaranteed and no acknowledgment is sent if the data is received.
Windows Sockets (WinSock)	WinSock is an API that enables applications to access transport protocols such as TCP/IP and NWLink.
RPCs	RPCs enable the various components of distributed applications to communicate with each other via the network.
Network dynamic data exchange (NetDDE)	NetDDE is an older version of a RPC that is based on NetBIOS.

continues

Table 4.1   Continued

IPC Mechanism	Typical Uses
Distributed Component Object Model (DCOM)	DCOM is a RPC based on Microsoft ActiveX technology and enables the components of a distributed application to be located on multiple computers across a network simultaneously.

Figure 4.3 shows where the various interprocess communications mechanisms fit into the overall Windows NT 4.0 network architecture.

Figure 4.3

Network Application Programming interfaces.

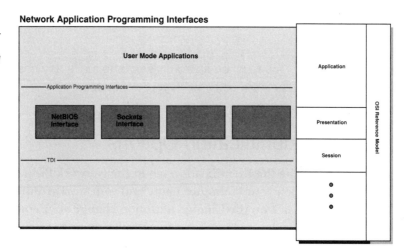

Adding and Configuring the Network Components of Windows NT Workstation

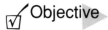 Objective

You can configure all your network components when you first install Windows NT Workstation 4.0. If you want to examine how your network components are configured, or make changes to your network configuration, double-click on the Network program in Control Panel to view the Network properties dialog box (see fig. 4.4).

Figure 4.4

The Network program in Control Panel.

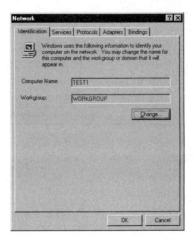

Note You must be an administrator to make any changes to the network settings on your computer.

Identification Options

Use the Identification tab in the Network Properties sheet to view your computer name and your workgroup or domain name. Click on the Change button to change your computer name—maximum length for a computer name is 15 characters—or to join a workgroup or domain—maximum length for a workgroup or domain name is 15 characters (see fig. 4.5).

Figure 4.5

Joining a domain.

The Windows NT security system requires that all Windows NT computers in a domain have accounts. Only domain administrators and other users that have been granted the user right of Add workstations to domain by a domain administrator can create computer accounts in a Windows NT domain.

 Note

If you are a domain administrator, you can give any user or group the user right of Add workstations to domain. Open User Manager for Domains. In the Policies menu, choose User Rights. Make sure that you check the Show Advanced User Rights box.

The following two methods enable you to change your domain name:

▶ If a domain administrator has already created a computer account for your computer, type the domain name into the Domain box and click on OK.

▶ Alternatively, you can create your computer account in the domain, as previously shown in figure 4.5. To create your own computer accounts, the user name specified must be a domain administrator or have been granted the user right of Add workstations to domain by a domain administrator.

Regardless of which method you use to join a domain, you should see a status message welcoming you to your new domain. You then must restart your computer to complete the process of joining the new domain.

 Caution

To join a domain, you must have network connectivity to the primary domain controller (PDC) in the domain that you wish to join. Also, make sure that you do not have a network session open with that PDC. If you must have open network sessions with that PDC, close all open files. Then join that domain, restart your computer, and reopen the files.

Services Options

Use the Services tab in the Network Properties sheet to view and modify the network services for your computer (see fig. 4.6).

Figure 4.6

Network services in Windows NT Workstation 4.0.

You might want to add some of the following network services to a Windows NT Workstation 4.0:

▶ **Client Services for NetWare (CSNW).** Enables you to access files and/or printers on a NetWare server.

▶ **Microsoft Peer Web Services.** Installs an intranet web server on your computer.

▶ **Microsoft TCP/IP Printing.** Configures your computer to act as a print server to which TCP/IP-based clients, such as Unix systems, can submit print jobs.

▶ **Remote Access Server.** Enables your computer to connect via telephone lines or the Internet to remote networks.

▶ **SNMP Service.** Enables your computer to transmit status information via TCP/IP to network management stations.

Protocols Options

Use the Protocols tab in the Network Properties sheet to view and modify the transport protocols for your computer (see fig. 4.7).

Figure 4.7

Transport protocols in Windows NT Workstation 4.0.

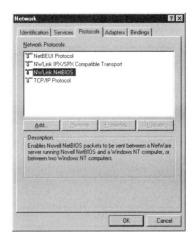

Windows NT Workstation 4.0 allows an unlimited number of network transport protocols. You might want to add some of the following network transport protocols to a Windows NT Workstation 4.0:

▶ **TCP/IP.** The default protocol for Windows NT Workstation 4.0. It is required for Internet connectivity.

▶ **NWLink IPX/SPX Compatible Transport.** Required for connectivity to NetWare servers.

▶ **NetBEUI.** Typically only allows connectivity to other Microsoft-based computers.

You can also add "third-party" transport protocols compatible with TDI and NDIS, which have not been developed by Microsoft.

Adapters Options

You can use the Adapters tab in the Network Properties sheet to add, remove, view properties of, or update your network adapter drivers (see fig. 4.8). Windows NT Workstation 4.0 allows an unlimited number of network adapters.

Figure 4.8

Viewing current network adapters.

 Tip

If you don't have a network adapter, you can still practice installing some of the network services that will not install without a network adapter. Select the MS Loopback Adapter from the Network Adapter list. (Keep in mind that although the services will install, they will not do much without an actual network adapter.)

Bindings Options

Network bindings are the connections between network services, transport protocols, and adapter card drivers. You can use the Bindings tab in the Network Properties sheet to view, enable, disable, and change the order of the bindings on your computer (see fig. 4.9). The current default protocol for each network service appears at the top of each section in the display. The default protocol for the Server service in figure 4.9, for example, is TCP/IP.

Notice that the binding from the Server service to the NetBEUI protocol has been disabled in figure 4.9. With this configuration, client computers that are only configured with the NetBEUI protocol cannot establish network sessions with this computer. This computer can still establish network sessions with servers configured with the NetBEUI protocol only, however, because the Workstation service is still bound to the NetBEUI protocol.

Figure 4.9

Viewing the net-work bindings on your computer.

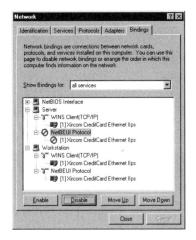

 Tip

For maximum performance, remove any unnecessary proto-cols and always make sure that your most frequently used protocol is configured to be your default protocol.

Using Various Methods to Access Network Resources

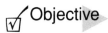 **Objective**

Windows NT Workstation 4.0 gives you different methods to work with network resources. You have different ways to determine what network resources are available to you and different types of connections that you can make to those network resources.

Universal Naming Convention

The *Universal Naming Convention* (UNC) is a standardized way of specifying a share name on a specific computer. The share names can refer to folders or to printers. The UNC path takes the form of *computer_name**share_name*. The UNC path to a share called Accounting on a server called ACCTSERVER is \\\\ACCTSERVER\\Accounting.

 Note

Connections made via UNC paths take place immediately and do not require the use of a drive letter.

You can also use UNC connections to connect to network printers. For example, \\ACCTSERVER\ACCTPRINT is the UNC path to a printer named ACCTPRINT on a server named ACCTSERVER.

 Caution

> Many 16-bit applications do not work with UNC paths. If you need to work with a 16-bit application that doesn't work with UNC paths, you must map a drive letter to the shared folder or connect a port to the network printer.

Network Neighborhood

If your Windows NT Workstation 4.0 computer has a network card installed, the Network Neighborhood icon appears on your desktop. When you double-click on the Network Neighborhood icon, the list of all computers in your workgroup or domain appears. By double-clicking on the Entire Network icon, you can also view all computers connected to your network that are not members of your workgroup or domain.

When you view lists of computers in Network Neighborhood, you are actually viewing a graphical representation of what is called a *browse list*. The browse list is actually maintained by a computer that has been designated as a *Browse Master*. All computers in the network (that have an active Server service) periodically announce their presence to the Browse Master to keep the browse list current.

 Key Concepts

> The *Browse Master* in a Microsoft network receives periodic broadcasts from all servers on the network and maintains the *browse list*, which lists all available servers.

Tip

> Windows 95 computers in a workgroup with the same name as a Windows NT domain, display together with the Windows NT computers when the browse list is viewed.

Net View Command

You can also access the current browse list from the command prompt by typing: **NET VIEW**. The current browse list will be displayed on your screen. A sample browse list looks like this:

```
C:\>net view
Server Name            Remark

-------------------------------------------------
\\TEST1
\\TEST2
\\TESTPDC
The command completed successfully.
```

Net Use Command

You can assign network resources to drive letters from the command prompt by using the Net Use command and the UNC path of the resource. To connect drive letter X: to a share called Good-Stuff on a server named SERVER1, for example, you would type the following command at a command prompt:

```
Net Use X: \\SERVER1\GoodStuff
```

You can also use the Net Use command to connect clients to network printers. If you want to connect port Lpt1: to a network printer named HP5 on a server named SERVER1, use the following command:

```
Net Use Lpt1: \\SERVER1\HP5
```

To disconnect the network resources for these two, use the following two commands:

```
Net Use X: /d
```

```
Net Use Lpt1: /d
```

Implementing Windows NT Workstation as a Client in a NetWare Environment

 **Objective**

To enable a Windows NT Workstation 4.0 computer to access and share resources on a NetWare server, it may be necessary to install additional software besides the NWLink protocol on the Windows NT Workstation 4.0 computers. The type of access that you are trying to establish determines whether additional software needs to be installed. NWLink can establish client/server connections, but does not provide access to files and printers on NetWare servers.

If you want to be able to access files or printers on a NetWare server, you must install the Microsoft Client Service for NetWare (CSNW), which is included with Windows NT Workstation 4.0. CSNW enables Windows NT Workstation 4.0 to access files and printers at NetWare servers running NetWare 2.x or later (including NetWare 4.x servers running NDS). CSNW installs an additional network redirector.

Windows NT Workstation 4.0 computers that have NWLink and CSNW installed, gain the following capabilities:

- ▶ A new network redirector compatible with NetWare Core Protocol (NCP). NCP is the standard Novell protocol for file and print sharing.

- ▶ Long file names, when the NetWare server is configured to support long file names.

- ▶ Large Internet Protocol (LIP) to automatically determine the largest possible frame size to communicate with NetWare servers.

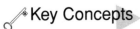 **Key Concepts**

The Microsoft *Client Service for NetWare* (CSNW) enables Windows NT Workstation 4.0 to access files and printers on NetWare servers.

Caution

Although NWLink and CSNW enables a Windows NT Workstation 4.0 to access files and printers on a NetWare server running NDS, it does not support administration of NDS trees. Also, although CSNW enables a Windows NT Workstation 4.0 to access files and printers on a NetWare server, it doesn't enable NetWare clients to access files and printers on a Windows NT Workstation 4.0.

If you need NetWare clients to be able to access files and printers on a Windows NT 4.0 computer, you must install Microsoft File and Print Services for NetWare (FPNW), available separately from Microsoft, on a Windows NT Server 4.0.

 Note

Windows NT Workstation 4.0 can access files and printers on a NetWare server without adding CSNW by connecting through a Windows NT Server configured with Gateway Services for NetWare (GSNW). GSNW can only be installed on Windows NT Server.

Installing CSNW

CSNW is installed the same way as any other network service, through the Network program in the Control Panel. After you install CSNW, you will notice a new CSNW program listed in the Control Panel. Exercise 4.4 details the full instructions on how to install CSNW.

 Caution

If after you install NWLink and CSNW you cannot establish connectivity to your NetWare servers, you should check to see what IPX frame type they are configured for. There are actually two different, incompatible versions, 802.2 and 802.3. Windows NT Workstation 4.0 attempts to automatically determine the correct frame type, but you might have to manually specify the frame type to make the connection work (see exercise 4.5).

Configuring CSNW

After you have installed CSNW on your computer, each user that logs on receives a prompt to enter the details of his or her NetWare account. Each user can enter either a preferred server for NetWare 2.x or 3.x, his or her default tree and context for NDS, or the user can specify <None> if he doesn't have a NetWare account. Each time the same user logs on to that computer, he automatically connects to his NetWare account in addition to his Windows NT account.

Each user is requested to enter his NetWare account information only once. The only way to change each user's recorded NetWare account information is to double-click on the CSNW program in Control Panel. You can also use the CSNW program in Control Panel to modify your print options for NetWare printers—adding form feeds or print banners, for example (see fig. 4.11).

Figure 4.11

Modifying NetWare account information.

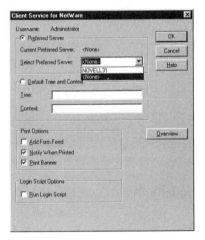

 Note

Even though Windows NT Workstation 4.0 attempts to automatically connect you to your NetWare system, there is no direct linkage between the two account databases. If you change either network password, the other password does not automatically change to match your new network password.

Connecting to NetWare Resources

After you install NWLink and CSNW, the NetWare servers in your network are accessed using the same methods that you use to connect to any other Windows NT Server. You can connect to files and printers on the NetWare servers without any special procedures.

Browsing

After you install NWLink and CSNW, when you double-click on Network Neighborhood, and then double-click on Entire Network, you can choose to browse either the Microsoft Windows Network or the NetWare or Compatible Network (see fig. 4.12).

Figure 4.12

Browsing NetWare servers.

Map Command

After you install NWLink and CSNW, right-click on Network Neighborhood and Choose Map Network Drive from the menu. You can then assign any drive letter to any shared directory on a NetWare server (see fig. 4.13).

Figure 4.13

Mapping network drives to NetWare servers.

Connecting to NetWare Printers

Installation of NWLink and CSNW enables you to connect also to NetWare print queues (see fig. 4.14 and exercise 4.9).

Figure 4.14

Connecting to a NetWare print queue.

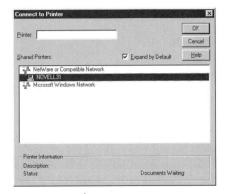

Using Various Configurations to Install Windows NT Workstation as a TCP/IP Client

 Objective

TCP/IP, the default protocol for Windows NT Workstation 4.0, is a suite of protocols designed for WANs. TCP/IP is supported by most common operating systems and is also required for connectivity to the Internet. When you manually configure a computer as a TCP/IP host, you must enter the appropriate settings, which are required for connectivity with your network. The most common network settings are as follows:

▶ **IP Address.** A logical 32-bit address used to identify a TCP/IP host. Each network adapter configured for TCP/IP must have a unique IP address, such as 10.100.5.43.

▶ **Subnet Mask.** A subnet is a division of a larger network environment typically connected with routers. Whenever a TCP/IP host tries to communicate with another TCP/IP host, the subnet mask is used to determine whether the other TCP/IP host is on the same network or a different network. If the other TCP/IP host is on a different network, the message must be sent via a router that connects to the other network. A typical subnet mask is 255.255.255.0. All computers on a subnet must have identical subnet masks.

▶ **Default Gateway (Router).** This optional setting is the address of the router for this subnet that controls communications with all other subnets. If this address is not specified, this TCP/IP host can only communicate with other TCP/IP hosts on its subnet.

▶ **Windows Internet Name Service (WINS).** Computers use IP addresses to identify each other, but users generally find it easier to use other means, such as computer names. Some method must be used to provide *name resolution,* which is the process where references to computer names are converted into the appropriate IP addresses. WINS provides name resolution for Microsoft networks. If your network uses WINS for name resolution, your computer needs to be configured with the IP address of a WINS server (the IP address of a secondary WINS server can also be specified).

▶ **Domain Network System (DNS) Server Address.** DNS is an industry standard distributed database that provides name resolution and a hierarchical naming system for identifying TCP/IP hosts on the Internet and on private networks. A DNS address must be specified to enable connectivity with the Internet or with Unix TCP/IP hosts. You can specify more than one DNS address and the search order that specifies the order in which they should be used.

Key Concepts

Name resolution is the process of translating user-friendly computer names to IP addresses.

Caution

If the settings for the TCP/IP protocol are incorrectly specified, you will experience problems that keep your computer from establishing communications with other TCP/IP hosts in your network. In extreme cases, communications on your entire subnet can be disrupted.

You can specify all the settings for the TCP/IP protocol manually, or they can be automatically configured through a network service called *Dynamic Host Configuration Protocol* (DHCP).

Understanding DHCP

One way to avoid the possible problems of administrative overhead and incorrect settings for the TCP/IP protocol—which are caused by manual configurations—is to set up your network so that all your clients receive their TCP/IP configuration information automatically through DHCP. DHCP automatically centralizes and manages the allocation of the TCP/IP settings required for proper network functionality for computers that have been configured as *DHCP clients*. One major advantage of DHCP is that most of the configuration of your network settings only needs to happen once, at the DHCP server. Also, the TCP/IP settings that the DHCP client receives from the DHCP server are only *leased* to it and must be periodically renewed. This lease and renewal sequence enables a network administrator to change client TCP/IP settings, if needed.

Using DHCP

To configure a computer as a DHCP client, all you must do is to specify Obtain an IP address from a DHCP Server in the TCP/IP properties box (see fig. 4.15). Exercise 4.2 contains complete instructions.

Figure 4.15

Specifying a TCP/ IP host to be a DHCP client.

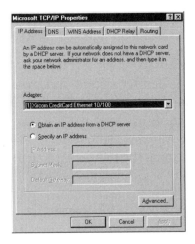

Testing DHCP

To determine the network settings that a DHCP server has leased to your computer, type the following command at a command prompt:

IPCONFIG /all

```
The following is sample output from the IPCONFIG
program:C:\>ipconfig/all
Windows NT IP Configuration
Host Name . . . . . . . . . : TEST1
DNS Servers . . . . . . . . : 10.1.45.1
Node Type . . . . . . . . . : Hybrid
NetBIOS Scope ID. . . . . . :
IP Routing Enabled. . . . . : No
WINS Proxy Enabled. . . . . : No
NetBIOS Resolution Uses DNS : No
Ethernet adapter CE31:
Description . . . . . . . . : Xircom CE3 10/100 Ethernet Adapter
Physical Address. . . . . . : 00-10-45-81-5A-96
DHCP Enabled. . . . . . . . : Yes
IP Address. . . . . . . . . : 10.100.5.140
Subnet Mask . . . . . . . . : 255.255.255.0
Default Gateway . . . . . . : 10.100.5.1
DHCP Server . . . . . . . . : 10.100.5.16
```

```
Primary WINS Server . . . . : 10.100.5.16
Lease Obtained. . . . . . . : Saturday, August 09, 1997 12:31:29 PM
Lease Expires . . . . . . . : Sunday, August 10, 1997 6:31:29 PM
```

Note that IPCONFIG also gives you full details on the duration of your current lease. You can verify whether a DHCP client has connectivity to a DHCP server by releasing the client's IP address and then attempting to lease an IP address. You can conduct this test by typing the following sequence of commands from the DHCP client at a command prompt:

IPCONFIG /release

IPCONFIG /renew

Manually Configuring TCP/IP

To manually configure your TCP/IP settings, you must enter all the required values into the TCP/IP properties sheet (see fig. 4.16). For complete details, see exercise 4.1.

Figure 4.16

Manual configuration of a TCP/IP host.

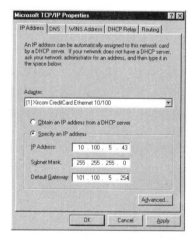

Name Resolution with TCP/IP

DNS and WINS are not the only name resolution methods available for Windows NT Workstation 4.0 TCP/IP hosts. Microsoft also provides for two different lookup files, LMHOSTS and HOSTS. You can find both LMHOSTS and HOSTS in the

\winnt_root\SYSTEM32\DRIVERS\ETC folder. Read the contents of each file for instructions on how to use them.

Note

> Although the sample LMHOSTS file, in the *\winnt_root*\SYSTEM32\DRIVERS\ETC folder is named LMHOSTS.SAM, it must be renamed LMHOSTS without any file extension. Otherwise, it will not be used for name resolution.

Configuring and Installing Dial-Up Networking in a Given Situation

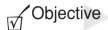**Objective**

Remote Access Service (RAS) and *Dial-Up Networking* (DUN) enable you to extend your network to unlimited locations. RAS servers and DUN clients enable remote clients to make connections to your LAN via either ordinary telephone lines or through higher-speed techniques, such as ISDN or X.25. The incoming connections can also be via industry standard *Point-to-Point Protocol* (PPP) or the newer *Point-to-Point Tunneling Protocol* (PPTP) that makes use of the Internet. DUN also supports the use of *Serial Line Internet Protocol* (SLIP) to initiate dial-up connections with SLIP servers.

Key Concepts

> The *Point-to-Point Tunneling Protocol* (PPTP) is an extension to PPP that enables clients to connect to remote servers over the Internet.

After clients establish a connection to a RAS server, they are registered into the local network and can take advantage of the same network services and data that they could if they were actually physically connected to the local network. The only difference that clients could notice is that WAN connections are much slower than a direct physical connection to their LAN.

Line Protocols

The network transport protocols (NetBEUI, NWLink, and TCP/IP) were designed for the characteristics of LANs and are not suitable for use in phone-based connections. To make the network transport protocols function properly in phone-based connections, it is necessary to encapsulate them in a line protocol. Windows NT Workstation 4.0 supports two different line protocols: SLIP and PPP.

Serial Line Internet Protocol (SLIP)

SLIP is an industry standard that supports TCP/IP connections made over serial lines. Unfortunately, SLIP has several limitations, as follows:

- ▶ Supports TCP/IP only, no support for IPX or NetBEUI

- ▶ Requires static IP addresses, no support for DHCP

- ▶ Transmits authentication passwords as clear text, no support for encryption

- ▶ Usually requires a scripting system for the logon process

 Tip   Windows NT Workstation 4.0 supports SLIP client functionality only; operation as a SLIP server is not supported.

Point-to-Point Protocol (PPP)

The limitations of SLIP prompted the development of a newer, industry standard protocol, Point-to-Point Protocol (PPP). Some of the advantages of PPP include the following:

- ▶ Supports TCP/IP, IPX, NetBEUI, and others

- ▶ Has support for DHCP or static addresses

- ▶ Supports encryption for authentication

- ▶ Doesn't require a scripting system for the logon process

Note

New to NT Workstation 4.0 is support for PPP multilink, which enables you to combine multiple physical links into one logical connection. A client with two ordinary phone lines and two 28.8 Kbps modems, for example, could establish a PPP multi-link session with a RAS server with an effective throughput of up to 57.6 Kbps. The two modems do not have to be the same type or speed.

Both the RAS server and the DUN client must have PPP multi-link enabled.

Point-to-Point Tunneling Protocol

New to Windows NT Workstation 4.0 is an extension to PPP called Point-to-Point Tunneling Protocol (PPTP). PPTP enables a DUN client to establish a communications session with a RAS server over the Internet. PPTP enables multiprotocol virtual private networks (VPNs), so remote users can gain secure encrypted access to their corporate networks over the Internet. Because PPTP encapsulates TCP/IP, NWLink, and NetBEUI, it enables the Internet to be used as a backbone for NWLink and NetBEUI.

To use PPTP, first establish a connection from the DUN client to the Internet and then establish a connection to the RAS server over the Internet.

Installing the Dial-Up Networking Client

**Objective**

Installation of DUN can happen when you install Windows NT Workstation 4.0, or later. If you select Remote Access to the network during setup, both RAS and DUN will be installed. Either, or both, services can be installed separately after installation of Windows NT Workstation 4.0.

To install DUN after installation of Windows NT Workstation 4.0, you should double-click on the Dial-Up Networking icon in My Computer and click on Install to start the Installation wizard. Then just follow the wizard's instructions.

Note

Windows NT Workstation 4.0 is limited to one RAS session at a time, either dial-out or receive. If you need to support more than one simultaneous RAS session, you should purchase Windows NT Server 4.0.

Configuring the Dial-Up Networking (DUN) Client

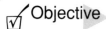**Objective**

As detailed in Exercise 4.6, the first step in configuring the Dial-Up Networking (DUN) client is to install the DUN software and a modem. The entire installation process is automated and is invoked when you double-click on the Dial-Up Networking program in My Computer. When you click on Yes to start the Modem Installer, the Install New Modem wizard appears (see fig. 4.17).

Figure 4.17

The Install New Modem Wizard.

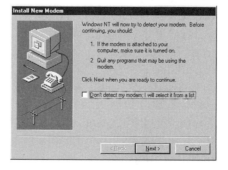

You can allow the Install New Modem Wizard to automatically detect your modem, or you can select your modem from a list, or you can supply a manufacturer's installation disk.

The next step in the installation process is to add the modem as a RAS device (see fig. 4.18).

Figure 4.18

Selecting a modem as a RAS device.

After you add the modem as a RAS device, you must configure it (see fig. 4.19).

Figure 4.19

Configuring your modem for RAS.

After you configure your modem, you must specify how RAS should use the phone line (see fig. 4.20). You have the following options:

▶ Dial out only (the default setting for Microsoft Windows NT Workstation 4.0)

▶ Receive calls only

▶ Dial out and Receive calls

Figure 4.20

Configuring RAS port usage.

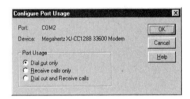

You can also select which of the network transport protocols (TCP/IP, IPX, or NetBEUI) you want to use after you have made a connection to the remote network (see fig. 4.21).

Figure 4.21

Selection of dial-out protocols for DUN.

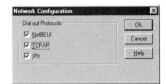

Tip

The steps to change your RAS configuration after you finish the installation process are as follows:

1. Double-click on the Network program in Control Panel.

2. Click on the Services tab.

3. Double-click on the Remote Access Service in the list.

4. In the Remote Access Setup box:

   ▶ Click on Configure to configure port usage.

   ▶ Click on Network to select dial-out protocols.

You must restart your computer after you change your RAS configuration.

Authentication

Security is a major consideration in the design of DUN. As shown in figure 4.22, you can choose from several different security settings, including the following:

▶ **Accept any authentication including clear text.** Use this setting when you don't care about security.

▶ **Accept only encrypted authentication.** RAS supports several industry standard encrypted authentication procedures to support connections to non-Microsoft remote networks, including RSA, DES, and Shiva.

▶ **Accept only Microsoft encrypted authentication.** If you select this option, you can also choose to have your entire session with the remote network encrypted, not just your logon. This setting is possible only if you are connecting to a Windows NT RAS server.

Figure 4.22

Selecting the authentication and encryption policy.

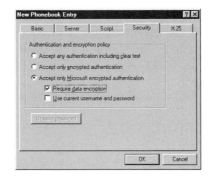

The authentication and encryption settings are set individually for each phonebook entry.

Creating a Phonebook Entry

You can create new phonebook entries by starting Dial-Up Networking and clicking on New. The New Phonebook Entry wizard then appears. If you then select the I Know All About Phonebook Entries and Would Rather Edit the Properties Directly check box, the New Phonebook Entry property box appears (see fig. 4.23). Each user on a computer has a unique phonebook stored as part of his or her User Profile.

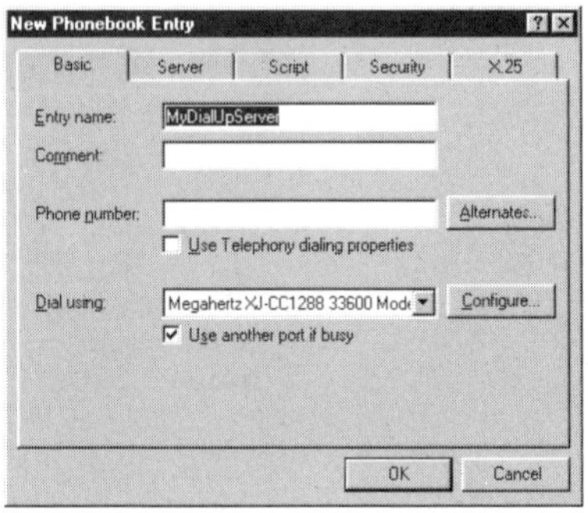

Figure 4.23

Manual entry of a new phonebook entry.

Tip

If you select manual phonebook entry and would like to be able to use the New Phonebook Entry wizard again, follow these steps:

1. Double-click on the Dial-Up Networking icon in My Computer.

2. Click on More.

3. Click on User Preferences.

4. Click on the Appearance tab.

5. Click on Use wizard to create new phonebook entries.

The New Phonebook Entry wizard automatically starts the next time that you run Dial-Up Networking.

Configuring a Location

When you double-click on the Telephony program in Control Panel, the Dialing Properties dialog box appears (see fig. 4.24).

You can enter Calling Card information by clicking on the Dial using Calling Card check box, and then clicking on Change.

Figure 4.24

Configuring Dial-Up Network locations.

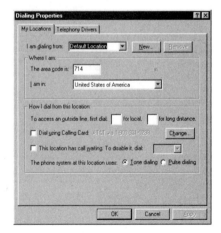

Configuring Peer Web Services in a Given Situation

Peer Web Services (PWS) gives users the ability to publish information on private intranets. PWS includes capabilities for hypertext documents, interactive web applications, and client/server applications and is optimized for use as a small scale web server. PWS supports the following industry standard Internet services:

▶ **HyperText Transfer Protocol (HTTP).** Used for the creation and navigation of hypertext documents.

▶ **File Transfer Protocol (FTP).** Used to transfer files between TCP/IP hosts.

▶ **Gopher.** A hierarchical indexing system that identifies files in directories to make searching for data easier.

PWS also supports Microsoft's *Internet Server Application Programming Interface* (ISAPI). You can use ISAPI to create interactive web-based applications that enable users to access and enter data into web pages.

> **Note**   Internet Information Server (IIS), which is included with Windows NT Server 4.0, should be deployed for larger scale requirements.

Installing Peer Web Services

Before you start the installation of Peer Web Services (PWS) make sure that you remove all other Internet services (Gopher, FTP, and so on) already installed. Make sure also that you have properly configured your computer to function as a TCP/IP host. Then start the installation process of PWS through the Network program in Control Panel. Then select the installation of Peer Web Services, which starts the PWS Installation wizard (see fig. 4.25).

Figure 4.25

*Installing Peer
Web Services
(PWS).*

The PWS installation wizard also asks you to choose which of the
PWS services to install (see fig. 4.26).

Figure 4.26

*Selecting which
PWS services to
install.*

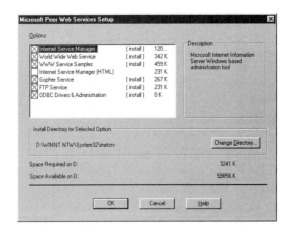

Exercise 4.10 gives complete details on the installation of PWS.

Configuring Peer Web Services

After you install PWS, a new program group containing the PWS
utilities is added to your desktop (see fig. 4.27).

Figure 4.27

Peer Web Services configuration utilities.

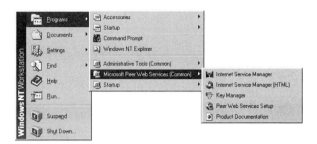

The Internet Service Manager enables management of multiple web servers from any location on your network (see fig. 4.28). Some of the capabilities of the Internet Services Manager include the following:

▶ Find and list all PWS and IIS servers on your network

▶ Connect to servers and view their installed services

▶ Start, stop, or pause any service

▶ Configure service properties

Figure 4.28

Peer Web Services Internet Services Manager

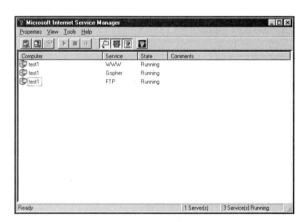

You can also choose to install a version of the Internet Services Manager accessible via HTML that enables you to manage your PWS server with any standard web browser.

Exercises

The following exercises detail step-by-step procedures on various ways to install and configure the networking components of Windows NT Workstation 4.0. Other lab exercises show you how to interoperate with Novell NetWare servers and to install a Peer Web Server on your computer.

Exercise 4.1: Add the TCP/IP Protocol

This exercise shows you the steps to add and configure the TCP/IP protocol.

Objective

Add and configure the network components of Windows NT Workstation

Time Estimate: 10 minutes

Steps

1. Double-click on the Network program in Control Panel.

2. Click on the Protocols tab in the Network properties box.

3. Click on Add.

4. Select the TCP/IP Protocol and click on OK.

5. In the TCP/IP Setup box, click on No to the question about DHCP.

6. When prompted, insert your installation CD and click on Continue.

7. When the Network properties box appears, click on Close.

8. In the Microsoft TCP/IP Properties box, specify the IP address **10.100.5.27**.

9. Specify the Subnet Mask of **255.255.255.0**, and then click on OK.

10. Restart your computer when prompted.

Exercise 4.2:   Change TCP/IP Properties to Use DHCP

This exercise shows you how to change the properties of the TCP/IP protocol from a static IP address to be DHCP client.

Objective

Use various configurations to install Windows NT Workstation as a TCP/IP client

Time Estimate: 10 minutes

Steps

1. Double-click on the Network program in Control Panel.

2. Click on the Protocols tab in the Network properties box.

3. Select the TCP/IP protocol.

4. Click on Properties.

5. Select Obtain an IP Address from a DHCP server.

6. Click on Yes to enable DHCP.

7. In the TCP/IP Properties box, click on OK.

8. In the Network Properties box, click on Close.

9. If prompted, restart your computer.

10. To verify whether DHCP is functional, at a command prompt, type **IPCONFIG /ALL**.

11. If you don't see a valid IP address and lease information and you didn't already restart your computer, restart your computer now.

Exercise 4.3:   Add a New Network Adapter Driver

This exercise shows you the steps required to add a new network adapter driver.

continues

Exercise 4.3: Continued

Objective

Add and configure the network components of Windows NT Workstation

Time Estimate: 10 minutes

Steps

1. Right-click on Network Neighborhood.

2. Click on Properties in the menu.

3. Click on the Adapters tab.

4. Click on Add.

5. Select MS Loopback Adapter from the Network Adapter list.

6. Click on OK.

7. In the MS Loopback Adapter Card Setup box, click on OK.

8. Insert your Windows NT Workstation 4.0 installation CD when requested, and then click on Continue.

9. Click on Close in the Network properties box.

10. Answer any questions having to do with any protocols that you might have installed.

11. Click on Yes to restart your computer.

Exercise 4.4: Install Client Service for NetWare (CSNW)

This exercise shows you how to enable your computer to access files and printers on a NetWare server.

Objective

Implement Windows NT Workstation as a client in a NetWare environment

Time Estimate: 20 minutes

Steps

1. Double-click on the Network program in Control Panel.

2. Click on the Services tab.

3. Click on Add.

4. Select Client Service for NetWare in the Network Service list and click on OK.

5. Insert your Windows NT Workstation 4.0 installation CD when prompted, and then click on Continue.

6. Click on Close and wait while the bindings are reset.

7. Click on Yes to restart your computer.

8. Press Ctrl+Alt+Delete and log on to your computer.

9. When the Select NetWare Logon box appears, select your NetWare 3.x preferred server or your NetWare 4.x default tree and context. Then click on OK.

10. When your desktop appears, right-click on Network Neighborhood.

11. In the Network Neighborhood menu, choose Who Am I.

12. Your NetWare user information appears.

Exercise 4.5:   Change the Frame Type of the NWLink Protocol

This exercise shows you how to adjust the properties of the NWLink protocol to change the frame type from auto-detect to 802.2.

Objective

Implement Windows NT Workstation as a client in a NetWare environment

continues

Exercise 4.5: Continued

Time Estimate: 10 minutes

Steps

1. Double-click on the Network program in Control Panel.

2. Click on the Protocols tab in the Network properties box.

3. Select the NWLink IPX/SPX Compatible Transport protocol.

4. Click on Properties.

5. In the Frame Type drop-down box, select Ethernet 802.2.

6. Click on OK.

7. In the Network properties box, click on Close.

8. Restart your computer when prompted.

Exercise 4.6: Install DUN and Configure Modem

This exercise shows you how set up your computer to access remote networks via a modem.

Objective

Add and configure the network components of Windows NT Workstation

Time Estimate: 15 minutes

Steps

1. Double-click on the Dial-Up Networking program in My Computer.

2. Click on the Install button to start the installation wizard.

3. Insert your installation CD when prompted.

4. Click on Yes to start the Modem installer.

5. Click on the Don't detect my modem, I will select it from a list check box, and then click on Next.

6. Select your modem from the list, or click on Have Disk.

7. Point the Installation wizard to your modem's install files.

8. Click on Next to install the modem.

9. Select the port to which the modem is connected, and then click on Next.

10. Wait while the modem is installed.

11. Click on Finish.

12. In the Add RAS Device screen, click on OK.

13. In the Remote Access Setup box, click on Configure.

14. Notice that the default setting for Microsoft NT Workstation 4.0 is Dial out only.

15. Click on OK to return to the Remote Access Setup box.

16. Click on Network.

17. Notice in the Network Configuration box that you can choose which of the protocols you want to use after you connect to the remote network.

18. Click on OK to return to the Remote Access Setup box.

19. Click on Continue.

20. Wait while the remainder of the RAS software is installed and the bindings are reset.

21. Press Restart to restart your computer, which finishes the installation of DUN.

Exercise 4.7: Add a New Dial-Up Networking (DUN) Phonebook Entry

This exercise leads you through the steps of adding a new DUN phonebook entry.

Objective

Configure and install dial-up networking in a given situation

Time Estimate: 5 minutes

Steps

1. Double-click on the Dial-Up Networking program in My Computer.

2. Click on New.

3. Enter **New Server** for the name of the new phonebook entry, and then click on Next.

4. Click on Next, for the Server settings.

5. Enter the phone number **555-5555**, and then click on Next.

6. Click on Finish.

7. Click on the Phonebook Entry to Dial drop-down box.

8. See how you can choose which phone number to use.

9. Click on Close.

Exercise 4.8: Add a new Dial-Up Networking (DUN) Dialing Location

This exercise shows you how to add a new dialing location so that you can use your DUN client from a new location.

Objective

Configure and install Dial-Up Networking

Time Estimate: 5 minutes

Steps:

1. Double-click on the Dial-Up Telephony program in My Computer.

2. Click on New.

3. Click on OK in the dialog box that tells you a new location was created.

4. Change the area code to your new area code.

5. Specify Dial 9 for an outside line and Dial 8 for long distance.

6. Check the Dial using Calling Card check box, and then click on Change.

7. Select your Calling Card from the list, and then click on OK.

8. Click on OK to close the Dialing Properties box.

Exercise 4.9:   Connect to a NetWare Print Server

This exercise shows you how to connect your computer to a NetWare print server.

Objective

Implement Windows NT Workstation as a client in a NetWare environment

Time Estimate: 10 minutes

Steps

1. Double-click on the Printers program in My Computer.

2. Double-click on Add Printer.

3. In the Add Printer wizard, select Network Printer Server, and then click on Next.

continues

Exercise 4.9: Continued

4. In the Connect to Printer box, select the desired network printer, and then click on OK. Note, double-click on the desired print server to see a list of the printers available on that print server.

5. In the Connect to Printer box, click on OK.

6. Select the proper printer from the list, and then click on OK.

7. Insert your installation CD when prompted, and then click on OK.

8. Select whether you want this new printer to be your default Windows printer, and then click on Next.

9. Click on Finish.

Exercise 4.10: Install Peer Web Services (PWS)

This exercise details the step-by-step process required to install a Peer Web Server on a Windows NT Workstation 4.0.

Objective

Configure Microsoft Peer Web Services

Time Estimate: 20 minutes

Steps

1. Before starting the installation of Peer Web Services, make sure that the TCP/IP protocol is installed and properly configured.

2. Double-click on the Network program in Control Panel.

3. Click on the Services tab.

4. Click on Add.

5. Select Microsoft Peer Web Services from the Network Service list, and then click on OK.

6. Insert your NT Workstation 4.0 installation CD when prompted, and then click on OK.

7. Click on OK to start Peer Web Services Setup.

8. Click on OK to select which PWS services to set up.

9. Click on Yes to create the Inetsrv directory.

10. Click on OK to specify the names for the publishing directories.

11. Click on Yes to create the publishing directories.

12. Wait while the PWS files are installed.

13. Click on OK in the Install Drivers box.

14. Click on OK to end the installation of PWS.

15. Click on Close in the Network Properties box.

16. You do not have to restart your computer. PWS is now active.

Review Questions

The following questions test your knowledge of the material in this chapter.

1. You have a laptop computer configured with Dial-Up Networking and you want to configure your system to use a calling card. Which is correct?

    a. You can't program calling card numbers.

    b. Enter the calling card number after the phone number that you want to dial.

    c. Edit the Dialing Location, click on Dial using Call Card, click on Change, and enter the number.

    d. Go to Control Panel, Network program, Services tab, and edit the properties for the Remote Access Service.

2. What three components enable a Windows NT Workstation 4.0 computer to access files and printers on a NetWare server?

    a. Client Services for NetWare

    b. Gateway Services for NetWare

    c. NWLink IPX/SPX Compatible Transport

    d. File and Print Services for NetWare

3. What do you need to do before you install Peer Web Services?

    a. Install NetBEUI

    b. Download the files from the Microsoft web site

    c. Remove all other Internet services from the computer

    d. Create a dedicated FAT partition

4. You have a TCP/IP network connected to the Internet. What name resolution service enables you to connect to web sites?

    a. WINS

    b. DHCP

    c. DNS

    d. Browser service

5. Which components must be installed on Windows NT Workstation 4.0 to enable it to access a print queue on a NetWare server?

    a. Client Services for NetWare

    b. Gateway Services for NetWare

    c. NWLink IPX/SPX Compatible Transport

    d. File and Print Services for NetWare

6. What tool should you use to configure Peer Web Services (PWS) after it is installed on your Windows NT Workstation 4.0?

    a. Internet Service Manager

    b. The Network program in Control Panel

    c. Windows Setup

    d. You can only configure PWS during installation.

7. Which of the following are characteristics of the NetBEUI protocol? Choose all that apply.

    a. Fast performance on small LANs

    b. Small memory overhead

    c. No tuning options

    d. Support for routing

8. Which of the following are limitations of SLIP for Dial-Up Networking (DUN) clients?

    a. DUN doesn't support use as a SLIP client.

    b. SLIP doesn't support NWLink or NetBEUI.

    c. SLIP doesn't support DHCP.

    d. SLIP doesn't support encrypted authentication.

9. What methods are supported by Dial-Up Networking to establish sessions with remote networks?

    a. ISDN

    b. X.25

    c. Dial-up with modems and ordinary phone lines

    d. XNS

10. Which network environments are supported by Windows NT Workstation 4.0? Choose all that apply.

    a. Microsoft networks

    b. TCP/IP networks

    c. Novell NetWare 3.x and 4.x (including NDS)

    d. AppleTalk

11. What service enables a Windows NT Workstation 4.0 to establish connections to other computers on a network?

    a. Session service

    b. Server service

    c. Workstation service

    d. Routing service

12. In distributed processing, the front-end process does what?

    a. Runs on a server and requires extensive resources

    b. Runs on a client and requires extensive resources

    c. Runs on a server and requires minimal resources

    d. Runs on a client and requires minimal resources

13. Each time you print to a printer on a NetWare server, an extra page is printed that contains your user name. How can you prevent this extra page from being printed?

    a. From a Command Prompt, type **NO BANNER**.

    b. In the CSNW program in Control Panel, clear the Print Banner check box.

   c. In the CSNW program in Control Panel, clear the Form Feed check box.

   d. Clear the Print Banner check box in the printer's property box.

14. After you have installed Client Services for NetWare (CSNW) on your Windows NT Workstation 4.0, what can you now do? Choose all that apply.

   a. Allow NetWare clients to access files on your computer

   b. Allow you to access files on NetWare servers

   c. Allow NetWare clients to access printers on your computer

   d. Allow you to access printers on NetWare servers

15. You have a Windows NT Workstation 4.0 with two modems and two ordinary phone lines. You wish to establish the fastest possible connection to a remote network. Which protocol should you use?

   a. Serial Line Internet Protocol (SLIP)

   b. Point-to-Point Tunneling Protocol (PPTP)

   c. Point-to-Point Multilink Protocol

   d. Remote Access Service (RAS)

16. What service enables other computers on a network to establish connections with a Windows NT Workstation 4.0?

   a. Session service

   b. Server service

   c. Workstation service

   d. Routing service

17. You need to purchase a new network adapter for your Windows NT Workstation 4.0. Which types of device drivers are supported? Choose all that are correct.

    a. ODI 3.0

    b. NDIS 3.0

    c. NDIS 3.1

    d. NDIS 4.0

18. Which Windows NT service provides support for remote users that make connections via ordinary phone lines?

    a. Dial-Up Service

    b. PPP Service

    c. SLIP Service

    d. Remote Access Service

19. Which of the following network settings are needed to manually configure a Windows NT Workstation 4.0 to communicate in a routed, WAN configuration? Choose all that apply.

    a. IP address

    b. Subnet mask

    c. DHCP server address

    d. Address of the default gateway

20. Which transport protocol provides connectivity with the Internet?

    a. DLC

    b. NetBEUI

    c. NWLink IPX/SPX Compatible Transport

    d. TCP/IP

Review Answers

1. C is correct. You enter your calling card information when you edit your Dialing Location. For more information, see the section entitled "Configuring a Location."

2. A, B, and C are correct. FPNW enables NetWare clients to access files and printers on a Windows NT Server. For more information, see the section entitled "Implementing Windows NT Workstation as a Client in a NetWare Environment."

3. C is correct. PWS requires TCP/IP. For more information, see the section entitled "Installing Peer Web Services."

4. C is correct. Unix TCP/IP hosts do not support WINS. For more information, see the section entitled "Using Various Configurations to Install Windows NT Workstation as a TCP/IP Client."

5. A and C are correct. GSNW is only supported for Windows NT Server. For more information, see the section entitled "Implementing Windows NT Workstation as a Client in a NetWare Environment."

6. A is correct. The Microsoft Internet Service Manager is used to configure PWS after installation. For more information, see the section entitled " Configuring Peer Web Services."

7. A, B, and C are correct. NetBEUI does not support routing. For more information, see the section entitled "NetBEUI."

8. B, C, and D are correct. Windows NT Workstation 4.0 supports usage as a SLIP client, but not usage as a SLIP server. For more information, see the section entitled "Serial Line Internet Protocol."

9. A, B, and C are correct. DUN doesn't support XNS. For more information, see the section entitled "Configuring and Installing Dial-Up Networking in a Given Situation."

10. A, B, and C are correct. Services for Macintosh are only supported by Windows NT Server. For more information, see the section entitled "Network Protocols."

11. C is correct. The Workstation service is used to initiate I/O requests to network servers. For more information, see the section entitled "File System Drivers."

12. D is correct. A front-end process runs on a client. For more information, see the section entitled "Distributed Processing."

13. B is correct. You need to stop printing print banners. For more information, see the section entitled "Configuring CSNW."

14. B and D are correct. CSNW enables you to access files and printers on a NetWare server, it doesn't allow NetWare clients to access files and printers on a Windows NT computer. For more information, see the section entitled "Implementing Windows NT Workstation as a Client in a NetWare Environment."

15. C is correct. The Point-to-Point Multilink Protocol enables you to combine multiple physical links into one logical connection. For more information, see the section entitled "Point-to-Point Protocol."

16. B is correct. The Server service is used to receive I/O requests from network clients. For more information, see the section entitled "File System Drivers."

17. B and D are correct. Although NDIS 4.0 is the newest version, Windows NT 4.0 is also backward compatible with NDIS 3.0. For more information, see the section entitled "NDIS-Compatible Network Adapter Card Drivers."

18. D is correct. The Remote Access Service enables Windows NT computers to accept connections from remote clients. For more information, see the section entitled "Configuring and Installing Dial-Up Networking in a Given Situation."

19. A, B, and D are correct. You need to configure the default gateway to enable TCP/IP connectivity in a WAN. For more information, see the section entitled "Using Various Configurations to Install Windows NT Workstation as a TCP/IP Client."

20. D is correct. The TCP/IP protocol provides connectivity with the Internet. For more information, see the section entitled "TCP/IP."

Answers to Test Yourself Questions at the Beginning of the Chapter

1. Windows NT does not support the use of any 16-bit device drivers. You must use a device driver written to support Windows NT. For more information, see the section entitled "NDIS-Compatible Network Adapter Card Drivers."

2. NetBEUI is not normally supported by routers. Either configure your router to support NetBEUI or switch your network protocol to IPX or TCP/IP. For more information, see the section entitled "NetBEUI."

3. NWLink is not sufficient to support file and print connectivity to a NetWare server. You must also install CSNW. For more information, see the section entitled "NWLink IPX/SPX Compatible Transport."

4. Network bindings are the initial connection made between each protocol being used and the network card driver. For more information, see the section entitled "NDIS 4.0."

5. Windows NT supports an unlimited number of network adapters. (Your hardware, however, limits how many cards you can actually use.) For more information, see the section entitled "NDIS 4.0."

6. A Browse Master is responsible for maintaining a list of all the servers available on the network. For more information, see the section entitled "Network Neighborhood."

7. Net Use Lpt1: \\PRINTSERVE\HP5. For more information, see the section entitled "Universal Naming Convention."

8. You need to specify a default gateway when your TCP/IP computer needs to communicate with a computer located on a different physical network. For more information, see the section entitled "Using Various Configurations to Install Windows NT Workstation as a TCP/IP Client."

9. SLIP supports only TCP/IP. For more information, see the section entitled "Serial Line Internet Protocol (SLIP)."

10. Peer Web Services is intended for use as a small-scale web server. For more information, see the section entitled "Configuring Peer Web Services in a Given Situation."

Chapter

Running Applications

This chapter prepares you for the exam by covering the following objectives:

> ▶ Start applications on Intel and RISC platforms in various operating system environments
>
> ▶ Start applications at various priorities

Understanding how the Windows NT architecture handles applications from different operating systems enables an administrator to better work with the Windows NT operating system. Knowing what operating system's applications are supported and on what platforms of Windows NT is a major area of using the Windows NT operating system.

This chapter discusses the following areas of managing applications:

▶ Windows NT's architectural design, which enables Windows NT to support applications from other operating systems

▶ Specifics on how Windows NT handles DOS, Win16, Win32, OS/2, and POSIX applications on Intel and RISC platforms

▶ Starting applications at various priorities and changing the priority of a running application

Test Yourself! Before reading this chapter, test yourself to determine how much study time you will need to devote to this section.

1. What type of OS/2 character-based applications can a RISC-based Windows NT Workstation run?

2. Which environment subsystem requires case-sensitive file naming?

3. Which, by default, handles Symmetric Multi-Processing better: two MS-DOS–based applications or two Win16 applications?

4. How do you run a Windows 16-based application in its own memory space?

5. What three components of DirectX does Windows NT have support for out of the box?

6. Windows 32-bit applications are _____ compatible across platforms.

7. Windows 16-bit applications are _____ compatible across platforms.

8. What other operating systems' applications does Windows NT support with environment subsystems?

Answers are located at the end of the chapter...

Windows NT Architecture

 Objective

The Windows NT operating system was designed to handle applications from other operating systems. This capability was implemented by using environment subsystems.

The applications believe that they are running in their native environment because the environment subsystems provide application programming interfaces (APIs) that the foreign programs can recognize. The environment subsystems translate calls made by the application into commands that the Windows NT Executive can perform for the application.

Windows NT provides two subsystems that provide support for applications meant for other operating systems. The following operating systems are supported:

▶ OS/2 subsystem

▶ POSIX subsystem

These subsystems receive all programmatic calls from the applications that they support (see fig. 5.1). They either handle the request themselves or pass the request on to the Windows NT Executive Services or to the Win32 subsystem. The Win32 subsystem handles all error handling, application shutdown, and console applications display.

All basic operating systems' functions are handled by the Windows NT Executive Services, which resides in the Kernel mode. By being located in Kernel mode, the Executive Services provides stability in that no application can directly access the Executive Services. This prevents a malfunctioning user application from causing a Kernel-mode component from functioning.

All graphics-related requests are passed to the Win32K Windows Manager and GDI component of Executive Services. Using a common executive service ensures that users of applications are provided a consistent user interface.

Figure 5.1

The Windows NT architecture.

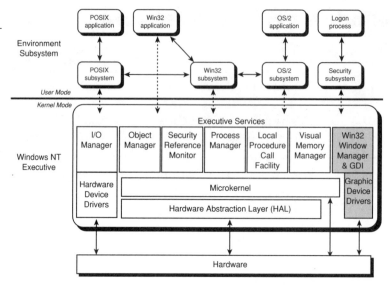

 Note

The moving of the Win32K Windows Manager and GDI to the Kernel mode is a major change in the Windows NT architecture. In version 3.x of Windows NT, this component was located in User mode. By moving this component to Kernel mode, great enhancements in GUI speed were achieved.

Building each subsystem into the Windows NT architectural model eliminates duplication of services in the environment subsystems. The I/O Manager executive service, for example, handles any disk input/output activity. Having each subsystem rely on the Executive Services makes possible the easier creation of future environment subsystems. It also makes maintenance easier because only Executive Services needs to be updated rather than every environment subsystem.

Windows NT Supported Subsystems

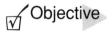 Objective

Windows NT is designed to run applications originally designed to run under other operating systems. Windows NT can support running applications designed for the following operating systems:

- Windows 95 and Windows NT

- MS-DOS

- Windows 3.x

- OS/2

- POSIX

Windows NT accomplishes this by using the subsystems discussed in the following sections.

Win32 Subsystem Support

The Win32 subsystem (also known as the Client/Server subsystem) supports all 32-bit Windows applications and the rest of the environment subsystems.

Some of the primary features of Win-32 bit applications include the following:

- Reliability due to each application having its own 2 GB address space

- Support of multithreaded applications

- Take advantage of multiprocessor systems

- Take advantage of preemptive multitasking

Each Windows 32-bit application runs in its own 2 GB address space (see fig. 5.2). This design prevents one 32-bit application from overwriting the memory space of another 32-bit application. In other words, a failure of one 32-bit application does not affect other running 32-bit applications.

The major advantage of 32-bit applications over 16-bit applications is that they can be multithreaded. Each Windows NT process requires at least one thread. These threads enable execution to be scheduled. 32-bit applications can have more than one thread of execution.

Figure 5.2

Memory spaces for 32-bit programs.

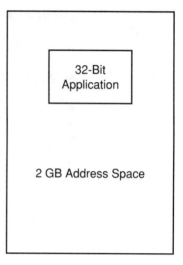

The most common example of a multithreaded application is a 32-bit setup program. A 32-bit setup program generally has the following three threads of execution:

▶ A decompression thread that decompresses all files from a centralized archive file

▶ A copying thread that copies the decompressed files to the appropriate installation directory

▶ A system configuration thread that modifies all necessary configuration files to enable the application to execute correctly

The threads of execution, while independent of each other, must be timed correctly by the developer of the application. The copying thread must wait for the decompression thread to have expanded the necessary file before placing it in the proper directory. Likewise, the system configuration thread must ensure that a file has been copied to the proper directory if it needs to execute the program to enable configuration to take place. Figure 5.3 shows a typical setup progress meter for a 32-bit setup program. Note that there are separate setup bars for progress of expansion, copying, and configuration.

Figure 5.3

*A 32-bit setup
program progress
meter.*

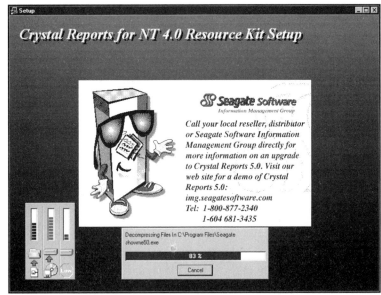

Note

Multiple threads in a process share the same memory space. It is imperative that they do not overwrite other threads' address space.

Having multiple threads also enables 32-bit applications to take full advantage of Windows NT's capability to support Symmetric Multi-Processing (SMP). SMP enables each thread of an application to execute on the first available processor. Figure 5.4 shows how the capability of using Symmetric Multi-Processing can lead to improvements on execution time by splitting threads between processors. Both threads 1 and 2 display an improvement in execution time due to less time spent in wait states waiting for the other thread to relinquish control of the processor. Windows NT 32-bit multithreaded applications can take full advantage of a multi-processor system.

Figure 5.4

Comparison of a single processor and multi-processor system.

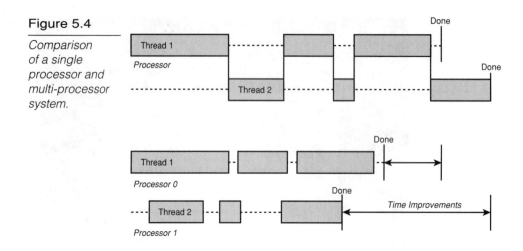

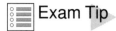 **Exam Tip**

One of the most common exam questions relates to multi-processing. Remember that Windows NT supports *Symmetric Multi-Processing* (SMP). This enables Windows NT to use whichever processor is available instead of scheduling the O/S to use one processor and applications to use the other processor(s). Under *Asymmetric Multi-Processing* (ASMP), operating systems set aside one or more processors for the exclusive use of the operating system. Windows NT uses SMP because it provides better load balancing between processors. It also provides a degree of fault tolerance. This is because a processor failure in a multi-processor system results only in a degradation of performance. In an ASMP system, this can lead to the entire operating system crashing.

Finally, 32-bit applications can take part in preemptive multitasking. Rather than having the operating system wait for a thread to voluntarily relinquish control of the processor (as Windows 16 applications did), the operating system can interrupt a thread when one of the following events occurs:

▶ A thread has run for a specified length of time.

▶ A thread with a higher priority has become ready to execute.

The scheduling of threads by the operating system makes it more unlikely that an application will monopolize the processor.

OLE / ActiveX

Windows NT 32-bit applications are capable of performing object linking and embedding (OLE) with other 32-bit applications and 16-bit applications. The OLE is not limited to just other 32-bit applications.

Object linking and embedding makes creating compound documents possible. An object from one application can be embedded or linked into another application's data. By embedding an object, the data can be edited in its native format. Linking an object enables changes to the original object to be reflected in the host document.

Figure 5.5 shows an example of a linked Excel chart in Microsoft Word.

Figure 5.5

A linked Excel chart in Microsoft Word.

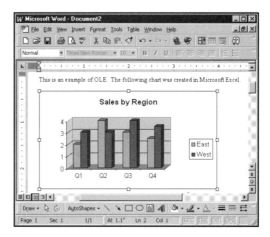

Because the spreadsheet is linked into the Word document, any changes made to the original Excel spreadsheet are reflected in the Word document when it is opened. Likewise, double-clicking on the linked chart can make changes to the Excel chart easily. This will lead to the chart being edited in Microsoft Excel and the original source data document will be opened for editing.

ActiveX, like OLE, is based on the Component Object Model. ActiveX specializes in embedding control into web-based sites, enabling web pages to respond to events instead of remaining static at all times.

ActiveX adds new innovations to the Internet. ActiveX controls enable web developers to implement many features in a web page, including the following:

▶ Designating a life span on an embedded object on a web page. After an object's deadline passes, it no longer displays on the page. This works very well for limited-time offers on a web page.

▶ Adding additional animation to a web page.

▶ Adding preprogrammed ActiveX objects to a web page that are readily available instead of developing them yourself. In fact, you need no knowledge whatsoever about how the control was actually developed.

▶ Adding increased functionality to web pages, more like that commonly found in dialog boxes, such as combo boxes and scroll bars.

 Note

The ActiveX Control Pad can be used to easily add prefabricated ActiveX controls into your web pages. You can download the ActiveX Control Pad for free from Microsoft's web site.

When a web page that has an ActiveX control within it is accessed, the user should be warned that an ActiveX control is about to be downloaded to his or her system. Depending on the security level set in Internet Explorer, the user is then asked whether the download should proceed. If the control makes use of Authenticode, a digital certificate displays (see fig. 5.6).

The digital signature information is stored within the control itself. The end user has the option of downloading or not downloading the control. The user can also set the automatic downloading of any further controls from the same developer.

Figure 5.6

*VeriSign
Authenticode
certificate for an
ActiveX object.*

Caution

ActiveX controls have the potential to be quite harmful. Be wary of installing ActiveX controls if you are uncertain of their origin. It is possible for damage to occur to your system if a "suspect" ActiveX control is downloaded. One of the best ways of protecting yourself is by setting your security level in Internet Explorer. On the Security tab of the View Options in Internet Explorer you can set the safety level (see fig. 5.7). Internet Explorer 3.02 changed the default level to a high safety level. This prevents any ActiveX control from being downloaded to your system, because they may be a danger to your computer.

Figure 5.7

*Setting the safety
level in Internet
Explorer.*

OpenGL

Windows NT supports the industry-standard graphics language known as OpenGL. OpenGL provides a software interface for creating two-dimensional and three-dimensional graphics. The only difference between OpenGL in Windows NT and Unix and other Windows implementations is that Windows NT supports VGA 16-color mode graphics.

Several OpenGL screen savers ship with Windows NT. Although these savers are good examples of the OpenGL capabilities, they are also quite resource intensive. You should not implement them on production file, print, or application servers.

 Note

The OpenGL screen savers contain several "Easter eggs." Two of the better-known Easter eggs are as follows:

▶ The OpenGL 3D Text screen saver has several hidden message text strings over the versions of Windows NT. Windows NT 4 includes an Easter egg that displays all the volcanoes located in Washington. To view these volcano names, set the text field to "volcano" as shown in figure 5.8. This causes the screen saver to display a random list of volcanoes.

Figure 5.8

The Volcano Easter egg.

▶ The OpenGL Mixed Pipes screen saver has another Easter egg hidden within its settings. If you set the joint type to Mixed in the 3D Pipe screen saver settings, the screen saver periodically draws a teapot as an elbow joint. Figure 5.9 shows the settings for this.

Figure 5.9

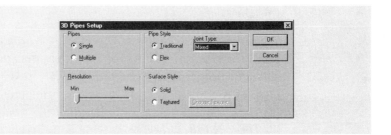

Mixed Pipe drawing the Teapot Easter egg.

Windows NT supports the following three graphics modes for OpenGL:

▶ Software rendering mode

▶ 3D accelerated mode

▶ OpenGL accelerated mode

Software rendering mode enables OpenGL to work with any Windows NT–supported video adapter. All OpenGL calls are executed using the Windows NT GDI. This mode does not take advantage of accelerated video cards.

3D accelerated mode is required when the user need to do serious graphics work such as animation or computer aided design (CAD). In this mode, graphic card vendors provide device drivers optimized for performance of OpenGL applications. The 3D drivers convert OpenGL calls to functions supported on the video card. This removes the execution from software calls to the actual hardware, resulting in a performance gain.

OpenGL accelerated mode is used by Windows NT Workstation when the workstation has workstation-class 3D graphics hardware. These adapters contain 3D OpenGL functionality, and any OpenGL calls are passed straight to the hardware. This is the best performing mode for OpenGL support because it removes all execution from software to hardware.

DirectX

Windows NT now supports DirectX for Win32 applications. DirectX for Windows NT 4 supports the application entry points called by programs designed for DirectX in Windows 95. This enables you to run DirectX programs unchanged under Windows NT even though they are not handled the same as under Windows 95. DirectX is designed to provide better response times to the following areas:

▶ DirectDraw provides accelerated drawing to the screen. This version of the DirectDraw API does not directly access the hardware as in Windows 95. Instead, it provides a thin layer above the actual hardware that maintains Windows NT device independence from the actual drivers. This more closely follows the Windows NT architecture. The GDI mediates the DirectDraw functions.

▶ DirectSound provides accelerated audio features. The DirectSound API gives you control over volume and real-time mixing of audio streams. Under Windows NT, there is no actual acceleration. Application entry points are provided for DirectSound calls, but these functions are emulated and are not in an accelerated format.

▶ DirectPlay provides easier communication over a network. It provides simpler methods for allowing communication to take place over networks using TCP/IP or NWLink IPX/SPX. Support is also provided for modem connections using the Windows Telephone API (TAPI).

Supporting MS-DOS Applications

Windows NT supports any MS-DOS applications that do not attempt to directly access hardware. The Windows NT architecture does not allow any User mode processes to directly access the system hardware.

MS-DOS applications run in a special Win32 application known as a Windows NT Virtual DOS Machine (NTVDM). The NTVDM creates a pseudo MS-DOS environment in which the application is capable of running. Each NTVDM has a single thread of execution and its own address space. This enables preemptive multitasking between MS-DOS applications and protection from other MS-DOS application failure. The following components make up the NTVDM:

▶ **NTVDM.EXE**—Provides the MS-DOS emulation and manages the NTVDM.

▶ **NTIO.SYS**—The NTVDM's equivalent of IO.SYS in MS-DOS.

▶ **NTDOS.SYS**—The NTVDM's equivalent of the MS-DOS kernel.

▶ **Instruction Execution Unit (IEU)**—On RISC systems, this emulates an Intel 80486 microprocessor. On x86 computers, the IEU acts as a trap handler. Any instructions that cause hardware traps have their control transferred to the code in Windows NT that handles them.

 Note

Prior to Windows NT 4.0, NTVDMs provided only 80286 emulation. This did not greatly affect MS-DOS applications, but it did affect Win16 applications because they could only run in Standard mode, not 386 Enhanced mode.

Figure 5.10 shows the components of the NTVDM and the communication between the various components.

Because applications cannot directly access the hardware in the Windows NT architectural model, the NTVDM's virtual device drivers intercept any attempt by an application to access the hardware. The Virtual Device Drivers translate the calls to 32-bit calls and pass them to the Windows NT 32-bit device drivers. This entire process is hidden from the MS-DOS–based applications. Provided Virtual Device Drivers include drivers for the mouse, keyboard, parallel ports, and COM ports.

Figure 5.10

The components of an NTVDM.

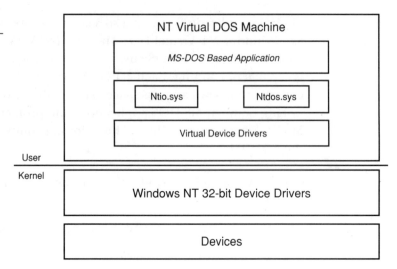

Caution

If a Virtual Device Driver does not exist for a hardware device, any application trying to access this hardware directly cannot run in an NTVDM. Many MS-DOS applications do not execute in Windows NT for this reason.

Configuration of an Windows NT Virtual DOS Machine is performed through customizing the application's Program Information File (PIF). A shortcut created to any MS-DOS application is assigned the extension PIF. To modify an application's PIF settings, just right-click on the shortcut to the application and choose Properties from the pop-up menu.

Configuring the Program Properties of a PIF

The Program dialog box of a PIF enables you to configure default locations for where a program is located on the hard disk and the directory in which the program will execute (see fig. 5.11).

Figure 5.11

The Program dialog box of PIF settings.

Table 5.1 shows the settings that you can configure in the Program Property dialog box.

Table 5.1

Program Property Settings

Setting	Meaning
Cmd Line	The full path to the MS-DOS application's executable file.
Working	Default directory to which you want to save an application's data files.
Batch File	The name of a batch file that runs each time the application is run (only functional in the Windows 95 operating system).
Shortcut key	Used to set a shortcut key combination to launch the application. To remove a shortcut key combination, use the Backspace key.
Run	Determines what windows state the program starts in. Choices include normal windows, minimized, or maximized.
Close on Exit	When selected, automatically closes the MS-DOS window in which the MS-DOS application runs.
Windows NT	Enables the application to specify tailored Autoexec and Config files that are processed every time the application is run.
Change Icon	Enables the user to change the icon displayed for the shortcut.

Each MS-DOS shortcut can point to a different Autoexec and Config file. By default, these are Autoexec.nt and Config.nt located in the %Systemroot%\System32 directory. These configuration files must follow MS-DOS 5.0 conventions. This does not include multiple configurations.

Configuring the Memory Properties of a PIF

Running MS-DOS applications under Windows NT does ease one area of configuration. MS-DOS applications use one of two methods for providing additional memory beyond conventional memory:

▶ Expanded memory

▶ Extended memory

To configure these types of additional memory, configuration changes had to be made to the Config.sys file by modifying the Himem.sys and Emm386.exe drivers. In addition, you had to reboot the system every time a configuration change was made to see the results.

In Windows NT, these configuration changes have been moved from the Config.sys to the Memory Property tab of a PIF (see fig. 5.12).

Figure 5.12

The Memory tab of PIF settings.

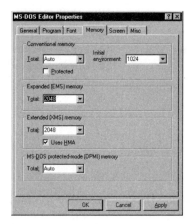

You can use the Memory dialog box of a PIF to allocate the exact amount of expanded memory specification (EMS) or extended memory specification (XMS) to allocate to a program. Rather than having to reboot the system, the application needs only to be restarted for the new settings to take effect. You can also use the Memory page to set the amount of environment space that will be allocated to the Windows NT Virtual DOS Machine. The environment space is used to store all environment variables declared for the application.

Tip

One of the most difficult configurations for a DOS application is the proper memory setting. Most applications support only EMS or XMS memory. Be certain to select the appropriate type of memory to provide. If an application states that it is LIM compatible, you need to provide EMS memory. If the application uses DPMI, you need to provide XMS memory.

Configuring a PIF's Miscellaneous Settings

Because Windows NT supports multitasking, one key setting to change for a PIF is to enable an application to run in the background. To do this, clear the Always Suspend option on the Misc tab of a PIF (see fig. 5.13).

Figure 5.13

The Misc tab of PIF settings.

Another area commonly configured is the Windows Shortcut Keys section. By clearing any of the key combinations in this section, the user removes that key combination from the set of predefined Windows NT key combinations. Table 5.2 shows the Windows NT definitions of the provided key combinations.

Table 5.2

Windows NT Special Key Combinations	
Key Combination	Windows NT Meaning
Alt+Tab	This key combination is commonly used for switching between running applications. It makes use of a pop-up window that shows the icons of the running applications.
Ctrl+Esc	This key combination activates the Start menu.
Alt+PrtSc	This key combination is used to capture the active window to the Windows NT clipboard.
Alt+Space	This key combination activates the Control menu of the running applications.
Alt+Esc	This key combination also enables the user to switch between running applications. It is processed by pulling each application to the foreground.
PrtSc	This key captures the entire screen to the Windows NT clipboard. This is the most commonly disabled Windows NT key. Many MS-DOS programs require the capability to have the Print Screen key print the current window to the printer. This is accomplished by clearing the PrtSc option.
Alt+Enter	This key combination switches an MS-DOS application between full screen and windowed mode.

Supporting Win16 Applications

Windows 16-bit applications are supported in Windows NT using Win16 on Win32 (WOW). Figure 5.14 shows the Win16 on Win32 architecture.

Note that the WOW environment runs within a Windows NT Virtual DOS Machine. This is just like Windows 3.x, which ran over MS-DOS. Table 5.3 describes the WOW components.

Figure 5.14

The Win16 on Win32 (WOW) architecture.

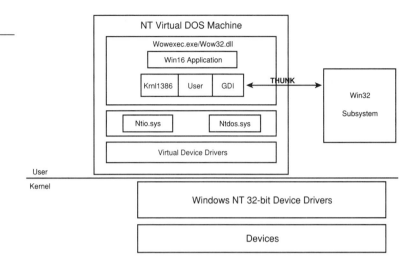

Table 5.3

WOW Components

Component	Functionality
Wowexec.exe	The Wowexec provides the Windows 3.1 emulation for the NTVDM.
WOW32.dll	The supporting dynamic link library for the Wowexec.
Win16 application	The Windows 16-bit application that is being executed. This application must not use any Windows 16-bit VxDs. Support may not be provided for them in Windows NT.
Krnl386.exe	This is a modified version of the Windows 3.x kernel. It translates calls meant for the Windows 3.x kernel to Win32 calls. Basic operating system functions are handled by Krnl386.exe.
User.exe	The User.exe is a modified version of the Windows 3.x User.exe. It handles all user interface API calls and translates them to Win32 calls.
Gdi.exe	The Gdi.exe captures API calls related to graphics and printing. These calls are translated to Win32 calls.

Based on the API calls that an application makes, either the Krnl386.exe, User.exe, or Gdi.exe intercepts the calls and translates them into Win32 calls. This process is known as *thunking*. Also, any responses from the Win32 services must be translated back to 16-bit responses. The time spent translating the calls is offset by the speed increases of executing 32-bit instructions.

Running Multiple Win16 Applications

By default, the WOW environment provides non-preemptive multitasking as provided in Windows 3.x. This means that control of the processor is voluntarily given up by one application to give another application access to the processor. The implication of this is that one 16-bit application can cause another 16-bit application to fail.

By default, Windows NT starts each 16-bit Windows application in the same Windows NT Virtual DOS Machine. All Win16 applications share a single thread of execution. If one Win16 application were to hang, all other Win16 applications would also hang. Figure 5.15 demonstrates how Windows NT handles multitasking with Windows 16- and 32-bit applications.

Figure 5.15

Multitasking with Win16 and Win32 applications.

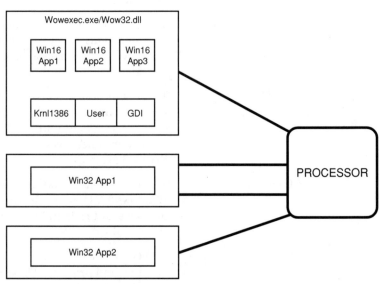

Win16 App1, Win16 App2, and Win16 App3 are all running within a single NTVDM. Within the NTVDM, the three Win16 applications are non-preemptively multitasked. The NTVDM does have one thread of execution. This thread is preemptively multitasked with the two threads of Win32 App1 and the one thread of Win32 App2. If one of the Win16 applications were to fail, they would affect only the other Win16 applications that share its memory space within the NTVDM. They would not affect the two Win32 applications because they are being run in their own memory space.

 Note

You can determine what Win16 applications are running by viewing the processes in the Task Manager. Figure 5.16 shows that Spind16.exe, Capture.exe, and Badapp16.exe are all running within the same NTVDM.

Figure 5.16

Viewing Multiple Win16 applications running within a Common NTVDM.

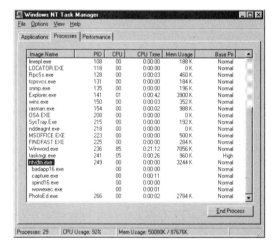

Running Win16 Applications in Individual NTVDMs

Win16 applications can be executed within their own individual NTVDM under Windows NT. This is done by configuring the Win16 application to run in a separate memory space. Architecturally, this generates a separate NTVDM with its own WOW environment for each Win16 application. This enables Win16 applications to now preemptively multitask because each Win16 application's NTVDM will have a separate thread of execution.

Figure 5.17 shows the same three Win16 applications executing under Windows NT, but now configured to each run in its own NTVDM.

Figure 5.17

Viewing multiple Win16 applications running in separate NTVDMs.

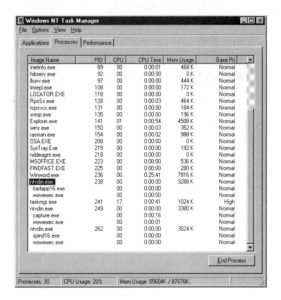

The reasons for running Win16 applications in their own memory space include the following:

▶ Win16 applications will now use preemptive multitasking. An ill-behaved Win16 application will now enable other Win16 applications to continue to execute normally because each Win16 application will have its own memory space and thread of execution.

▶ Win16 applications will now be more reliable because they will not be affected by the problems of other Win16 applications.

▶ Win16 applications can now take advantage of multi-processor computers. When Win16 applications are run in a common NTVDM, they must share a single thread of execution. The generation of individual NTVDMs also creates individual threads of execution. Each thread can potentially be executed on a different processor. The operating system could now schedule each NTVDM's thread of execution to run on whichever processor is available. When multiple processors exist, this can now lead to multi-processing. If the Win16 applications were running in a common NTVDM, their single thread of execution would only be able to run on a single processor, no matter how many processors existed on the computer.

▶ Windows NT will enable Win16 applications running in separate memory spaces to continue to participate in OLE and dynamic data exchange (DDE).

As with any configuration change, there are some trade-offs for the advantages gained by running Win16 applications in separate memory spaces. These trade-offs include the following:

▶ There is additional overhead in running each separate NTVDM. In figure 5.16, for example, 3244 K was allocated to the shared NTVDM. In figure 5.17, however, where each Win16 application is run in a separate memory space, there is a total of 9648 K of memory to support the three separate NTVDMs. If you do not have enough memory installed on the server, this could result in a decrease in performance of the system.

▶ Some older Win16 applications did not use the standards of OLE and DDE. These applications would not function properly if they were run in separate memory spaces. These applications must be run in a common memory space to function correctly. Lotus for Windows 1.0 is an example of this type of application.

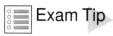 Exam Tip

Expect at least one question on running Win16 applications in separate memory spaces. The key concept is that you can only load multiple Win16 applications into the same memory space if it is the initial Win16 NTVDM. It is not possible, for example, to run Word for Windows 6.0 and Excel for Windows 5.0 in one shared memory space and PowerPoint 4.0 and Access 2.0 in another shared memory space.

Note You have several ways to kill a non-responsive program. These include ending the process by using Task Manager or the POSIX Kill command from the Windows NT Resource Kit. You can also use the Remote Kill command from the Windows NT Resource Kit to kill processes on a remote computer running the Remote Kill Service.

Configuring Win16 Applications to Run in Separate Memory Spaces

There are a few ways to run Win16 applications in separate memory spaces. These include the following:

▶ Any time you start a Win16 application from the Start menu using the Run option, you can select the Run in Separate Memory Space option (see fig. 5.18).

Figure 5.18

Running a Win16 application in its own memory space by using the Start menu.

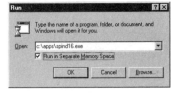

Note The Run in Separate Memory Space option is available only when you type in the path to a Win16 application. This is not available for any other types of applications because by default they run in their own memory space. Only Win16 applications will share the same memory space by default.

▶ At a Command prompt, you can start a Win16 application by typing **start /separate application**.

▶ Any shortcuts that point to Win16 applications can be configured on the Shortcut tab of the Spinner Properties dialog box to always run in a separate memory space (see fig. 5.19).

Figure 5.19

*Configuring a
shortcut to run a
Win16 application
in a separate
memory space.*

▶ The final way to configure a Win16 application to run in a separate memory space enables you to configure any file with the same extension to always run in a separate memory space when the data document is double-clicked on in the Windows NT Explorer. Editing the File Types tab of the View, Options properties, does this. To configure this type of process, follow these steps:

1. Start the Windows NT Explorer.

2. From the View menu, choose Options.

3. Click on the File Types tab.

4. If your default application to display bitmap images was a 16-bit Windows application, you can change its properties for execution, by first selecting Bitmap Image from the Registered File Types list and then clicking on the Edit button.

5. From the list of possible actions, select Open and click on the Edit button to modify the Open action.

6. Figure 5.20 shows how the Application Used to Perform Action option was changed to run the executable Imgmgr.exe in a separate memory space. The executable was set to be cmd /c start /separate c:\cw\imgmgr.exe %1.

Figure 5.20

Configuring the Open action to always run in a separate memory space.

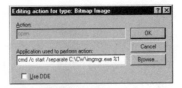

Supporting OS/2 Applications Under Windows NT

Windows NT has limited support for OS/2 applications. By default the following is supported under Windows NT:

▶ OS/2 1.x-character-based applications are supported only on the Intel platform running the OS/2 subsystem.

▶ If the OS/2 applications make any calls to the Presentation Manager, they are not by default supported in the OS/2 subsystem.

▶ OS/2 applications can be executed on RISC-based Windows NT systems if the OS/2 applications are *Bound* applications. Bound applications are applications that have been written to execute in either OS/2 or MS-DOS. Because there is no OS/2 subsystem for RISC-based systems, these bound applications execute only in an NTVDM.

You can force a Bound application to execute in a NTVDM on an Intel-based Windows NT system by using the *Forcedos* command. By default though, Bound applications always choose to run in the OS/2 subsystem because they execute faster in their native environment.

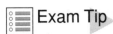

Expect at least one exam question that deals with the concept of Bound applications and the Forcedos command. Remember also that the only way to execute OS/2 applications on RISC-based systems is to use the Forcedos command for Bound applications.

Configuring OS/2 Applications

As with all Windows NT configurations, the configuration data is stored within the Windows NT Registry. This configuration data is stored in the following two locations:

▶ Hkey_Local_Machine\System\CurrentControlSet\Control\Session Manager\Subsystems

▶ Hkey_local_machine\Software\Microsoft\OS/2 Subsystem for NT

OS/2 itself stores all its configuration information in the files Config.sys and Startup.cmd. When the OS/2 subsystem is started (when an OS/2 application is executed), Windows NT interprets the Config.sys and Startup.cmd files and adds the necessary configuration information to its Registry.

The suggested method to configure the OS/2 subsystem is to edit the Config.sys file with an OS/2 text editor. It is imperative that an OS/2 text editor is used because it places a header into the file that indicates that it is an OS/2 configuration file.

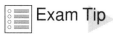 Exam Tip

A common scenario question on the exam tests your knowledge of configuring the OS/2 subsystem. Typical questions test you on the fact that the Config.sys file must be edited with an OS/2 text editor.

Windows NT Add-On Subsystem for Presentation Manager

Windows NT 4 added supported for 16-bit OS/2 1.x Presentation Manager applications. Previous versions of Windows NT provided no support for Presentation Manager–dependent applications. This support is provided by the Add-on Subsystem for Presentation Manager. This subsystem replaces the OS/2 Subsystem on Intel-based Windows NT systems. It is not available for RISC-based systems.

Note This add-on subsystem is not provided free of charge. You must purchase it separately in addition to Windows NT.

Table 5.4 shows the components of the Add-on Subsystem for Presentation Manager. An executed Presentation Manager application generates a separate Presentation Manager desktop. This desktop is *not* integrated with the Windows NT desktop.

Table 5.4

Add-On Subsystem for Presentation Manager

Component	Functionality
OS2.exe, OS2srv.exe, OS2ss.exe, and Netetapi.dll	Updated versions of the OS/2 Subsystem support files that now support Presentation Manager applications.
Pmntdd.sys Pmwindll, Display.dll, Pmgre.dll, and others	The Presentation Manager Device Driver. 16-bit OS/2 support DLLs for Presentation Manager applications.
Pmshell.exe	The Presentation Manager desktop that is executed first so that a Presentation Manager application has a desktop in which to function.
Pmspool.exe	The Presentation Manager Print Manager application.
Pmcpl.exe	The Presentation Manager Control Panel.
Sample applications	Some sample Presentation Manager applications are provided with the Add-on Subsystem.

Removing Support for OS/2 Subsystem

The Windows NT Resource Kit includes a utility called the C2 Configuration Tool. The National Computer Security Center has created a set of security standards that have been called the Orange Book. Windows NT 3.5x was evaluated as being C2 secure according to the specifications of the Orange Book. The Windows NT operating system supports security that is not part of the C2 security definition.

The OS/2 Subsystem is not included in the current C2 security definition. To meet the C2 security standards, the OS/2 Subsystem should be disabled. The C2 Configuration Tool accomplishes this by deleting the OS2.exe and OS2ss.exe files from the %systemroot%\system32 subdirectory.

 Note

Another reason to disable the OS/2 Subsystem is because you are not using any OS/2 applications. If you need to restore the OS/2 Subsystem, OS2.exe and OS2ss.exe must be restored from the original Windows NT distribution files. To do this, you use the Expand command.

The steps to disable the OS/2 Subsystem are as follows:

1. Start the C2 Configuration Tool. By default, it is located by choosing from the Start menu, Programs, Resource Kit 4.0, Configuration, C2 Configuration.

2. In the list of Security Features, select the OS/2 Subsystem entry.

3. Double-click on the OS/2 Subsystem entry. A dialog box appears (see fig. 5.21).

Figure 5.21

Disabling the OS/2 Subsystem.

4. Click on the OK button to disable the OS/2 Subsystem. A confirmation dialog box asks you to verify that you do wish to remove the OS/2 Subsystem from the computer and tells you that this is not reversible. If this is acceptable, click on the OK button.

5. The icon to the left of the OS/2 Subsystem now appears as a red, closed lock, indicating full C2 Orange Book compliance.

Supporting POSIX Applications

POSIX (Portable Operating System Interfaced based on Unix) support is provided in Windows NT due to a U.S. government requirement for government computing contracts. By including support for POSIX applications, Windows NT can be considered for government quotes. The implementation of POSIX in Windows NT enables portability of common applications from a Unix system to Windows NT running the POSIX subsystem.

Table 5.5 describes the components that comprise the POSIX Subsystem.

Table 5.5

POSIX Subsystem Components

Component	Functionality
Psxss.exe	The POSIX server, which is the main component of the POSIX Subsystem. It is initialized when the first POSIX application is run.
Posix.exe	The Console Session Manager is a Windows NT 32-bit application that handles all communication between the POSIX Subsystem and the Windows NT Executive Services.
Psxdll.dll	The dynamic link library support files that handle communications between POSIX applications and the Psxss.exe, the POSIX server.

 Note

The POSIX Subsystem does not load until a POSIX application is executed. The POSIX Subsystem can support up to 32 concurrent POSIX applications.

Windows NT provides POSIX.1 support in its POSIX Subsystem. POSIX.1 defines a C language, source-code-level application programming interface (API) to an operating system environment. To have full POSIX.1 compliance, the NTFS file system must be implemented on the computer that will be executing POSIX applications. This provides the user with the following POSIX.1 compliance features:

- ▶ **Case-sensitive file naming.** NTFS preserves case for both directories and file names.

- ▶ **Hard links.** POSIX applications can store the same data in two differently named files.

- ▶ **An additional time stamp on files.** This tracks the last time the file was accessed. The default on FAT volumes is when the file was last modified.

Modifying Support for the POSIX Subsystem

For full POSIX.1 compliance, one of the Windows NT user rights must be modified. By default the user right Bypass Traverse Checking is granted to the special group Everyone. This right enables a user to change directories through a directory tree even if the user has no permission for those directories. This user right must be disabled for any accounts that will be using POSIX applications.

To disable the Bypass Traverse Checking right, follow these steps:

1. Start the User Manager. Be certain to be logged on as a member of the Administrators local group.

2. Create a Global group that contains all users that will *not* be running POSIX applications. It is imperative that no POSIX users be members of this Global group.

3. From the Policies menu, choose User Rights.

4. Ensure that the Show Advanced User Rights check box is selected.

5. Select the User Right Bypass Traverse Checking User Right.

6. Click on Remove to remove the Everyone Group.

7. Click on the Add button and select the New Global Group of Non-POSIX users that you created in step 2, and then click on the OK button to add this group.

8. Click on the OK button to complete this user rights change.

Removing Support for the POSIX Subsystem

Like the OS/2 Subsystem, you can also disable the POSIX Subsystem through the C2 Configuration Tool in the Windows NT Resource Kit because it is not included in the current C2 security definition. The C2 Configuration Tool accomplishes this by deleting the Psxss.exe file from the %systemroot%\system32 subdirectory.

To disable the POSIX subsystem, follow these steps:

1. Start the C2 Configuration Tool. By default, it is located by choosing from the Start menu, Programs, Resource Kit 4.0, Configuration, C2 Configuration.

2. In the list of Security Features, double-click on the POSIX Subsystem entry.

3. Click on the OK button to disable the POSIX Subsystem.

4. Click on the OK button to confirm that you do wish to permanently remove support for the POSIX Subsystem.

5. The icon to the left of the POSIX Subsystem now appears as a red, closed lock, indicating full C2 Orange Book compliance.

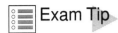 Exam Tip

Most exam questions on the POSIX Subsystem focus on what features of NTFS provide support for POSIX.1 requirements. These are case-sensitive file naming, hard links, and access date information. Remember that if a POSIX application does not access file system resources, they can run on the FAT file system.

Application Support on RISC and Intel Platforms

Although you can run Windows NT on both the Intel and RISC platforms, there are compatibility issues when considering applications to support. Applications are either *source-compatible* or *binary-compatible*. Source-compatible applications must be recompiled for each hardware platform that they are going to be executed on. Binary-compatible applications can run on any Windows NT platform without recompiling the application. Table 5.6 outlines application compatibility on the Windows NT platforms.

Table 5.6

Application Compatibility Across Windows NT Platforms

Platform	MS-DOS	Win16	Win32	OS/2	POSIX
Intel	Binary	Binary	Source	Binary	Source
Alpha	Binary	Binary	Source*	Binary**	Source
Mips	Binary	Binary	Source	Binary**	Source
PowerPC	Binary	Binary	Source	Binary**	Source

* Third-party utilities such as Digital FX!32 enable Win32-based Intel programs to execute on Digital Alpha AXP microprocessors. Although these utilities are interpreting the code on the fly, they end up performing faster on the Alpha due to the increase speed of the processor.

** Only Bound applications can be run on the three RISC hardware platforms. They will run in a Windows NTVDM because the OS/2 Subsystem is not provided in RISC-based versions of Windows NT.

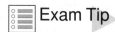 **Exam Tip**

Typically, the exam tests your knowledge of the terms *source* and *binary compatible.* Be certain to know the difference and how each type of application is supported on each platform.

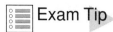 **Exam Tip**

Although products such as Digital's FX!32 exist, the exam still considers that Win32-based applications are source-compatible across platforms.

Building Distributed Applications Across Platforms with DCOM

Distributed application development is based on creating applications made up of multiple components that can be spread across multiple platforms. The Distributed Component Object Model (DCOM) integrates the following features to make the rapid development of distributed applications possible:

▶ Communications between components over connection and connectionless network transports. These include TCP/IP, UDP/IP, IPX/SPX, AppleTalk, HTTP, and Remote Procedure Calls (RPCs). These objects can communicate over public networks such as the Internet.

▶ DCOM is an open technology capable of running on multiple implementations of Unix-based systems, including Solaris.

▶ DCOM can lead to lower integration costs because DCOM is based on a common set of interfaces for software programs. This will lead to a lesser requirement for customization when implementing components from outside vendors.

▶ DCOM supports remote activation. A client can just start an application by calling a component on another computer.

▶ DCOM is capable of implementing Internet certificate-based security or Windows NT–based Challenge/Response security. This ensures the best of both worlds for security. Security is supported for the launch of objects, access to objects, and context. Security can also be based on whether the application is launched locally or remotely.

In a pure Windows NT environment, RPCs can be used to allow communication between and interoperability between various DCOM objects. RPCs make it possible for an application to execute procedures and call objects on other remote computers.

Figure 5.22 shows how a client application can call an object on a remote server.

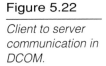

Figure 5.22

Client to server communication in DCOM.

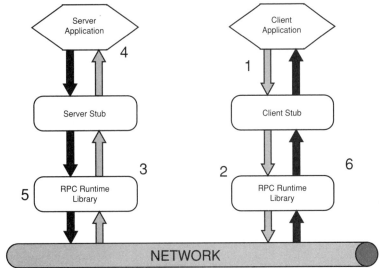

The flow of communication for a DCOM application is as follows when a client makes a call to a DCOM object located on another server:

1. A client initiates a Remote Procedure Call.

2. The RPC client stub packages the call for transport across the network. The RPC runtime library on the client transmits the package to the indicated server. The server is found by using a name resolution method. This could include NetBIOS Name Server or Domain Name Server methods.

3. The RPC runtime library on the server receives the package, forwards it to its own RPC stub, which converts the package into the same RPC that was sent from the client.

4. The Remote Procedure Call is carried out at the security level specified in the Server object.

5. The RPC Server stub packages the results of the procedure call and the Server's RPC runtime library transmits this package back to the calling client application.

6. The RPC runtime library on the client receives the package, forwards it to the client's RPC stub, which unpacks the data for the client application to use.

Windows NT 4 includes DCOM support out of the box. The DCOM configuration tool including with Windows NT is called Dcomcnfg.exe (see fig. 5.23).

Figure 5.23

Configuring DCOM properties for a DCOM-enabled application.

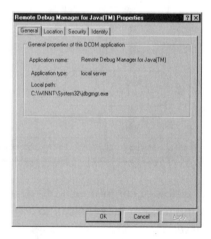

You can configure the following parameters for an application with the DCOM Configuration tool:

▶ **The General tab.** Indicates the name of the DCOM application, whether the application is located on the local system or on a remote computer, and the path to the application's executable.

▶ **The Location tab.** Enables you to set the distributive properties for an application. The administrator can set whether the application is to run on the local computer, the computer where the data is located, or on another computer designated on the network.

▶ **The Security tab.** Enables you to set the permissions for accessing the DCOM application, launching or executing the DCOM application, and configuration, which determines which users can modify the application's DCOM configuration.

▶ **The Identity tab.** Enables the administrator to specify what security context the object will be executed in. The choices include the *Interactive User* who is logged on at the system where the DCOM object resides, the *Launching User* who made the call to the DCOM object, or a *Specific User* account that is identified on this tab.

 Note

Both the client and the server computer must be configured using the DCOM Configuration Tool. The client computer must indicate the server where the DCOM object will be accessed. The server computer must specify the access level for the user and which users will be allowed to execute the DCOM object.

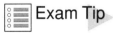 **Exam Tip**

The DCOM Configuration Tool is not tested too deeply on the exam. Know the basic configuration of DCOM objects. This includes where the application resides; who can access, launch, or modify a DCOM object; and whose security context is used to run the DCOM object.

Starting Applications at Different Priorities

 **Objective**

Under preemptive multitasking, Windows NT determines which application should get access to the processor for execution by using priority levels. Each application starts at a base priority level of eight. The system dynamically adjusts the priority level to give all applications access to the processor. The process or thread with the highest priority base at any one time has access to the processor. Some of the factors that cause Windows NT to adjust the priority of a thread or process include the following:

▶ Windows NT boosts the base priority of whichever process is running in the foreground. This ensures that the response time is maximized for the currently used application.

▶ Windows NT randomly boosts the priority for lower-priority threads. This has two major benefits. The first benefit is that low priority threads that would normally not be able to run can do so after their priority base is raised. The second benefit is that if a lower-priority process has access to a resource that is to be shared with a higher priority process, the lower priority process could end up monopolizing the resource. The boost in the lower priority thread's base priority frees up the resource sooner.

▶ Any time that a thread has been in a voluntary wait state, Windows NT boosts its priority. The size of the boost depends on how long the resource has been in a wait state.

Figure 5.24 shows how Windows NT handles different priority levels.

Figure 5.24

Base priority levels in Windows NT.

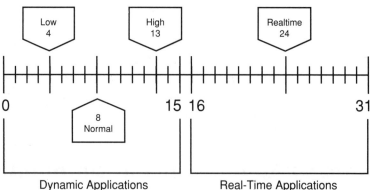

Priority levels 0 to 15 are used by dynamic applications. Anything running at a dynamic level can be written to the Windows NT Pagefile. This includes user applications by default and operating system functions that are not imperative to the performance of the operating system. Priority levels 16 to 31 are reserved for real-time applications that cannot be written to the Windows NT Pagefile. This includes all Executive Services and the Windows NT Kernel.

Starting Applications at Different Levels

Windows NT enables the user to change the default priority level from Normal by either using the command prompt to start an application or to adjust the priority level after the application has started by using the Task Manager.

Table 5.7 shows the four priority levels that the user can set.

Table 5.7

Base Priority Levels Under Windows NT		
Priority Level	Base Priority	Command Line
Low	4	Start /low executable.exe
Normal	8	Start /normalexecutable.exe
High	13	Start /high executable.exe
Realtime	24	Start /realtime executable.exe

 Warning

Be very careful about running any application at the Realtime base priority. This could slow down the performance of your system, because no other applications will be able to access the processor for I/O. Windows NT protects against the usage of Realtime base priority by only allowing members of the Administrators group to run applications at this level.

After an application is running, the Task Manager can change the base priority (see fig. 5.25).

To change the priority of a running application, follow these steps:

1. Right-click on the taskbar to bring up its Property menu.

2. Click on the Task Manager option on the taskbar.

3. Click on the Processes tab to view all running processes.

4. If the Base Priority column is not visible, add it to the view by choosing Select Columns from the View menu. Ensure that Base Priority is selected in the ensuing dialog box.

5. Right-click on the process in the Process list.

6. Click on Set Priority and then click on the desired priority at which you want the process to run.

Figure 5.25

Changing base priorities of running applications by using Task Manager.

Changing the Default Priority Boost for Foreground Applications

It may be desired on some Windows NT computers to improve the responsiveness of background applications. By default, the foreground application is given a priority boost of two levels. This changes the base priority for foreground applications to 10 from the default of 8 in the case of Normal priority applications. If you wish to change this level, follow these steps:

1. In Control Panel, double-click on the System applet.

2. In the System Properties dialog box, click on the Performance tab.

3. The Performance tab contains an Application Performance setting that determines whether foreground applications are given a priority boost over background applications (see fig. 5.26).

Figure 5.26

Changing the default priority boost for foreground applications.

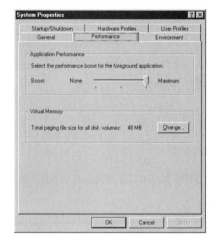

You can select from three settings. If the slider is set to None, no boost is given to foreground applications over background applications. This setting is preferred for file and print servers and application servers so that running a utility on the server will not affect any client connection performance. If the slider is set to the middle setting, the foreground application only receives a boost of one over background applications. The default setting is to have the priority boost set to Maximum. This gives a foreground application a priority increase of two over background applications. This is the preferred setting for Windows NT Workstation acting as a client's workstation.

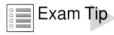 Exam Tip

Common questions about base priorities include how to start an application at a different base priority using the start command with the /low, /normal, /high, or /realtime switches.

Exercises

These lab exercises provide practice at configuring Windows NT to support DOS, Win16, and Win32 applications. They also investigate changing the priory levels of running applications. You can find the applications used in Exercise 5.2 and Exercise 5.3 on the CD that accompanies this book.

Exercise 5.1: Configuring a Windows NT Virtual DOS Machine

This exercise investigates some of the configuration that can be done to a NTVDM.

Objectives

Create a shortcut to a MS-DOS application

Modify a PIF for an MS-DOS application

Time Estimate: 5 minutes

Steps

1. Right-click on the desktop and choose to create a New Short-cut.

2. Enter **c:\winnt\system32\edit.com** as the command line. (This assumes that Windows NT is installed in the c:\winnt directory. Substitute your directory if this differs.)

3. Click on the Next button and the Create Shortcut dialog box should suggest MS-DOS Editor as the shortcut name.

4. Click on Finish to complete the creation of the shortcut.

5. Double-click on the newly created shortcut to start the MS-DOS Editor. Press the Esc key to bypass the display of the survival guide.

6. The MS-DOS Editor runs in a DOS window and, by default, enables you to use the mouse. By pressing the Alt and Enter keys simultaneously, you can switch to Full-screen mode. Note that the mouse pointer switches to a box on-screen.

You will now modify the NTVDM to automatically run full screen and to disable the capability to switch between Full-screen and Windowed mode.

7. Exit the MS-DOS Editor by choosing Exit from the File menu.

8. Right-click on the shortcut to the MS-DOS Editor and choose Properties from the pop-up menu.

9. On the Program tab, change the command line to read **c:\winnt\system32\edit.com /h** to change the display of the editor to 32 lines.

10. On the Screen tab, set the Usage to Full Screen. Also increase the initial size to 43 lines.

11. On the Misc tab, deselect the check box next to Alt-Enter. This prevents the switching between Full-screen and Windowed mode.

12. Click on the OK button to apply all your changes to the MS-DOS Editor's NTVDM, and then double-click on its shortcut to start the MS-DOS Editor. Note that the MS-DOS Editor now runs full screen with 43 lines of display. Try switching to Windowed mode by using the Alt+Enter key combination. This should not work!

Exercise 5.2:   Running Win16 Applications in Separate Memory Spaces

This exercise makes use of the Ntsrv16.exe utility found on the accompanying CD to investigate how Windows NT by default runs Win16 applications in the same memory space. It then investigates how Windows NT can run Win16 applications on a separate memory space.

Objectives

Running Win16 applications in the same memory space

Running Win16 applications in separate memory spaces

Using Task Manager to view running processes

continues

Time Estimate: 10 minutes

Steps

1. Locate the Ntsrv16.exe file on the accompanying CD, and then double-click on it.

2. Double-click on the Ntsrv.exe file again to open a second instance of the program. Notice that there are now two instances of thte progam running on the taskbar.

3. Right-click on the open space the taskbar and choose Task Manager from the pop-up menu.

4. On the Process tab, look for the NTVDM.EXE process. Note that both instances of Ntsrv16.exe are running in the same NTVDM.EXE.

5. Close both instances of Ntsrv1116.exe by selecting Exit from this Program from the program's option menu.

6. From the Start menu, choose Run.

7. Using the Browse button, select the Ntsrv16.exe executable from the accompanying CD and click on OK to return to the Run dialog box.

8. Select the Run in Separate Memory Space option and click on the OK button to start Ntsrv16.exe.

9. Repeat steps 6 through 8 again to run a second instance of Ntsrv16.exe in a separate memory space.

10. Start the Task Manager. Note that each instance of Ntsrv16.exe is running in its own NTVDM. In fact, you should also see the default NTVDM running with only Wowexec.exe running in it.

11. Close all instances of Ntsrv16.exe using the Exit this Program button on the program's option menu.

Exercise 5.3:   Testing Reliability When Win32 and Win16 Applications Fail

This exercise uses the Ntsrv16.exe, POW_16.exe, and POW_16.exe files from the accompanying CD. Using these files, you investigate what the effect of an ill-behaved application has on other running applications if the ill-behaved application is 16-bit or 32-bit.

Objectives

Understanding how Win16 and Win32 applications protect themselves from other program crashes

Understanding how running Win16 applications in a separate memory space gives better protection from system hangs

Time Estimate: 20 minutes

Steps

1. Using the accompanying CD, start the following applications by double-clicking on each application:

   ▶ Ntsrv16.exe

   ▶ POW_16.exe

   ▶ POW_32.exe

   From the Start menu, select Run. Type in MSpaint.exe as the program name. The paint program included with Windows NT is 32-bit program and the NT Server Simulator (Ntsvr16.exe) is a 16-bit program that we will use for our testing.

2. Now it is time to investigate the crash of a Win32 program. Switch to the running version of POW_32.exe. Click the pow button to cause a general protection fault. Note that you can no longer do anything in the POW_32.exe window, but you can still operate Ntsvr16.exe and MSpaint.exe. This is because each Win32 application has its own 2 GB address

continues

space. The crash of one Win32 application does not affect other programs. Click the OK button in the Dr. Watson window to close the POW_32.exe application.

3. Next, switch to the POW_16 program. Click the POW button to cause a general protection fault. You can still continue to draw in the mspaint.exe program. On the other hand, you cannot operate the NT server simulator. This is because it is running in the same memory space as Badapp16.

4. For a final test, run both POW_16.exe and Ntsrv16.exe in separate memory spaces. When you cause a general protection fault in the POW_16.exe program's execution. This is due to each Win16 application running in it's own memory space.

Exercise 5.4: Changing Priorities of Applications

This final exercise investigates starting programs at different base priority levels and then changing the base priority on the fly.

Objectives

Starting programs at base priorities other than normal

Changing the base priority of a running program

Time Estimate: 5 minutes

Steps

1. Log on as the administrator of your Windows NT Workstation computer.

2. Start a command prompt by choosing Start, Programs, Command Prompt from the Start menu.

3. Type **start /low sol.exe** to start Solitaire at a low base priority. This sets the base priority to four.

4. Type **start /realtime freecell.exe**.

5. Close the command prompt.

6. Start the Task Manager.

7. Change focus to the Processes tab. If you do not see the Base Priority Column, you must add it by choosing Select Columns from the View menu. In the Select Columns dialog box, select the check box next to Base Priority.

8. Note that the Freecell.exe process is currently running at a base priority of Realtime. Right-click on the Freecell.exe process in the Process list to change the base priority. In the pop-up menu, choose Set Priority and then select Normal to reset the base priority to the default level.

9. Change the base priority for Sol.exe to Normal as well.

Review Questions

1. Select all the advantages that running Win16 applications in their own separate memory spaces provides:

    A. OLE runs more efficiently

    B. Preemptive multitasking

    C. Non-preemptive multitasking

    D. More reliable in that one Win16 application crashing does not affect other Win16 applications

    E. Support for multiple processors

2. Which of the following are valid switches for the Start command?

    A. /base

    B. /separate

    C. /high

    D. /kernel

3. What methods can you use to stop a non-responsive program?

    A. Task Manager

    B. Control Panel's System applet

    C. Kill.exe

    D. Server Manager

4. Which groups have the capability to run applications at the Realtime base priority?

    A. Server operators

    B. Administrators

    C. Account operators

    D. Replicator

5. An OS/2 application that can also be executed in an NTVDM is known as a _____ application.

    A. Dynamic

    B. 32-bit

    C. Flexible

    D. Bound

6. The command that causes an OS/2 application to execute in a NTVDM is:

    A. start /ntvdm os2app.exe

    B. start /separate os2app.exe

    C. Forcedos

    D. Forcecmd

7. POSIX.1 support in Windows NT includes which of the following features?

    A. Additional time stamp

    B. Hard links

    C. Binary compatible

    D. Case-sensitive naming

8. What utility is used to configure DCOM applications?

    A. DCOMCONF.EXE

    B. SRVMGR.EXE

    C. REGEDT32.exe

    D. Dcomcnfg.exe

9. What files are used to configure a NTVDM by default?

    A. Autoexec.bat

    B. Autoexec.nt

    C. Config.sys

    D. Config.nt

10. After making changes to the Config.sys file to reflect the configuration changes you want for the OS/2 subsystem, the changes are ignored. What caused this?

    A. Boot-sector virus

    B. The OS/2 Subsystem is configured by modifying the Registry

    C. An OS/2 configuration editor must not have been used to edit Config.sys

    D. OS/2 configuration is saved to the %systemroot%\system32\config.os2 file.

11. You download a new POSIX utility from the Internet to run on your Dec Alpha AXP system running Windows NT. The application does not run. Why?

    A. POSIX applications are binary compatible.

    B. The POSIX Subsystem must be configured to auto start in the Control Panel to run POSIX applications

    C. POSIX applications are source compatible

    D. The POSIX Subsystem must be unloaded

12. MS-DOS applications are compatible across which platforms? Pick any that apply.

    A. Source

    B. Processor

    C. Thread

    D. Binary

13. You have several macros in Excel that you want to run faster in the background when you are working on other applications. How do you accomplish this?

    A. Run the foreground processes using the /separate switch

    B. Run Excel in its own memory space

C. Increase the base priority for Excel spreadsheets in the Registry

D. Use the System option in the Control Panel to lower the boost given to foreground applications

Review Answers

1. B, D, and E are correct. Running Win16 applications in their own separate memory space enables them to participate in preemptive multitasking because each Win16 application will now have a separate thread of execution. Running the application in a separate memory space also prevents the crash of one Win16 application from affecting other Win16 applications. Finally, with each Win16 application having a separate thread of execution, they could now take advantage of multiple processors in the system because Windows NT could now schedule each thread independently. For more information, refer to the section entitled "Running Win16 Applications in Individual NTVDMs."

2. B and C are correct. The /separate switch is used to start Win16 applications in a their own separate memory space and the /high switch is used to start an application with a base priority of 13 rather than the default of 8. For more information, refer to the sections entitled "Configuring Win16 Applications to Run in Separate Memory Spaces" and "Starting Applications at Different Levels."

3. A and C are correct. You can stop most applications by using the Task Manager. The Resource Kit's Kill utility enables you to kill any process. For more information refer to "Running Win16 Applications in Individual NTVDMs."

4. B is correct. Only administrators can start an application using the /realtime switch. This level is normally reserved for operating system functions. For more information, refer to the section entitled "Starting Applications at Different Levels."

5. D is correct. Bound applications run more efficiently under OS/2 environments, but they can also run in MS-DOS environments. This is the only type of OS/2 application that can be run on a RISC-based Windows NT system. For more

information, refer to the section entitled "Supporting OS/2 Applications Under Windows NT."

6. C is correct. The Forcedos command must be used to run Bound applications in MS-DOS mode on RISC-based Windows NT systems. For more information, refer to the section entitled "Supporting OS/2 Applications Under Windows NT."

7. A, B, and D are correct. By using the NTFS file system, Windows NT provides hard links, or the capability to store the same data in two files with different names. Changing the data in one, also changes the data of the other. Case-sensitive naming is also supported for POSIX applications, which means that Data.txt and DATA.txt will be two different files. Finally, POSIX support provides not only for a last-modified time stamp, but also a last-accessed time stamp. For more information, refer to the section entitled "Supporting POSIX Applications."

8. D is correct. The Dcomcnfg.exe utility is used to configure DCOM applications. It must be run on both the client computer that will call the DCOM object and the server computer that will host the DCOM object. For more information, refer to the section entitled "Building Distributed Applications Across Platforms with DCOM."

9. B and D are correct. The Autoexec.nt and Config.nt files are stored in the %systemroot%\System32 subdirectory. Remember that each PIF can have its own Config and Autoexec files. These are set by using the Advanced button on the Program tab of the PIF. For more information, refer to the section entitled "Configuring the Program Properties of a PIF"

10. C is correct. The Config.sys file is not simply a text file as under MS-DOS, and must be saved using an OS/2 configuration editor. For more information, refer to the section entitled "Configuring OS/2 Applications."

11. C is correct. POSIX applications must be compiled for each platform on which they are going to run. Be careful, most applications that you find by default on the Internet for Windows NT are compiled for the Intel platform. For more information, refer to the section entitled "Application Support on RISC and Intel Platforms."

12. D is correct. MS-DOS applications are binary compatible across platforms and do not need to be recompiled to run under RISC systems. The Intel Instruction Unit provides the Intel emulation and the NTVDM provides an environment for the MS-DOS applications to run under. For more information, refer to the section entitled "Application Support on RISC and Intel Platforms."

13. D is correct. Even though the Excel application is running in the background, affecting the priority boost for foreground applications works in this case because you are lessening the boost for the application that you are working on as the macro executes in the background. For more information, refer to the section entitled "Changing the Default Priority Boost for Foreground Applications."

Answers to Test Yourself Questions at the Beginning of the Chapter

1. RISC-based Windows NT Workstations can only run bound OS/2 applications, because the OS/2 Subsystem is not supported on RISC systems. Bound applications can be run in an NTVDM by using the Forcedos command.

2. The POSIX Subsystem provides support for case-sensitive file naming as long as the NTFS file system is being used.

3. Two MS-DOS-based applications handle Symmetric Multi-Processing better by default because each MS-DOS application will have a separate thread of execution. By default, Win16 applications share a common memory space with only one thread of execution. For more information, refer to the sections entitled "Supporting MS-DOS Applications" and "Running Multiple Win16 Applications."

4. You can do this by running the Win16 application and at the command prompt typing the command **start / separate app.exe**. Another method is to select the Run in Separate Memory Space check box in the Run option from the Start Menu. For more information, refer to the section entitled "Configuring Win16 Applications to Run in Separate Memory Spaces."

5. DirectSound, DirectDraw, and DirectPlay are the three components shipped with Windows NT. Other DirectX components not shipped with Windows NT include Direct3D and Autoplay. For more information, refer to the section entitled "DirectX."

6. Win32 applications are source compatible across platforms. This means that they must be recompiled for every platform on which they are going to run. You cannot use the same version of the software on Intel, Alpha, Mips, or PowerPC systems. For more information, refer to the section entitled "Application Support on RISC and Intel Platforms."

7. Win16 applications are binary compatible across platforms. This means that they can be run "as is" on all versions of Windows NT. For more information, refer to the section entitled "Application Support on RISC and Intel Platforms."

8. The OS/2 Subsystem and the POSIX Subsystem are provided with Windows NT to support applications for these operating systems.

C h a p t e r

6

Monitoring and Optimization

This chapter prepares you for the exam by covering the following objectives:

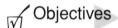 Objectives

> ▶ Monitoring system performance
>
> ▶ Identifying and resolving performance problems
>
> ▶ Optimizing system performance

Monitoring and optimization of the Windows NT Workstation 4.0 product can be broken down into three parts. The first is to understand the tools within Windows NT used to monitor system activity and performance. The second is to interpret symptoms and to know which tool can help diagnose the situation. The third is to understand the complete effects of one Windows NT component on others before making changes.

The Windows NT Workstation 4.0 product, running as a stand-alone system or networked in an Windows NT domain, will have very different issues to be considered. This chapter focuses on Windows NT Workstation 4.0 in a simple Windows NT domain networked environment.

Two basic Windows NT Workstation 4.0 tools are discussed in this chapter: the Task Manager and the Performance Monitor. Additional tools are mentioned as supportive roles. Each tool is discussed as to its merits and purpose. Along with detailed descriptions of the features of these tools, this chapter contains recommended techniques and suggested uses.

Note

The Windows NT Resource Kit and third-party utilities mentioned in this chapter are for information only, and will be elaborated on later in this chapter.

To implement changes, you must make use of several Windows NT features. For this reason, a fair understanding of Windows NT is required before you can start to monitor and modify performance.

Test Yourself! Before reading this chapter, test yourself to determine how much study time you will need to devote to this section.

1. You have an application that has stopped responding. How can you shut down this application?

2. When several applications run simultaneously, your system slows down considerably. How can you verify the amount of memory being used by each application?

3. You are planning to upgrade the amount of RAM in your computer. How can you find out how much memory you need to purchase?

4. Your computer runs on a network and you are sharing folders. You find your machine tends to slow down every once in a while for no apparent reason. How can you monitor the activity caused by other network users on your system?

5. You are experiencing an intermittent "out of memory" problem and cannot reproduce it for your support department. How can you save the performance monitoring screens that you have seen to show the support department?

Answers are located at the end of the chapter...

Monitoring System Performance

 Objective ▶

This section takes a close look at the activities going on behind the scenes of Windows NT Workstation 4.0. Unfortunately, no absolute correct answer or value can be given to a specific reading. The goal here is to explain the purpose and use of each tool.

The only method used to evaluate a given result is to compare it to a benchmark value. These benchmarks will be gathered over time and should be kept on record. Microsoft as well as third-party magazines do publish some guideline values that are mentioned in this chapter. These guidelines are examples and suggestions. Remember that each system and situation differs. Thus you may not be able to implement some of the suggestions mentioned in this chapter.

Using the Task Manager

The Task Manager tool offers a quick overview of key system resources such as memory and CPU usage, the status of applications currently running, and processes in use on the system (see fig. 6.1).

You can invoke the Task Manager in several ways, including the following:

▶ Right-click on the taskbar and select Task Manager

▶ Press Ctrl+Alt+Delete, and then select Task Manager

▶ Press Ctrl+Shift+Esc

Using the Applications Tab

The Applications tab is used to list all DOS, 16-bit, and 32-bit Windows applications. The application name is listed under the Task column and the status of running or not responding appears under the Status columns (see fig. 6.2).

Here the terms *task* and *application* are interchangeable. You can use the Applications tab to end a task, start a task, or to switch to a task.

Figure 6.1

The three tabs that appear for Task Manager are Applications, Processes, and Performance.

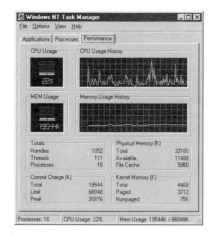

Figure 6.2

The application status column identifies a failed application that needs to be ended.

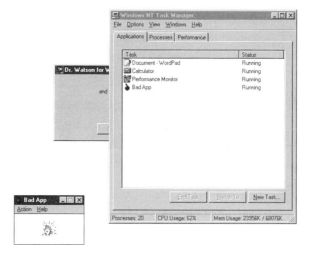

If an application fails, it can tie up critical resources such as memory and the CPU. It is in the best interest to end the task as soon as possible. When your word processor stops responding, are you more likely to be aware of it than if a background application fails? The Task Manager's Applications tab identifies the application as not responding.

To end an application not responding, complete the following steps:

1. Select the application to end.

2. Click on the End Task button.

3. A dialog box appears warning of possible lost data. Click on Wait to allow the application five more seconds to shut down properly.

4. If the application does not terminate, the same dialog box re-appears. Click on End Task to end it immediately.

DOS, 16-bit, and 32-bit applications are ended the same way. The big difference is in the resources that may be released. DOS and 32-bit applications run in their own memory address space with very little sharing of resources between them.

16-bit applications on the other hand are much more intertwined with all other 16-bit applications. All 16-bit applications share the same memory address space and message queue. When one application fails to respond to the user or the operating system, it blocks all other 16-bit applications from responding as well because they all share the same message queue.

By terminating a failed 16-bit application, the system releases the resources that may have been tied up and returns all memory to the common pool. For more information on how applications run under Windows NT Workstation 4.0, see Chapter 5, "Running Applications."

 Note

Windows NT is designed to prevent application failures from corrupting the entire system. There may be instances when it appears that Windows NT has crashed. Always verify the Applications tab in the Task Manager and end any task not responding. Windows NT will continue to function properly. What may have happened is that a failed application was using a resource needed by the operating system.

If you do not close down an application properly, you risk losing data. When you use Task Manager to close a currently running application, you receive a prompt to save the current data if desired. You cannot save any data when you are ending an application that is not responding. The applications themselves, however, may have an auto-save feature that might be able to salvage some data.

Using the Processes Tab

Each application may run several processes simultaneously. The Windows NT operating system runs several processes at a time. You can consider a process a subset of programming code used to run applications.

NT services are also processes. They use system resources such as memory and CPU time. You can monitor each process in the Processes tab of the Task Manager. To free system resources for other applications and processes, you should end services not being used (see fig. 6.3 and the section entitled "Running Windows NT Services").

Figure 6.3

This system currently has only one application running, but several processes still exist and take up system resources.

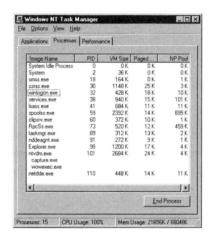

The processes in the Task Manager can be sorted in ascending or descending order based on any visible column. You can change columns to reflect different information. Fourteen information columns are available. By changing the sort order or the columns listed, you can organize information by importance; thus less time is wasted on idle or low-impact processes. The Processes tab of the Task Manager has four default-selected columns (see table 6.1).

Table 6.1

Default-Selected Columns in the Processes Tab of Task Manager

Column	Description
Image name	The process running.
PID	Process identifier. This is a unique number.
CPU Usage	Current percent of CPU's usage allocated to this process.
CPU Time	Total time the process has used on the CPU.
Memory Usage	The amount of memory allocated to this process.

To add all other columns to the list, choose Select Columns under the View menu (see fig. 6.4). The Task Manager screen can only display five columns of information at a time. To view additional columns, use the Scroll button.

To sort the information by a specific column, click on the column heading, and then click on the column a second time to change between ascending and descending. Listing processes in ascending or descending order of memory usage can help identify an application's usage even if idle or to identify a process tying up the CPU sort by CPU usage.

Figure 6.4

A list of all possible columns that can be displayed on the Processes tab of Task Manager.

Microsoft does not explain each column directly in the dialog box. You can always obtain more information through the Help menu (F1), specifically the Glossary book. Another good source is Microsoft's TechNet CD as discussed in Chapter 7, "Troubleshooting."

Each application or service is a process running on the system and takes up some system resources. An application can be made up of several processes; Windows NT's several services, however, can fall under one process.

Several Windows NT services fall under the Services.exe process; others have their own process. The Spoolss.exe process, for example, identifies printing. With this in mind, it becomes important to monitor processes and possibly stop a process that might be using up too many resources.

Not all processes can be ended by using the Task Manager. Using the Services icon in the Control Panel stops only some services. You should end applications by using the Applications tab of the Task Manager (stopping the Explorer.exe process, for example). The desktop shuts down, but not the operating system. This would be necessary if the desktop seems to have stopped responding to user input.

To end a process, complete the following steps:

1. Change to the Processes tab of Task Manager.

2. Click on the process to end.

3. Click on End Process.

If you end a process by mistake, you can restart it by accessing New Task (run) in the File menu and typing the task name. Otherwise restarting the computer returns the system to normal.

Using the Performance Tab

The Performance tab is used to display a summary of memory, CPU usage, and general indicators. A more complete analysis of these items can be done by using the Performance Monitor seen later in this chapter (see the section entitled "Using the Performance Monitor"). Refer back to figure 6.1 to see the Performance tab.

The first part of the Performance tab that is seen is the CPU usage and CPU history. These indicators show the total usage of the CPU by either the operating system or an application. The CPU usage indicates the percentage of the CPU in use at the last update count. The history displays the last few updates. The default update time is approximately one second. You can change this value by using the Update Speed under the View menu. Selecting a low update count allows for a longer time in the history window.

If the computer has several CPUs, you can set up the history portion to show one chart for all CPUs or one chart per CPU. Choose CPU History in the View menu to see the options. Additional detail on CPU history can be broken down to show the CPU usage of the Windows NT kernel (core of the operating system), by choosing Show Kernel Times in the View menu.

The Totals area of the Performance tab shows the total number of file handles, threads, and processes running. If you compare these counters before and after a new application starts, the difference indicates resource usage for this application.

The balance of the screen has to do with memory consumption. Table 6.2 lists the four main categories in the Performance tab.

Table 6.2

Main Categories in the Performance Tab	
Category	Description
Totals	
Handles	The number of file handles opened on the system.
Threads	The total number of application threads in use by all applications.

Category	Description
Processes	Total number of processes in use by all applications.
Physical Memory	
Total	Actual RAM in the computer.
Available	Physical RAM available that can be allocated to a process.
File Cache	The amount of physical RAM used by the file cache.
Commit Charge	
Total	The total amount of memory allocated. This includes physical and virtual memory.
Limit	Total amount of memory the system can use before the pagefile needs to be increased. This is using the current size of the pagefile, not the maximum or minimum necessarily.
Peak	The largest amount of memory that has been used this session.
Kernel Memory	
Total Paged	This is the amount of memory that the kernel is using and can be swapped to the pagefile.
Nonpaged	The memory that cannot be paged while in use.

The Performance Monitor tool shows all these counters in much more detail. The Task Manager is used to obtain a quick overview of the system. Information cannot be logged or printed from the Task Manager.

Using the Performance Monitor

The Performance Monitor takes the Task Manager to the next level of detail. The entire system's operations as well as the application's performance can be monitored, charted, logged, or displayed in a report. The Performance Monitor enables remote monitoring of other Windows NT 4.0 systems, assuming that administrative rights are available for the remote system.

Information is presented under the following three components:

▶ Items are categorized as objects.

▶ Each object has counters that can be monitored.

▶ There may be several instances of each counter.

An object is broken down into several counters and counters are broken down in to instances. There are three types of counters: instantaneous, averaging, and difference. Windows NT 4.0 now includes a total instance for most counters as well as individual instances for more detail. Instances shown may vary depending of the applications or feature running. The number of objects available depends on the Windows NT features installed. A special set of TCP/IP counters shows up only if SNMP protocol is loaded along with Service Pack 1 or later. Disk performance counters show up only if DISKPERF -y is run.

The object Physical Disk, for example, is broken down into counters such as Avg. Disk Bytes/Read, Disk writes per second, and %Disk Time—all of which can be shown for all physical disks combined or each physical disk separately (each instance). See figure 6.5 for a sample. This approach of breaking down into objects, counters, and instances is seen in all aspects of the Performance Monitor.

Figure 6.5

A sample of an object, its counters, and the instances of a specific computer.

Objects found in the Performance Monitor may vary depending on the current configuration of NT. Table 6.3 shows common objects that are always available.

Table 6.3

Common Objects Always Available in the Performance Monitor

Cache	The file system cache is an area of physical memory that holds recently used data.
Logical Disk	Disk partitions and other logical views of disk space.
Memory	Random access memory used to store code and data.
Objects	Certain system software objects.
Paging File	This file is used to support virtual memory allocated by the system.
Physical Disk	Hardware disk unit.
Process	Software object that represents a running program.
Processor	Hardware unit that executes program instructions.
Redirector	File system that diverts file requests to network servers.
System	These are counters that apply to all system hardware and software.
Thread	The part of a process that uses the processor.

Using Charts

The Performance Monitor can show the system's performance in an easy-to-read chart format. The default view is the Chart view. It is the easiest to use initially. Data can be viewed in a chart format as live data or from a pre-recorded log file. Live data must be monitored constantly and evaluated on the spot. A pre-recorded log file could have been gathering data for several hours or more and can be monitored at a more convenient time. Current or live data is explained in this section; log files are covered in a following section entitled "Using Logs."

To decide which data is going to be presented on the chart, use the Data From command under the Options menu. Two choices are presented: Current Activity, to view live data; and Log File, to open a previously recorded log file. Using the ellipse button (…), you can obtain the log file name by browsing the hard drive.

With both sources of data, you must add object/counters/instances to the chart. For the logged data source, only objects captured in the log can be displayed. The current data source, however, can use any and all objects/counters/instances available.

The following steps show how to add an instance of a counter within a specific object:

1. Use the Add Counter button on the toolbar or the Add To Chart command in the Edit menu.

2. Select the Object from the drop-down list.

3. Select the Counter. Each counter is explained in the Explain button on the right side of the dialog box. The expanded Explain area (Counter Definition) makes it easier to decide which counter to use. Reading the definition of several counters should clarify the definition and purpose of an initially obscure counter definition.

4. If an instance is relevant, select it or use Total for all instances.

To remove items from the chart, select a counter and press the Delete key.

Note

Each counter definition may be longer than the three lines allocated to it in this dialog box. Always scroll all the way to the end of the explanation. Also read the definitions of several similar counters to get a more detailed understanding. The definitions do not repeat themselves. If a term is explained in the first counter, it is not explained in following counters of the same object.

More information may be obtained on key words by searching through Help or the TechNet CD.

All selected counters display on the same screen using a 0–100 scale. All counters that refer to percentages are perfect under this 0–100 scale. A value of 50 shows a 50 percent use of the resource. Counters that measure exact figures such as Memory, Available Bytes are scaled down or up to fit on the screen between 0 and 100. The challenge is to figure out whether the value on the chart shows 50—is that 50 bytes or 50,000 bytes?

Each charted value uses a scale shown at the bottom of the screen just before the counter name. A scale of 1.000 indicates this counter was not scaled up or down. A scale ratio of 0.100 shows the 50 has been multiplied by 0.1 (divided by 10) for a true value of 5. A ratio of 10 shows the value was multiplied by 10 for a true value of 50. Multiply the value on the chart by the scale to get a true value.

Changing the scale ratio can be a little tricky. Only change the ratio if the chart line is flat at 0 or 100. You can change the default value by double-clicking on the counter name found at the bottom of the chart. The current value for the ratio is not shown; only the word default appears. Thus, it is not always obvious what the current ratio is. Using the drop-down list to select an appropriate scale re-charts this counter only. You may need to test several scale ratios before a relevant chart displays.

Another way to improve the readability of the chart is to change the maximum value of the chart's scale. The initial values are always 0 to 100. From the Chart command in the Options menu, change the Vertical Maximum. If all entries are 110–120 on your chart, they will appear as a flat line at 100 with a maximum of 100. Change the maximum to 150, or for a flat line around 20 set the maximum at 50, and the fluctuations become more apparent. Figure 6.6 shows all chart options.

Chart options affect all counters currently shown. Items such as Vertical Grid or Horizontal Grid can be set under Options to make reading easier. Do not remove Vertical Labels or Legend if you need accurate counts.

Figure 6.6

A list of all chart options is viewed from the Chart command in the Options menu.

You can obtain further statistics on any chart line by clicking on the counter name at the bottom of the screen. Just above the list of counters being displayed is the last, average, minimum, and maximum values of the current item. To highlight a chart item on the screen, click on the item name and press Ctrl+H. The emphasized counter is shown in a thick white line.

You cannot print charts from Performance Monitor, but you can export them to a tab separated value .TSV or comma separated value .CSV file. These files contain the data, not chart lines. The Export Chart menu is found under File. You can open these files from a spreadsheet or database for analysis and further charting. To print a quick chart, use the PrintScreen button on the keyboard, open a paint program such as MS-Paint, and paste. This places a copy of the image in MS-Paint that you can then save or print.

Using Logs

In most cases, just watching current data flowing across the screen is not a thorough analysis. Log files are designed to watch the system and record activity in a file that may be reviewed later. You can also use log files to compare the system at different times. All object information that can be monitored live can also be logged to a file.

Creating a log and analyzing data from a log are two distinct processes. Creating a log involves selecting the objects to be monitored, the file name to store the logged information, and an interval time at which to collect data. Notice here that you are not selecting counters or instances for each object. All counters and instances are recorded in the log file. Selecting these individual counters and instances is done when the log file is analyzed.

Tip

> You may want to create a separate partition just for storing log files. The maximum size of the log file cannot be set. Log files can grow very quickly and may fill up an entire hard drive. To prevent a log file from crashing the system, always make sure it is stored on a partition other than the system or boot partition.

You must always start a new log file from the Log view. Figure 6.7 shows the Log Options dialog box. The following steps show how to start recording a log file to monitor disk activity:

1. Choose Log from the View menu.

2. Choose the Add to Log command from the Edit menu or use the Add Counter button.

3. To analyze disk activity, add the LogicalDisk and PhysicalDisk counters.

4. From the Options menu, choose the Log command.

5. Enter a file name and the location in which to save the logged information.

6. The update interval should be set properly. The default is to take a reading every 15 seconds.

7. Click on the Start Log button to begin.

8. Minimize the Performance Monitor. The computer should be used normally while being careful not to close the Performance Monitor.

9. While the log is being created, you can insert bookmarks to identify the current activity. To add a bookmark, use the Bookmark command in the Options menu and type a short comment. This comment will be used later in the Time Window feature.

Figure 6.7

A list of all log options is viewed from the Log command in the Options menu.

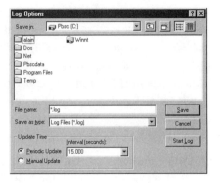

 Note The smaller the update time interval, the larger the file will become. It will, however, offer a lot of detail. A larger interval will show a trend, but may not reflect a specific problem. If a log is to run overnight, do not use a 15 second interval. Try a 15 (900 seconds) or 30 (1,800 seconds) minute interval instead.

After a log file has been stopped, it cannot be restarted. If a new log file is created using the same name, it overwrites the old one. To stop a log file, use the same Log command in the Options menu. Stop the log only when all data has been collected. You can view the log file after a log has been stopped or while the log file is still running.

Performance Monitor also enables you to view or analyze the data captured in a log file. You can display the logged file through the Chart or Report views.

The following steps show how to view a log file (after it has been stopped) in a Chart view and change the data source:

1. In the Options menu, choose Data From.

2. Change from Current Activity to Log File with the name of the log file to be viewed. Using the ellipse button (…), you can obtain the log file name by browsing the hard drive.

3. Add the counters by using the Add Counter button or the Add to Chart command in the Edit menu.

To remove items from the chart, select a counter and press the Delete key.

The process of viewing data is similar to using the Chart view in Current Data mode. Notice that only objects selected to be logged appear in the list. All counters and instances of those objects, however, are available.

The log file may have recorded information over several hours or days. The width of the chart screen is not any wider and cannot be scrolled. The mechanism used to focus the view on any given time frame can be enabled by choosing the Time Windows command from the Edit menu. The Time Window is a graphical tool that can be dragged to indicate the start and end of a section within the log file to be viewed. You can use a Time Window to view the data one hour at a time by continuously moving the Time Window graph. If bookmarks were recorded during the logging process, you can use them to mark the start or end of the Time Window.

All other chart options such as scales and grid lines mentioned earlier in this chapter apply to viewing logged data in the Chart view.

 Tip

To view data from a logged file that has not been stopped, you must open a new copy of Performance Monitor, and then follow the same procedure as described earlier. The original log file is untouched and continues to function properly. A slight increase in CPU and memory activity is recorded in the original log while the second copy of Performance Monitor runs.

Using Reports

The Report view just displays data in a numeric format. With current data, an average of the last three updates displays. Data viewed from a log file shows the average value for the Time Windows selected.

Reports are viewed from the Reports command under the View menu. To choose the source of the data, use the Data From command in the Options menu. You must add each counter/instance to the report through the Add Counter button or Add to Report under the Edit menu. To remove items from the report, select a value and press the Delete key.

The Reports view cannot show trends or large fluctuations. You cannot print a report from Performance Monitor, but you can export it as a .CSV (comma separated value) or .TVS (tab delimited file) and open it in a spreadsheet or word processor.

Report options contain only one item; it is often the update interval. The interval determines how often the report is updated with new information. This update interval can only be set on a report displaying current data, not logged data.

Using Alerts

The Alerts view is very different from the three previous views of Charts, Logs, and Reports. No data is reported or displayed until a system passes a threshold set by the administrator. There can up to 1,000 alerts set up on a given system. The same objects/counter/instances are used, except one additional item is added as a condition. When an alert is generated, the system sends an administrative alert message or runs a program. You can set the alerts to react on the first occurrence of the threshold being attained only or on each and every time.

You may set, for example, the following condition.

> Only alert the administrators if the computer's hard drive space falls below 10 percent free.
>
> or
>
> Alert the administrators when the server's total logons are above 150.

In both these cases, you could set up the system to send a message to the administrator informing him of the situation.

The alert's destination must be set separately using the Alerts command in the Options menu. All alerts are sent to the same destination. You can enter the destination either as a user name or a computer name.

The following steps describe how to set up the alert's destination:

1. Change to the Alerts view by choosing the Alerts command in the View menu.

2. Select Options menu, and then choose Alerts.

3. Enter the user or computer name to notify in case of an alert.

4. Select Log Event in Application Log to enable this log feature for all alerts.

Note

For the alerts to be generated from a computer, both the Alerter and Messenger service must be started. For a computer to receive an alert message, the Messenger service must be running. You can start all these services from the Services icon in the Control Panel or remotely from a Windows NT Server's Server Manager.

For alerts to function, the Performance Monitor must be running at all times. This may slow down a workstation and thus should be used for short-term monitoring and troubleshooting only.

Using Remote Monitoring

You can use the Performance Monitor to monitor other computers on the network. Each time a counter is added to a chart, log, report, or alert, the current computer is used. Any computer that can be remotely administered can be remotely monitored as well.

To select a remote computer to monitor, select the specific computer from the ellipse button (…) or type the computer name in the Add Counter dialog box. The full computer name is usually preceded by two backslashes (\\). To add a counter for a computer named salesvr1, for example, you use \\salesvr1. The person doing the remote monitoring must be a member of the Administrators group of the target computer. In a Windows NT domain environ-ment, the group Domain-Admins is always a member of each workstation's local Administrators group and thus can remotely administer/monitor the system.

Saving Settings

Charts, reports, logs, and alerts are modified each time a counter is added or removed and each time options are set. You can save all these settings in a separate Settings file. This will allow charts, reports, logs, or alerts to be generated one time; they could, how-ever, be used several times on current data or several log files, offering consistency when trying to compare systems or situations.

The Performance Monitor can be shut down and restarted quick-ly when a Settings file is opened. You can even move the Settings from computer to another. The Settings page stores the objects/counters/instances for the computer on which they were set up. Just copying the file to another computer does not monitor the new computer; it just makes remote monitoring a little easier to set up.

Using the Server Tool

The Server tool can be found in the Control Panel. This tool is used to monitor network activity related to sharing folders or printers, to set up the Replication utility, and to set up alert desti-nations for an Windows NT Workstation 4.0.

The monitoring section of interest here is the number of remote users and the types of access they are getting on the system. A few remote users accessing a few shares will not have any ill effect on the system. You should be more concerned with understanding this tool so that you can pinpoint any excessive number of con-nections. All remote network accesses are performed as back-ground processes; they may not be readily noticeable to the user.

The Server tool offers three methods of viewing remote users and their activity on the system. The three methods offer pretty much the same information with a slight different focus. These methods are listed and described in table 6.4 and also shown in figure 6.8.

Figure 6.8

The Server dialog box displays one session connected and one file opened.

Table 6.4

Three Remote User Monitoring Tools Found in the Server Manager

Button	Description
Users	This lists all users remotely connected to the system. Selecting a specific user lists all the shares to which the user is connected. Additionally, information such as how long the user has been connected and whether he is using the Guest account is available. From the Users button, you can disconnect any user from the share.
Shares	The Shares button shows the same information as the Users button except the shares are listed initially. Selecting a specific share lists all the users connected to it. You can also use the Shares button to disconnect someone from a given share.
In Use	The In Use button goes one step further than the two previous item: It lists the resource being connected to and the type of access. A list of files that may be opened with read-only permission is listed as such. You can close off resources. This disconnects the current users.

The Server dialog box exists on all Windows NT Workstations and Servers alike. A Windows NT domain controller also includes a Server Manager icon that can perform the same tasks as the Server dialog box on all Windows NT systems in the domain.

Disconnecting a user or a share has little effect initially on remote users because Windows NT and Windows 95 use a persistent connection technique to reconnect lost connections as soon as the resource is needed. Disconnecting a user will be used to close connections from systems after hours or to prepare for a backup where all files must be closed. To completely remove someone permanently from a share, you must change the share permissions beforehand, and then disconnect the user. When the persistent connection is attempted, the permissions are re-evaluated and access may be denied.

Using the WinMSD Utility

The WinMSD utility stands for Windows Microsoft Diagnostic. This utility is part of Windows NT Workstation 4.0 and can be run from the Start Run menu. The utility is not used to make changes to a system. Its primary function is to provide a summary report on the current status of the system. This utility displays nine categories of information, from the services' status to the size of the current pagefile as well as device drivers used on the system (see fig. 6.9).

Figure 6.9

The System tab of Windows NT's Windows Diagnostic.

A printed report can be produced with all details showing from all the tabs. This information is only accurate at the time WinMSD is started. It does not monitor or update automatically its information while running. There is a Refresh button at the bottom of the dialog box to update information.

Table 6.5 shows each tab from the WinMSD utility and its purpose. WinMSD will prove very useful when comparing two systems. Network administrators can use WinMSD to view information on remote systems. Slightly less information is available with remote viewing of WinMSD.

Table 6.5

WinMSD Summary Information	
WinMSD Tab	Information Displayed
Version	The Licensing screen showing the registered owner and the CD key. The product version and build is also displayed here. This same information is available from the Properties of the My Computer icon.
System	Shows the type of computer and CPU chip used. The system BIOS date and version can also be found here.
Display	The display adapter BIOS information and the current adapter settings, including memory on the card and display drivers being used.
Drive	All local drives on the system. The properties of each drive reveal the usage in bytes and clusters.
Memory	The Memory screen is similar to the Task Manager's Memory tab. The pagefile size and usage is displayed in kilobytes.
Services	All Windows NT services are listed with their current status. The properties of each service show the executable running the service and services that depend on the current service.
Resources	The four critical resources are listed for each device: IRQ, I/O port, DMA, and memory. Information can also be listed per device.
Environment	The environment variables for the system as well as the local user. These variables can be set through the System icon in the Control Panel.
Network	Shows general information about the logon status, transport protocols in use on the system, device settings of the network card, and overall statistics of network use.

Most of the information available in WinMSD can be configured through the Control Panel and the Registry Editor. You can run this diagnostic tool from DOS as MSD.com. From the Start Run menu, type **MSD**. This DOS version offers slightly different information such as a list of TSRs and a list of all device drivers.

Using Resource Kit Utilities

You can use Resource Kit utilities to augment the built-in tools such as Task Manager and Performance Monitor. These tools are not available on the Windows NT Workstation CD. The Windows NT Workstation 4.0 Resource kit is either purchased separately in a book format, which includes a CD, or accessed through Microsoft TechNet.

These utilities go beyond everyday analysis. They usually provide a behind-the-scenes look at system activities. Programmers will find this information useful. You can find the three mentioned here in the \i386\perftool\meastool directory of the utility CD for Intel-based computers.

The Resource Kit text explains in detail the purpose and use in far more detail than is expected for the exam (and thus provided this book). Table 6.6 shows a sample of utilities from the Windows NT Resource Kit.

Table 6.6

Windows NT Resource Kit Sample Utilities	
Utility	Purpose
Process Explode (Pview)	A full breakdown of each process as to all thread used with each priority, memory address space allocated, and security rights.
Process Viewer (Pviewer)	Contains less information per process than Pview, but enables remote monitoring of other Windows NT Workstations (assuming the proper access rights have been granted).

Utility	Purpose
Process Monitor (Pmon)	A command line utility showing processes information much like the Processes tab of Task Manager.

These are not all the tools available on the market today. With the exception of the Resource Kit tools, this was a complete list of built-in tools always available within Windows NT Workstation 4.0. Several third-party vendors have their share of utilities that you can purchase. In some cases, these perform better than the built-in items described in this section. Microsoft does not always support these third-party tools and may not be willing to assist someone whose system may have been damaged by these utilities.

Identifying and Resolving Performance Problems

 Objective

The Task Manager and Performance Monitor are used to determine whether performance is suffering in any way. A major cause of performance degradation is bottlenecks—that is, one or more resources operating at or near 100 percent of capacity.

The four major components that can be monitored and enhanced fall under the following groupings:

- ▶ Memory
- ▶ Processor
- ▶ Disks
- ▶ Network

Each of these items listed are expanded on in the following sections.

Identifying Bottlenecks

By properly identifying one or more bottlenecks, you can help focus the attention on the appropriate resources and help determine a course of action. The tricky part is that a resource may seem to be the culprit and thus the bottleneck when in fact another resource is really at fault.

Consider, for example, a CPU running at or near 100 percent consistently. At first it would seem a new and faster CPU is in order. When you look deeper, you may find that the CPU is so busy swapping memory pages from RAM to the pagefile and back that it has no time for anything else (see fig. 6.10). Adding more RAM reduces page swapping. Thus this would be the solution in this scenario, not a faster CPU.

Figure 6.10

The Performance Monitor is showing heavy CPU usage due to memory paging.

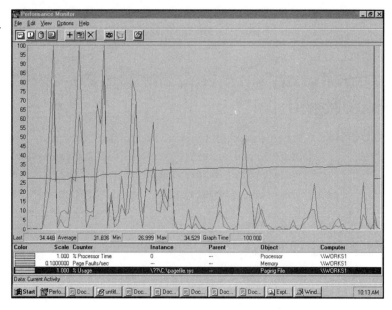

Figure 6.10 shows how only one reading of CPU usage may lead you to believe the CPU is inadequate when in fact the CPU is very busy each time an application is started due to lack of memory. There are three lines on this chart; the two lines that spike are CPU usage and PageFaults; the third line is the size of the pagefile. Each time an application is started, in this example, the system cannot find room in physical memory to load it into physical memory and must page information to the pagefile. The CPU is mostly used to perform the paging, not to run the application. Memory bottlenecks are described in full detail later in this chapter.

Tip
You should always look at all bottlenecked resources, not just the first one found, because resources are often dependent on each other.

To determine what constitutes a bottleneck, each resource must be understood and its baseline or optimum-operating level must be known. Is it a bottleneck if the hard drive is reading 150 bytes per second, or if the CPU is at 75 percent? No exact figure can be given for each resource, but Microsoft has a few guidelines that you can follow. The best method for an individual to analyze a given situation is to maintain a Baseline log of appropriate resource counters under normal or basic operating use of the system. You can compare the Baseline log to situations of extreme stress or to determine whether a change to the system has any impact on performance.

Creating a Baseline Log

You can create a Baseline log by using the Log feature from Performance Monitor as shown in the section entitled "Using Logs" earlier in this chapter. A log file does not have to be very large to show pertinent information, so long as a log has been created while the system is being used in its normal or basic state. If a log can be created when a system is freshly installed, you can use it to determine the impact of configuration changes or additional components added at a later date. You can create a Baseline log for each object individually or as a complete set. Creating a complete set is more flexible, but the file will be larger (see fig. 6.11).

To create a Baseline log, follow these steps:

1. Get the system into its initial state. Do not have any applications or additional items running. The system should be at rest.

2. Start a log file on all objects to be tested.

3. Let the log run for at least five minutes, and then stop it.

4. Keep this file on hand. You will use it to compare with current activities or new logs at a later date.

Figure 6.11

All objects ready to be logged as Baseline.log.

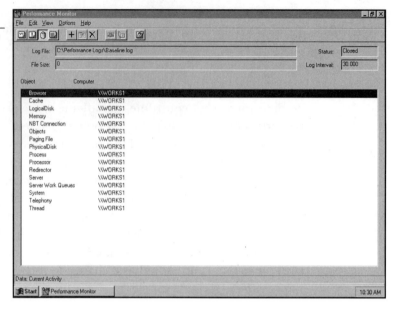

The following four sections show which counter to follow and log to pinpoint possible bottlenecks and system deficiencies.

Pinpointing Memory Bottlenecks

The amount of physical memory (RAM) in a computer is probably the most significant factor when it comes to system performance. More is definitely better in respect to memory. The amount of RAM will depend of the typical use of the workstation (running applications or sharing folders) and expectations of the user.

Windows NT Workstation 4.0 uses a virtual memory mechanism to store and retrieve information for the processor. Along with real memory capacity that is the amount of physical RAM, Windows NT also makes use of a pagefile system. As soon as Windows NT Workstation runs out of RAM to store information, it makes up virtual memory by using space on the hard drive. All information presented to the processor always comes from physical memory. When information is required and is not found in the physical memory, Windows NT has to read the pagefile on the hard drive and transfer the information to physical memory before it can be used.

The action of moving information between the pagefile and physical memory is called *paging*. Windows NT always returns to physical memory and tries to retrieve any information deposited there earlier. If the information cannot be found, the system returns a *page fault*. A soft page fault is returned if the information is just found in a different area of physical RAM. A hard page fault is returned when Windows NT has to look in the pagefile on the hard drive to find the information requested. Hard page faults take more time, CPU usage, and system resources than soft page faults and should be monitored.

Every application that runs under Windows NT 4.0 is allocated a linear 4 GB address space in which it can store data. Most systems today will not have 4 or more gigabytes of RAM, so a pagefile is used to handle the supplement. By allocating each application its own set of memory space, it prevents a poorly written application from trying to use another application's memory. This problem might still be encountered with 16-bit application because they share the same 4 GB space.

The Virtual Memory Manager is responsible for keeping track of each application's address space, the real list of physical memory, and pagefile memory used to store the information. When physical memory reaches its limit, Windows NT moves some information from the physical space that it occupies to the pagefile. When the information is needed again, it is paged back into physical space.

 Note   Exercises at the end of this chapter demonstrate a technique to identify a memory bottleneck. See exercises 6.1 through 6.3.

The memory object is definitely of interest, but you cannot forget that Windows NT Workstation uses logical disks to create a pagefile (used as virtual memory) as well as processor time to perform the paging.

The Performance Monitor objects of interest are as follows:

- ► Memory

- ► Paging File

- ► Process

- ► Logical Disk

- ► Processor

These item are listed in order of importance and if monitored as a group will indicate whether a bottleneck has occurred due to lack of physical memory. As you should remember, selecting an object for a log will include all the counters and instances as well. A Memory Baseline log file could be created with these four objects and used in a comparison.

You can use all the memory counters to determine a bottleneck. From the memory objects, three specific counters should be monitored: Page Faults, Pages Input/sec, and Page Reads/sec. See table 6.7 for a list of all object/counters/instances and their purpose.

You should monitor the size of the pagefile to see whether it is always increasing. Excessive paging may just be a short-term phenomenon and could be due to a one-time increase in demand. When the pagefile is constantly pushing the upper limits, there may be cause for concern. Each time the system is started, a pagefile of the minimum parameter is generated. As more pagefile is required, the pagefile is allowed to grow until it reaches the maximum parameter setting. The default size of the pagefile is based on the amount of physical RAM present when Windows NT Workstation was installed. The installation procedure creates a pagefile with a minimum size of RAM + 11 MB, and a maximum of RAM + 11 + 50 MB.

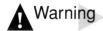 **Warning**

All Microsoft documentation shows the pagefile calculation to be RAM + 12 for the minimum and RAM + 12 + 50 for the maximum on Windows NT Workstation. In the exam, always quote Microsoft's numbers. There would never be a choice of answers showing 11 and 12, only 12 will be listed.

From the Paging File objects, the % Usage Counter is used to monitor the percentage of the pagefile being used. From the Process object, the Page File Bytes (using the instance total) shows the current amount of the pagefile being used in bytes. These two counters in effect show the same information. It may be easier for some to see the actual numbers rather that having to calculate the size of the percentage.

The Process object identifies the activity performed by an individual process or total processes on the system. The same counters are found in other areas and may reflect the same results. The Process object helps determine which process (application or operating system) may be causing a problem on the system. The counters to keep under observation are as follows: Page File Bytes (as mentioned earlier), Pool Nonpaged bytes, and Page Faults/ sec.

The Pool Nonpaged Bytes represents the amount of physical memory an application is using that cannot be moved to the pagefile. If this number keeps increasing while an application runs, it can indicate that a poorly written application is using up more physical memory and forcing the system to use more pagefile space. In this scenario, the pagefile counters and CPU usage may be showing a memory bottleneck when in fact the culprit may only be one application. Microsoft refers to these types of applications as *leaky memory applications.*

The logical disk object will not have the same significance as the previous objects do, but may help point out inefficiencies from the disks rather than from memory. The pagefile is stored on one or more physical disks. It is important to identify where the pagefiles are being stored. Each counter shows an instance of total disk as well as each logical disk.

To identify the location of the pagefile, follow these steps:

1. From the Start menu, choose Settings, Control Panel.

2. Double-click on the System icon.

3. Select the Performance tab.

4. Click on the Virtual Memory Change button.

A physical disk may contain several logical disks if the disk has been partitioned. The logical disks counters are used to identify the access to a particular storage area, not the entire disk. For more information on how to improve virtual memory disk usage, see the section entitled "Optimizing System Performance" later in this chapter.

The Average Disk Queue Length counter shows the amount of entries waiting to be read or written to the disk. Pagefile items fall into the queue like any other request. If the queue is too slow and cannot process paging request fast enough, the system seems to be slow due to paging when in fact it is the disk that cannot handle the request. In this case, you want to make sure the bottleneck is being caused by a lack of sufficient memory and that the disks performance is adequate. You are looking for a small disk queue or at least no different than under normal circumstances. This number should be less than 2 under an optimum scenario.

Finally, the CPU object may show the amount of work being done to satisfy the paging request on the system. If the CPU is very busy before paging starts, it will have an effect on overall performance. Similar to the Logical Disk object, you are not interested in the performance of the CPU as such. Instead, you need to make sure the processor is not slowing down the paging process and is not the real cause of the bottleneck.

The counters to follow for the processor are the %Processor Time, %Privilege time, and DPC Rate. The percent of processor time shows just how busy the processor is performing all tasks. The percent of privilege time excludes all tasks being performed for applications. Most device drivers and paging is performed in privilege processor time—all display and printing tasks are in user processor time. The DPC stands for Deferred Procedure Call. These are tasks waiting to be processed and are placed in a queue. Another indicator of the processor queue is found in the System object as Processor Queue Length. This counter should not remain above 2 for any significant length of time.

Another indicator of memory bottleneck is found in the Task Manager's main screen. It indicates the Total Commit Bytes and Total Physical Memory. If the Total Commit is larger than Total Memory, a memory bottleneck may exist.

Table 6.7 enumerates all the counters that may be used to determine a memory bottleneck. The first few items (Memory and Paging File) offer a significant insight into a bottleneck scenario. The last few (Process, Logical Disk, and Processor) are meant to rule out other possible factors that may be slowing down the system.

Table 6.7

Counters Summary		
Object	Counter	Purpose
Memory	Page Faults	Page faults include both soft and hard page faults. Microsoft suggests that a count of more than five page faults per seconds on an ongoing basis is problematic.
Memory	Pages Input/sec	Represents the number of pages the system had to retrieve from the hard drive to satisfy page faults. Thus itrepresents the number of hard page faults per second. This number is compared to the total page faults/sec counter to determine the percentage of hard page faults.
Memory	Page Reads/sec	This shows the number of times pages are transferred into

continues

Table 6.7 **Continued**

Counters Summary

Object	Counter	Purpose
		memory from the pagefile per second. This indicator can also be used to show a disk bottle-neck that might be created by a memory shortage.
Paging File	%Usage	The percentage usage shows the percentage of the pagefile in use.
Process	Page File Bytes	Make sure to use the instance Total to get a full reading. The actual size measure in bytes of the pagefile in use.
Process	Pool Nonpaged Bytes	The amount of physical memory being used that cannot be moved to the pagefile.
Process	Page Faults/sec	This same counter appears under Memory. In the Process object, it can be further broken down to show the number of faults being generated per process.
Logical Disk	Avg. Disk Queue Length	The number of items waiting in a queue to be read from or written to the disk. This number should be less than 2 under optimum usage.
Processor	%Processor Time	The total amount of time the CPU is performing tasks other than the idle process.
Processor	%Privilege Time	The time used by the operating system only to perform system tasks such as paging.
Processor	DPC Rate	A Deferred Procedure Call queue that indicates how many procedures are placed in the queue waiting for the processor.

For more information on memory bottleneck, refer to Chapter 12, "Detecting Memory Bottlenecks," in Microsoft's *Windows NT Workstation 4.0 Resource Kit.*

Pinpointing Processor Bottlenecks

The processor (CPU) on any computer will always be busy processing information. Even when no real process is running, Windows NT runs an idle process. Most counters take this idle process into account and display information on all processes except the idle process. A bottleneck may occur if too many items are waiting in a queue to get processed at one time or if an item takes a long time to make it through the queue. With so much emphasis put on NT's capability to run multithreaded applications in a multitasking environment, the CPU must be performing at its peak capacity not to slow the overall system down.

The processor may run fine for most applications and situations, and a log file should be generated during these times. When a problem does manifest itself, there will be a baseline value to use in comparison. For more information on creating a Baseline log, see the section entitled "Creating a Baseline Log" earlier in this chapter.

As described in the preceding section, memory bottlenecks may sometimes have the effect of excessive use of the CPU and lead someone to believe the CPU is too slow. Always try to eliminate the suspicion of memory bottlenecks before spending too much time evaluating the CPU.

Each computer has at least one processor; much more powerful systems may have two or more. Windows NT Workstation supports up to two processors in its original configuration. Even when a system has multiple processors, a bottleneck can still occur. A system with two processors that share the work equally is less likely to be the source of a bottleneck under multithreaded applications.

Microsoft's recommendation is that a single processor system should not be above 90 percent usage for any significant length of time. A multiple processor system should not exceed 50 percent usage for any significant length of time. Another main component of CPU usage is the queue of items waiting to be processed. Microsoft's guideline on the queue is that it be less than two entries most of the time. See figure 6.12 for a sample chart showing a system with a CPU usage well below the 90 percent in some cases, but then at 100 percent. The chart also shows a large number of entries in the queue (20 to 35 on average).

Figure 6.12

CPU usage of 100 percent and queue of 30 clearly indicates a processor bottleneck. If this situation persists, a new or faster processor is in order.

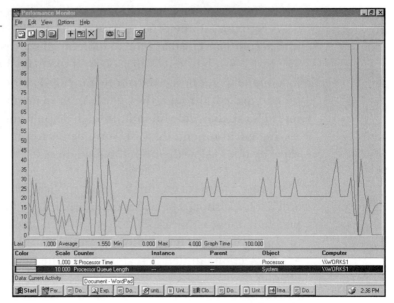

Applications that are single threaded—this includes all DOS and 16-bit as well as some 32-bit applications—behave the same way on a single or multiple processor system. When several processes are being executed at the same time coming from different applications, it can cause the CPU utilization to increase. A quick temporary solution to this situation is to close down applications not being used at the present time and re-open them as needed. 32-bit applications that are multithreaded, however, will run several processes at once and may tie up a processor even if it is the only application running.

In a multiprocessor system, there can be two types of processing: synchronous and asynchronous. Windows NT Workstation uses a synchronous environment in which all processors can be used simultaneously. Several single threaded applications can share both processor, and multithreaded applications can run several threads on one or spread across processors. An asynchronous processing system would run only the OS on one processor while applications run on the second. Even when the OS is not using its processor, it is not released for applications to use.

A few counters can be used to determine a processor bottleneck. Most counters use a process of sampling rather than a full count. This sampling may be misleading during a short monitoring period that uses averages. The average CPU usage in a 15 second interval may be very low or very high just because the sampling has taken few readings. A longer sampling period usually deals with this problem. Counters that deal with counts or exact numbers will not be as affected by the sampling errors.

The following objects/counters listed in table 6.8 are monitored to determine a possible processor bottleneck.

Table 6.8

Objects/Counters Used to Monitor Processor Bottlenecks

Object	Counter	Description
Processor	%Processor Time	The total amount of time the processor is busy excluding the idle process. This includes user processing and privilege processing time. This counter should be below 90 percent over time.
System	Processor Queue Length	The number of threads waiting to be processed by all processors on the system. This does not include threads being processed.

The solution to resolving CPU bottlenecks depends on the number of processors as well as their speed and the type of applications (single-threaded or multithreaded) being run on the system. A multithreaded application benefits more from multiple processors just because many tasks are performed simultaneously. The processor is overrun in the short term as the application is executing. With multiple processors, threads can be spread across the processors. For single threaded applications, multiprocessors would only help if several applications are running simultaneously; otherwise a faster CPU helps process information faster, thus reducing the amount of entries in the queue.

After a bottleneck caused by the processor has been shown, you need to complete a further investigation on processes, threads, and priorities. This additional investigation will help clarify whether a single application or thread is generating the bottleneck. In the case of a specific application causing the problem, there may be an alternative to upgrading the application rather than the CPU. Some 16-bit applications monopolize the CPU while the 32-bit counterpart works quite well.

Although the exam does not get into this level of detail, more information on processor bottlenecks as well as details on threads and priorities can be found in Chapter 13, "Detecting Processor Bottlenecks," of the *Windows NT Workstation 4.0 Resource Kit.*

Pinpointing Disk Bottlenecks

Disk performance has effects on many components on Windows NT Workstation 4.0. The pagefile system runs of a disk, the processor is busy searching or seeking for information on a disk, and file sharing uses the disk along with disk caching to provide information to clients.

These same components may be creating disk bottlenecks due to their limitations. When at all possible, eliminate memory or CPU bottlenecks before trying to monitor disk performance. All components such as memory, CPU, caches, and disk must work together to accomplish proper overall system throughput. Calculating the speed of a disk may not be very relevant. A faster disk may not always enable the overall system to perform any faster if other bottlenecks are present.

A log of disk activity can help compare results on several disks under similar circumstances. The Save Settings feature should be used to start tests on different machines or several hard drives. More information on how to use saved settings can be found in the section entitled "Saving Settings" earlier in this chapter.

The most important object/counters are not available by default in Windows NT Workstation 4.0. They must be activated with the DiskPerf utility. The only reason these objects/counters are not active is that they use system resources and slow down most systems. If they are needed, you can activate them and then deactivate them after completing the analysis. Table 6.9 shows the DiskPerf utility and its switches.

Table 6.9

DiskPerf.exe and Its Switches

Command	Description
diskperf	Shows whether the DiskPerf objects are active
diskperf -y	Activates the disk counters
diskperf -ye	Activates the disk counters on mirror, stripe sets, and other noncontiguous partition sets
diskperf -n	Deactivates disk counters

 Note   Only a member of the Administrators groups can run the Disk-Perf utility on a stand-alone Windows NT Workstation 4.0. The DiskPerf utility requires the computer to be restarted if it is being activated or deactivated for the change to take effect. Do not forget to deactivate the DiskPerf objects by using diskperf -n.

Another method to activate the DiskPerf utility is to start it using the Device Manager in the Control Panel. After the appropriate objects and counters have been activated, two main objects are available: Physical Disk and Logical Disk. Without DiskPerf, these counters show up in the Performance Monitor but have readings of 0. The Physical Disk refers to the actual hard drive placed in the system. This hard drive would be identified as disk 0 for the first one, the second is disk 1, and so on. The logical disks can be subsets of the physical disks. Disk or drive C: may be the full size of disk 0 or only take up a portion in a primary or extended partition. All counters shown under both Physical Disk and Logical Disk are identical. Several counters appear only under one or the other.

Two types of possible bottlenecks exist when it comes to disks. The amount of disks space available, and the access time of the disk. The counters used and solutions required differ greatly.

When a system's disks become too full, there may be other symptoms such as the pagefile has no room to grow or an application cannot save or update files. Hard drives are also used for temporary files created by applications and the operating system. Checking the hard drive by using the disk's properties shows only the current free disk space. Using Performance Monitor, you can set up an alert to create an entry in the Event Viewer.

To monitor the amounts of available hard drive space, use the Free Megabytes counter in the Logical Disk object. You can use this counter to show free space for each drive separately, or a total instance can be used.

 Tip

> A basic rule of thumb for hard drive space is that a hard drive should not be at more than 85 percent of capacity after all necessary applications are installed and configured.

The second area of concern is the efficiency at which requests are being handled by the hard drive and the overall usage of the hard drive. Microsoft makes the following three recommendations regarding usage of a typical hard drive:

▶ Disk activity should not be above 85 percent usage as shown by the % Disk Time counter in the Physical or Logical Disk object.

▶ The number of requests waiting in the queue should not exceed two, as shown in the Current Disk Queue Length counter of the Physical or Logical Disk object.

▶ Paging should not exceed five page faults per second as shown in Page Reads/sec, Page Writes/sec, and Page Faults counters of the Memory object. (Refer back to the section on memory bottlenecks for a more thorough discussion.)

Monitoring drives for a comparison is fairly simple as long as the same conditions apply to both disks. Certain factors might affect how one disk performs compared to another. Some of the factors are as follows:

▶ The type of disk partition could be FAT or NTFS.

▶ The controller card and type of drive might be IDE, SCSI, or SCSI-2.

Keep all this in mind when two test results are compared. Changing just one of these factors might have the desired result of improving overall system performance, but might also be hiding other areas of inefficiency.

 Note

Performance Monitor is an application as any other, and as such uses system resources. Be aware of the activity you might be creating on a disk as you are monitoring or logging information. Monitoring disk writes of drive C: using a log that is also being stored on drive C: will increase disk activity and alter the results.

Table 6.10 shows a list of common counters used in determining a bottleneck situation.

Table 6.10

Disk Bottleneck Counters

Object	Counter
Logical Disk/Physical Disk	% Disk Time
Logical Disk/Physical Disk	Avg. Disk Queue Length
Logical Disk/Physical Disk	Current Disk Queue Length(known in previous versions as Disk Queue Length)

continues

Table 6.10 Continued

Disk Bottleneck Counters

Object	Counter
Logical Disk/Physical Disk	Avg. Disk sec / Transfer
Logical Disk/Physical Disk	Disk Bytes / sec
Logical Disk/Physical Disk	Avg. Disk Bytes / Transfer
Logical Disk/Physical Disk	Disk Transfers / sec
Logical Disk/Physical Disk	% Free Space
Logical Disk/Physical Disk	Free Megabytes

You can use several other counters to interpret disk activity. This may not necessarily show a bottleneck, but can help in understanding how the system resources are being used by certain applications. For a complete list of all counters and explanations, always refer to the counters list in the Performance Monitor and the Explain button.

 Caution

Several counters seem to complement each other. Yet when you add up their figures, you can obtain results that surpass the 100 percent mark or overall capacity.

The over-calculation is due to the Performance Monitor methods of gathering information. Performance Monitor does not time the actual disk activity, it times the I/O requests (which includes processing and queuing time). When many items are in the queue, the numbers tend to be larger. When the queue is properly serviced, this exaggeration is not as significant.

An example is the %Disk Read Time added to the %Disk Write Time should equal the %Disk Time. But it does not always work out this way. For more information on this discrepancy, see the article titled "Troubleshooting the Disk Activity Counters" in Chapter 14, "Detecting Disk Bottlenecks," in the *Windows NT Workstation 4.0 Resource Kit.*

Pinpointing Network Bottlenecks

Monitoring network activity can only be done on a system connected to the network. Network terminology is used within this chapter and there is an expectation of networking basics on the part of the reader. Non-networked systems do not require monitoring of network activities, and this section may be skipped.

Network activity on certain systems causes bottlenecks even if all other aspects of the system are performing in an optimum state. The network components pertain to information being shared from the system of information accessed from a remote system. Typically a Windows NT Workstation's primary function is not that of a file or print server, and the number of request being made of the system does not have any negative effects.

Understanding network traffic though can help in eliminating overall network congestion. Network activity uses system resources and could lead to conclusions of inadequate memory, disk, or processor usage when the source of the bottleneck is in fact the network card.

In the earlier sections on pinpointing bottlenecks, it has been mentioned several times to focus the attention on very few items simultaneously to get a better understanding of the activity of a particular resource. In the case of network efficiency, the focus is not on the system itself but mostly on the number of remote hosts connected to the system and the amount of information being requested.

You have two main tools to monitor network activity on the system: the Performance Monitor, and the Server tool in the Control Panel. The Performance Monitor offers counters that can monitor the amount of bytes transmitted as well as errors encountered over several protocols, the Server service, and the Redirector service (client). These counters, however, cannot show the remote computers or users involved in this network activity. The Server icon in the Control Panel can display all the shares on a system as well as which user at which computer is connected to that share. Figure 6.13 shows a sample system's Server icon with a user connected to a shared folder.

Figure 6.13

All Windows NT Workstations can behave as small server in a domain or work-group environment to share folders or printers with remote users.

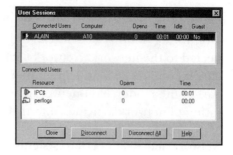

The Server icon can only be used to monitor local resources. For more information on all the sharing components of the Server icon, see the section entitled "Using the Server Tool" earlier in this chapter.

The Performance Monitor counters are not all initially present for network monitoring. Some counters that deal specifically with TCP/IP network traffic are not installed and must be added separately. Installing the SNMP (Simple Network Management Protocol) service adds the TCP/IP counters. The network or system administrators are the only users able to add network services.

To add SNMP services, follow these steps:

1. From the Control Panel open the Network icon.

2. Select the Services tab.

3. Select the Add button and select SNMP services.

4. Accept all dialog boxes and identify the Windows NT Workstation 4.0 source files if needed.

5. Restart the computer.

After the SNMP service is loaded, a TCP/IP system has five additional counters available: TCP, UDP, IP, ARP, and ICMP. The full detail of these counters is beyond the scope of this book. The focus here is on counters that show information transmission.

Regardless of the network protocol being used, there are counters to monitor simple read or write request from the network card. These counters are always available under the Redirector and Server object. Individual protocol counters are under the protocol name itself. Table 6.11 displays a list of relevant counters from various objects used to monitor network activity on the system.

Table 6.11

Network Counters

Object	Counter	Description
Server	Bytes Total/sec	This indicates the total activity of the system as a peer server on the network.
Server	Files Opened Total	The total number of files opened by remote systems. This calculates the amount of I/O requests.
Server	Errors Access Permission	This counter shows the number of client request that have failed. A remote user may be attempting to access resources that have been restricted. The system must process these requests, thus taking up system resources for nothing. It may also identify possible hackers trying to gain access to the system.
Redirector	Bytes Total/sec	The Redirector is the client portion of the network initiated by the local system.
NetBEUI	Bytes Total/sec	The Bytes handle the NetBEUI protocol only. This can be useful in determining which protocols are not used much and could be removed.

continues

Table 6.11   Continued

Network Counters

Object	Counter	Description
TCP	Segments/sec	The amount of information being handled by the TCP/IP protocol.
NWLink	Bytes Total/sec	There are three object for NWLink: IPX, SPX, and Net BIOS. All three have the same counter of bytes transferred per second using the NWLink protocol.

Monitoring with the Event Viewer

A part of the operating system is constantly monitoring for possible errors either committed by applications or other parts of the operating system. It should be noted that only 32-bit applications can log errors in the Application log. Event monitors are always active and keeps track of these errors in three separate logs, which you can view with the Event Viewer. The logs are as follows:

▶ System log

▶ Security log

▶ Application log

The System log reports errors originating from the operating system. By no means is this to say the Windows NT Workstation has crashed or is misbehaving. This log keeps track of services or devices that may not have started because of equipment failure or configuration errors.

The Security log is unavailable unless the Auditing feature is active in the System Policy of the User Manager. By default, the Windows NT Auditing feature is not active on a new system installation. This log does not provide relevant information as to system performance; it monitors users' and system activities with respect to user rights and permissions. When Auditing is active, it may require the use of several system resources. Auditing should be disabled to reflect a true reading of processor, disk, and memory performance.

The Application log keeps track of 32-bit application errors. A misbehaving application could be tying up system resources consistently with little benefit to the overall system performance. You may need to upgrade these applications or just restart to correct the situation. Applications under Windows NT have very little interaction directly with devices or device drivers. They can, however, report whether an error has occurred as the device was being requested or used.

Reading Event Viewer Logs

In both the System and Application log, Windows NT categorizes the entries as Information, Warning, or Error. In the Security log, there are Success or Failure entries to perform the activity sections.

Table 6.12

Event Viewer Icons

Icon	Description
	Mostly information about successful activities.
	The warnings are indirectly the result of critical errors. The system can still function properly, but some features may not be available. These warnings should be used to support or understand critical errors.
	The error message indicates a service or device that failed to start up properly. The system may still function, but none of the dependent features are available. You should address these errors quickly.

Figure 6.14

The Service Control Manager reported an error of the event type 7000 by the system.

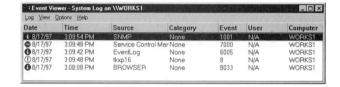

Understanding the error codes and types can make it easier to solve the problem. Each log entry can be expanded by double-clicking anywhere on the line. The Event Detail page is presented as in figure 6.15. This example shows that the network device driver for the INTEL TokenExpress adapter failed to started due to a device not functioning properly. The network card or cable may be defective.

Figure 6.15

The Intel network card driver failed to initialize due to hardware problems.

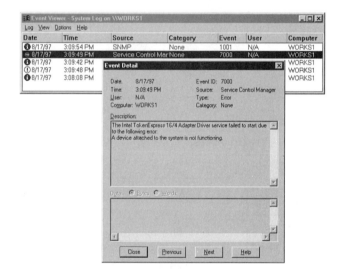

Additional information displays in the log to help clarify the source and type of message. The Event ID is found in the top right corner of the detail screen and can be used during searches in the Help system, using Microsoft's TechNet CD, or when communicating with a support center. The TechNet CD is a compilation of current information about all Microsoft's products. It is an invaluable tool. For more information on using Microsoft's Tech-Net CD system, see Chapter 7, "Troubleshooting." Table 6.13 offers a complete list of additional information in the Event Detail page.

Table 6.13

Event Details

Item	Description
Date	The date the event was logged.
Time	The time the event was logged.
User	The user name responsible for the event being logged. If N/A appears, in means the error was not a result of user interaction. Each Windows NT Workstation has a built-in hidden system account responsible to start up the system and perform system-wide functions.
Computer	The name of the computer from which the event was initiated. Most of the time, it is the local computer name that displays. If an alert was set up in Performance Monitor and the Server icon had a computer destination for alert in place, the name of the computer would be a remote system, not the local one.
Event ID	The code that has been assigned to the error. It is used in searches or support calls. A recurring error always displays the same event ID and can be easily recognized.
Source	The source indicates which part of Windows NT or which application found the event and reported it to the log.
Type	The type is the same as the icon shown in the list: Information, Warning, and Error.
Category	Several errors will not have a category. The Audit feature categorizes the event such as logon, logoff, policy change, and so on.

Filtering for Events

The size of a current log or an archive file can make it very difficult to find a specific problem. Using a filter can remove from the view all events that do not match a criteria. You can set criteria based on any of the detail options shown previously in table 6.12.

The filter performs only on the current information being displayed. The log may need to be re-filtered if new information has been added while it was being analyzed. The full list of events does not have to be displayed between filtered views; the system always bases the filter criteria on all events currently in the log. See figure 6.16 for a sample filter criteria.

Figure 6.16

The filter is based on all events with and Event ID of 7000. The event 7000 is "Network Card Failed to Start Up Properly."

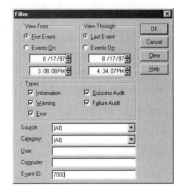

To filter using a log, follow these steps:

1. Select the log or open an archive file.

2. Choose Filter Events from the View menu.

3. Complete the dialog box. All selections are cumulative and an event must meet all conditions for it to be listed.

4. Open Events and evaluate the situation.

5. Return the view to all events by choosing the All Events in the View menu.

Managing Log Settings

All three logs have settings that you can manage separately. The size of the logs as well as the actions to be taken when a log is full are set for each log in the Log Settings item of the Log menu. The default values for a log are to use up to 512 KB of memory to store events and remove entries that have been in the log for seven days. Three options can be set to clear up logs: Overwrite Events as Needed, Overwrite Events Older than X Days, and Do Not Overwrite Events (Clear Log Manually). The system warns with a message box that the log is full except if the Using the Overwrite Events as Needed is used. If the log is full and not cleared manually, new events cannot be logged (see fig. 6.17).

Figure 6.17

The settings for the system log uses a 512 KB buffer and keeps entries for up to seven days.

A larger log keeps track of more information, but uses more system resources. Clearing and saving logs is a more efficient method to keep track of events and possible trends.

Archiving and Retrieving a Log

The file format used is an .EVT file format and can only be viewed from the Event Viewer.

Archiving a log refers to saving the event log in a separate file. You can do this while clearing or through the Save As item in the Log menu. The Event Viewer is a 32-bit utility. Its Save As routine uses all the standard 32-bit saving features such as long file names and Create New Folder. All three logs must be saved separately.

Saving the log file cannot be automated; it is an administrator's task to save the log files at least before they reach their maximum size. All logs can be saved in the same folder and used to determine whether a trend of errors or warnings is occurring.

To open an archived log file, use Open in the Log menu and select the appropriate .EVT file. An archive file contains only one of the three types of logs. Upon opening an archive file, the system prompts for the type of log being opened. The Categories column does not display properly if the log type is not valid. In that case, just re-open the file using a different type.

Current logging does not stop when an archive log is being viewed. To return to an active log of the current computer, choose the log type from the Log menu.

Although the steps to performance monitoring cannot be laid out exactly, the tools and method described in these sections will help identify problem areas. The resources available and the time constraints do not always make it possible to analyze a system and tune it to 100 percent efficiency. There will always be a trade off between system performance and providing the time and money to make it happen.

Optimizing System Performance

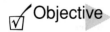 Now that the tools and areas of concern are understood, it is time to look at techniques to improve the overall performance of the Windows NT Workstation 4.0 operating system. Not all the techniques listed here are appropriate in all situations or for all users. Microsoft has shipped Windows NT Workstation 4.0 optimized for the majority of users working in a typical environment. The improvement in performance might only be a slim one or two percent, but could require a lot of work and money to make it happen.

Messing around with system configuration can be hazardous. In all cases, a backup of critical system files and settings should be performed before any changes are made. The effect of the changes should also be monitored and compared with a Baseline log created before the changes were implemented. See the section entitled "Creating a Baseline Log" earlier in this chapter.

Making a Safe Recovery

A safe recovery can be made if the proper steps were taken before any major changes were made to the system. Recovery techniques take time and are often overlooked by impatient users. Unless the machine can be completely torn down and rebuilt, it is much faster to recover a damaged system than to start all over.

The Registry files form the core of the Windows NT operating system. Windows NT 4.0 has several Registry files that contain specific information about the hardware, software, and user settings.

These files are stored in the %Winroot%\system32\config folder. The %winroot% is a system variable that represents the folder where Windows NT is installed. It is usually named WINNT. The system variable %winroot% is used to refer to this directory in batch files or configuration screens. The Admin$ name is the share name of this WINNT folder on all Windows NT systems and can be accessed only by members of the Administrators group from remote systems.

Several methods enable users to recover from system configuration changes: creating an Emergency Repair Disk, using NT's Backup to store the Registry, Last Known Good Configuration, and Hardware Profiles.

Creating and Maintaining an Emergency Repair Disk

The best way to make a copy of all necessary Registry files is to create and maintain an Emergency Repair Disk (ERD). The disk includes all hardware and software configuration items as well as security account database information. You can use this disk to restore a corrupted Registry. The backup copy of these files can be stored in two locations when an ERD is created. The disk has a copy and the %winroot%\repair folder has a second identical copy. The copy on the hard drive is not very useful if the system has crashed.

There is no menu or icon to create the Emergency Repair Disk. The RDISK utility is run from a command prompt or from Start/ Run. This brings up a graphical tool used to create the disk or just update the repair folder (see fig. 6.18).

Figure 6.18

RDISK is used to create an Emergency Repair Disk. All disks are unique to the system they were created on.

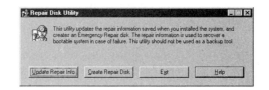

The RDISK utility presents two option: Update Repair Info, and Create Repair Disk. Update Repair Info updates the repair folder and then prompts to create a disk. Create Repair Disk creates a disk without updating the repair folder. You should create and maintain an Emergency Repair Disk. You should also have a back-up copy of the disk on a system dealing with critical information.

Creating Hardware Profiles

Creating a hardware profile is one of the safest and fastest methods for making and testing changes to a system without the dangers of loosing system integrity. Hardware profiles are also used to control when the network settings are loaded on laptops that may be connected to the network or set up to run as a stand-alone. This setting can be done quickly through the Properties button of the profile.

A hardware profile starts off as an identical copy of the current system's configuration. Part of the Registry is duplicated. All device and device-related configuration changes are made to the copy profile and tested. If a particular configuration fails, the system can just be rebooted into the original configuration without any ill effects. Only device and device-related items are stored in a profiles. Most Registry settings are always available to all profiles. The Registry Editor should not be used to modify profiles. Using the devices or services icons provides safer methods to change a profile.

All systems have a hardware profile initially named Original Configuration. The systems starts up using this configuration without prompting the user. A hardware profile copy is not modified by the system, only by current configuration changes that are made when the copy is in use.

Once a copy exists, Windows NT brings up a prompt prior to logon but after the Boot.ini displays the list of operating systems as to which hardware profile is to be used for this session. If no choice is made, the system has a time out of 30 seconds and will load the default profile. Figure 6.19 shows the system's Performance tab with two hardware profiles defined. You can modify the time out period as well as the default choice in the system's Properties dialog box.

Figure 6.19

The default Original Configuration loads in 30 seconds when no choice is made at startup.

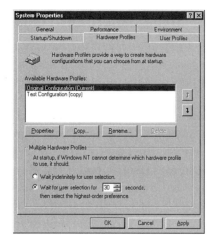

To create a hardware profile for testing system changes, follow these steps:

1. From the Control Panel, select the System icon.

2. Select the Hardware Profiles tab.

3. Click on the Copy button.

4. Enter a new name for the new profile.

5. Select a Wait for Selection time, or set Wait Indefinitely. The default hardware profile is always the first listed. You can use the arrows on the side of the list to change the order.

The profile is now in place and can be selected when the system restarts. Always restart the system using the testing profile before making any changes to the system. When all the testing is completed, the copy profile can be deleted. A successful testing profile can be renamed and the original configuration deleted. As long as there are two or more configurations, Windows NT prompts for a profile during startup.

The hardware profiles are easier to use than the ERD. The ERD may still be needed if changes are made to the system that corrupt the Registry. The hardware profiles are stored in the Registry.

Exercise 6.4 and 6.5 at the end of this chapter make use of hardware profiles to test new configuration.

Using the Last Known Good Configuration

A temporary copy of the hardware's Original Profile is made after a successful logon. This temporary copy is called the Last Known Good Configuration. It is replaced each time the user logs on.

Configuration changes get written to the Registry in the Current Control Set. Upon successful logon, a copy of this Control Set is copied to the LastKnownGood set. This set can be retrieved when a system is restarted after failed configuration changes. During the startup procedure, Windows NT displays the message `Press the space bar now to load Last Known Good Configuration`. This message appears for a short time only. If the Last Known Good Configuration is loaded, it replaces the last set that failed. All the changes to the system made during the last session are lost.

NT's startup procedure can be misleading. Services and devices are started before, during, and after the Ctrl+Alt+Delete logon security box appears. After a user has logged on to the system, it updates the Last Known Good even if devices or services fail after logon. Always wait for the system to load all devices and services before logging on. If a device or service fails, Windows NT displays an error message. The system's power can be turned off and restarted with the Last Known Good still intact.

To invoke the Last Known Good Configuration, follow these steps:

1. Do not log on to the system if an error appears or the last configuration changes have caused problems.

2. Power off the computer and wait 10 seconds before powering on again.

3. Choose Windows NT from the Boot menu.

4. Press the space bar when the message appears `Press the space bar now to load Last Known Good Configuration`.

5. Press L to invoke the Last Known Good Configuration.

6. Log on to the system normally. All settings should be restored to their state prior to the last set of failed changes.

Because the Last Known Good is not always very reliable, hardware profiles and Emergency Recovery Disks are recommended as well.

Configuring the Operating System

You can tune several aspects of Windows NT. Having faster hardware is always an asset, but is not always realistic in the short term. From the operating system's perspective, Windows NT is a set of services that run devices to provide resources to the user. Tuning these items can be done quickly without having to upgrade or invest a large amount of money. The following sections cover areas such as Windows NT services, Windows NT device drivers, and Registry components. These components can be modified on the system and their benefits can be seen instantly. There is always a warning that goes along with tampering with default system values. Be careful and always have backup mechanisms in place to recover from any unexpected results.

Running Windows NT Services

Windows NT Workstation 4.0 is made up of a series of services that run in conjunction with each other to provide the operating system. A default set of services is loaded with a typical installation, and the user or applications can install additional services. Not all services are required to run Windows NT Workstation 4.0. The default set of services is chosen to satisfy most common users and systems. Disabling unused services frees up system resources such as memory and the CPU. You cannot disable all services through hardware profiles, but you can stop them manually.

 Caution

Several services depend on one another. Stopping a service may have very significant effects on the overall system's operations. Consult the WinMSD utility for service dependencies before stopping a service. Always use hardware profiles when possible to test the effects of stopping a service.

Table 6.13 lists some of the services that you disable using hardware profiles. The information displayed in this table is extracted from Microsoft's TechNet CD and shows memory usage of certain Windows NT services. Stopping these services reduces Windows NT Workstation's functionality, but frees up memory.

Table 6.13

Sample Memory Usage Per Service

Service Pool	Nonpaged Bytes	Private Bytes	Working Set Bytes
AtSrv	10,308	253,952	765,952
ClipBook Server	1,908	237,568	1,114,112
Network DDE	11,142	368,640	1,286,144
Nmagent	2,532	1,810,432	2,727,936
Alerter (thread in services.exe)	52	4096	24576
Messenger (thread in services.exe)	156	16384	49152
Spooler	11,452	618,496	1,105,920
Telephony Services	12,624	499,712	1,433,600

Disabling Devices

Devices, like services, can be disabled on a per hardware profile basis. Most devices set up initially are required to run the hardware attached or included in the system. During normal operation of the system, there may be devices that are not used. They are using system resources for nothing. To disable a device, always use the hardware profiles first to test their impact on the system.

The following steps show how to disable a device safely:

1. Open the Devices icon in the Control Panel.

2. Select the device from the list.

3. Click on the HW/Profiles button.

4. Select a test profile, if one exists.

5. Click on the Disable button.

The Original Configuration should be left intact. You can use this profile to return the system to a proper working order at any time.

Running Tasks and Applications

Each application runs one or more tasks in the Task Manager. You should close unused tasks to free up system resources. Some tasks are required to operate Windows NT, and others are applications themselves. Windows NT services are also shown as tasks, but cannot be closed with the Task Manager. Windows NT services should be closed using the Services icon in the Control Panel. (See the preceding section, "Running Windows NT Services.")

You should close applications when they are not in use or at least minimized. Surprisingly, an application running in a window takes up significantly more memory than the same application that is minimized. When moving from one application to another, do not use the Alt+Tab or the Taskbar button; they just move the selected application to the foreground.

To see the effects of memory consumption of full-screen versus minimized applications, follow these steps:

1. Start the Task Manager and view the Processes tab.

2. Select Start, Programs, Accessories, WordPad.

3. With the application maximized, return to the Task Manager. Note the amount of memory being used from the Mem Usage column.

4. Minimize WordPad and compare the memory usage in the Task Manager.

Not all applications run as effectively under Windows NT Workstation 4.0. DOS, 16-bit, 32-bit, OS/2, and Unix applications are treated very differently on the system. A 32-bit application designed to run on Windows NT performs better and more efficiently than any other type. That is because only 32-bit applications run in the main subsystem without additional effort. 32-bit applications are designed to take advantage of the Pentium processor, and they are most likely multithreaded. For all other types, Windows NT emulates their native operating system environment. This emulation requires more system resources to maintain, but offers better compatibility.

All DOS applications are run in an NTVDM. This is a Windows NT Virtual DOS Machine that represents all the aspects of single computer. The DOS application believes it is the only application running on the computer. All 16-bit applications run in a WOW on top of an NTVDM. WOW stands for Windows on Windows. The WOW is meant to represent Windows 3.1/3.11.

OS/2 and Unix-based applications run in their respective subsystems that start along with the application. The Task Manager shows these NTVDMs and other subsystems in use along with their memory requirements.

Running applications as foreground tasks will have a higher priority on the workstation and seem to be more responsive to the user. Windows NT Workstation 4.0 offers a foreground/background priority setting. All applications are written with a set of base priorities for each of its threads. The base priority of the thread is used to determine how much CPU time that it can have in relation to other threads. A thread running at a priority of 12 runs before a thread with a priority of 8. Windows NT dynamically modifies the priority of threads to ensure all threads get some time on the CPU.

Priorities range from 1 to 31 and are set by the programmer. A normal thread level is 8 for most user-based application tasks. Most operating system tasks run at a priority above 15. Although the user cannot change the exact value of the thread's priority, it can be boosted.

A simple method to change the overall responsiveness of foreground versus background tasks is to set the Application Performance Boost found in the System icon's Performance tab.

A Maximum boost increases the thread's priority by two levels when running in the foreground. The Minimum boost increases the priority by one and the None boost does not increase the thread priority at all (see fig. 6.20).

Figure 6.20

The Boost setting may be set to None to prevent foreground applications from dominating the CPU.

You can boost individual applications by using the command line. The command line is accessed through the Start menu by choosing Command Prompt in the Programs menu. An alternative way is to use Start/Run and type **CMD**.

Four start command switches used to change the priority of a given application. They all use the Start command and are listed in table 6.14.

Table 6.14

Start Command Switches to Change Priority

Start Switch	Effects on priority
Start /low	This actually lowers the base priority of the application to 4. The effect is to increase the overall performance of other applications. Running an application with a priority 4 as a background application takes longer to complete any task.
Start /Normal	This switch runs the application using the normal priority of 8. It can be used for applications that normally run at value lower than 8.

continues

Table 6.14 Continued

Start Command Switches to Change Priority

Start Switch	Effects on priority
Start /High	The High priority sets application priority to a value of 13. Most applications run much faster if they require a lot of CPU time. This improves the performance of an application that reads and writes to the hard disk.
Start /Realtime	This switch increases the base priority to 24. Realtime is not recommended for applications that use the CPU extensively. You may not be able to interact with the system. The mouse or keyboard commands may not be able to interrupt the CPU. Only users with Administrator privileges can use the /Realtime switch.

To start the Notepad application with a priority of 13, follow these steps:

1. From the Start menu, choose Programs, Command Prompt.

2. Type **Start/High Notepad.exe**.

You can see a process' current priority with utilities such as the Process Monitor and Process Viewer from the Windows NT Resource Kit. See the section entitled "Using Resource Kit Utilities" earlier in this chapter. The only situation in which the option of running applications in a higher priority level will manifest itself is on a system where the CPU is very busy. The same example could be repeated using the /Realtime switch.

Virtual versus Physical Memory

You can almost always add physical memory to a computer with positive results. *Memory is the single most significant factor in overall system performance.* Adding more memory may not be possible in the short term for several reasons: the cost of upgrading can be a barrier, or the system may not have any space to quickly add additional memory chips.

There are alternatives to purchasing more memory. After Windows NT has been tuned to make the best use of its current memory levels, modifying the location and size of the pagefile may have an effect on the system.

The pagefile is defined using a minimum and maximum size on a given hard drive. On a system with several hard drives, moving the pagefile to a drive that is faster or not used as much improves read and write requests. Placing the pagefile on a drive other than the operating system can result in problems during a memory dump. Memory dumps cause the information in physical memory to be stored in the pagefile during a crash. If the pagefile is on a different drive from the operating system, the dump will not be successful.

When the system starts, a pagefile is created at the minimum level. The operating system increases the size of the file to accommodate demand up until the maximum level is attained. You can monitor the current usage of the pagefile in Performance Monitor and the Task Manager. Growing the pagefile requires system resources and may result in a fragmented pagefile. These factors affect system performance. The minimum size of the pagefile should be large enough to accommodate current uses.

Another technique is to create additional pagefiles stored on different drives. The read/write operations may be handled faster. This depends of the current activity on the drives and the drive's own performance issues. Windows NT supports one pagefile on each logical disk. Placing pagefiles on multiple logical drives contained on the same physical disk does affect system much. Because there is only one physical reader on each physical disk, it takes longer to read.

You can make all changes to the pagefile from the Performance tab of the System properties. Select the Change button in the Virtual Memory section. See figure 6.21 for details on virtual memory assignment.

Figure 6.21

The initial size of the pagefile was 43 MB. That is 32 MB RAM + 11 MB. The new values increase performance.

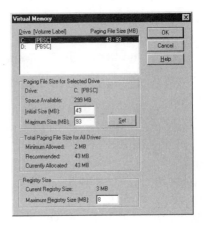

The maximum size of the pagefile could be left intact. The recommendation is to always keep a 50 MB buffer between the minimum and maximum sizes. This buffer ensures that the pagefile can grow to accommodate short-term demands.

Reviewing Disk Usage

Other than pagefile activity, the disks are used constantly by the operating system to read information and write data. The speed and efficiency of the drive is important. Hardware issues are very important when selecting a type and speed of hard drive.

Making Hardware Choices

Hard drive and controller types can make a big difference on performance. The following are some examples of transfer rates: some IDEs (integrated drive electronic) have a 2.5 MB/sec throughput; ESDI has a 3 MB/sec; SCSI-2 has a 5 MB/sec throughput; and a Fast SCSI-2 can have a 10 MB/sec throughput. Exact figures can be seen in the manufacturer's documentation. Using a 32-bit controller card rather than a 16- or 8-bit controller will have significant impact on the system.

Although these options improve performance, they may not be realistic in the short term. The cost of these new controller cards may prevent an upgrade.

Choosing Partition Size and Disk Format

You can partition each hard drive into different sizes and format them using FAT or NTFS. Large partitions may be easier to use because a single drive letter references them. It is not always better to use one logical disk per physical disk. The size and format of the partition determines the size of the cluster being used for storage. A *cluster* is the smallest storage unit on a hard drive.

While using a FAT partition, a larger partition must use a larger cluster; that can result in inefficient use of the hard drive. If a 12 K amount of data is stored to a hard drive that uses a 4 K cluster, it uses up 3 full clusters with none wasted. If the same 12 K is stored in a 32 K cluster, however, it uses only one cluster but wastes 20 K of space in the cluster. NTFS partitions are not bound by the same cluster size limitation that FAT has. NTFS is designed for larger partitions. The maximum size of an NTFS partition is 2 terabytes.

Creating two 500 MB partitions will prove more beneficial than a 1 GB partition on the same drive. There are limits to the amount of partitions that can be supported by each physical drive. With Windows NT, you can have up to four partitions on each drive. There are two types of partition: primary and extended. There can only be one extended partition per physical drive. Logical drives can be created in the extended partition to allow for even smaller storage areas. It is all based on the size of the cluster being used.

FAT partitions are supported by DOS and NT. NTFS partitions can only be accessed from within NT. NTFS offers much more security and data integrity features. NTFS uses a B-tree method for file access. This method is much faster than traditional FAT searches on large partitions. Disk access on FAT partitions are actually faster for small partitions.

Partitions larger than 512 MB should be converted to NTFS to reduce the size of the cluster being used. Partitions smaller than 512 MB can be converted to NTFS, but because NTFS requires additional space to operate it may in fact offer less disk space. There are many other reasons to choose between FAT and NTFS. This discussion, however, focuses on disk space only.

Disk Access Issues

During the analysis period, certain counters are enabled for the disk. The diskperf-y command is used to enable those counters. Although the counters are necessary during an analysis, they are detrimental to system performance. Always remove these counters when the analysis is complete. Use the diskperf-n command to disable the counters and restart the computer.

The operating system, the pagefile, programs, and data may be stored on a single hard drive. This may not be very efficient and can slow down overall system performance.

Placing the operating system on a separate partition improves the I/O request. When a pagefile is used constantly, it should be placed on a partition other than the operating system. On a system with multiple disks and multiple controller cards, the improvements can be substantial.

Applications and data files should share the same physical disk— at least all data files being used by an application. When the disk reads information from one file and then must move the disk heads to a completely separate area of the disk, it takes a little longer.

Disk compression has an effect on disk access. Windows NT Workstation 4.0's compression can be implemented on NTFS partitions only. The compression is done on a per drive, per folder, or per file basis. Although compressing information on the drive improves disk storage capacity, it reduces access time. Finding the information on the disk remains the same, but uncompressing it to pass it on to the CPU takes a little more time.

You should never compress heavily used files and programs that access the hard disk frequently. Compression under NTFS was designed for the NT Workstation and does not have a major impact but can be noticeable is some cases. The pagefile will not be compressed even if it is selected. Applications and common data file should not be compressed. Data files and application that are seldom used may be compressed while they sit idle. They can always be uncompressed before use or Windows NT can uncompress them while they are being used. Considering the low price of hard drives these days, compressed drives should be used at a minimum.

NT Workstation 4.0 creates a backward compatible short file name (8.3) for each long file name. This takes up little space on the drive, but uses processor time to perform. This short name generation can be disabled on a system running only Windows NT and using only 32-bit programs that do not require the traditional 8.3. Short names can still be used, but NT will not create short names when a long name is used.

To disable short name generation, use REGEDT32.EXE to set a Registry DWORD value of 1 in the following Registry location:

```
SYSTEM\CurrentControlSet\Control\Filesystem\NtfsDisable8dot3NameCreation
```

Always be careful when making Registry changes. The Registry Editor does not warn you of any syntax errors or missing entries.

Cleaning Up Disk Space

Fragmentation occurs in all cases when the operating system saves, deletes, and moves information to a hard drive. A file is fragmented if it is stored in several non-consecutive clusters on the hard drive. Windows NT attempts to store information in the first continuous block of clusters. When a continuous block is not available, the file is stored in several non-consecutive blocks and is said to be fragmented. The disk can be fragmented even if files are not fragmented. There may be clusters unused in areas not large enough to store any one complete file.

Fragmentation slows down disk access time because the read heads must move to several locations on the disk to read one file. Currently, Windows NT Workstation 4.0 does not offer a de-fragmentation tool. There are third-party disk utilities that can do the job. From within Windows NT, just moving large amount of information from one drive to another and back again re-creates a larger continuous block of clusters that will store data more efficiently.

When multiple users share a computer, Windows NT creates a separate user profile, and all users share the same Recycle Bin. These two items may not amount to much for one user. By default, Windows NT uses up to 10 percent of each drive to store deleted files. On a system with a 2 GB drive, the space used could be up to 200 MB. User profiles maintain a separate list of files for each user in the Recycle Bin if file security has been applied. If a file is marked as No Access to user1 on drive C:, it is not visible by user1 in the Recycle Bin.

To reduce disk usage for a multiple user workstation, follow these steps:

1. Reduce the size of the Recycle Bin that is available per user.

2. Only use one hard drive for the Recycle Bin.

3. Review the content of the Recycle Bin regularly and delete older items.

4. Delete unused User Profiles.

To modify the properties of the Recycle Bin, right-click on the Recycle icon and select Properties. To delete unused user profiles, open the System icon in the Control Panel and select the User Profiles tab. Every new user to log on to an Windows NT Workstation automatically gets his or her own profile. This profile is a copy of the default profile. A roaming profile is stored on the server as well as copied down to each NT computer used during logon.

All improvements in performance come at a price. As pointed out earlier, there will always be faster and newer hardware available. Changing NT's internal configuration may improve performance slightly, but in some cases at the expense of losing a service or resource. Always consider the changes before implementation and be prepared to reverse them if problems occur. The basic configuration generated with a standard install may be more than adequate for most systems.

Exercises

These exercises provide practice for you at using performance monitoring tools effectively to pinpoint bottlenecks. They also demonstrate safe methods to reconfigure a system to maximize its potential.

Exercise 6.1:   Reducing Available Memory

This exercise demonstrates how to modify the Boot.ini file to enable Windows NT to access a restricted amount of memory.

Before you can create a situation that results in a memory bottleneck, you may need to reduce the amount of RAM a computer has. On an Intel-based computer, there is a startup switch called MAXMEM that is added to the Boot.ini and used to limit the amount of memory the system can use. The same bottleneck may result without having to resort to the MAXMEM switch, but on computers with 16 MB of RAM or more it may take more time to manifest itself.

To reduce the amount of physical RAM that Windows NT uses, change the startup command in the Boot.ini file by adding the /Maxmem switch. The minimum amount of RAM that Windows NT Workstation will run on is 12 MB. Reduce the amount of RAM to 12, and the system will almost immediately show a memory bottleneck. This MAXMEM command is only to test or simulate a shortage of memory and should not be left on the system after the test.

 Note   The /Maxmem switch can only be used on an Intel-based computer.

Objective

Set up the objectives in the remaining exercises.

continues

Time Estimate: 5–10 minutes

Steps

To reduce the system's memory to 12 MB, follow these steps:

1. Run the Windows NT Explorer found under Start/Programs.

2. Open the C: drive and locate the Boot.ini file in the right pane.

3. Always make a copy of files that you intend to modify in case the file needs to be restored later. Right-click on the file and select Copy. Right-click anywhere on the C: drive and select Paste. The copy of the file is now called "copy of BOOT."

4. Right-click on the original Boot file and select Properties. Remember that if the extensions are hidden you will not see the Boot.ini only Boot.

5. Click once to remove the Read-only check box so that the file may be modified. Close Properties.

6. Double-click on the Boot file to open and edit it. If the file is not associated with any program, you can select Notepad from the dialog box presented.

7. At the end of the first line in the [operating system] section, add the following entry: /**maxmem:12**.

8. Exit and save the file with the new entry. The Boot file is now ready to start up Windows NT with only 12 MB of RAM available.

9. Restart the computer.

Exercise 6.2: Creating a Memory Log

Exercise 6.2 demonstrates how to create a log to monitor memory usage and determine whether a bottleneck is being created by lack of memory on the system. Exercise 6.2 is guaranteed to show a bottleneck if exercise 6.1 has been completed beforehand. For a true test of the system, either do not complete exercise 6.1 or reverse the effects before proceeding.

Objective

Monitor system performance by using various tools.

Time Estimate: 20–30 minutes

Steps

To create a memory bottleneck log, complete the following steps:

1. Start Windows NT under basic conditions. No additional software or hardware conflicts are occurring. This may not always be possible, but you should try and reduce as many factors as possible to focus the analysis on the memory component.

2. Open Performance Monitor, found under Start Programs, Administrative Tools (Common).

3. Change to the Log view. Choose Log from the View menu.

4. Select the Add Counter icon or Add under the Edit menu.

5. From the list of objects, select the following and add them to the log.

   Memory

   Process

   Page File

   Logical disk

6. Choose the Log item from the Options menu.

7. Give the log file a name such as **Memtest.log** and select a folder for storage. The size of this log should not be considerable. (Always make sure the hard drive used to store the log file has sufficient space if the log is going to run overnight.)

continues

Exercise 6.2: Continued

8. Change the interval to 30 seconds and press the Start Log button.

9. Let the log record for at least 20 to 30 minutes while the system is performing normal tasks. A longer logging period offers more accurate averages and trends.

10. Minimize the Performance Monitor and startup programs that are used frequently on the system.

 Tip   The log file may have bookmarks inserted to help decipher the information later during analysis.

11. Return to Performance Monitor and stop the log.

 Note   Do not overdue this test—a memory bottleneck can always be shown if enough applications are started simultaneously. You do not want to show a bottleneck if none really exist. Run the system under normal circumstances.

Exercise 6.3:   Evaluating the Log File

This exercise helps you understand and interpret the results found in the log that was recorded in exercise 6.2.

Objective

Identify and resolve a given performance problem.

Time Estimate: 10–15 minutes

Steps

1. From the Performance Monitor, choose Data From in the Options menu.

2. Select to view data from a log and type in or browse for the log file **Memtest.log**.

3. Choose Chart from the View menu.

4. Add the following counters to the chart.

   Memory: Page Faults/sec

   Memory: Page Inputs/Sec

   Paging File: %use

5. If the Page Faults/sec are consistently above 10 and the Page Inputs/sec are also spiking, this indicates that the system is low on RAM. Verify the %use of the pagefile to see whether it is increasing over time. This indicates whether the pagefile demands are becoming more extensive as new applications are loaded or whether it is only used when the application starts up. Additional paging that occurs when an application starts up may not be much of a concern as long as paging demands return to lower or normal levels after the application is running.

Exercise 6.4: Creating a Hardware Profile

This exercise creates a hardware profile that will be used to make and test hardware and software changes without the risk of permanently damaging the Windows NT Workstation 4.0 operating system. You must complete this hardware profile before you can start exercise 6.5.

Objective

Optimize system performance in various areas.

Time Estimate: 5–10 minutes

Steps

1. Right-click on the My Computer icon and select Properties. (This is the same as opening the System icon in the Control Panel.)

continues

Exercise 6.4: Continued

2. Select the Hardware Profiles tab.

3. Click on the Copy button.

4. Type **Test Configuration** as the new name for the test profile.

5. Select Wait Indefinitely to enable you the time to make a choice and not load any default configuration. The default hardware profile is always the first listed.

6. Restart the system. Choose the Windows NT Workstation 4.0 item from the Boot menu.

7. A list of two new hardware configurations will be listed. The Original Configuration and your Test Configuration. At this first logon, the Test Configuration is identical to the Original Configuration because no changes have been made.

Exercise 6.5: Improving Memory Performance

You must complete exercise 6.4 before attempting this exercise. The changes that are made can be quickly reversed if the desired results are not achieved. This exercise shows the impact in memory usage when certain services are stopped.

Objective

Optimize system performance in various areas.

Time Estimate: 10—15 minutes

Steps

1. The Memtest.log file created in Exercise 6.2 can be used here as a Baseline log before changes are made to the system. If the Memtest.log file is not available, create one.

2. Boot the computer in the Test Configuration. No changes have been made yet to this profile.

3. From the Control Panel, select the Services icon.

4. Click on the Spooler service.

5. Click on the HW Profile button and disable only the Test Configuration. Disabling the Spooler removes printing capabilities.

6. Click on the Server service and disable it for the Test Configuration. Administrators cannot remotely administer your system and you will not be able to share folders.

7. Click on any other service you think is not required and disable it as well for the Test Configuration.

8. Restart the computer using the same Test Configuration.

9. Create a new memory log called **MemTestAfter.log** and perform the same operations as for MemTest.log for about the same amount of time.

10. Compare the values in the MemTest.log (no system improvements) with MemTestAfter.log (with the system improvements). If the values are not significantly better, it may not have been worth making the improvements.

11. Reboot the computer using the Original Configuration. If the changes did not improve, delete the Test Configuration from the System icon in the Control Panel.

Review Questions

The following questions test your knowledge of the information in this chapter. For additional questions, see the MCP Endeavor and the Microsoft Roadmap/Assessment Exam on the CD that accompanies this book.

1. Which tool can provide information about CPU utilization? (Choose all that apply.)

   A. Performance Monitor

   B. WinMSD

   C. Task Manager

   D. CPU Manager

2. Which counters could be used to identify a physical memory shortage? Pick two.

   A. Thread: % of User Time

   B. Memory: Page Faults/sec

   C. Processor: % Processor Time

   D. LogicalDisk: % Free Space

3. Where can someone find a list of all applications currently running on the system?

   A. From the Start menu

   B. Using the Task Manager

   C. Using the Control Panel's Application icon

   D. Looking at the taskbar

4. You are thinking of stopping an unused service. Before doing so you want to check on service dependencies. Which Windows NT tool could you use?

   A. Services icon in the Control Panel

   B. The Task Manager's Services tab

C. Using WinMSD and the properties of a service

D. The System icon

5. You are looking at the Processes tab of Task Manager. There is some information regarding memory usage that is not listed. How can you get more information displayed in this same window? (Choose all that apply.)

A. Use the Performance Monitor's memory counters.

B. Open two Task Managers.

C. From the View menu, use Select Columns.

D. Change the size of the window using the mouse.

6. You have decided to optimize your Windows NT Workstation 4.0. How can you safely make the changes?

A. Record a log on the system. The log can be used to reconstruct the system at a later time.

B. Use the HardWare Profiles feature and make a test configuration. If a failure occurs, the system can be restarted using the Original Configuration.

C. Document all changes in the WinMSD utility. The system will recover automatically.

D. Make sure the User Profiles are enabled. All changes made to the system will only affect the current user.

7. What is the relationship between counters, instances, and objects in Performance Monitor?

A. Objects are categories that contain specific counters for all instances.

B. An object is a unit of each instance. A counter is only used to determine the number of events occurring on a system.

C. Performance Monitor uses counters only.

D. All objects are divided into counters. Each counter can be monitored for a given instance or a total instance.

8. A baseline log was created a few week ago and is stored on the local hard drive in a logs folder. Which tool could you use to view this log? (Choose all that apply.)

   A. From the System icon, use Log view and select the log file.

   B. Using the Performance Monitor.

   C. A log file can only be viewed by Microsoft.

   D. Using the Event Viewer.

9. What are the two objects used to monitor disk activity?

   A. DiskPerf

   B. Physical Disk

   C. Hard Disk

   D. Logical Disk

10. You have decided to stop unused service using hardware profiles. Which services can be stopped without preventing the user from connecting with other computers? (Choose all that apply.)

    A. Browser

    B. Redirector

    C. Spooler

    D. Server

11. You have been monitoring disk activity in a log for the last eight hours. Yet when you display the counters they all read 0. What is the meaning of these readings?

    A. The disk has been still for the entire logging period.

    B. The Performance Monitor is not functioning correctly and needs to be reinstalled.

    C. The DiskPerf utility was not enabled.

    D. The PhysicalDisk Counter was not enabled.

12. After making several configuration changes to the system, you reboot and log on. Several seconds after you have logged on, the system presents an error dialog box. You reboot again and use the Last Known Good command. The same error appears. What could be the problem?

   A. The Last Known Good works only with hardware profiles.

   B. The Last Known Good was updated after you logged on, replacing the good configuration with the current one.

   C. The Last Known Good was not told to update on exit. You must boot up using the letter L and tell the system to update the Last Known Good.

   D. None of the above.

13. What are some of the factors that affect disk performance? (Choose all that apply.)

   A. The partition size

   B. The amount of information on the disk

   C. The name of the files

   D. The DiskPerf utility

14. You need to monitor activity on your system. You suspect a lot of network activity. How can you substantiate your suspicions? (Choose all that apply.)

   A. Use the Performance Monitor, making sure DiskPerf is enabled.

   B. Using the Server Service icon in the Control Panel.

   C. Using the Task Manager's Network tab.

   D. Using the Server icon in the Control Panel.

15. How does upgrading to 32-bit applications make a difference on the system? Pick all that apply.

   A. 32-bit applications run faster because they are only written by Microsoft.

    B. 32-bit applications run directly in the system's win32 module and no emulation is required.

    C. 32-bit applications cannot run under Windows NT.

    D. 32-bit applications run faster because they can be multithreaded, are designed to make better use of the processor, and run at a higher priority.

16. The hard drive on your Windows NT 4.0 computer seems to be full. You investigate the C: drive using Explorer and find very little software loaded. What could be using up so much hard drive space? (Choose all that apply.)

    A. The disk is fragmented.

    B. There are several Recycle Bins at full capacity.

    C. The DiskPerf utility is active.

    D. The size of a FAT partition is very large, using large clusters.

17. You have lost your Emergency Recovery Disk. You can create a new one from any other Windows NT Workstation 4.0 computer. True or False?

    A. True

    B. False

18. The system has generated an error code. What tool can you use to review the error code? (Choose all that apply.)

    A. The Performance Monitor

    B. The System icon in the Control Panel

    C. The Event Viewer

    D. The Task Manager

19. You need to quickly free up system memory without restarting the system. What can be done? (Choose all that apply.)

    A. Close any applications or files that are not required

    B. Minimize all background applications

    C. Run a 16-bit application in its own memory address space

    D. Increase the size of the pagefile

20. You have been logging disk objects for the last few days. What are you looking for in the log to indicate whether a disk bottleneck is occurring?

    A. CPU activity is above 85 percent consistently.

    B. PageFaults/sec counter is above 2.

    C. The Pagefile increases consistently.

    D. Disk usage is above 85 percent.

Review Answers

1. A and C are correct. The Performance Monitor offers CPU usage counters and Task Manager shows the CPU usage in a chart. For more information, see the sections entitled "Pinpointing Processor Bottlenecks" and "Using the Performance Tab."

2. B and C are correct. The Page Faults counter shows the number of requests that are not found in physical memory and processor time may indicate a lot of paging activity being processed. For more information, see the section entitled "Pinpointing Processor Bottlenecks."

3. B and D are correct. The Task Manager shows an Application tab that list all running applications and the taskbar at the bottom of the screen shows all opened windows. For more information, see the section entitled "Using the Application Tab."

4. C is correct. The WinMSD offers a list of all services, and their properties show the dependencies. For more information, see the section entitled "Running Windows NT Services."

5. C is correct. The View menu offers a Select Column item that offers up to 14 columns of information. If all columns

are selected, a scroll bar is available. The size of the window cannot be changed. For more information, see the section entitled "Using the Processes Tab."

6. B is correct. The hardware profile can be used to make changes to a given profile without affecting the original profile. For more information, see the section entitled "Creating Hardware Profiles."

7. D is correct. For more information, see the section entitled "Using the Performance Monitor."

8. B is correct. Performance Monitor logs can only be viewed using the Performance Monitor. For more information, see the section entitled "Using Logs."

9. B and D are correct. DiskPerf is not an object; it only activates objects. The hard disk is not an object either. For more information, see the section entitled "Pinpointing Disk Bottlenecks."

10. A, C, and D are correct. The Redirector is the client software that connects the workstation to a Server service on another system. For more information, see the section entitled "Running Windows NT Services."

11. C is correct. The DiskPerf utility enables disk counters. For more information, see the section entitled "Pinpointing Disk Bottlenecks."

12. B is correct. For more information, see the section entitled "Using the Last Known Good Configuration."

13. A, B, and D are correct. Large FAT partitions may waste disk space. A full disk tends to be fragmented because there is less room to store data continuously and running the Disk-Perf utility will slow down the disk. For more information, see the sections entitled "Choosing Partition Size and Format" and "Disk Access Issues."

14. A and D are correct. The DiskPerf can show file and print sharing accessing the drives. The Server icon can show users that are connected and resources being used. For more

information, see the sections entitled "Using the Server Tool" and "Pinpointing Network Bottlenecks."

15. B and C are correct. For more information, see the section entitled "Running Tasks and Applications."

16. A, B, and D are correct. Disk fragmentation creates holes on the disk that are not used. NT can use one Recycle Bin per hard drive. The default size is 10 percent of space. Large clusters on a FAT partition may waste disk space. For more information, see the section entitled "Choosing Partition Size and Disk Format."

17. B is correct. Parts of Registry are stored on the ERD and are unique to each system. For more information, see the section entitled "Creating and Maintaining an Emergency Repair Disk."

18. C is correct. The Event Viewer stores errors generated by applications and the operating system. For more information, see the section entitled "Monitoring with the Event Viewer."

19. A and B are correct. Applications that are opened will be stored in memory and full-screen applications take up more memory than minimized. For more information, see the section entitled "Running Tasks and Applications."

20. D is correct. The Disk Usage counter may spike above 85 percent, but should not remain that high. Page faults and the pagefile have to do with memory bottlenecks. CPU usage reflects CPU or memory bottlenecks. For more information, see the section entitled "Identifying and Resolving Performance Problems."

Answers to Test Yourself Questions at the Beginning of the Chapter

1. Use the Task Manager's Applications tab, select the application, and then click on End Task. For more information, see the section entitled "Using the Task Manager."

2. Use the Task Manager and compare the memory column of each process. Each application uses one or more processes. For more information, see the section entitled "Using the Task Manager."

3. Under normal use of your computer, compare the total physical memory with the total committed memory in the Performance tab of the Task Manager. If total committed and peak are always higher than physical memory, you may want to purchase RAM to bring your physical memory up to the total commit or peak values. For more information, see the section entitled "Pinpointing Memory Bottlenecks."

4. Use the Performance Monitor to track the amount of bytes read or bytes written to your disk under the Network object. For more information, see the section entitled "Pinpointing Network Bottlenecks."

5. Use the Performance Monitor and create a log file during normal use of your computer. If an error occurs, you can pass on the log file. Include objects such as Processor, Memory, Physical Disk and Paging File. The support department can then analyze this log file. For more information, see the section entitled "Using Logs" in the "Using the Performance Monitor" section.

Chapter

Troubleshooting

7

By the end of this chapter, you should be able to execute the following test objectives relating to troubleshooting a Windows NT Workstation 4.0:

▶ Choose the appropriate course of action to take when the boot process fails

▶ Choose the appropriate course of action to take when a print job fails

▶ Choose the appropriate course of action to take when the installation process fails

▶ Choose the appropriate course of action to take when an application fails

▶ Choose the appropriate course of action to take when a user cannot access a resource

▶ Modify the Registry using the appropriate tool

▶ Implement advanced techniques to resolve various problems

The modern digital computer contains numerous components that interact with each other: both hardware and software. The potential for malfunctions, poorly performing systems, and general system failure always exists. The key to successful troubleshooting is to isolate the component or module responsible for the trouble, fix or modify the problem, and test the results. Often the issue at hand isn't easily isolated, and may not arise out of one simple factor. Catastrophic failure is the easiest problem to fix, because the problem is always there to be analyzed. It is the intermittent problems that are the most troublesome, and challenging.

The best weapon that any professional can have in his or her arsenal when attempting to troubleshoot a system problem is the knowledge of how the underlying system is supposed to work. With that knowledge, and using the various diagnostic tools that Microsoft includes with Windows NT Workstation 4.0, you can fix many, if not most of the common problems you encounter.

This chapter builds on the information that you learned about in Chapter 6, "Monitoring and Optimization," using many of the same tools and techniques. The basic difference between the information presented in that chapter, and in this one is that problems discussed in this chapter are essentially showstoppers that require a solution before your client can proceed with additional work.

Test Yourself! Before reading this chapter, test yourself to determine how much study time you will need to devote to this section.

1. What phase of the startup process displays the blue screen with a series of dots added to the screen?

2. How do you return to your workstation's previous configuration?

3. How do you create a boot floppy?

4. How do you share a printer so that it is available to others on the network?

5. What is a service pack?

6. What are the most common reasons that a user can't log on to a domain?

7. How can you tell which service has failed?

8. What is a user profile, and what does it control?

9. Who "owns" a resource?

10. Why is much of the Windows NT Registry not worth backing up?

11. How long do events remain in an Event Log?

12. What utility is useful in determining resource conflicts?

Answers are located at the end of the chapter...

Assessing Boot Process Failures

When you know that your workstation's hardware is correctly functioning, the failure of Windows NT Workstation to start up properly and load the Windows NT shell may be a boot process problem. The key to solving problems of this type is to understand the logical sequence that your workstation uses when starting up. Windows NT shows you various boot sequence errors, the meaning of which should help you determine the problem with your system. You can also diagnose the boot.ini file to determine the nature of any potential problems, and you can apply your emergency repair disks to boot your system and repair common boot process failure problems.

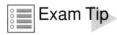 **Exam Tip**

This is likely to be on the exam because a boot failure often requires the direct intervention of support personnel to alleviate the problem as a priority.

A boot failure is a very obvious error, and one of the most common problems that you will encounter. When you or your client can't start your computer up, you know you have a problem. It's also the kind of problem that forces you to stop what you are doing and fix it before you can go on to further work.

The Boot Sequence

Your computer begins the boot sequence after the Power On Self Test (POST) completes itself. The first series of messages that you see when you turn the power on to your computer are hardware related, and are not associated with the boot process. Your memory is tested, for example, and then your bus structure is tested. Your computer runs a series of tests. These tests signal to peripheral devices and sense their reply to check for successful I/O performance. You may see a series of messages that your mouse and keyboard are detected, the appearance of an IDE drive, whether a SCSI adapter is detected, response from any devices on that SCSI chain, and so forth. Failure at this stage isn't a boot sequence problem.

The boot sequence initiates when the hard drive Master Boot Record (MBR) is read into memory and begins to load the different portions of the Windows NT operating system. Windows NT Workstation runs on different microprocessor architectures. The exact boot sequence depends on the type of microprocessor on which you have installed Windows NT Workstation.

The NT Loader

Windows NT loads on an Intel x86 computer by reading a file called the NTLDR or NT Loader into memory from the boot sector of the startup or active partition on your boot drive. The NTLDR is a hidden system file set to be read-only. NTLDR is located in the root folder of your system partition, and can be viewed in the Windows NT Explorer when you set the View All File Type option.

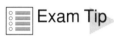 Exam Tip

This is likely to be on the exam because by understanding the boot sequence you can detect and correct many common configuration errors that prevent users from accessing their machine.

NTLDR does the following things:

▶ Turns on the 32-bit flat memory model required by the Windows NT kernel to address RAM.

▶ Turns on the minifile system driver to access the system and boot partitions.

▶ Displays the Boot Loader menu system on your monitor that provides you a selection of the operating system to use. These selections are contained in the boot.ini file in your systemroot directory.

You can install Windows NT Workstation over a previous installation of MS-DOS or Windows 95. These operating systems will appear in the menu, and call the bootsect.dos file when they are loaded and executed. bootsect.dos loads and hands off at the end of the boot process to the operating system component responsible for I/O communication. In Windows 95 that file is the io.sys file.

▶ After you select an operating system, a hardware detection routine is initiated. For Windows NT, the NTDETECT.COM program is responsible for this routine, and creates a hardware list passed to the NTLDR program.

▶ The operating system kernel is then loaded. The ntoskrnl.exe file located in the %systemroot%\System32 folder is called to load the kernel of Windows NT. The menu is replaced by the OS Loader V4.00 screen.

▶ A blue screen appears that loads the Hardware Abstraction Layer (HAL). To execute this the hal.dll is called with a set of routines that isolate operating system functions from I/O.

▶ The HKEY_LOCAL_MACHINE\System hive of the Registry is read and the system is loaded. Registry hives are stored as files in the %systemroot%\System32\Config folder.

▶ The boot time drivers HKEY_LOCAL_MACHINE\System\ CurrentControlSet\Control\ServiceGroupOrder are loaded. For each driver loaded, a dot is added to the OS Loader screen.

By entering the /SOS switch in the boot.ini file Windows NT will list the driver's name in the OS Loader screen as Windows NT Workstation starts up.

▶ The list of supported hardware devices is handed off from ntdetect.com to ntoskrnl.exe.

▶ After ntoskrnl.exe executes, the computer's boot phase finishes and the software you have installed begins to be loaded.

A RISC computer contains the NTLDR software as part of its BIOS. Therefore, the boot phase of a RISC-based computer is both simpler and faster than the boot phase of an Intel x86 computer. A RISC computer keeps its hardware configuration in its BIOS, which obviates the need for the ntdetect.com file. Another item kept in firmware is the list of any valid operating system and how to access it. This means that a RISC computer doesn't use a boot.ini file as well.

A RISC computer boots by loading a file called the osloader.exe file. After reading the hardware configuration from the BIOS and executing, osloader.exe hands off the boot process to the ntoskrnl.exe. Then the hal.dll is loaded, followed by the system file, which ends the RISC Windows NT boot process.

Since the boot.ini file is a text file, you can edit this file to control aspects of the boot process. Open the Windows NT Explorer and remove the read-only attribute from this file (which is located in the %systemroot% top-level folder) before you begin. There are two sections to the boot.ini: the [boot loader], and [operating systems] sections.

You will see parameters that control the time a user has to decide on an operating system (timeout) as well as the default location in an ARC- (Advanced RISC) compliant path nomenclature. Although you can change the default operating system and the timeout by editing the boot.ini file, you will probably find it easier to change these parameters on the Startup/Shutdown tab of the Systems Properties dialog box.

To change system startup parameters, complete the following steps:

1. Right-click on the My Computer icon and choose the Properties command from the Shortcut menu.

2. Click on the Startup/Shutdown tab of the Systems Properties dialog box if necessary (see fig. 7.1).

Figure 7.1

The Startup/ Shutdown tab of the Systems Properties dialog box.

3. Enter the operating system desired in the Startup list box.

4. Change the timeout parameter in the Show List for ... Seconds spinner.

5. Click on the OK button.

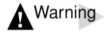 **Warning**

> The advantage that making changes in the Systems Properties dialog box has to editing the boot.ini file is that any mistake entering information into the boot.ini file can cause your system to fail at boot up.

When you encounter a blue screen error, you may need to employ a *memory dump* of your system for diagnostic purposes. A memory dump is a copy of the data held in RAM. To save that file, you need free disk space equal to your installed RAM plus an additional MB of space.

To take a memory dump, check the Write debugging information to and Overwrite any existing file check boxes in the Startup/ Shutdown tab of System Control Panel. Close that Control Panel and confirm any alerts about page file size should they occur. Then reboot your computer. The memory dump file is written to the location displayed in the Startup/Shutdown tab text box.

The Load Process

After the boot portion of the operating system loads, your device drivers are loaded and the boot process is handed off to the operating system kernel. In Windows NT, this portion of the startup occurs when the screen turns a blue color and the text shrinks. At that point, the kernel is initializing. The operating system begins to read various hives in the Windows NT Registry. One of the first hives read is the CurrentControlSet, which is copied to the Clone-ControlSet and from which a HARDWARE key is written to RAM. The System hive is read to determine whether any other additional drivers need to be loaded into RAM and initialized. This ends the kernel initialization phase.

The Session Manager then reads the System hive in the Registry to determine which programs are required prior to Windows NT itself being loaded. Commonly the AUTOCHK.EXE program (a stripped down version of CHKDSK.EXE) runs and reads the file system. Other programs defined in the HKEY_LOCAL_MACHINE\SYSTEM\CurrentControlSet\Control\SessionManager\BootExecute key are run, and a page file is then created in the location stored in the HKEY_LOCAL_MACHINE\SYSTEM\CurrentControlSet\Control\Session Manager\Memory Management key. The Software hive is read, and the Session Manager then loads other required subsystems as defined in the HKEY_LOCAL_MACHINE\SYSTEM\CurrentControlSet\Control\SessionManager\Subsystems\Required key. This ends the portion of the boot process where services are loaded into RAM.

 Tip

> The *Windows NT Resource Kit* contains a more detailed description of the boot process than that presented here. That kit also contains some additional tools for determining which drivers have loaded, and other diagnostic functions.

After services are loaded, the Windows WIN32 Subsystem starts to load. This is where Windows NT Workstation switches into a Graphics (GUI) mode. The WINLOGON module runs and the Welcome dialog box appears. The Windows operating system is still loading at this point, but the user can enter his user name, domain, and password to initiate the logon process. After the Service Controller (SERVICES.EXE) loads and initializes the Computer Browser, Workstation, Server, Spooler, and so on, the request for logon is passed to the domain controller for service.

The SERVICES.EXE program is a central program in the Windows NT operating system. It initializes various system DLL files. Should this file be damaged, you must reinstall Windows NT Workstation.

The following DLLs provide operating system services:

- ▶ **Alerter (alrsvc.dll).** Provides messaging services and event alerts.

- ▶ **Computer Browser (browser.dll).** Provides a way for locating resources on the network.

- ▶ **EventLog (eventlog.dll).** Notes and enters events into the three log files.

- ▶ **Messenger (msgsvc.dll).** Provides interapplication communications that enable one application to communicate with another.

- ▶ **Net Logon (netlogon.dll).** Has the code required to request resource validation from domain servers.

- ▶ **NT LM Security Support Provider (ntmssos.dll).** Provides security support.

- ▶ **Server (srvsvc.dll).** Enables Windows NT Workstation to provide limited network services to other computers.

- ▶ **TCP/IP NetBIOS Helper (lmhsvc.dll).** Handles IP address resolution.

- ▶ **Workstation (wkssvc.dll).** Enables a Windows NT Workstation computer to access resources on the network. Workstation includes services that enable the computer to log on to a domain, to connect to shared resources such as printers and directories, and to participate in client/server applications running over the network.

Key Concepts

A successful logon is considered the completion of the boot process. To mark the event, Windows NT Workstation updates the LastKnownGood control set key in the Registry with information about what got loaded and the current system configuration at startup.

Last Known Good Recovery

The Last Known Good configuration provides a method for recovering to your preceding system setup. When you create a specific configuration for Windows NT, that information is stored in a particular control set. The LastKnownGood control set enables you to recover from a boot process error—provided that you use this method immediately after discovering the error on the first boot up attempt and do not log on a second time. Subsequent boots (if they proceed and you log on to the system again) remove this option as a recovery method.

The information contained in the LastKnownGood configuration is stored in the Registry in the HKEY_LOCAL_MACHINE\ SYSTEM\CurrentControlSet key.

To boot to the Last Known Good configuration, follow these steps:

1. Reboot your system.

2. Press the spacebar when a message appears asking you whether you want to boot the Last Known Good configuration.

3. When the Hardware Profile/Configuration Recovery menu appears, select a hardware profile and press the L key for the Last Known Good configuration.

In instances where a critical system error was encountered, Windows NT Workstation defaults to the Last Known Good configuration on its own accord. This doesn't always occur, but is a frequent occurrence. Should basic operating system files be damaged, you must boot up using a boot floppy and recover your system as described in the next few sections.

Boot Sequence Errors

The most common boot sequence errors occur when the operating system components required for the boot process cannot be found or are corrupted. Often a modification of the boot.ini file leads to a failure to boot properly. If you or your client have recently made a modification to the startup files, you should suspect that problem first.

Catastrophic hardware failure is not a common problem, but it is encountered—particularly in older equipment. If a hard drive stops operating, it is obvious because your computer sounds differently. Also, when you open the case of the computer and listen to it, you won't hear the hard drive spin up and achieve its operating speed.

Much less obvious are hardware errors that damage the capability of your system to start up without appearing to alter the performance of your system noticeably. If your hard drive develops a bad disk sector, which contains the operating system components responsible for booting your computer, for example, the computer appears to function correctly. This problem is solved by re-establishing the boot files on another portion of your hard drive.

The following error messages appear when there is a problem with the boot.ini file. If you get one of these error messages and the Windows shell doesn't load, you should suspect the boot.ini file and use a boot disk or an Emergency Repair Disk (ERD) to repair the boot.ini file. Later in this chapter, you learn how to create an ERD.

This message indicates that the Windows NT Loader file is either damaged or corrupted:

```
BOOT: Couldn't find NTLDR
Please insert another disk
```

Typically, the error with the NTLDR file occurs early on in the boot process. When you see a repeated sequence of error messages indicating that Windows NT Workstation is checking hardware, the error is a problem with the ntdetect.com file. These messages appear as follows:

```
NTDETECT V1.0 Checking Hardware…
NTDETECT V1.0 Checking Hardware…
NTDETECT V1.0 Checking Hardware…
```

It is possible for Windows NT to load even if the boot.ini file is missing. If that is the case, the NTLDR starts Windows NT loading files it finds in the <default>\WINNT folder. If the operating system was installed in another location, an error message appears indicating that the ntoskrnl.exe file is missing or corrupt. The following error message appears when the boot.ini file is damaged or when it points to a location that no longer contains the Windows NT Workstation operating system files:

```
Windows NT could not start because the following file is missing
or corrupt:
\<winnt root>\system32\ntoskrnl.exe
Please re-install a copy of the above file.
```

This message indicates that the Windows NT operating system kernel has failed to load. The problem most often occurs when someone inadvertently renames the folder containing the operating system files without realizing the consequences of that action. The solution is to use your boot disk to gain access to the system and to rename the folder back to the location contained in the boot.ini file. It is less common to see a change in the boot.ini file giving rise to this problem, as that requires a knowledgeable user's action.

Another potential explanation for the inability of the kernel to load could be that you used the Disk Administrator to create a partition with free space. If you changed the partition number that contains your Windows NT operating system files, the pointer in the boot.ini file no longer points to the correct location. To fix this problem, you need to edit the pointer to the partition to correct the partition number so that it correctly locates your Windows NT operating system files.

When there is a problem with the boot sector, the following error message appears during startup:

```
I/O Error accessing boot sector file
Multi(0)disk(0)rdisk(0)partition(1):\bootsect.dos
```

This error message may indicate a problem with your hard drive. You should boot from a boot disk and run the RDISK utility.

Windows NT Workstation also posts a more specific message when it can determine that the error in locating the boot sector is hardware related. The operating system checks hardware (as you have just seen) by testing it during startup. Failure to respond to one of these tests generates the following message:

```
OS Loader V4.00
Windows NT could not start because of a computer disk hardware
configuration problem.
Could not read from the selected boot disk. Check boot path and
disk hardware.
Please check the Windows NT™ documentation about hardware disk
configuration and your hardware reference manuals for additional
information.
```

The preceding message indicates that the pointer in the boot.ini file that locates the Windows NT operating system references a damaged or nonexisting device, or a partition that doesn't contain a file system that Windows NT can access with the boot loader.

Finally, you may see a STOP error when the Windows NT Loader cannot resolve the appropriate partition that contains your operating system files. This error takes the following form:

```
STOP: 0x000007E: Inaccessible Boot Device
```

This error appears when the hard disk controller has difficulty determining which is the boot device—if your computer contains an Adaptec SCSI disk controller, for example, and there is an ID number conflict. Other instances where this error occurs is when the Master Boot Records (MBR) is corrupted by a virus or a disk error.

If you have an internal IDE drive on the workstation and a SCSI disk drive with an ID number set to 0, you will also see the inaccessible boot device problem appear. The 0 ID number is used to specify which disk is the internal disk, and this drive conflicts with a boot partition on the IDE drive. Any bootable SCSI disks may also be booted in preference to your internal IDE drive, so you may want to make all SCSI drives non-bootable to prevent the SCSI disk controller from booting that SCSI drive. (Some disk adapters dynamically assign SCSI device numbers, but they aren't particularly common.) If Windows NT DETECT program in the boot loader assigns the SCSI bus adapter the number 0, this too makes the reference in the boot.ini file to your internal IDE drive inaccurate.

Tip
As a general rule, SCSI drives are faster than IDE drives and preferred by the operating system. Don't mix and match these two different drive types. If you have a SCSI disk controller and SCSI drives, use those to locate your boot partition on.

Key Concepts
If your system proceeds through the load phase and boots correctly but still seems to be malfunctioning, you should check the System Event Log to see whether any system messages were written to the log.

The System Log may display errors, warnings, or informational events that contain an explanation of the conditions leading to the anomaly that you observe due to an error in the boot sequence. Use the Event Viewer program in the Administrative Tools folder on the Program submenu of the Start menu to view the System Log. Choose the System Log command on the Log menu to open the System log. Figure 7.2 shows a System Log with various events.

Boot Disk Recovery

If your hard disk boot partition fails, you can start up from a floppy disk provided you create a Windows NT boot disk prior to the error condition occurring. If you have installed a multi-partition system and your boot partition contains Windows NT, you can also use your boot disk to start up from your floppy disk drive. After you have started your system using the floppy disk drive, you can perform procedures to test and repair any errors that exist.

Figure 7.2

*The System Log
in the Event
Viewer applica-
tion.*

Date	Time	Source	Category	Event	User	Computer
8/15/97	5:16:09 AM	Srv	None	2021	N/A	LUIGI
8/15/97	5:14:43 AM	NETLOGON	None	5719	N/A	LUIGI
8/15/97	4:59:25 AM	NETLOGON	None	5719	N/A	LUIGI
8/15/97	4:59:18 AM	Service Control Mar	None	7024	N/A	LUIGI
8/15/97	4:59:12 AM	Srv	None	2012	N/A	LUIGI
8/15/97	4:59:12 AM	Srv	None	2012	N/A	LUIGI
8/15/97	4:58:51 AM	Serial	None	11	N/A	LUIGI
8/15/97	4:58:51 AM	Serial	None	24	N/A	LUIGI
8/15/97	4:58:51 AM	Serial	None	24	N/A	LUIGI
8/15/97	4:58:51 AM	Serial	None	11	N/A	LUIGI
8/15/97	4:58:51 AM	Serial	None	22	N/A	LUIGI
8/15/97	4:58:51 AM	Serial	None	22	N/A	LUIGI
8/15/97	4:58:38 AM	EventLog	None	6005	N/A	LUIGI
8/15/97	4:58:51 AM	Serial	None	3	N/A	LUIGI
7/30/97	9:23:56 AM	NETLOGON	None	5719	N/A	LUIGI
7/30/97	9:08:37 AM	NETLOGON	None	5719	N/A	LUIGI
7/30/97	9:08:29 AM	Service Control Mar	None	7024	N/A	LUIGI
7/30/97	9:08:24 AM	Srv	None	2012	N/A	LUIGI
7/30/97	9:08:24 AM	Srv	None	2012	N/A	LUIGI
7/30/97	9:08:02 AM	Serial	None	11	N/A	LUIGI
7/30/97	9:08:02 AM	Serial	None	24	N/A	LUIGI

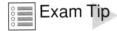 **Exam Tip**

> This is likely to be on the exam because the maintenance of a
> boot disk and an Emergency Recovery Disk set is one of the
> most powerful methods for resolving many startup problems.

Most computers are started up from their floppy disk drives—
commonly given the volume label A. If your computer is set up to
start up from your hard drive, you must change this in your computer's BIOS setup. Press the keystroke displayed in the startup
sequence to open your computer's setup. Then change the boot
sequence to start up from the floppy disk drive prior to attempting to boot from a boot floppy disk. If your Windows NT Workstation is a NetPC computer and does not have a floppy disk, you
cannot boot from a floppy disk.

To create a floppy boot disk, do the following:

1. Insert a blank floppy disk in your floppy disk drive.

2. Double-click on My Computer on your Desktop.

3. Right-click on the icon for your floppy disk drive, and then
   select the Format command from the shortcut menu.

4. Click on the OK button to begin the formatting, and then
   click on the OK button to confirm that formatting occurred.

5. Select the Windows NT Explorer command from the Programs submenu of the Start menu.

6. Select the boot.ini, NTLDR, ntbootdd.sys, and ntdetect.com files in the root directory of your hard drive in the Windows NT Explorer. This directory is commonly the C:\ drive.

7. Right-click on any of the selected files and drag them to the icon for your floppy disk drive.

8. Choose the Copy Here command from the shortcut menu.

9. Restart your computer with the boot floppy disk in the floppy disk drive to test the disk.

The Emergency Repair Disk (ERD)

When a portion of the Windows NT Registry becomes corrupted, your workstation can become unstable and crash. In some instances, these errors even prevent you from starting your computer up and booting the Windows NT operating system itself. You can repair the Windows NT Registry by creating an ERD that contains the important system Registry information and using that disk to repair your system configuration.

An ERD contains backup information about your workstation's security account manager (SAM) database, your system configuration, and important system configuration parameters. Also copied to the ERD are the two files required to create a virtual DOS machine (NTVDM): autoexec.nt and config.nt.

You are prompted to create an ERD when you install Windows NT Workstation. If you prefer, you can create an ERD at a later time. Regardless of whether you choose to create an ERD, the appropriate files are copied to the %systemroot%\Repair directory.

If you search for the topic of the Emergency Repair Disk in the online Help system, Windows NT Workstation's Help system steps you through the process of either creating or updating your ERD. You can also open a Command Prompt window and create or update your ERD by using the rdisk.exe command.

RDISK performs the following functions:

► Copies the Registry default hive (HKEY_USERS\DEFAULT)

► Copies the Registry security hive (HKEY_LOCAL_MACHINE\Security)

► Copies the Registry software hive (HKEY_LOCAL_MACHINE\Software)

► Copies the Registry system hive (HKEY_LOCAL_MACHINE\System)

► Copies the workstation SAM

► Copies the Registry autoexec.nt file

► Copies the config.nt file

These files are copied into the %systemroot%\REPAIR folder. After these files are copied into the REPAIR folder, the RDISK utility prompts you for a floppy disk on which to create an ERD. The information in the REPAIR folder is copied on to this disk.

 Caution

The ERD is only useful if you update it on a regular basis. You should consider updating the ERD before any major software installations or upgrades are performed, before any changes to your security policy occurs, and before the hardware configuration of your workstation changes. If this information is not current on your ERD, the restoration you can perform using the ERD is of limited value. The ERD doesn't take the place of a full volume backup, it saves only data that can help re-establish your system configuration based on information contained in the Registry.

To create an ERD, follow these steps:

1. Choose the Command Prompt command from the Programs submenu of the Start menu.

2. Enter **RDISK /S** at the command prompt, and then press Enter.

3. Click on the Create Repair Disk button in the Repair Disk Utility dialog box (see fig. 7.3).

Figure 7.3

The Repair Disk Utility dialog box.

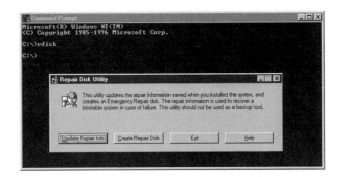

4. Insert a formatted floppy disk, and then click on the OK button.

5. After Windows NT Workstation creates the ERD, remove the floppy disk, write-protect the disk, and store it away.

6. Click on the Exit button to close RDISK.

7. Click on Close.

The information copied to the ERD is in compressed format. To restore a Registry key by using the Registry Editor and the ERD data, expand the files by using the Windows NT Expand program. The following list of files are found on an ERD:

▶ **autoexec.nt and config.nt.** The two files responsible for a Virtual DOS Machine. They correspond to the autoexec.bat and config.sys files on MS-DOS. The first runs a batch file; the second sets an environment.

▶ **default._.** The compressed copy of the System's default profile.

▶ **ntuser.da_.** The compressed copy of the ntuser.dat file, which stores user profiles.

▶ **sam._.** The compressed copy of the SAM hive of the Registry with a copy of the Windows NT accounts database. A workstation's SAM doesn't contain as much information as a server's (especially a domain server) SAM does. Missing is information about other machine and user accounts that the workstation doesn't know about.

▶ **security._.** The compressed copy of the Security hive with SAM and security policy information for your workstation's users.

▶ **setup.log.** This text file has the names of the Windows setup and installation files, and checksums for each file. The file is used to determine whether essential system files are either missing or corrupt. If so, it replaces them in a recovery operation.

▶ **software._.** A compressed copy of the Software hive with information about installed programs and associated files and configuration information for those programs.

▶ **system._.** A compressed copy of the System hive of the Registry. This hive contains the Windows NT control set.

To update the ERD, run the RDISK program and select the Update Repair Info button and confirm that you want to overwrite the current repair information.

The importance of using the S switch for the RDISK program is worth noting. This switch updates the DEFAULT._ SECURITY, and SAM changes without requiring that you go through the Create Repair Disk? dialog box first. Without it, changes to your account information are not noted. If you have a lot of accounts, updating this information can take some time. Also, your ERD will likely expand beyond the single floppy disk limit. In that case, the RDISK program asks you for additional disks, as needed.

Restoring Your System Using the ERD

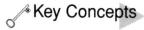

When you use the ERD to repair a damaged Windows NT Workstation, the procedure essentially reinstalls the sections of the operating system that are required for your particular setup. The data that you copied to the ERD contained in the Windows NT Registry determines which files need to be replaced, and how the configuration should be re-established.

Among the things that the ERD does are the following:

▶ Runs CHKDSK to determine the validity of the partition containing your Windows NT system files

▶ Determines whether the individual files on a system partition are valid, as determined by the use of a checksum

▶ Restores missing or corrupt files from your Windows NT installation disks

▶ Replaces your default system and security Registry hives

▶ Replaces the Security Account Manager hives

▶ Reinstalls the files responsible for booting your system in the Boot Loader: boot.ini, NTLDR, ntbootdd.sys, and ntdetect.com.

Note

Before you begin to restore your system, make sure you have your Windows NT Setup floppy disks handy. If you can't find those disks, you can create them from the installation CD by using the WINNT /O or the /OX switch. You can find online documentation for the WINNT.EXE program in the Help system.

To restore Windows NT Workstation on an Intel x386 system, complete the following steps:

1. Insert the Windows NT Workstation Setup boot disk into your floppy disk drive. (Make sure your system boots from a floppy disk first.)

2. Turn on your system, and then insert Setup Disk 2 when asked. Press the Enter key.

3. Press the R key to perform a repair.

4. Press the Enter key to mark any options that you wish to restore, press Tab to move to the Continue button, and press the Enter key again.

5. Press Enter to detect devices.

6. Insert the Setup Disk 3 into your floppy disk when requested.

7. Insert additional disks with device drives when the Other Disk option appears, and then replace that (those) disk(s) with Setup Disk 3 again.

8. Press Enter and insert your ERD when requested, and then press Enter again.

9. Press Enter to select each Registry hive you wish to restore, and then move to the Continue button and press Enter again.

10. Press the A key to replace all modified system files.

11. Insert any required device driver files requested.

12. Press the Esc key to have Setup ignore the Windows NT Workstation DRVLIB disk, if you wish.

13. When the program is complete, reboot your computer.

You can choose the following four main options to repair in the recovery process:

▶ **Inspect Registry Files.** By using your ERD, you can repair corrupt portions of the Registry. You can select to repair any or all of the following hives: Default, Security/SAM, Software, and/or System. Changes to the Registry do not require the use of the Windows NT installation CDs.

▶ **Inspect Startup Environment.** Any boot files are inspected, dissected, and potentially rejected. Because all default boot files are equivalent, you can use any ERD to replace startup files.

▶ **Verify Windows NT System Files.** This option compares any system file (with the system attribute) in the Windows NT directory and any subdirectories and verifies them using the checksum values in the setup.log file. You need your installation disks to perform this repair.

▶ **Inspect Boot Sector.** The prime reason that the boot sector becomes invalid is by upgrading MS-DOS, or Windows 95 using the SYS command. Use an ERD (any ERD) and the installation disks to repair this problem.

Each ERD that you create is specific to the type of computer (vendor and CPU type) on which it is created. An ERD that you create on one system does not work on another system. The process of restoring a RISC system containing the Windows NT Workstation as its operating system is similar in concept to the procedure previously described. The individual sequence differs, however, depending on the specific manufacturer for your system.

To restore a RISC-based Windows NT system, complete the following steps:

1. Start the Windows NT Setup program as your computer's manual instructs you to.

2. Insert the ERD, and then follow your computer's instructions that appear on your monitor.

After the repair is complete, remove the ERD and reboot your system. Creating and maintaining an ERD is one of the most effective troubleshooting tools that you have in your arsenal. It cures a host of ills. It is only effective, however, if you remain diligent in updating it whenever a workstation's configuration changes.

Assessing Print Job Failures

One of the benefits of Windows printing is that the operating system handles all print job output in a standardized manner, regardless of the application from which you are printing. Windows NT, being a network operating system, enables you to define network printers that are available as shared resources for other Windows NT Workstations to print to. Any client or server on a network can serve as the print server to a network printer. Additionally, you can have local printers that are not shared resources to other network computers, but that need to be managed and troubleshooted by their owner.

The centralization of printing services is a beautiful thing; you must admit. A single standardized print model under Windows replaces the individual print models of applications under MS-DOS, something more easily understood. The down side is that when problems do arise they affect your entire application suite and maybe an entire workgroup.

Keep in mind that Windows still retains the older model for printing for MS-DOS application that run in Windows NT Workstation from the command prompt. These applications require their own printer drivers to print anything other than ASCII output. If you are using WordPerfect 5.1, for example, you require that both a WordPerfect and printer driver be installed. Some MS-DOS applications may require that you turn on the printer port by using a command such as:

    NET USE LPT1: \\servername\printername

prior to printing.

Understanding the Windows Print Subsystem

The printing subsystem is modular and works hand-in-hand with other subsystems to provide printing services. When a printer is a local printer and a print job is specified by an application, data is sent to the Graphics Device Interface (GDI) for rendering into a print job in the printer language of the print device. The GDI is a module between the printing subsystem and the application requesting the printing services. This print job is passed to the spooler, which is a .DLL. The print job is written to disk as a temporary file so that it can survive a power outage or your computer's reboot. Print jobs can be spooled using either the RAW or EMF printer languages.

The client side of the print spooler is winspool.drv, and that driver makes a Remote Procedure Call (RPC) to the spoolss.exe server side of the spooler. When the printer is attached to the same computer, both files are located on the same computer. When the printer is attached to a Windows NT Workstation in a peer-to-peer relationship, those files are located on different computers.

spoolss.exe calls an API that sends the print job to a route (spoolss.dll) that sends the print job to the computer with the local printer where the localspl.dll library writes the file to disk as a spooled file. At this point, the printer is polled by localspl.dll to determine whether the spooled print job is capable of being processed by the printer, and altered if required.

The print job is then turned over to a separator page processor and despooled to the print monitor. The print device receives the print job and raster image processes it to a bitmap file that is then sent to the print engine to output.

For network printers the process is very much the same, but client requests and server services are more clearly defined and separate. The routers found in the spooler modules: winspool.drv, spoolss.exe, and spoolss.dll are identical to the ones used for a local printer. A local print provider on the client localspl.dll is matched to a remote print provider win32sp.dll (for Windows print servers), nwprovau.dll (for NetWare print servers) on the server side. In a network printer process, the print processors and print monitors may use several different server DLLs, each one required by a supported operating system.

You generally install a printer using the Add Printer wizard that you find in the Printer folder accessed from the Settings submenu of the Start menu. After you step through the wizard you create a virtual printer with a name that you provide. You can create any number of virtual (or logical, if you will) printers that use the same physical printer for a number of purposes. If you wish to print differently, have different security schemes, or provide different access times, multiple virtual printers provides a means to do this. You manipulate printers by:

▶ Double-clicking on the printer to see any spooled jobs, provided you have the privilege to do so.

▶ Right-clicking on a printer to view a shortcut menu that provides several actions. You can use this menu to delete a printer that no longer exists, for example. You can use the Default Printer command to set the default printer for a Windows NT Workstation from the shortcut menu.

▶ Right-clicking on a printer and selecting the Properties command from the shortcut menu to access the Printer Properties and control any number of settings.

Using a Basic Error Checklist

Any number of things can go wrong when you attempt to print to a printer. In many cases, Windows NT alerts you to an error, and in some cases Windows NT actually tells you what the error type is.

Here is a standard checklist of the most common solutions to print problems.

Your print job spools, but it will not print:

❏ Check that your printer is turned on and that all the connections are secure.

❏ The paper tray is empty and needs to be refilled.

❏ A piece of paper is jammed in the printer and needs to be removed.

❏ The printer has an error condition that prevents print processing.

The preceding problems are so simple that its easy to waste time and overlook them. It is amazing the percentage of printer problems that disappear when you restart your printer. If that fails to work, restart Windows NT Workstation. That is, assuming that your printer worked before you specified the print job.

If none of these solutions seems to work, try the following:

❏ Verify that the printer you think you printed to is either the default printer or was selected within the application from which the print job comes.

❏ Print a simple text file from Notepad. This often verifies whether the print problem is application specific. Try printing from DOS to test the DOS subsystem, if that is the problem environment.

❏ Print to a different printer, or substitute another printer on the same printer port. This helps determine whether the printer is malfunctioning.

❏ Check the amount of available hard disk space on your system partition to see whether there was room to create the temporary spooled print file.

❏ Print to a file, and then copy that file to the printer port in question. If you can print in this manner, you should suspect the spooler or a data-transmission error. Otherwise, you are probably dealing with a hardware, device driver, or application error.

At the very worst, you can try reinstalling the printer and supplying a new or updated printer driver.

These are the usual sources of printer drivers:

▶ The Windows NT operating system distribution disks.

▶ The setup disks that come with your printer.

> ▶ The printer manufacturer's BBS or web site.

> ▶ Microsoft's technical support line. You can contact Microsoft at 206-882-8080. Microsoft's current printer driver library is on the Windows NT Driver Library disk.

> ▶ The Microsoft web site. Use the Search button to search for the keyword "NT driver," or search for the name of your particular model of printer.

> ▶ CompuServe. Enter **GO WINNT** or **GO WDL** (Windows Driver Library) to go to that area of the service.

If the problem printing to a printer is observed after you have installed the printer, you should probably suspect a configuration issue. Check that you assigned to the correct serial port in the Configure Port dialog box of the Add Printer wizard. You can open a printer's Properties sheet to check port settings after the fact. Make sure that you have assigned the appropriate communication settings: baud rate, data bits, parity, start and stop bit, and flow control that your printer requires. These settings should be listed in your printer's manual. Failure to configure these settings properly may result in your printer operating too slowly, improperly processing print jobs, or not working at all.

Printers as Shared Resources

Network printers are shared resources. You must either own the printer (have created or installed it), be an administrator, or be assigned the rights to use a printer in some way to be able to view, modify, and use a printer. Different levels of rights can be assigned by an owner or an administrator. You assign shared rights by using the Sharing command on a printer's shortcut menu, which brings up the Sharing tab of the Printer Properties dialog box.

Creating additional printer shares for the same physical printer proves useful for the following reasons:

> ▶ Each share can have different printer setups.

- ▶ It enables you to assign different access privileges to groups of users.

- ▶ Each group can have different printing priorities.

- ▶ You can control access to the printer at different times for each group.

- ▶ You can use one share for a network printer, and another share name for a local printer.

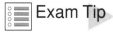 **Exam Tip**

> This is likely to be on the exam because the control of a network printer is one of the essential functions that a system administrator is expected to manage in an NT network.

If a user cannot see a printer, he may not have been given the right to access that printer. An administrator should be able to view and modify printers on any Windows NT Workstation.

If you have MS-DOS clients on the network and you want them to see a printer share, you must use a file naming convention that DOS recognizes. Names must be up to 12 characters long without spaces or any of the following characters:

> ? * # | \ / = > < %

To hide a printer share, add a dollar sign character to the end of the share name, as in *sharename*$. Any printer with that kind of a name will not show up in the Connect To Printer dialog box that is one of the steps in the Add a Printer wizard. A user must know that this printer share exists and be able to enter both the correct name and path to the printer share name to connect to that printer.

Solving Print Spooler Problems

Any print job spooled to a printer is written as a temporary file to the %systemroot%\System32\Spool\Printers folder. The file is deleted after the printer indicates that the job has been printed. The primary print spool problem encountered is a lack of available disk space. If you print high-resolution graphics, you might have print jobs as large as 20 MB to 80 MB per file for a 32-bit image at standard page size. Not surprisingly, it doesn't take many print jobs to overwhelm the typical Windows NT Workstation configuration.

When you print to the spooler, you create two files for each print job. The .SPL file is the actual print job spool file. You also create a shadow file, given the .SHD extension. The shadow file contains additional information about the print job that is not part of the print job itself, such as owner, priority, and so forth. If your computer crashes, .SPL and .SHD files remain in the default spool file until the service restarts and they are processed and printed. After being printed, these files are deleted from disk.

Should your spooled files become corrupted, they will be orphaned and remain in the spool folder taking up valuable space.

You can print directly to a printer from your application by turning off the print spooling feature. Before you print, open the Scheduling tab of the Printer Properties dialog box and select the Print directly to the printer radio button. When the printer next becomes available, your document prints. Until that point, you cannot use the application that originates the print job. You can task switch to another application and continue working until your printing application becomes available.

Spooler Performance Problems

You can solve spooler performance problems by increasing the priority that Windows NT Workstation assigns to the Spooler service. By default, Windows NT assigns this service a rating of 7, which is consistent with other background processes that run. Increase the rating to 9 to improve the performance of the spooler to the level of a foreground operation. Only consider doing this as a temporary measure to print a large print job, or if your workstation is used heavily as a print server. Changing this rating on a permanent basis degrades the performance of other services and applications on that workstation.

To change the priority of the Spooler service, open the RegEdit32 application and change the value of the PriorityClass of type REG_DWORD in the following key:

HKEY_LOCAL_MACHINE\System\CurrentControlSet\ Control\Print

Set that value to the priority class required. A value of 0, or no value entered, is substituted with the default value of a background process of 7 for Windows NT Workstation. (For Windows NT Server background processes, take a value of 9.)

 Tip

One very simple and effective procedure that improves printer performance is to defragment your hard drive on a regular basis.

Changing the Default Spool Folder

Should you run out of room on your system partition for spooled print jobs, you can specify a different default spool folder. To do so, make the change in the Advanced tab of the Server Properties dialog box. Open that dialog box by double-clicking on the Server Control Panel.

To change the location of spooled documents, complete the following steps:

1. Create a new spool directory.

2. Choose the Printers command from the Settings menu of the Start menu.

3. Choose the Server Properties command from the File menu.

4. Click on the Advanced tab, and then enter the location of the spool file directory

5. Click on the OK button.

You may want to create the spool folder on an NTFS volume and set security for this folder.

You can also edit the Registry to change the value of the Default-SpoolDirectory of type REG_SZ. The path is entered into the following key of the Registry:

> HKEY_LOCAL_MACHINE\System\CurrentControlSet\
> Control\Print\Printers

After you enter the new folder and its path, save the change and restart your machine for the change to take effect. Any spooled job in the original location will be lost, but will not be deleted. You need to delete the TEMP file manually.

If you wish to have individual spooled folders for each virtual printer, you can assign them. Find your printers in the following key:

> HKEY_LOCAL_MACHINE\System\CurrentControlSet\
> Control\Print\~Printers*printername*

Then enter the folder and its path as the data in the SpoolDirectory value for that key. Again, you need to restart the workstation to effect the change.

Enabling Printer Logging

You can enable event logging to your spooler by adding a check mark to the Enable spooler event logging check box on the Advanced tab. Doing so enables you to track who has used a printer and when, and what was requested.

To turn on auditing of a printer share, complete the following steps:

1. Enable File and object access auditing in the User Manager.

2. Then enable printer auditing for a specific printer share. Open the Security tab of the Printer Properties dialog box and click on the Auditing button.

3. In the Printer Auditing dialog box click on the Add button (see fig. 7.4).

4. In the Add Users and Groups dialog box, select a group or user to be audited.

Figure 7.4

The Printer Auditing dialog box.

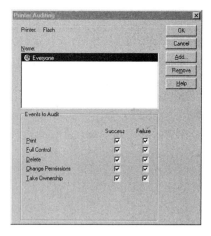

5. Click on the OK button to return to the Printer Auditing dialog box.

6. Select a user or group and click on the check boxes in the Events to Audit section to track events you wish to log for that user and group.

7. Click on OK.

Use the Event Viewer utility in the Administrative Tools folder to view logged events.

Installing Print Pooling

If you have adequate printer resources and wish to distribute the print queue load, you may want to install printer pooling. Printer pooling enables you to take two or more *identical* printers and print to them as if they were a single printer. The print job goes to the first available printer and is managed as if it is a single print queue.

To use printer pooling, complete the following steps:

1. Choose the Printers command from the Settings submenu of the Start menu.

2. Right-click on a printer icon and select the Properties command.

3. Click on the Ports tab and select the logical printer to which you wish to print.

4. Click on the Enable Print Pooling check box, and then close the Printer Properties dialog box.

To set up a logical printer you can use the Add Printer wizard to add a printer to a port and use the same share name. Although the printers need to be identical, the ports do not. You can mix and match local, serial, and parallel ports in the same logical printer.

Scheduling a Print Job

You cannot specify when a particular job will print on a printer within the current Windows NT Workstation architecture. You can control when a printer is available for printing, however, as part of a printer share's definition. Use two differently named printer shares for the same printer, and have one printer always be available. Restrict the availability of the second printer and use that printer share to schedule your print job.

To set availability times, complete the following steps:

1. Click on the printer icon in the Printers folder and press Alt+Enter to open the Printer Properties dialog box.

2. Click on the Scheduling tab of the Printer Properties dialog box (see fig. 7.5).

Figure 7.5

The Scheduling tab of the Printer Properties dialog box.

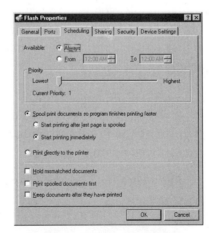

3. Click on the From radio button in the Available section, and then enter the starting and ending times that the printer is available.

Any print job printed off-hours is left in the print queue until the printer becomes available.

Using the Print Troubleshooter

To aid in solving printer problems, Windows NT comes with an interactive print troubleshooting aid as part of the online Help system.

To access the Print Troubleshooter, complete the following steps:

1. Choose the Help command from the Start menu.

2. Click on the Index tab and enter the keyword **troubleshooting** into the 1 Type the first few letters text box. Figure 7.6 shows this topic in the Help system.

Figure 7.6

The Print Trouble-shooter topic in the Help system.

3. Double-click on the problem type and follow the instructions in the Help system.

Printers are one of the most important network resources in many organizations. Therefore, you will be called on often to solve problems that crop up with printer shares and printer hardware. This section reviewed some of the most common problems.

Assessing Installation Failures

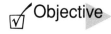Objective

The Windows NT Setup program makes installation errors much less common than they use to be. Several categories of errors may

still occur after an installation has been made, but they are also easier to track down and eliminate.

Installation Disk Errors and Upgrades

Infrequently there will be a problem with the CD that you have obtained to perform the Windows NT Workstation installation. Typically a read error is posted, but less frequently the installation may not complete itself and you may not be able to determine why this is so.

To obtain a replacement disk, contact Microsoft at 800-426-9400. Have your registration number handy; the sales and support staff requires this to process your request. New media requests under the warranty are generally sent without cost. If the upgrade is a slipstream upgrade, you may be charged postage.

A note about slipstream upgrades and service packs is also in order. Many small problems are often repaired as part of a minor version change in the operating system. If you have a problem related to an installation, either get the latest version of the operating system from Microsoft or download any available service packs from the Microsoft web site.

Key Concepts

A service pack is a self-running program that modifies your operating system. It isn't uncommon within the lifetime of an operating system to have two or three service packs. Windows NT Server 4.0 prior to the release of beta for Windows NT Server 5 had Service Pack 3 available, for example. You should try to install the latest service pack because it generally solves a lot more problems than it creates. (It is not unknown, however, for a service pack to create error conditions that didn't previously exist in your workstation's configuration.)

Inadequate Disk Space

The Windows NT Setup program examines the partition that you specify you wish Windows NT Workstation to be installed in for the amount of free space it contains. If there isn't adequate free space, the installation stops and fails. You need to take corrective action to proceed with the installation.

In some respects the Setup program is both smart and stupid. It protects your files in the Recycle Bin by not deleting them, which is wise. It leaves any number of TEMP files that could be safely deleted scattered about your disk.

To free up some room on your disk, consider doing any of the following:

▶ Empty your Recycle Bin.

▶ Delete any TEMP files that you find in the various locations that they are stored in (for example, the Print Cache folder).

▶ Delete any files that you find in your Internet browser's cache folder or any other cache folder that you have.

▶ Uninstall any programs that you no longer need.

▶ Compress any files that you use on an infrequent basis.

▶ Go into the Disk Administrator and change the size of the system partition that you wish to use for your installation.

▶ Create a new partition with adequate room for the installation.

▶ Compress your NTFS partition to make more room.

Several other methods enable you to reclaim or recover lost disk space, and it's possible to get really creative in this area. These, however, are often sufficient to help you get over the crunch.

Disk Configuration Errors

If you have inherited a configuration with a non-supported SCSI device adapter, you may not be able to boot your newly installed Windows NT Workstation operating system. In that instance, boot to a different operating system and try starting WINNT on the installation CD. You can also use a network installation to try and rectify the problem. Short of these solutions you may be forced to replace the adapter with one recommended on the Hardware Compatibility List.

Cannot Connect to a Domain Controller

The error message `Cannot Connect to a Domain Controller` is one of the more common error messages that you see when you install Windows NT Workstation, change your hardware configuration, or change network settings. There are a number of explanations for this problem.

Carefully verify that you are entering the correct user name and password and that the Caps Lock key is not on. The first thing you should check is that the account name that you are using is listed in the User Manager for Domains on the primary domain controller. An incorrect password generates a different error message than the lack of the user account.

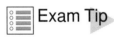

This is likely to be on the exam because the inability of a user to connect to a domain controller is one of the most common problems that a user encounters. It also arises from a variety of causes.

You should also check to see whether the machine account has been added to the User Manager for the primary domain controller.

Next, open the Network Control Panel and check that the network bindings are properly installed on the Bindings tab. Some bindings such as TCP/IP require not only computer names but IP addresses and subnet masks as well. If there is a conflict with two machines on the network having the same IP address, you get an error condition. Failure to enter the subnet mask also leads to your workstation being unable to find and connect to a domain controller and get its network identity properly verified.

The failure to connect to a domain controller is such a common problem that it is really unfortunate that the message isn't more descriptive of the problem.

Domain Name Error

If you make a mistake selecting the domain name, you get an error message when you attempt to log on. The solution is obvious when you realize what the problem is. Just reselect the correct domain name.

Assessing Application Failures

 Objective Unlike MS-DOS and earlier versions of Windows, an application failure won't bring your system to a complete halt. Most application failures are recoverable, and in many cases you won't even need to reboot your computer to re-establish a working configuration. That is not to say that a system crash is impossible. It happens very infrequently.

Most often the worst actors are applications written for MS-DOS or 16-bit Windows applications. These programs tend to crash more frequently than 32-bit Windows applications—a good reason to upgrade.

If you have a malfunctioning application, bring up the Task Manager and close the process down. You can access the Task Manager by either using your mouse or your keyboard (useful in case either is hung up by a malfunction).

To use your keyboard to close an application, complete the following steps:

1. Press Ctrl+Alt+Delete to open the Windows NT Security dialog box.

2. Click on the Task Manager button there to open the Task Manager.

3. Click on the Applications tab (see fig. 7.7).

Figure 7.7

The Applications tab of the Task Manager.

4. Select the offending application and click on the End Task button.

5. Close the Task Manager.

You can also open the Task Manager by moving the cursor over the Status bar area and right-clicking, and then selecting the Task Manager command.

If you need to end a 16-bit Windows or an MS-DOS application, you must close the entire session. When you close a 32-bit Windows application, only the process or thread needs to be closed.

Using the Application Log

Many errors are logged into the Application log for native
Windows NT application. The developer of the application determines the events that are logged, their codes, and meanings.
Often an application's manual or online Help system documents
the events you see in the Application log, as well as your ability to
control the events that are noted.

Service Failures

✎ **Key Concepts**

> Some applications run as services on Windows NT Worksta-
> tion. Internet Information Server's three tools WWW, FTP, and
> Gopher, for example, all are services. Services are started,
> stopped, and paused from within either their central adminis-
> trative tool (for IIS that tool is the Internet Service Manager), or
> from within the Services Control Panel. If you want to configure
> a service so that it runs automatically when your workstation
> boots, more often than not you will set this behavior in the
> Services Control Panel.

Sooner or later, sad to say, you will see the command and infa-
mous error messsage when your Windows NT Workstation starts
up after the load phase:

```
One or more services failed to start. Please see the Event
Viewer for details.
```

Well at least if the error message isn't going to tell you anything
useful, the Event Viewer will. Open the System log using the Event
heading in the Event Viewer and look for an Event code that has a
value of 6005. That event is an informational message that indicates that the EventLog service has started up. Any event prior to
that is a boot event and should be resolved. Double-click on the
event message to view an Event Detail dialog box.

Figure 7.8 shows the Event Detail dialog box for a `Cannot Connect
to a Domain Controller` error message. This detail indicates the
problem is that Windows NT Workstation is attempting to act as

the master browser. Resolution of this error would likely remove this problem and enable the user to log on to the domain.

Figure 7.8

The Event Detail dialog box.

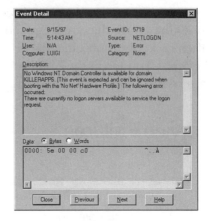

Assessing User Resource Access Failures

Key Concepts

Windows NT's security system controls access to network resources through user and machine accounts. Your logon to a particular domain is validated by a domain controller and provides you with certain privileges and rights that are registered in the Security Accounts Manager (SAM) database.

When you log on to Windows NT, the system provides a Security Access Token (SAT) based on your user name and password. This SAT is a key that enables you to access objects that Windows NT manages by maintaining a Security Descriptor (SD) file. That SD file contains the access control list (ACL) for each resource.

Two types of accounts are created and managed in Windows NT: machine accounts and user accounts. Both of these accounts are stored in the Security Account Manager (SAM) database stored on the primary domain controller (PDC) and replicated to any backup domain controllers (BDC) on the system. Accounts are assigned an internally held System Identification number (SID).

You create and manage accounts in the User Manager for Domains. Log on as an administrator so that you can fully access accounts for machines and different users. Other levels of users also have privileges, but what they can do is more limited. An account is specified by the machine and user name, as in <computername>\<username>.

A *group* is an account that contains other accounts. Every computer contains a Users group to which all user accounts belong. There is also a Guest group that allows limited privileges to users who log in without a password (if you allow it).

The logon provides the definition of your group membership and other properties assigned to you. Groups are a set of users as well as other groups that are given the same access rights to resources. Access privileges are cumulative. Local groups can be created to provide control over resource access. Windows NT also comes with some pre-built global groups that are available system wide. You can also define additional global groups. Users, groups, and domains offer a flexible system for managing resource access through security settings that you make either in the file system or on your desktop for various system objects.

Passwords Issues

Passwords enable you to log on to a particular user account. To log on successfully, you must know both the user name and the exact password. The important thing to know about passwords is that they are *case sensitive*. Therefore, one of the most commonly encountered errors is when the Caps Lock key is pressed accidentally. A user can enter the correct password and still have his entry to the system denied because the password is entered in uppercase.

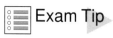 Exam Tip

This is likely to be on the exam because the control of user passwords is the key to making network resources available through the challenge/response mechanism.

To protect passwords, Windows NT has an option that enables you to retire a password after a certain period. You can also set an option that requires that Windows NT Workstation users change the assigned password the first time they log on to the system. Users logging on after that time are required to change their password. Windows NT also allows a "no password" password for anonymous access that provides limited access to system resources. This password is used for a web server running an FTP service, which enables a user to access a PUB folder, as one example of its use.

To change your users' password options, complete the following steps:

1. Select the User Manager for Domains from the Administrative Tools folder on the Programs submenu of the Start menu.

2. Select the account name in the Username panel of the User Manager for Domains.

3. Choose the Account command from the Policies menu.

4. In the Account Policy dialog box, select the options you desire, and then click on OK (see fig. 7.9).

Figure 7.9

The Account Policy dialog box.

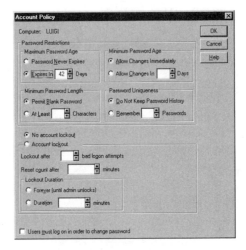

The options of interest are as follows:

▶ Minimum and maximum password age before a password expires

▶ The minimum length of a password

▶ Whether blank or no character passwords are permitted

▶ Whether a password list is maintained for an account and allows the user to cycle between passwords

▶ How many failed attempts to log on with a user name results in an Account Lockout

If you use the Account Lockout feature, it is important to enter a Lockout Duration. After that duration, the account can be used again after a set of failed logons invalidates the account.

It is important not to have a very large number of workstation passwords expire at the same time in a domain. The changing of 2,000 passwords at a time will require that the entire SAM be re-synchronized across the domain—a time consuming procedure.

By the way, the common method used to change your own password is to press Ctrl+Alt+Delete, and then click on the Change Password button in the Windows NT Security dialog box (see fig. 7.10). The use of the Ctrl+Alt+Delete keystroke to initiate a logon or password change is meant to prevent the posting of a spoofed Password Change dialog box and theft of a user account and associated password.

Figure 7.10

The Windows NT Security dialog box.

Troubleshooting Profiles and System Policies

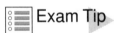**Key Concepts**

A user profile is created whenever a user logs on to Windows NT Workstation the first time. User profiles can be created that provide a specific configuration of the desktop, programs, accessories, printers, a taskbar and Start menu configuration, Help system bookmarks, and options in the Windows NT Explorer. This enables an administrator to provide a default profile that is used by a standard user in a domain.

Profiles offer a method for creating an environment based on the user account. To set this option, or to check to see whether a problem with the environment can be corrected, select the user account in the User Manager for Domains, and then click on the Profile button. Check the User Environment Profile dialog box for the startup script that modifies the environment at logon. Scripts can be a BAT (batch), CMD (OS/2), or EXE (program or executable) file. You can also create a new script and specify its location.

Exam Tip

This is likely to be on the exam because profiles and system policies are an efficient way of managing user access to network resources.

Profiles can be stored on the server and retrieved as a cached copy on a local machine when a user logs on. A stored local profile can be used when a problem occurs with a network connection or with a logon. To enable a user to have his profile and configuration travel with him regardless of which workstation that he logs on to in the domain, you can create *roaming profiles*.

You can find user profile settings in the Windows NT Registry in the HKEY_CURRENT_USER key. To modify a user profile, complete the following steps:

1. Log on to the system with the user name whose profile you wish to modify.

2. Open the Registry Editor (regedit32.exe).

3. Choose the Read Only Mode command on the Options menu if you don't intend to make changes (optional).

4. Click on the HKEY_CURRENT_USER key to expand the settings; then alter the setting you desire.

5. Close the Registry Editor.

Close the Registry Editor to have your new settings take effect. The actual information that the Registry reads for a user profile is contained in the ntuser.dat file of the User Profile folder. This file is cached on a local computer when the user profile is read.

If you wish to modify your user profiles, you can find them stored in the C:\WINNT\Profiles folder. The default profile is in the Default User folder, with other user accounts contained in folders with the same name as the user account. Each user profile folder contains a directory of shortcuts or link (.LNK) files to desktop items and the ntuser.dat file. Figure 7.11 shows the structure of an individual user's profile folder.

The following shortcuts are contained in these folders:

- ▶ **Application Data.** Any application data or settings are stored in this folder.

- ▶ **Desktop.** Shortcuts to files or folders are contained in the Desktop folder.

- ▶ **Favorites.** Any shortcuts to programs, folders, or favorite locations on the web are stored in this folder.

- ▶ **NetHood.** This folder stores shortcuts to Network Neighborhood objects. This is a hidden folder.

- ▶ **Personal.** This folder contains program items.

- ▶ **PrintHood.** Any network printer connections and settings are stored in this folder. This is a hidden folder.

▶ **Recent.** The list of files that appear on the Documents menu are stored as shortcuts in this folder. This is a hidden folder.

▶ **SendTo.** This contains shortcuts to document items.

▶ **Start Menu.** Any items that appear on the Start menu are stored in this folder.

▶ **Templates.** Any template items stored to disk by a user are contained in this folder. This is a hidden folder.

Figure 7.11

The directory structure of a user profile folder.

A user profile can be opened and read in any text editor, because a .DAT file is a simple text file. The information contained in the<USERNAME>\NTUSER.DAT file is stored in the following subkeys of the HKEY_CURRENT_USER:

▶ AppEvents (sounds)

▶ Console (Command Prompt and installed applications)

▶ Control Panel (which Control Panels are accessible and their settings)

▶ Environment (system configuration)

▶ Printers (Printer connections)

▶ Software (which software programs are available, and their settings)

Working with System Policies

To enforce a set of rules on a computer, a network administrator can create a system policy that applies to a single user, group of users, or all users in a domain. You create a specific policy with custom options in the System Policy Editor. This utility enables you to edit portions of the Windows NT Registry or edit system policy. Policies that you see in the System Policy Editor are contained in the winnt.adm and common.adm system policy template files. Template files are a set of stored Registry entries. You can modify a template file in the System Policy Editor, or create new template files.

System policy settings are stored in the Windows NT Registry in the HKEY_CURRENT_USER and HKEY_LOCAL_MACHINE keys. When you open the System Policy Editor in the Registry mode, you expose various keys in this area of the Registry.

System policy can restrict network logon or access, customize the desktop, or limit access to settings in the Control Panel. A system policy can be applied to a single user, a group of users, or all the users in a domain. Windows NT comes with two standard policies: Default Computer and Default User, both of which control options applied to all computers and users in a domain. You can create and enforce additional system policies.

To create a system policy, do the following:

1. Log on to the computer as an administrator.

2. Select the System Policy Editor from the Administrative Tools folder on the Programs submenu of the Start menu.

3. Choose the New Policy command from the File menu.

Two icons appear in the System Policy Editor window: Default Computer and Default User (see fig. 7.12).

Figure 7.12

*The System
Policy Editor.*

4. Select the Add User, Add Computer, or Add Group commands to add a policy.

5. Enter a name for the user, computer, or group in the Add User, Add Computer, or Add Group dialog box; then click on the OK button.

6. Select the Exit command on the File menu to close the System Policy Editor.

With the System Policy Editor in Policy File mode, you create or modify system policy files (.POL) for the domain. Any modifications you make for a user, group, or computer in the system policy is written as an entry into the ntconfig.pol file. To be enforced, you must save this file in the NETLOGON share on the primary domain controller (PDC).

To have more than one system policy in a domain, you need to change the Remote Update setting from automatic to manual in the computer policy section of the system policy. Then the local policy is enforced instead of the default action of Windows NT searching the ntconfig.pol file on the domain controller to validate a user logon.

When a lot of users log on to the network at the same time, there can be long delays when a large number of different policies are contained in the netlogon.pol file. To improve performance on Windows NT Workstation, enable manual updating and create system policy files on workstations other than the domain controllers to balance the load.

When a user presses Ctrl+Alt+Delete, the Logon Information dialog box shows the name of the person who last logged on to the system in the User Name text box. To suppress this default action, change the DontDisplayLastUserName in the \Microsoft\Windows NT\Current Version\Winlogon key of the HKEY_LOCAL_MACHINE\SOFTWARE to off. The value should be set to 1, and the key is of the REG_SZ type. This setting suppresses the display of the last user name.

Accessing Shared Resources

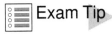 **Key Concepts**

Files, shared folders (or simply shares), printer shares, and other shared resources require resource permissions. To create a share for an object, typically you right-click on the object and select the Sharing command. In many instances, the Sharing tab of the object appears and enables you to specify users, groups, and access privileges that are allowed.

The person who creates the resource "owns" the resource and has full privileges to it. The administrator also has full access to resources and can take ownership of it. When an administrator takes ownership of a resource, access to the resource from the original owner is denied. This is a safety mechanism to make it obvious that ownership has been removed and that the resource has been fully taken over.

When a user can't access a shared resource, he may not have the privileges required to do so. Try logging on under a different account to attempt to access that resource. If the resource has been accessed in the past under a particular user account, make sure that the resource is spelled correctly, and that it has been located properly.

Exam Tip

This is likely to be on the exam because the management of shared resources is one of the central tasks that an administrator is expected to be responsible for. Failure to access a share is one of the most common problems requiring resolution by an administrator.

If there is a general problem accessing shared resources, you may want to open the Control Panel folder and check the Services Control Panel to see whether the various services responsible for validation services are running properly. These services are the following:

▶ NetLogon service

▶ Server service

▶ Workstation service

You should also check the Network Control Panel to ascertain whether the network bindings are correctly bound. These binding are contained on the Bindings tab, and individual binding settings are determined by selecting that binding and clicking on the Properties button.

Inadvertent changes or even purposeful changes to a user's group memberships in the User Manager for Domains or a change in System Policy can also lead to denied access to resources that were previously permitted.

Modifying the Registry

Key Concepts

Windows NT 4.0 introduced the Registry database to this operating system, building on an early version in Windows NT 3.1 that stored OLE location information on object servers. The first complete Registry appeared in Windows 95, although the versions of both are different. The Registry is a database of settings and parameters. Among the features set by the Registry are the nature of the interface, operating system hardware and software settings, user preferences, and other settings. Prior to Windows NT Workstation 4.0 and Server 4.0, these settings appeared as sections and lines in various .INI files.

The Registry is hierarchical and each branch is referred to as a hive. Individual sub-branches are called keys, which is a binary file. The top or first key of a hive is the primary key, with each key composed of subkeys that take value entries. Most Registry entries are permanent, although some are session dependent, transient, and never written to disk. An example of a transient key is the HKEY_LOCAL_MACHINE\Hardware as generated by automatic hardware detection by the Hardware Recognizer (ntdetect.com for Intel computers). The Hardware key is an example of a session value. Another transient value is the information written as part of a logon for a session, including security tokens.

When you install software, either a program or a part of the operating system such as a device driver or service, new subkeys and value entries are written to the Registry. Uninstall these components to remove the information. Subkeys and value entries store information about hardware settings, driver files, environmental variables that need to be restored, anything the application developer requires reference to.

 Exam Tip

This is likely to be on the exam because many troubleshooting operations require access to the Windows NT Registry.

Only members of the Administrators or Power Users group can access the Registry by default. You can assign other users rights to modify all or part of the Registry by hives, but you should think long and hard before doing so. The potential to compromise security or corrupt an installation is high. By default, any user can see the Registry files, but cannot edit, delete, or copy Registry files without specific permission to do so.

Using the Registry Editor

You use the Registry Editor to view and modify the Windows NT Registry. Of the two versions of the Registry Editor, regedit32.exe and regedit.exe, the former is more generally useful and offers more options.

These programs are not listed on the Start menu and are not found in the Administrative Tools folder where you might expect to find them to discourage their casual use. Their programs are located in the WINNT folder, and you can add them to your Start menu, if you wish.

Whenever you change a setting in a Control Panel or alter your desktop, you are writing changes to the Registry associated with the user account profile with which you logged on. If you wish to view and modify Registry information relating to services, resources, drivers, memory, display, or network components, you can use the Windows NT Diagnostic program (WINMSD). This utility is found in the <System Root>\System32 folder, or in the Administrative Tools folder on the Programs submenu of the Start menu. When you make a change in WINMSD, you are limited in what you can alter, and protected from making destructive changes.

 Caution

When you alter a value in the Registry using the Registry Editor, the changes you can make are unlimited and can be hazardous to your computer's health. If you delete or modify a required key, you could cause your computer to malfunction. The only recovery method that you can count on in that instance is to reinstall Windows NT or to use the Repair disk. Proceed with caution when working in the Registry, and consider wandering around with the files opened as read-only (use the Read Only menu command in the Registry Editor to achieve this) to begin with.

The six root keys and their subtrees are as follows:

▶ **HKEY_CLASSES_ROOT.** This subtree stores OLE, file, class, and other associations that enable a program to launch when a data file is opened. Although the HKEY_CLASSES_ROOT is displayed as a root key, it is actually a subkey of HKEY_LOCAL_MACHINE\Software.

▶ **HKEY_CURRENT_USER.** All user settings, profiles, environment variables, interface settings, program groups, printer connections, application preferences, and network connections for each user are stored in the subkeys of this root key.

▶ **HKEY_LOCAL_MACHINE.** This subkey contains information that identifies the computer on which the Registry is stored. Information in this key includes settings for hardware such as memory, disk drives, network adapters, and peripheral devices. Any software that supports hardware—device drivers, system services, system boot parameters, and other data—is contained in this subkey.

▶ **HKEY_USERS.** All data on individual user profiles is contained in this subkey. Windows NT stores local profiles in the Registry, and the values are maintained in this subkey.

▶ **HKEY_CURRENT_CONFIG.** The current configuration for software and any machine values are contained in this key. Among the settings stored in this root key are display device setup and control values required to restore the configuration when the program launches or your computer starts up.

▶ **HKEY_DYN_DATA.** Transient or dynamic data is stored in this last key in the Windows NT Registry. This root key cannot be modified by the user.

When the system loads the Registry, most of the data is contained in the HKEY_LOCAL_MACHINE and HKEY_USERS keys.

As an example of the kinds of changes you can make, individual settings that you make in the Control Panels are written back to different keys in the Registry. You can modify those settings directly. Table 7.1 shows you the location of the different Control Panel settings. When you install a program using the Add/Remove Programs Control Panel, the data isn't written directly to the Registry, but the installer creates delete Registry entries in the Software hive.

Table 7.1

Control Panel Relations to Registry Keys	
Control Panel	Registry Data Location
Accessibility Options	HKEY_CURRENT_USER\Control Panel\Accessibility
Add/Remove Software	HKEY_CURRENT_USER\Console\Application Console
Date/Time	HKEY_LOCAL_MACHINE\System\CurrentControlSet\Control\TimeZoneInformation
Devices	HKEY_LOCAL_MACHINE\System\CurrentControlSet\Services
Display (Machine settings)	HKEY_LOCAL_MACHINE\Hardware\ResourceMap\Video
Display (User settings)	HKEY_CURRENT_USER\Control Panel\Desktop
Fast Find	HKEY_LOCAL_MACHINE\Software\Microsoft\Shared Tools\Fast Find
Fonts	HKEY_LOCAL_MACHINE\Software\Microsoft\Windows NT\CurrentVersion\Fonts
Internet	HKEY_LOCAL_MACHINE\Software\Microsoft\Windows\CurrentVersion\Internet Settings
Keyboard	HKEY_CURRENT_USER\Control Panel\Desktop
Mail	Several places
Modems	HKEY_LOCAL_MACHINE\Software\Microsoft\Windows\CurrentVersion\Unimodem
Mouse	HKEY_CURRENT_USER\Control Panel\Mouse
Multimedia	HKEY_LOCAL_MACHINE\Software\Microsoft\Windows\Multimedia
Network	Several locations

Control Panel	Registry Data Location
PC Card	HKEY_LOCAL_MACHINE\Hardware\Description\System\PCMCIA PCCARDs
Ports	HKEY_LOCAL_MACHINE\Hardware\ResourceMap
Printers	HKEY_CURRENT_USER\Printers
Regional Settings	HKEY_CURRENT_USER\Control Panel\International
SCSI Adapters	HKEY_LOCAL_MACHINE\Hardware\ResourceMap\ScsiAdapter
Server	Several locations
Services	HKEY_LOCAL_MACHINE\System\CurrentControlSet\Services
Sounds	HKEY_CURRENT_USER\AppEvent\Schemes\Apps\Default
System	Several locations
Tape Devices	HKEY_LOCAL_MACHINE\Hardware\ResourceMap\OtherDrivers\TapeDevices
Telephony	HKEY_LOCAL_MACHINE\Software\Microsoft\Windows\CurrentVersion\Telephony
UPS	HKEY_LOCAL_MACHINE\System\CurrentControlSet\Services\UPS

When you make a mistake and delete a key or value in the Registry Editor, you cannot use an Undo command to recover from this error. The Confirm On Delete command on the Options menu offers a limited safeguard. As everyone knows, it is easy to confirm a deletion and repent the mistake later.

To correct a critical deletion, complete the following steps:

1. Close the Registry Editor.

2. Immediately restart your computer.

3. Hold down the spacebar as Windows NT loads and select the Last Known Good option.

When Windows NT boots your system, it uses the backup copy of the Windows NT Registry. Any changes you made to your system since your last startup are discarded. The Last Known Good configuration, however, at least enables you to recover from any critical deletion in the Registry that you made—provided that you recognize the error before logging on to your computer successfully again.

Backing Up the Registry

The most important thing you can do to protect your investment in your system's configuration is to back up the Registry files. When you create an ERD, as described earlier in this chapter, you back up specific hives of the Registry. You should keep a full backup of the Registry on hand.

You find the Registry file in the %system root%\System32\Config folder. For most installations the %system root% is typically C:\WINNT. Individual user's Registry data is written to the ntuser.dat file contained in that user's folder at the location C:\WINNT\Profiles\<username>\NTUSER.DAT. When a user logs on to his workstation, a Profile folder for him is created with an ntuser.dat file to hold his user profile. Roaming profiles for a domain are stored as the original copy of the ntuser.dat file on the domain controller.

The following CONFIG folder files store direct information on Registry hives:

▶ DEFAULT

▶ NTUSER.DAT

▶ SAM

▶ SECURITY

▶ SOFTWARE

- ▶ SYSTEM

- ▶ USERDIFF

- ▶ USERDIFR

Several files are associated with each Registry hive in the CONFIG folder. The first and primary file takes no extension. The CONFIG directory also contains auxiliary files for the Registry that are the backup, log, and event files. These files have the same names as the list above, but take the .LOG, .EVT, or .SAV extensions. The System file also has a system.alt file associated with it. The .EVT or event files are viewable in the Event Viewer, and contain audited events. Log files store changes that can be rolled back. The .SAV files are part of the Last Known Good boot configuration that enables you to restore your Registry based on your last booted session. The Last Known Good option was described earlier in this chapter.

The LOG file is a backup file that enables changes to be rolled back. It is a fault tolerance feature, as changes are written to the LOG file first. When the data is completely written in the LOG file, updating of the matching Registry hive begins. The data section to be changed is marked, and the data is transferred. When the data transfer is completed, the update flag is reset to indicate successful transfer. Should there be a problem or should your computer malfunction during the transfer, the update is begun again from scratch.

The SYSTEM file is updated in a somewhat different manner because your computer relies on that key to start up. The duplicate system.alt file is used and operates as the replacement for a .LOG file. The entire file is mirrored and replicated. Then in the event of a crash the backup file is used and the entire file is replaced.

It is unnecessary to back up the entire Registry. Much of the information is transitory and session dependent. Only specific portions of the Registry need be protected. The files of greatest importance are the SYSTEM and SOFTWARE files. They are generally small and can be fit on a single floppy disk. You should also note that the SAM and SECURITY files can't be modified and cannot be copied or backed up.

To back up the Registry, use the RDISK program described earlier in this chapter and set that option. Do not try to copy the files directly to a disk. You can also back up individual hive files from within the Registry Editor by saving a branch using the Save Key command on the Registry menu. You can use the Restore Key command to load those backup files.

The hives of the Registry are locked and cannot be accessed to be copied directly. In a dual-boot system, or if you boot your system using MS-DOS or some other operating system, these files are not locked and may be copied directly. You could copy those files to another drive or volume.

You can view Registry files on a FAT volume from any other operating system. If the file system is an NTFS volume, only a Windows NT or Linux system running a disk access utility can view the files, read them, and copy them. On Windows NT, one program that can do this is NTFSDOS.EXE.

For a temporary copy of a key, use the Restore Volatile command rather than the Restore key command. This command loads the key in the Registry Editor, but it does not load that key again in a future session after your computer reboots.

Changing the Registry Size

Normally the default size of the Windows NT Workstation Registry is sufficient for most configurations. If you have a large organization and a lot of user profiles and application data configurations are stored, you may find that the Registry runs out of room. You may need to alter the allowed size of the Registry.

To change the maximum Registry size, complete the following steps:

1. Double-click on the System icon in the Control Panel folder.

2. Click on the Performance tab, and then click on the Change button in the Virtual Memory section to view the Virtual Memory dialog box (see fig. 7.13).

Figure 7.13

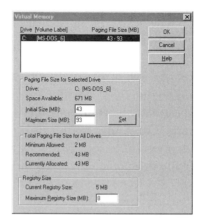

3. Enter a size in the Maximum Registry Size (MB) text box, and then click on OK.

The Registry size can be somewhat larger than the value entered in the System Control Panel. It is related to the size of your paging file, which is related to the amount of installed RAM in your system. When the Registry exceeds the size you set, it brings your system to a halt with a STOP error. This problem is very rarely encountered unless you attempt to reduce the size of the Registry artificially. Keep a maximum Registry size about 2 MB larger than the current size in the Virtual Memory dialog box.

Troubleshooting the Registry

Several problems may be directly related to Registry errors. The most common category of problems are the following:

▶ Your computer won't boot properly or at all.

▶ Your computer looks or works differently than it once did.

▶ Your computer won't shut down correctly.

▶ The "Blue Screen of Death" resulting from a STOP error.

▶ A software or hardware component that operated correctly stops working without any physical changes being made to the files or to the device.

> ▶ Something stops working after you add new software or hardware, and the two are not known to be incompatible with one another.

Most of these error conditions are at least correctable from backup. The one really frightening error is the STOP error because you can't access your machine. To correct the Blue Screen of Death, try booting from your boot disk and running the Check Disk program to repair these type of errors associated with disk and file problems. The CHDSK.EXE program is located in the <SYSTEM ROOT>\SYSTEM32 directory.

Utilizing Advanced Techniques

Windows NT comes with several diagnostic tools to help you optimize and tune the system and to correct error conditions. In many ways, the operating system is meant to be *self-tuning* and to require relatively few settings be altered to make the computer run well. To track errors, Windows has a system of events that are recorded in log files. These events can be tracked and controlled, and they prove very useful in troubleshooting. This section delves into the Event logs in some detail.

To aid in solving network problems, Windows NT also offers you the Network Monitor. This utility enables you to examine and analyze network performance and utilization. Common network issues are also discussed in this section.

Working with the Event Logs and Event Viewer

Key Concepts

Events are actions that occur on your system. The system itself generates events and records them in the System and Security log files. Applications record their events in the Application log. There are standard events that you see, and you can audit resources to add additional events. Many application developers use the event system to aid in analysis of their application. The Event Viewer enables you to view the Event logs and analyze them.

The Event logs are normally viewed by anyone who cares to see the information. You can also remote view an Event log if you have the permission to do so on another machine.

An administrator may want to restrict access to these logs so that the information is secure and can't be erased.

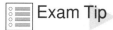 Exam Tip

This is likely to be on the exam because careful analysis of a systems Event log enables you to diagnose many problems.

To restrict who can open the System or Application logs, you can set the following key:

HKEY_LOCAL_MACHINE\System\CurrentControlSet\ Services\EventLog\<log_name>

so that the RestrictGuestAccess value of type **REG_DWORD** is set to 1. When the RestrictGuestAccess is set to 0 or doesn't exist, the default condition is for anyone to access these two logs.

The log files are a first-in, first-out (FIFO) system. When the ultimate limit of a log file is reached, the oldest events are deleted to make room for new events. The default size is 512 KB, and the oldest event stored is up to one week old. You can modify these settings from within the Event Viewer.

To change the settings of the Event logs, complete the following steps:

1. Open the Event Viewer (see fig. 7.14).

2. Choose the Log Settings command on the Log menu.

3. Select the log type in the Change Settings for... Log list box of the Event Log Settings dialog box (see fig. 7.15).

4. Set the size of the log in the Maximum Log Size spinner.

5. Select one of the radio buttons in the Event Log Wrapping section to determine what happens to old events.

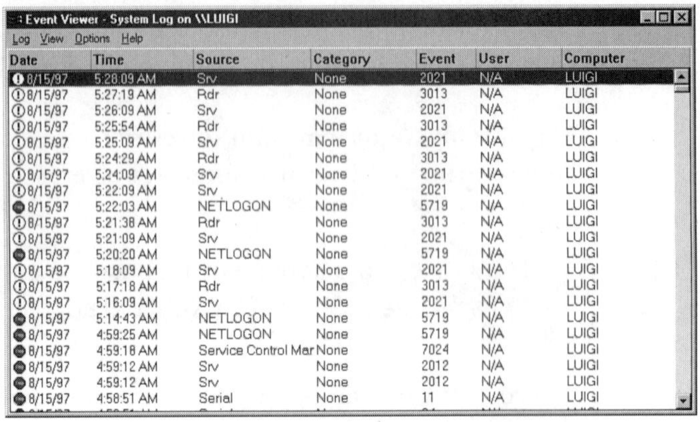

Figure 7.14

The Event Viewer.

Figure 7.15

The Event Log Settings dialog box.

6. Close first the Event Log Settings dialog box, and then the Event Viewer.

A prudent administrator makes a habit of checking the Event logs on a regular basis. Many events occur so frequently that they can overwhelm the Event logs and make it difficult to determine what other error conditions or trends exist. By analyzing the Event logs, you can determine what event types are worth keeping, and how often they should be noted.

Another useful option that the Event Viewer enables is the export of Event logs to data files. Several different output formats are offered to enable you to more easily analyze the data in the logs. You can export your log data out to text files (.TXT), Event log files (.EVT), spreadsheet (.SYLK), and database data file (.DBF) formats, among others. Numerous third-party tools help analyze Windows NT Workstation log files.

Tip

The Event Viewer (like the Performance Monitor) is one of the Windows NT operating system's central diagnostic tools. Learning how to use this tool well will reward the administrator with a better running workstation, less time spent tracking down errors, and a lower stress existence.

If you want additional information about an event, double-click on that event to view the Event Detail dialog box. You saw this dialog box earlier in figure 7.8. You will find the following information generated for an event:

- ▶ Date of event.

- ▶ Time of event.

- ▶ User account that generated the event. When applicable, this information is recorded in the Security log.

- ▶ Computer on which the event occurred.

- ▶ Event ID (the actual Event Code).

- ▶ Source or the component that recorded the error.

- ▶ Type of error: Error, Information, or Warning.

- ▶ Category of event.

- ▶ Description of event.

- ▶ Data describing the event in hexadecimal form.

You can find many of the error messages in the documentation and resource kits for Windows NT Workstation. Microsoft also keeps a technical database that contains many of the reasons that error messages are generated. You can search the Knowledge Base on the Microsoft web site (as a premium service) or on the Microsoft network to obtain error information stored in the logs.

Another database on CD-ROM is delivered to programmers as part of their subscription to the Microsoft Developer Network program. This database contains information about not only error conditions, but internal error codes of interest to programmers. All levels of participation in MSDN result in your receiving this database.

The Event log is very flexible. You can turn event logging on and off for a number of resources by specifying the auditing properties for that resource. Many developers use the event logs to record information specific to their applications.

The Event log is almost an embarrassment of riches. To help you find the particular event you need, the Event Viewer has a find and search function. You can also filter the Event log derived from your own computer by using the View menu by any of the following:

▶ Computer

▶ Event date and time

▶ Event ID

▶ Event type

▶ User

▶ Source of the event

Network Diagnostics

Numerous network problems arise relating to both hardware and software configuration. Some of these problems require that you experiment with cabling and couplings, others can be solved with software that comes with Windows NT Workstation.

If you have a complex network installation, you may require diagnostic equipment to test your hardware. Often you can test individual components by rearranging their position in the network (swapping cables or boards) and isolating the offending piece of hardware.

Windows NT comes with a utility called the Network Monitor that can be very useful in diagnosing network activity. This Administrative Tools utility collects and filters network packets and can analyze network activity. This utility diagnoses only the computer that it is running on.

The Network Monitor is a supplementary component of the Windows NT Workstation installation. To install this program, open the Network Control Panel's Service tab and click on the Add button. After Windows NT Workstation builds its list of services, you can select the Network Monitor from the list.

Network Monitor is both statistical and graphical. In the four panes of the Network Monitor, the current activity in real time appears (see fig. 7.16).

Figure 7.16

The Network Monitor utility.

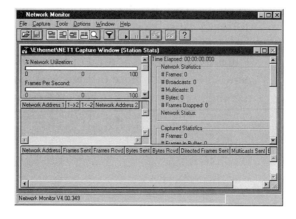

The Graph pane in the upper left shows the following bar graphs:

- ▶ % Network Utilization

- ▶ Broadcasts Per Second

- ▶ Bytes Per Second

- ▶ Frames Per Second

- ▶ Multicast Per Second

These parameters show you the level of activity that your network is experiencing, and how saturated your network bandwidth is.

The Session Stats pane shows you which nodes are communicating, and the number of frames (of the first 128 measured) sent and received from each.

The Total Stats pane (on the right half of the Network Monitor) shows complete network statistics in the following categories:

▶ Captured Statistics

▶ Network Card (Mac) Error Statistics

▶ Network Card (Mac) Statistics

▶ Network Statistics

▶ Per Second Statistics

You must scroll to see each of the panels in the pane for these different categories.

The last pane at the bottom of the window is the Station Stats pane. Information here displays what your workstation is communicating to the network. Click on a column head to sort by that category. The following categories appear:

▶ Broadcasts Sent

▶ Bytes Rcvd

▶ Bytes Sent

▶ Directed Frames Sent

▶ Frames Rcvd

▶ Frames Sent

▶ Multicasts Sent

▶ Network Address

An amazing number of network problems are relating to TCP/IP protocol addressing. Make sure that your workstation has a unique address, or uses a DHCP (Dynamic Host Configuration

Protocol) service for its TCP/IP assignment. Also check that the subnet address you entered into the TCP/IP Properties dialog box is correct.

To view TCP/IP settings, complete the following steps:

1. Double-click on the Network Control Panel.

2. Click on the Protocols tab of the Network dialog box.

3. Select the TCP/IP protocol, and then click on the Properties dialog box (see fig. 7.17).

Figure 7.17

The Microsoft TCP/IP Properties dialog box.

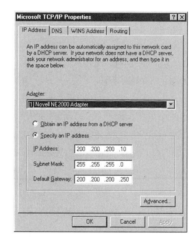

4. Examine the settings to see whether they are correct.

The PING utility is also included in Windows NT Workstation. You can ping other computers on the network to see whether they are active, your own workstation with the specific address, the default gateway, and any computer on the Internet or your intranet. Use the PING command in a Command Prompt session without any other parameters to see an informational screen detailing its use.

Resource Conflicts

Many configuration errors are resource conflicts. These take the form of duplicate interrupt or I/O assignment, or SCSI devices having duplicate assignments or improper assignments. You may see these problems when you first boot your system, or they may show up later when a device doesn't work properly.

Check the Event log to see what error events are listed. Also run the Windows diagnostic program WINMSD (in the Administrative Tools folder) to examine your resource settings. Errors in software can be rolled back using the Last Known Good Configuration.

Using the Windows NT Diagnostics Program

Key Concepts

The Windows NT Diagnostics program is the worthy successor to the MSD program found in Windows 3.1. This dialog box shows you information on many of the Registry items found in the HKEY_LOCAL_MACHINE subtree. Using WINMSD, you can obtain detailed information and reports on the state and configuration of your workstation. You cannot use this diagnostic tool to change any configuration settings, but you can use it to determine what conditions exist so that you can fix a problem.

Figure 7.18 shows the WINMSD dialog box.

Figure 7.18

The Windows NT Diagnostic tool.

This dialog box contains the following tabs:

- ▶ **Display.** Information on your video adapter, its firmware, and any adapter settings are found on this tab.

- ▶ **Drives.** A list of drives and volumes are contained in a hierarchical display. Drives include floppy disk drives, hard disk drives, CD-ROM, optical drives, and mapped drives through any network connections. If you double-click on a drive letter, the Drive Properties dialog box appears. The Drive Properties dialog box shows you cluster size, bytes per sector, the current status of the use of the disk, and the file system in use.

- ▶ **Environment.** Any environmental variables in use for a Command Prompt session appear on this tab.

- ▶ **Memory.** The installed memory, virtual memory, and usage of both is shown on this tab.

- ▶ **Network.** The network tab shows any installed logons, transports (protocols and bindings), settings, and statistics. Figure 7.19 shows the Transport display of the Networks tab.

Figure 7.19

The Transport listing of the Networks tab of the WINMSD dialog box.

▶ **Resources.** If you open this tab, the listing of device assignments appears. Shown here is the IRQ, port numbers, DMA channels, and UMB locations being used by each device. If you suspect a device conflict, this is the place to go to attempt to locate the suspect.

▶ **Services.** The information stored in the HKEY_LOCAL_MACHINE\System\CurrentControlSet\Services key is displayed on this tab. If you select a service and click on the Devices button, the information stored in the HKEY_LOCAL_MACHINE\System\CurrentControlSet\Control key appears, along with the status of that control.

▶ **System.** The information stored in the HKEY_LOCAL_MACHINE\Hardware key shows the CPU type and information on other installed devices.

▶ **Version.** The information stored in the HKEY_LOCAL_MACHINE\Software\Microsoft\Windows\NT\CurrentVersion key is shown on this tab. You will find the operating system version, build number, Service Pack update, and the registered owner of the software.

Windows NT ships with several utilities for evaluating a workstation's configuration and performance. A thoughtful administrator by being proficient at the use of these tools can solve many problems, and prevent others from occurring.

Exercises

These lab exercises provide practice for you at troubleshooting Windows NT workstation, as well as creating resources that will help you resolve a variety of problems.

Exercise 7.1: Creating a Boot Floppy Disk and Emergency Repair Disks

This exercise creates a set of disks that enable you to start your workstation in case of boot failure, and to repair a workstation that doesn't boot properly.

Objectives

Establish a course of action when the boot process fails

Time Estimate: 20 minutes

Steps

To create the boot floppy, follow these steps:

1. Insert a blank floppy disk in the disk drive and format that disk.

2. Open the Windows NT Explorer and select the boot.ini, NTLDR, and ntdetect.com.

3. Copy these four files to the floppy disk to create the NT boot floppy disk.

4. Restart your computer without removing the floppy disk from the drive. If disk is valid, it boots your computer.

5. Label the disk and store the disk in a secure location.

To create a set of emergency repair disks, follow these steps:

6. Choose the Command Prompt command from the Programs submenu of the Start menu.

7. Type **RDISK /S** and press the Enter key.

continues

8. Click on the Create Repair Disk button in the Repair Disk Utility dialog box (refer back to fig. 7.3).

9. Insert a formatted floppy disk, and then click on the OK button.

10. After Windows NT Workstation creates the ERD, remove the floppy disk, write-protect the disk, and store it away.

11. Click on the Exit button to close RDSIK.

12. Click on the Close box.

Exercise 7.2: Displaying Device Drivers at Startup

This exercise explores modifying the boot.ini file to enumerate your drivers when the kernel is loading.

Objectives

Set a course of action when the boot process fails

Set a course of action when the installation fails

Choose an action when access to a resource cannot be achieved

Time Estimate: 15 minutes

Steps

1. Choose the Notepad command from the Accessories folder on the Programs submenu of the Start menu.

2. Select the Open command from the File menu.

3. Select All Files in the File of type list box and select the boot.ini file in the root directory.

4. Find the line in the boot.ini file that reads Windows NT Server Version 4.00 [VGA] followed by /basevideo and /sos switches. If your system uses a VGA driver, skip to step 6.

5. Choose the Save As command from the File menu and save the boot.ini file to a different name, such as boot.bak.

6. Delete the /basevideo switch and leave the /sos switch intact. Modify the bracket text to read **Windows NT Server Version 4.00 [SOS].**

7. Select the Save As command on the File menu and save the file as the boot.ini file in the root directory. (Note that the file boot.ini is read-only, system, and hidden. You will probably have to change the attributes to be able to save the file.)

8. Exit Notepad and reboot your system.

9. Select the SOS option from the boot menu when it appears. Your device drivers appear listed on-screen as they load in ARC format.

10. Log on to Windows NT Workstation.

11. Restore the original boot.ini file with the VGA configuration and /basevideo switch; then reboot to test your system.

Review Questions

The following questions review your knowledge of the information presented in this chapter. For additional questions, see MCP Endeavor and the Microsoft Roadmap/Assessment exam on the CD that accompanies this book.

1. The Last Known Good Configuration is overwritten when?

   a. You indicate an update in the Startup/Shutdown tab of the Services Control Panel.

   b. You start up your computer.

   c. You shut down your computer.

   d. You log on successfully to your workstation.

2. An error message appears that a service failed to load. Where would you determine the nature of the problem?

   a. The Network Control Panel's Services tab

   b. The User Manager for Domains

   c. The System log in the Event Viewer application

   d. The Services Control Panel

3. Which SCSI address for an external hard drive is valid?

   a. 4

   b. 0

   c. 8

   d. 1

4. Which file is not required on a boot disk for an x86 Windows NT Workstation?

   a. boot.ini

   b. NTLDR

   c. ntdetect.com

   d. ntbootdd.bat

5. Which program creates an ERD?

    a. FORMAT

    b. RDISK

    c. RECOVER

    d. ERD

6. Your print job spools, but does not print. All the following could be reasons except?

    a. The printer is turned off.

    b. The paper tray is empty.

    c. The printer's memory is full.

    d. Your hard drive is full.

7. How do you hide a printer share?

    a. Move the file to your system WINNT folder.

    b. Add a dollar sign after the share name.

    c. Set an option in the Printer Properties dialog box.

    d. Create a hidden spool folder.

8. What happens when you don't have adequate space for an installation?

    a. The Setup program detects this and stops, canceling the operation.

    b. The space available is used to overwrite as many files as possible.

    c. Your installation is corrupted.

    d. You are given the choice of installing MS-DOS as a temporary measure.

9. Which one of the following should you not do to reclaim space on your disk?

   a. Delete any TEMP files that you find in the various locations that they are stored in (for example the print cache folder).

   b. Empty your Recycle Bin.

   c. Uninstall any programs that you no longer need.

   d. Change your file system.

10. Which methods can you use to open the Task Manager?

   a. Select the Task Manager from the Administrative Tools folder.

   b. Click on the Task Manager button in the Windows NT Security dialog box.

   c. Select the Task Manager command from the Start menu's Status bar shortcut menu.

   d. Press Ctrl+Esc.

11. Which user profile does not exist?

   a. Default user profile

   b. A user account profile

   c. Anonymous user profile

   d. Roaming profiles

12. How do you control what action to take when your workstation encounters a STOP error?

   a. Use the System Control Panel to specify the action.

   b. No action is possible. The computer logs an error and reboots.

   c. Use the Network Control Panel to specify the action.

   d. Reboot to MS-DOS and enter the RECOVER command.

Review Answers

1. D is correct. A successful logon overwrites changes in the Registry for the Last Known Good Configuration. For more information, see the section entitled "Last Known Good Recovery."

2. C is correct. Any system failure is written as an event in the System log. For more information, see the section entitled "Service Failures."

3. A and D are correct. SCSI can have 8 devices, 0 through 7. The number 0 is reserved for your computer; the number 8 falls outside of the allowed range. For more information, see the section entitled "Disk Configuration Errors."

4. D is correct. Choice D is fictitious. All the other choices are essential files that get copied to a floppy boot disk. For more information, see the section entitled "The NT Loader."

5. B is correct. RDISK creates and updates emergency repair disks. For more information, see "The Emergency Repair Disk (ERD)."

6. D is correct. A full hard drive has no effect on a previously spooled print file as that file has already been written to disk. For more information, see the section entitled "Solving Print Spooler Problems."

7. B is correct. When you add a dollar prefix to a sharename, you are hiding that share from view. For more information, see the section entitled "Printers as Shared Resources."

8. A is correct. One of the first things that SETUP does is to examine the file system, the disk size, and assess the amount of free space that you have and that is required. If you don't have enough free space, the installation is aborted. This is true even if you are overwriting enough files to free up sufficient disk space for the installation. For more information, see the section entitled "Assessing Installation Failures."

9. D is correct. Changing the file system permanently deletes all the data on your disk. In almost all instances, this is not either necessary or required. For more information, see the section entitled "Inadequate Disk Space."

10. B and C are correct. A is incorrect because there is no command for the Task Manager on the Start menu. D is incorrect because the keystroke used to open the Task Manager is Ctrl+Shift+Esc. For more information, see the section entitled "Assessing Application Failures."

11. C is correct. A, B, and D all exist and support both local and remote users on a network. Choice C is incorrect because there is no "guest" or anonymous user profile, only the default profile. For more information, see the section entitled "Troubleshooting Profiles and System Policies."

12. A is correct. The System Control Panel contains a setting for the action to be taken when a STOP error is encountered. For more information, see the section entitled "Boot Sequence Errors."

Answers to Test Questions at the Beginning of the Chapter

1. The blue screen that appears is when the Hardware Abstraction Layer (HAL) loads. Each dot is a device driver being loaded. For more information, see the section entitled "The NT Loader."

2. The Last Known Good configuration is offered as a step in the startup process. Hold the Shift key to return to that configuration. Each time you successfully log on to Windows NT Workstation the Last Known Good configuration is changed. For more information, see the section entitled "Last Known Good Recovery."

3. Format a floppy disk and copy the hidden system files: boot.ini, NTLDR, ntbootdd.sys, and ntdetect.com in your %systemroot% to that floppy disk. For more information, see the section entitled "Boot Disk Recovery."

4. You can specify that a printer is to be shared in the Add a Printer wizard. After the fact, you can select the Sharing command on a printer's shortcut menu and configure the printer share from the Sharing tab of the Printer Properties dialog box. For more information, see the section entitled "Printers as Shared Resources."

5. A service pack is a program that Microsoft releases that updates Windows NT Workstation (or another application). Service packs are numbered for each version of the operating system, with a greater number being a later version. It's a good idea to use service packs to stay current. For more information, see the section entitled "Installation Disk Errors and Upgrades."

6. Either the user name and password have been entered incorrectly, or the user account doesn't exist. For more information, see the section entitled "Password Issues."

7. Open the Event Viewer and examine the System log to see what error events are entered. Check for details to determine the cause. For more information, see the section entitled "Service Failures."

8. A user profile is a collection of Registry settings that control the look and feel of your workstation, commands on the Start menu, available applications, printers, and other resources. Profiles can be either a default, related to a specific user, or roam on the network as a user moves from workstation to workstation. For more information, see the section entitled "Troubleshooting Profiles and System Policies."

9. The creator of the resource owns that resource and has full rights and privileges to it. An administrator can access a resource and modify it, as well as take ownership of that resource away from the original owner. Doing so causes the original owner to be locked out of his ownership position. For more information, see the section entitled "Assessing User Resource Access Failures."

10. Much of the Windows NT Registry describes transient settings that are session dependent. Two of the Registry hives describing Security and SAM settings cannot be backed up. For more information, see the section entitled "Backing Up the Registry."

11. Events remain in the Event logs for seven days or until the log fills up and additional space is required. Events are removed in a first-in, first-out manner. For more information, see the section entitled "Working with Event Logs and the Event Viewer."

12. The Windows NT Diagnostic program lists the various devices that you have installed on your workstation, and the settings that they have for IRQs, I/O ports, DMA, and so forth. Through examination of this utility, you can determine what conflicts might exist. For more information, see the section entitled "Using the Windows NT Diagnostic Program."

Appendix

Overview of the
Certification Process

To become a Microsoft Certified Professional, candidates must pass rigorous certification exams that provide a valid and reliable measure of their technical proficiency and expertise. These closed-book exams have on-the-job relevance because they are developed with the input of professionals in the computer industry and reflect how Microsoft products are actually used in the workplace. The exams are conducted by an independent organization—Sylvan Prometric—at more than 700 Sylvan Authorized Testing Centers around the world.

Currently Microsoft offers four types of certification, based on specific areas of expertise:

▶ **Microsoft Certified Product Specialist (MCPS).** Qualified to provide installation, configuration, and support for users of at least one Microsoft desktop operating system, such as Windows NT Workstation. In addition, candidates may take additional elective exams to add areas of specialization. MCPS is the first level of expertise.

▶ **Microsoft Certified Systems Engineer (MCSE).** Qualified to effectively plan, implement, maintain, and support information systems with Microsoft Windows NT and other Microsoft advanced systems and workgroup products, such as Microsoft Office and Microsoft BackOffice. The Windows NT Workstation exam can be used as one of the four core operating systems exams. MCSE is the second level of expertise.

▶ **Microsoft Certified Solution Developer (MCSD).** Qualified to design and develop custom business solutions using Microsoft development tools, technologies, and platforms, including Microsoft Office and Microsoft BackOffice. MCSD also is a second level of expertise, but in the area of software development.

▶ **Microsoft Certified Trainer (MCT).** Instructionally and technically qualified by Microsoft to deliver Microsoft Education Courses at Microsoft authorized sites. An MCT must be employed by a Microsoft Solution Provider Authorized Technical Education Center or a Microsoft Authorized Academic Training site.

 Note

For up-to-date information about each type of certification, visit the Microsoft Training and Certification World Wide Web site at http://www.microsoft.com/train_cert. You must have an Internet account and a WWW browser to access this information. You also can call the following sources:

▶ Microsoft Certified Professional Program: 800-636-7544

▶ Sylvan Prometric Testing Centers: 800-755-EXAM

▶ Microsoft Online Institute (MOLI): 800-449-9333

How to Become a Microsoft Certified Product Specialist (MCPS)

To become an MCPS, you must pass one operating system exam. Passing the "Implementing and Supporting Microsoft Windows NT Workstation 4.0" exam (#70-73), which this book covers, satisfies the MCPS requirement.

Windows NT Workstation is not the only operating system you can be tested on to get your MCPS certification. The following list shows the names and exam numbers of all the operating systems from which you can choose to get your MCPS certification:

- ▶ Implementing and Supporting Microsoft Windows 95 (#70-63)

- ▶ Implementing and Supporting Microsoft Windows NT Workstation 4.0 (#70-73)

- ▶ Implementing and Supporting Microsoft Windows NT Workstation 3.51 (#70-42)

- ▶ Implementing and Supporting Microsoft Windows NT Server 4.0 (#70-67)

- ▶ Implementing and Supporting Microsoft Windows NT Server 3.51 (#70-43)

- ▶ Microsoft Windows for Workgroups 3.11-Desktop (#70-48)

- ▶ Microsoft Windows 3.1 (#70-30)

- ▶ Microsoft Windows Operating Systems and Services Architecture I (#70-160)

- ▶ Microsoft Windows Operating Systems and Services Architecture II (#70-161)

How to Become a Microsoft Certified Systems Engineer (MCSE)

MCSE candidates need to pass four operating system exams and two elective exams. The MCSE certification path is divided into two tracks: the Windows NT 3.51 track, and the Windows NT 4.0 track. The "Implementing and Supporting Microsoft Windows NT Workstation 4.0" exam covered in this book can be applied to the Windows NT 4.0 track of the MCSE certification path.

Table A.1 shows the core requirements (four operating system exams) and the elective courses (two exams) for the Windows NT 3.51 track.

Table A.1

Windows NT 3.51 MCSE Track		
Take These Three Required Exams (Core Requirements)	Plus, Pick One Exam from the Following Operating System Exams (Core Requirement)	Plus, Pick Two Exams from the Following Elective Exams (Elective Requirements)
Implementing and Supporting Microsoft Windows NT Server 3.51 (#70-43)	Implementing and Supporting Microsoft Windows 95 (#70-63)	Implementing and Supporting Microsoft SNA Server 3.0 (#70-13)
AND Implementing and Supporting Microsoft Windows NT Workstation 3.51 (#70-42)	OR Microsoft Windows for Workgroups 3.11-Desktop (#70-48)	OR Implementing and Supporting Microsoft SNA Server 4.0 (#70-85)
AND Networking Essentials (#70-58)	OR Microsoft Windows 3.1 (#70-30)	OR Implementing and Supporting Microsoft System Management Server 1.2 (#70-18)
		OR Microsoft SQL 4.2 Database Implementation (#70-21)
		OR Microsoft SQL Server 4.2 Database Administration for Microsoft Windows NT (#70-22)
		OR System Administration for Microsoft SQL Server 6.5 (#70-26)
		OR Implementing a Database Design on Microsoft SQL Server 6.5 (#70-27)
		OR Microsoft Mail for PC Networks 3.2-Enterprise (#70-37)

Take These Three Required Exams (Core Requirements)	Plus, Pick One Exam from the Following Operating System Exams (Core Requirement)	Plus, Pick Two Exams from the Following Elective Exams (Elective Requirements)
		OR Internetworking Microsoft TCP/IP on Microsoft Windows NT (3.5-3.51) (#70-53)
		OR Internetworking Microsoft TCP/IP on Microsoft Windows NT 4.0 (#70-59)
		OR Implementing and Supporting Microsoft Exchange Server 4.0 (#70-75)
		OR Implementing and Supporting Microsoft Exchange Server 5.0 (#70-76)
		OR Implementing and Supporting Microsoft Internet Information Server 3.0 and Index Server 1.1 (#70-77)
		OR Implementing and Supporting the Microsoft Proxy Server 1.0 (#70-78)
		OR Implementing and Supporting Microsoft Proxy Server 2.0 (#70-88)

Table A.2 shows the core requirements (four operating system exams) and elective courses (two exams) for the Windows NT 4.0 track. Tables A.1 and A.2 have many of the same exams listed, but there are distinct differences between the two. Make sure you read each track's requirements carefully.

Table A.2

Windows NT 4.0 MCSE Track		
Take These Three Required Exams (Core Requirements)	Plus, Pick One Exam from the Following Operating System Exams (Core Requirement)	Plus, Pick Two Exams from the Following Elective Exams (Elective Requirements)
Implementing and Supporting Microsoft Windows NT Server 4.0 (#70-67)	Implementing and Supporting Microsoft Windows 95 (#70-63)	Implementing and Supporting Microsoft SNA Server 3.0 (#70-13)
AND Implementing and Supporting Microsoft Windows NT Workstation 4.0 in the Enterprise (#70-68)	OR Microsoft Windows for Workgroups 3.11-Desktop #70-48	OR Implementing and Supporting Microsoft SNA Server 4.0 (#70-85)
AND Networking Essentials (#70-58)	OR Microsoft Windows 3.1 (#70-30)	OR Implementing and Supporting Microsoft Systems Management Server 1.2 (#70-18)
	OR Implementing and Supporting Microsoft Windows NT Workstation 4.02 (#70-73)	OR Microsoft SQL Server 4.2 Database Implementation (#70-21)
		OR Microsoft SQL Server 4.2 Database Administration for Microsoft Windows NT (#70-22)
		OR System Administration for Microsoft SQL Server 6.5 (#70-26)
		OR Implementing a Database Design on Microsoft SQL Server 6.5 (#70-27)

Take These Three Required Exams (Core Requirements)	Plus, Pick One Exam from the Following Operating System Exams (Core Requirement)	Plus, Pick Two Exams from the Following Elective Exams (Elective Requirements)
		OR Microsoft Mail for PC Networks 3.2-Enterprise (#70-37)
		OR Internetworking Microsoft TCP/IP on Microsoft Windows NT (3.5-3.51) (#70-53)
		OR Internetworking Microsoft TCP/IP on Microsoft Windows NT 4.0 (#70-59)
		OR Implementing and Supporting Microsoft Exchange Server 4.0 (#70-75)
		OR Implementing and Supporting Microsoft Exchange Server 5.0 (#70-76)
		OR Implementing and Supporting Microsoft Internet Information Server 3.0 and Index Server 1.1 (#70-77)
		OR Implementing and Supporting Microsoft Proxy Server 1.0 (#70-78)
		OR Implementing and Supporting Microsoft Proxy Server 2.0 (#70-88)

How to Become a Microsoft Certified Solution Developer (MCSD)

MCSD candidates need to pass two core technology exams and two elective exams. Unfortunately, the "Implementing and Supporting Microsoft Windows NT Workstation 4.0" (#70-73) exam does *not* apply toward any of these requirements. Table A.3 shows the required technology exams, and the elective exams that apply toward obtaining the MCSD.

 **Warning**

The "Implementing and Supporting Microsoft Windows NT Workstation 4.0" (#70-73) exam does *not* apply toward any of the MCSD requirements.

Table A.3

MCSD Exams and Requirements	
Take These Two Core Technology Exams	**And, Choose from Two of the Following Elective Exams**
Microsoft Windows Architecture I (#70-160)	Microsoft SQL Server 4.2 Database Implementation (#70-21)
AND Microsoft Windows Architecture II (#70-161)	OR Implementing a Database Design on Microsoft SQL Server 6.5 (#70-27)
	OR Developing Applications with C++ Using the Microsoft Foundation Class Library (#70-24)
	OR Microsoft Access 2.0 for Windows-Application Development (#70-51)
	OR Developing Applications with Microsoft Excel 5.0 Using Visual Basic for Applications (#70-52)
	OR Programming in Microsoft Visual FoxPro 3.0 for Windows (#70-54)
	OR Programming with Microsoft Visual Basic 4.0 (#70-65)

Take These Two Core Technology Exams	And, Choose from Two of the Following Elective Exams
	OR Developing Applications with Microsoft Visual Basic 5.0 (#70-165)
	OR Microsoft Access for Windows 95 and the Microsoft Access Developer's Toolkit (#70-69)
	OR Implementing OLE in Microsoft Foundation Class Applications (#70-25)

Becoming a Microsoft Certified Trainer (MCT)

To understand the requirements and process for becoming a Microsoft Certified Trainer (MCT), you need to obtain the Microsoft Certified Trainer Guide document (mctguide.doc) from the following WWW site:

```
http://www.microsoft.com/train_cert/download.htm
```

On this page, click on the hyperlink MCT GUIDE (mctguide.doc) (117 KB). If your WWW browser can display DOC files (Word for Windows native file format), the MCT Guide displays in the browser window. Otherwise, you need to download it and open it in Word for Windows or Windows 95 WordPad. The MCT Guide explains the four-step process to becoming an MCT. The general steps for the MCT certification are as follows:

1. Complete and mail a Microsoft Certified Trainer application to Microsoft. You must include proof of your skills for presenting instructional material. The options for doing so are described in the MCT Guide.

2. Obtain and study the Microsoft Trainer Kit for the Microsoft Official Curricula (MOC) course(s) for which you want to be certified. You can order Microsoft Trainer Kits by calling 800-688-0496 in North America. Other regions should review the MCT Guide for information on how to order a Trainer Kit.

3. Pass the Microsoft certification exam for the product for which you want to be certified to teach.

4. Attend the Microsoft Official Curriculum (MOC) course for the course for which you want to be certified. This is done so that you can understand how the course is structured, how labs are completed, and how the course flows.

 Warning

You should use the preceding steps as a general overview of the MCT certification process. The actual steps you need to take are described in detail in the mctguide.doc file on the WWW site mentioned earlier. Do not misconstrue the preceding steps as the actual process you need to take.

If you are interested in becoming an MCT, you can receive more information by visiting the Microsoft Certified Training (MCT) WWW site at http://www.microsoft.com/train_cert/mctint.htm, or by calling 800-688-0496.

Appendix

Study Tips

Self-study involves any method that you employ to learn a given topic, with the most popular being third-party books, such as the one you hold in your hand. Before you begin to study for a certification book, you should know exactly what Microsoft expects you to learn.

Pay close attention to the objectives posted for the exam. The most current objectives can always be found on the WWW site `http://www.microsoft.com/train_cert`. This book was written to the most current objectives, and the beginning of each chapter lists the relevant objectives for that chapter. As well, you should notice a handy tear-out card with an objective matrix that lists all objectives and the page you can turn to for information on that objective.

If you have taken any college courses in the past, you have probably learned what study habits work best for you. Nevertheless, consider the following:

▶ Study in bright light to reduce fatigue and depression.

▶ Establish a regular study schedule and stick as close to it as possible.

▶ Turn off all forms of distraction, including radios and televisions.

▶ Study in the same place each time you study so that your materials are always readily at hand.

▶ Take short breaks (approximately 15 minutes) every two to three hours or so. Studies have proven that your brain assimilates information better if you allow this break.

Another thing to think about is this: Humans learn information in three ways: visually, aurally, and through tactile confirmation. That's why, in a college class, the students who took notes on the lectures had better recall on exam day; they took in information both aurally and through tactile confirmation—writing it down.

Hence, use study techniques that reinforce information in all three ways. By reading the books, for example, you visually take in information. By writing down the information when you test yourself, you give your brain tactile confirmation. And lastly, have someone test you out loud, so you can hear yourself giving the correct answer. Having someone test you should always be the last step in studying.

Pre-Testing Yourself

Before taking the actual exam, verify that you are ready to do so by testing yourself over and over again in a variety of ways. Within this book, there are questions at the beginning and end of each chapter. On the accompanying CD, a number of electronic test engines emulate the actual Microsoft test and enable you to test your knowledge of the subject areas. Use these over and over and over again until you are consistently scoring in the 90 percent range (or better).

 Objective

> This means, of course, that you can't start studying five days before the exam begins. You need to give yourself plenty of time to read, practice, and then test yourself several times.

TestPrep, the electronic testing engine on the CD-ROM, is arguably the best one on the market. It is described in full detail in Appendix D, "All About TestPrep." Here it is just important for you to know that TestPrep prepares you for the exam in a way unparalleled by most other engines.

Hints and Tips for Doing Your Best on the Tests

In a confusing twist of terminology, when you take one of the Microsoft exams, you are said to be "writing" the exam. When you go to take the actual exam, be prepared. Arrive early and be ready to show your two forms of identification and sit before the monitor. Expect wordy questions. Although you have 90 minutes to take the exam, you must answer 51 questions. This gives you just over one minute to answer each question. This may sound like ample time for each question, but remember that most of the questions are lengthy word problems, which tend to ramble on for paragraphs. Your 90 minutes of exam time can be consumed very quickly.

It has been estimated that approximately 85 percent of the candidates taking their first Microsoft exam fail it. It is not so much that they are unprepared and stupid. It is more the case that they don't know what to expect and are immediately intimidated by the wordiness of the questions and the ambiguity implied in the answers.

Every exam that Microsoft offers requires a different passing score. The Windows NT Workstation score is 705, or 70.5 percent. Because the exam has 51 questions (randomly taken from a pool of about 150), this means that you must correctly answer 36 or more to pass.

Things to Watch For

When you take the exam, look closely at the number of correct choices you need to make. Some questions require that you select one correct answer; other questions have more than one correct answer. When you see radial buttons next to the answer choices, you need to remember that the answers are mutually exclusive and there is but one right answer. On the other hand, check boxes indicate that the answers are not mutually exclusive and there are multiple right answers. Be certain to read the questions closely to see how many correct answers you need to choose.

Also, read the questions fully. With lengthy questions, the last sentence often dramatically changes the scenario. When taking the exam, you are given pencils and two sheets of paper. If you are uncertain of what the question is saying, map out the scenario on the paper until you have it clear in your mind. You are required to turn in the scrap paper at the end of the exam.

Marking Answers for Return

You can mark questions on the actual exam and refer back to them later. If you get a wordy question that will take a long time to read and decipher, mark it and return to it when you have completed the rest of the exam. This saves you from wasting time on it and running out of time on the exam—there are only 90 minutes allotted for the exam and it ends when those 90 minutes expire, regardless of whether you are finished with the exam.

Attaching Notes to Test Questions

At the conclusion of the exam, before the grading takes place, you are given the opportunity to attach a message to any question. If you feel that a question was too ambiguous, or tested on knowledge you did not need to know to work with the product, take this opportunity to state your case. It is unheard of that Microsoft has changed a test score as a result of an attached message. It never hurts to try, however—and it helps to vent your frustration before blowing the proverbial 50-amp fuse.

Good luck!

Appendix

What's on the CD-ROM

This appendix briefly explains what you will find on the CD-ROM that accompanies this book. For a more detailed description of the newly developed TestPrep test engine, exclusive to Macmillan Computer Publishing, see Appendix D, "All About TestPrep."

TestPrep

A new test engine was developed exclusively for Macmillan Computer Publishing. It is, arguably, the best test engine available because it closely emulates the actual Microsoft exam and enables you to check your score by objective, which helps you determine what you need to study further.

Before running the TestPrep software, be sure to read CDROM.hlp (in the root directory of the CD-ROM) for late-breaking news on TestPrep features.

Copyright Information and Disclaimer

Macmillan Computer Publishing's TestPrep test engine:
Copyright 1997, Macmillan Computer Publishing. All rights reserved. Made in U.S.A.

Appendix

All About TestPrep

The electronic TestPrep utility included on the accompanying CD-ROM enables you to test your Windows NT Workstation 4 knowledge in a manner similar to that employed by the actual Microsoft exam.

Although it is possible to maximize the TestPrep application, the default is for it to run in smaller mode so that you can refer to your Windows NT Workstation desktop while answering questions. TestPrep uses a unique randomization sequence to ensure that each time you run the program you are presented with a different sequence of questions—this enhances your learning and prevents you from merely learning the expected answers over time without reading the question each and every time.

Question Presentation

TestPrep emulates the actual Microsoft "Implementing and Supporting Microsoft Windows NT Workstation 4.0" exam (#70-73), in that radio (circle) buttons are used to signify only one correct choice, while check boxes (squares) are used to imply multiple correct answers.

You can exit the program at any time by clicking the Exit button, or you can continue to the next question by clicking the Next button.

Scoring

The TestPrep Score Report uses actual numbers from the "Implementing and Supporting Microsoft Windows NT Workstation 4.0" exam. For Windows NT Workstation 4, a score of 705 or higher is considered passing; the same parameters apply to TestPrep. Each objective category is broken down into categories with a percentage correct given for each of the 7 categories.

Choose Show Me What I Missed to go back through the questions you incorrectly answered and see what the correct answers are. Click Exit to terminate the application.

I n d e x

MCSE Training Guide: Windows 95

ISBN: 1-56205-746-4 $59.99 USA/$84.95 CDN   784 pp.   1 CD-ROM

This resource contains all the insider tips, notes, tricks, strategies, and helpful advice users need to achieve Microsoft certification on Windows 95. The easy-to-read, concise format provides users with the most valuable information—quickly and efficiently. The CD-ROM contains New Riders' exclusive TestPrep test engine, which simulates the actual Microsoft exam better than anything else on the market.

Covers: Implementing and Supporting Microsoft Windows 95—Exam 70-63

MCSE Training Guide: Windows NT Server 4

ISBN: 1-56205-768-5 $49.99 USA/$70.95 USA   560 pp.   1 CD-ROM

This must-have guide to the Implementing and Supporting Microsoft Windows NT Server 4.0 exam will save users countless hours and thousands of dollars in MCSE courses. Filled with insider tips and notes from MCSEs and MCTs, the training guide also includes a CD-ROM with hundreds of questions to help users practice taking the exam.

Covers: Implementing and Supporting Microsoft Windows NT Server 4.0—Exam 70-67

MCSE Training Guide: Networking Essentials

ISBN: 1-56205-749-9 $49.99 USA/$70.95 CDN   512 pp.   1 CD-ROM

This updated edition has all the information users need to pass the Networking Essentials exam. Organized in a concise, easy-to-read manner, this must-have resource saves users countless hours and thousands of dollars in training courses. This series is the fastest, most effective, and least expensive study tool for achieving Microsoft certification. The CD-ROM contains New Riders' exclusive testing engine, TestPrep, with hundreds of questions to prepare users for the actual exam.

Covers: Networking Essentials—Exam 70-58

Inside Windows NT Server 4, Certified Administrator's Resource Edition

ISBN: 1-56205-789-8 $59.99 USA/$98.95 CDN   1,344 pp.   2 CD-ROMs

This book ensures you will have the skills you need to be a success. This proven bestseller is the best book available for the vast majority of Windows NT Server administrators. It contains numerous tutorials that quickly bring new administrators up to speed, but is organized as a reference that serves the needs of even the most technically savvy and experienced Windows NT administrator. Certified by Microsoft as an Approved Study Material, this book is ideal for those preparing for the MCSE Exam 70-67. Two CD-ROMs contain New Riders' official TestPrep testing software; an electronic version of the text; utilities, and administration tools.

Covers: Windows NT Server 4.0 and MCSE Exam 70-67

Inside Windows NT Workstation 4, Certified Administrator's Resource Edition

ISBN: 1-56205-790-1 $59.99 USA/$98.95 CDN   1,145 pp.   2 CD-ROMs

This book offers Microsoft-certified training material, enhanced with hands-on, performance-based exercises and includes advanced peer-to-peer discussions, in-depth Registry analysis, and troubleshooting scenarios. Two CD-ROMs contain New Riders' exclusive TestPrep testing software; an electronic version of the text; utilities, and administration tools.

Covers: Windows NT Workstation 4.0 and MCSE Exam 70-73

Networking with Microsoft TCP/IP, Certified Administrator's Resource Edition

ISBN: 1-56205-791-X $55.00 USA/$77.95 CDN   672 pp.   1 CD-ROMs

This bestselling title is enhanced with end of chapter review and self-test sections that greatly increase the reader's chance of passing the Microsoft TCP/IP certification exam. Key information markers provide the necessary testing information at the reader's fingertips. The CD-ROM contains New Riders' official TestPrep testing software; an electronic version of the text; utilities, and administration tools.

Covers: Microsoft TCP/IP for Windows NT Server 4.0 and MCSE Exam 70-59